Testing the Literary

Harvard-Yenching Institute Monograph Series 125

Testing the Literary

Prose and the Aesthetic in Early Modern China

ALEXANDER DES FORGES

Published by the Harvard University Asia Center
Distributed by Harvard University Press
Cambridge (Massachusetts) and London 2021

Printed in the United States of America

The Harvard University Asia Center publishes a monograph series and, in coordination with the Fairbank Center for Chinese Studies, the Korea Institute, the Reischauer Institute of Japanese Studies, and other faculties and institutes, administers research projects designed to further scholarly understanding of China, Japan, Vietnam, Korea, and other Asian countries. The Center also sponsors projects addressing multidisciplinary and regional issues in Asia.

The Harvard-Yenching Institute, founded in 1928, is an independent foundation dedicated to the advancement of higher education in the humanities and social sciences in Asia. Headquartered on the campus of Harvard University, the Institute provides fellowships for advanced research, training, and graduate studies at Harvard by competitively selected faculty and graduate students from Asia. The Institute also supports a range of academic activities at its fifty partner universities and research institutes across Asia. At Harvard, the Institute promotes East Asian studies through annual contributions to the Harvard-Yenching Library and publication of the *Harvard Journal of Asiatic Studies* and the Harvard-Yenching Institute Monograph Series.

Library of Congress Cataloging-in-Publication Data

Names: Des Forges, Alexander Townsend, 1970- author.
Title: Testing the literary : prose and the aesthetic in early modern China
  / Alexander Des Forges.
Description: Cambridge, Massachussetts : Harvard University Asia Center,
  2021. | Includes bibliographical references and index. |
Identifiers: LCCN 2020050237 | ISBN 9780674251182 (hardcover ; acid-free
  paper)
Subjects: LCSH: Chinese examination essays--History and criticism. |
  Chinese essays--Ming dynasty, 1368-1644--History and criticism. |
  Chinese essays--Qing dynasty, 1644-1912--History and criticism. |
  Chinese prose literature--Ming dynasty, 1368-1644--History and
  criticism. | Chinese prose literature--Qing dynasty, 1644-1912--History
  and criticism. | Aesthetics in literature.
Classification: LCC PL2405 .D47 2021 | DDC 895.14/4609--dc23
LC record available at https://lccn.loc.gov/2020050237

Index by Anne Holmes and Rob Rudnick, EdIndex

♾   Printed on acid-free paper
Last figure below indicates year of this printing

26 25 24 23 22 21

For Terry and Kai

CONTENTS

ACKNOWLEDGMENTS

This book was slow to get started. The idea of the eight-legged essay caught my imagination years ago: a genre that focused the intellectual energies of millions on a difficult canon of texts, produced in an environment in which poets may have been the acknowledged legislators of the world but administrators were selected in large part on the basis of their prose style. The consistency with which these essays, most commonly known in the Ming and Qing as *shiwen* or "modern prose," were excluded from the literary canon presented an interesting challenge. But the essays themselves did not speak to me clearly at first. It was not until I became thoroughly impatient with canonical Qing prose criticism that I began to invest the necessary time to hear their voices.

Had I not encountered the scholarship of Gong Duqing and Huang Qiang, the returns on that time invested would have remained slim. I am grateful for their willingness to tolerate naive questions no less than for their groundbreaking work, as well as for their enthusiastic participation in a conference Rui Magone and I organized in 2012, "The Literature of High Stakes and Long Odds: Locating Civil Service Examination Writings in the Late Imperial Cultural Landscape." I also thank the other presenters and discussants at this conference for their contributions to a panoramic view of examination writings and for their insightful critiques on this and other occasions: Iwo Amelung, Peter Bol, Cynthia Brokaw, Kai-wing Chow, Shiuon Chu, Hilde De Weerdt, Joseph Dennis, Wynn Gadkar-Wilcox, Paize Keulemans, Wai-yee Li, Liu Haifeng, Yasushi Ōki, Stephen Roddy, Bruce Rusk, Shang Wei, Ellen Widmer, Weili Ye, and Yu Li. This book draws on conversations that started at that conference in so many ways.

I began to discover the questions that would preoccupy me throughout this project as a postdoctoral fellow at the Pembroke Center for Teaching and Research on Women at Brown University. I owe a great debt to Ellen Rooney, Elizabeth Weed, Denise Davis, Brian Locke, and Monique Roelofs for their commitment to inquiry both literally and figuratively dialectical. Indeed, even as three days spent alone in the examination compound invariably built on the foundation of years of preparation in the company of friends and colleagues, this project has benefited immeasurably from extended discussions. Ann Waltner's classical Chinese reading group provided a haven in the Twin Cities more than twenty years ago; I learned a great deal from Benjamin Elman and Dorothy Ko in a semester at the Institute for Advanced Study in Princeton. I thank Siao-chen Hu for inviting me to the Institute of Chinese Literature and Philosophy at the Academia Sinica for fall 2004, a most congenial place to lose oneself in Ming and Qing literature, and Kyoto Seika University, particularly Rebecca Jennison, for hosting me in spring 2012.

I am grateful for the opportunity to receive feedback on various aspects of this project at the China Humanities Seminar at Harvard University, Tufts University, the Civil Service Examination Museum in Nanjing, the conference on Civil Service Examination Studies at Xiamen University, and the Nanjing Forum. Two conferences at the Karl Jaspers Centre, Heidelberg University, on Paratexts (2010) and Transcultural Framings (2014) pushed me to articulate ideas that were still hazy. A panel on comparative early modernities at the International Comparative Literature Association meeting in 2013 organized by David Porter inspired me to think of *shiwen* in a global context; Ning Ma and Sophie Volpp's comments on silver and capital were thought-provoking in this regard.

This book draws on the work of colleagues in many fields. Michael Gibbs Hill, Hu Ying, and Theodore Huters modeled the study of prose in its social context in the long nineteenth century; Katharine Burnett, Rivi Handler-Spitz, Liao Chao-heng, and Evelyn Chiung-yun Liu brought the Ming alive; Keith McMahon, David Rolston, and Chloe Starr made the significance of fictional narrative clear; Roger Des Forges, Susan Naquin, and Ono Kazuko reminded me of the importance of history; Wolfgang Behr, Timothy Clifford, Pierre-Henri Durand, Saitō Mareshi, and Nathan Vedal inspired with their attention to detail; Liu Dong, Joachim Kurtz, and Shengqing Wu encouraged cross-cultural and comparative framings; Dorothy Ko, Perry Link, David Wang, and Ellen Widmer offered continued support as I ranged ever further afield. Andrew Plaks sparked my interest in the modern prose essay, and Rui Magone has been a constant interlocutor and resource on all things examination-related.

My original debt is to my teachers of prose, without whom I could not have begun to read or write. I thank Michael Fuller, Stephen Owen, Yuan-fang Tung, and Judith Zeitlin for their instruction in classical Chinese. Alison Des Forges did not see this project take shape on the page, but her standards of English prose have been the compass and square throughout. Need it be said that the misreadings, strained interpretations, and stretches of bad writing in this book are my own?

I am indebted to Bob Graham and Kristen Wanner, as well as two anonymous readers, for their encouragement and support. As copyeditor and indexer, Laura Poole and Anne Holmes, respectively, have put this book in order.

Some of the works that are most important to this book have seen little interest over the past century. I thank librarians past for preserving them nonetheless, and librarians present for their tireless assistance, at Gest Library at Princeton University, Harvard-Yenching Library, the National Library in Beijing, Shanghai Library, Beijing University Library, Nanjing University Library, Fudan University Library, Academia Sinica, the National Central Library in Taipei, and Seikadō Library. I am grateful to the Library of the Institute for Advanced Studies on Asia at Tokyo University for the *Xixiang zhiyi* image that appears on the book jacket.

Over the years, this project has benefited greatly from financial support from the Pembroke Center and the Institute for Advanced Study, as well as from the Chiang Ching-kuo Foundation, the American Council of Learned Societies, and the office of the Dean of the College of Liberal Arts at the University of Massachusetts Boston. The intellectual sustenance provided by colleagues and friends in the Department of Modern Languages, Literatures, and Cultures and elsewhere on the University of Massachusetts Boston campus, though less material, has been that much more significant. I am thankful to my students for many things, not least their willingness to wrestle with essay translation and analysis.

This book is dedicated to Terry Kawashima and Kai Deshima, who leaven learning with humor; it means so much that joyful times and challenging times are shared.

ATD

A NOTE ABOUT TRANSLATIONS
AND CONVENTIONS

Although there has been substantial scholarship in English on the civil service examination system as an institution, there are relatively few translations of the essays. For this reason, in addition to Tan Yuanchun's essay translated in the introduction, four of these essays are translated in full in the Appendix. Unless otherwise noted, all translations are my own. I have marked lines that would be read as parallel with italics.

In translations of the essay topics, which function as well as the titles of the essays, I have for the most part drawn from James Legge's translations of the Four Books. For readers and writers of *shiwen*, essay topics would have been instantly recognizable as such, and would at the same time have stood at a noticeable remove from everyday speech, as well as from the language of the essays. Making use of the difference between Legge's English and the English we write in today is one way to allude to this remove. The difference between Legge's understanding of the originals and the scholarly consensus of today can similarly serve as a helpful reminder of the historicity of interpretation that any sophisticated essay would have taken as the horizon of its own possibility.

For editions in which pagination starts anew with each *juan*, the *juan* number and page number are separated by a period.

For modern reprint editions with continuous pagination, the *juan* number (when given) and page number are separated by a slash.

Introduction

From the beginning of the fifteenth century to the turn of the twentieth, one genre dominated classrooms and bookstores across China. *Shiwen* (modern or contemporary prose), later also known as *bagu wen* (eight-legged essays), commanded every student, candidate, and examiner's attention. As "the writing that is everyone's shared enterprise," the mode of expression in which educated individuals were schooled, this practice spread beyond its base in the examination regime to include philological study, philosophical reflection, political provocation, religious proselytizing and scriptural analysis, fictional narrative and literary criticism, jokes and parodies, family letters, and even autobiographical writing. For anyone who wanted his or her work to "emerge to the widest contemporary reading public like the moon among the peaks," rather than remaining "tucked away on a high shelf unread," writing in the *shiwen* genre had distinct advantages, not least its close identification with its moment (*shi*) of production and circulation.[1]

Shiwen accommodated a striking range in content and tone: the genre had room for both emotion-filled dramatis personae and dry treatises exploring metaphysical subtleties. Examples include a counterfactual imagination of a sarcastic and arrogant Confucius and a careful calculation of the specific numerical ratio between harvest yields of different domains as a mathematically correct justification for varied emoluments assigned to nobles of comparable rank.[2] Some essays focused on close reading and formal analysis of the assigned topic in terms that would not be out of place in a graduate seminar on literary criticism, whereas others explained the nature and uses of manure in extreme detail.[3] For critics and advocates alike, *shiwen* represented a distinctive and crucially significant part of Ming-Qing cultural production, notable for their pervasiveness and influence. The institutional and sociological significance of examination writing has been explored in detail; this book reads these essays and their criticism from a literary perspective.

Although modern scholars have focused on ideological reproduction and contestation in the examination regime, writers and critics in the Ming and Qing paid just as much attention to aesthetic concerns centered on spirit (*shen*) and tone of voice (*yuqi*). Where the moral logic that was the substance of the canonical tradition was considered solid, firmly grounded material, the real interest in essay composition was in how to bring this material to life through techniques characterized as "empty" (*xu*) for the space they allowed for lively imaginative work.[4] Against concrete detail, *xu* stands for generality and abstraction; against what has already been realized and is fully present, *xu* refers to the imaginative or creative potential that can result in something new; against content that is meaningful in a conventional sense, *xu* allows one direct access to sensations by leaving this rational discourse behind. These three aspects are evident in the orientation toward speculative and reflexive thinking in many modern prose essays, the creative liberties taken by *shiwen* authors, and the interest in *xuzi yan* (key empty words) in the writing process, including sighs and other wordless exclamations, of which one critic remarks that "their meaning is none other than the emotional force that they articulate."[5] In its juxtaposition of these diverse characteristics, the discourse of *xu* at work in the modern prose essay constitutes a striking analogue to the sense of the aesthetic that took shape in early modern European philosophical discourse, from its initial understanding as the rejoinder that sensuous experience could pose to rational thought within a philosophical framework, down to the imaginative free play of the faculties it eventually was thought to epitomize.[6]

It may seem surprising to emphasize the aesthetic so heavily. In the words of one Qing critic, pigs may appear in paintings, but no painter puts the effort into perfecting their representation that other animals inspire; similarly, phrases taken from *shiwen* are never found adorning decorative screens, even though a wide range of other genres of writing all serve as source material for this kind of calligraphic work.[7] *Shiwen* in most cases were also not included in the collected writings—*wenji*—that have ordinarily been thought to define an individual in literary terms.[8] Indeed, for some critics, modern prose marked the outer bounds of the literary in the Ming and Qing, whether as an inferior genre located at the very margins of the category or a type of writing to be definitively excluded from consideration as literary altogether. For other writers, as we will see in more detail in this introduction, *shiwen* constituted a kind of epitome of the literary enterprise in both positive and negative senses. This understanding of *shiwen* as an "exterior" frame that paradoxically also defines the literary from within is borne out by the fact that typical attacks leveled against *shiwen* as a genre could be (and frequently were) also used against the broader category of the literary as such. These apparently contradictory tendencies suggest that attempts to delineate and characterize *shiwen* as a genre are rarely concerned purely with questions of stylistics and genre distinctions in the literary sphere but rather tend to represent questions of literary and aesthetic autonomy that in eighteenth- and nineteenth-century Europe would be worked out between an emerging field of literary production and capitalist society in general.[9]

It is intriguing that modern Western theories of aesthetic value and conventional Ming-Qing discourses of literary quality alike often strive to obscure the significance of literary labor. Emphasizing consumption, the former extend the logic of commodity fetishism into the cultural sphere and find value to be embodied in objects; emphasizing production, the latter nonetheless deny the fabricated nature of culture products in the name of unmediated authorial authenticity. My aim is instead to return literary practice—the actual work of writing, reading, and commenting—to center stage. My focus throughout, over a series of close readings of a variety of texts, is on the processes by which features such as literary voice, parallelism, subjectivity, and aesthetic originality are constructed and interpreted in *shiwen*. By 1550, these features constituted a recognizable set of practices proper to modern prose as a genre in which writers wrote for other writers, and through their imagination of a literary creativity unique to each person played a key role in the literary and cultural efflorescence of the late Ming and the unfolding of new literary subjectivities over the course of the Qing. An epistemic shift occasioned by the traumatic fall of the Ming transformed the discourse on *shiwen*—and on literary sociality more generally—in negative fashion, but *shiwen* practice continued to develop in striking new directions through the eighteenth century.

A Contested Genre

With a few exceptions, the academic field of Chinese literature seems to have decided that *shiwen* are not real literature. Modern anthologies of Ming-Qing literature and literary theory generally pass over *shiwen* and *shiwen* criticism in silence; only a few essays have been translated into Western languages, hidden away in scholarly assessments of the genre read primarily by intellectual and institutional historians rather than literary critics.[10] Histories of Chinese literature often treat the genre as an embarrassment, about which the less said, the better.

As is the case with the study of so many other aspects of Chinese literary and cultural production, the very terms on which inquiry into *shiwen* has been conducted over the past century were set by early twentieth-century literary reformers, particularly the May Fourth generation, who aimed to distinguish clearly texts that merited critical attention and preservation from those that did not. Within a few short decades, the "eight-legged essay" joined the bound foot and the opium habit as monuments of a feudal culture to be jettisoned without question.[11] When Zhou Zuoren attempted to challenge this consensus in 1932, arguing for the central significance of *shiwen* to premodern literature and to the new literature yet to come, proposing that the essay be studied as part of colleges' "national literature" programs, the most common reaction was that this must be a rather elaborate joke. Indeed, by this point "eight-legged essay" had become an all-purpose term of abuse, with new coinages including the "foreign eight-legged essay" (*yang bagu wen*) and the "Party eight-legged essay" (*dang bagu wen*).[12] Once Mao Zedong popularized the latter phrase as a club with which to beat the conventionalized report styles that became common in the Chinese Communist Party in the 1940s, the fate of "the eight-legged essay" seemed sealed. Circulation of this pejorative usage in particular far outstripped the availability of actual examples of *shiwen* throughout the second half of the twentieth century.[13]

Unlike the May Fourth reassessments of other literary genres, which frequently balanced their harsh criticism of previous favorites with new enthusiasm for writing that had been neglected, modern attacks on the eight-legged essay seemed to continue an existing tradition of abuse. Many of the better-known Qing dynasty critics had found *shiwen* to be a particularly problematic literary genre, consisting of works inspired by questionable motives, produced under less than ideal circumstances, and apt to reproduce past successes rather than break new stylistic or conceptual ground. A short list of common critical tropes includes uselessness, excessive artfulness, inauthenticity, formal inflexibility, and emphasis on sound at the expense of meaning. Perceived distance from the examination regime could even be used as an argument for the distinctive value of women's writing.[14]

It is intriguing indeed that the first century of the Qing is generally understood in terms of a conservative and ideologically driven cultural turn; one might assume that this was an environment in which essays devoted to speaking on behalf of the Sages and Worthies would fit in particularly well.[15] Yet it is worth noting that criticism of *shiwen* was typically much sharper in this period than it had been in previous decades, and the genre was briefly downgraded in importance relative to other forms in the civil service examinations of the 1660s.[16] One of the most respected scholars of the seventeenth century, Gu Yanwu (1613–82), wrote that the examination essay was worse than the Qin dynasty burning of the books and burying of scholars nearly two thousand years earlier.[17] Significantly, criticism of *shiwen* in this period is often linked to a broader skepticism toward literary production as a whole, with literary sociality coming in for particularly harsh treatment. This suggests that the aesthetic significance of the modern prose essay—indeed, of the examination system as a whole—may be not only more substantial but also rather more complex than we have thought.

It turns out that we can trace this critical discourse in varying degrees of strength only back to the mid-seventeenth century before the trail grows cold. The contrast between the harshness of Qing critiques of *shiwen* and the appreciation of the genre characteristic of late Ming writers is striking, even if there are exceptions to this rule.[18] To give one example, Yuan Hongdao (1568–1610) writes of these essays in 1596 that

> In their form there is no mindless copying of precedent; their word choice necessarily pushes talent to its very limits; they change according to year and differ by month and demonstrate the widest range of individual styles; for the last two centuries, the government has used them to select from the literati, and the literati have used them to put forward that which makes them unique; all this is true of this genre of writing alone![19]

It is ironic indeed that twentieth-century scholars, ordinarily disposed to favor the late Ming over the literary "conservatism" of the following centuries, sided with their more immediate Qing predecessors in criticizing *shiwen* and overlooked earlier and more positive assessments. Many of the writers and thinkers championed by May Fourth intellectuals and succeeding generations of scholars as moderns out of time (or at least as worthy predecessors to a modern Chinese literature) were in fact either *shiwen* enthusiasts, skilled practitioners of the form, or both, Tang Xianzu (1550–1616) and Li Zhi (1527–1602) among them.[20]

Modern literary scholars' treatment of Li Zhi's famous "Tongxin shuo" (On the childlike mind), often considered a key document of the late Ming moment, is symptomatic of this blindness. In this polemic, Li makes a point of including *shiwen* as the most recent example in a lineage of outstanding literary genres. Although some modern scholars merely do Li the favor of ignoring this point, others are quite critical, and several have gone so far as to literally write the examination essay genre out of the passage in question, whether by replacing it with an ellipsis in quotations or by silently deleting it altogether, leaving no trace in the text as it is quoted in their literary histories.[21] From the perspective of literary and cultural history of the Ming and Qing, the consequence of the seventeenth-century epistemic shift—reinforced and removed of what nuance it had allowed to continue by the May Fourth movement, and reiterated by many scholars since—has been to nearly rule out serious and sustained inquiry into the largest and most charged arena of aesthetic production in this period. This book aims to sketch some of the key dynamics of that arena.

The Question of Terminology

The terms commonly used to refer to the essays that are the focus of this book have shortcomings, as each attempts to bring a wide variety of practices under a single rubric.[22] "Civil service examination essays," or more simply, "examination essays," the most generic choice, gives a strong sense of an original functional motivation behind the genre, but it makes no clear distinction between the essays we are interested in here on one hand and policy essays (*celun*) written in the second session on the other, perpetuating a confusion that does justice to neither form.[23] More significantly, it fails to address the many *shiwen* written outside of the examination context or even in direct confrontation with it.

It is important to note that although one can think of modern prose in generic terms as a response to the examination compound scenario, few of the examples circulated at the time or studied by later scholars are manuscript copies produced there.[24] Reworking one's compositions for publication was broadly accepted, and many of the best-known works in the genre were written expressly for pedagogical purposes as models at the author's leisure, not while he was confined in the examination compound.[25] To this we must add the many essays written with no intention of engaging with the civil service selection process, appropriating this form for entirely different purposes.

As we will see in detail in chapter 2, examination candidates often made use of concepts and terminology drawn from Buddhist and Daoist texts to add distinctiveness to their writing; even more striking, however, is the phenomenon of essays written entirely outside of the civil examination system that take their topics from these scriptures. According to Shen Defu's (1578–1642) *Wanli yehuo bian* (Miscellaneous notes on the Wanli period), monks were selected for promotion to positions of greater authority in at least one major monastery in the Ming on the basis of essays on quotes taken from the Diamond Sutra and the Surangama Sutra, among other texts. Other than the sources of their topics, these essays were "no different from those written by Confucian literati."[26] For the rather different purpose of proselytization in society at large, we find a collection of essays on topics drawn from the *Yinzhi wen* (Scripture of hidden good deeds), devoted to Wenchang, the god of literacy, literature, and examination success.[27]

Even the authors who kept to more canonical source material were not always writing or preparing to write examination papers. Another use of modern prose is to present political, philosophical, or philological arguments in a format in which these arguments would be most likely to gain wide and rapid circulation. As one mid-Qing scholar put it:

> Now experts in exegesis conduct wide-ranging philological inquiries, and since their vision is outstanding and distinctive, is it not better for them to make use of the language of everyone's shared enterprise to display their points, and cause the accumulated wisdom of the Sages and Worthies, as well as the aspects not yet illuminated by former scholars, to emerge like clouds along the ridge and the moon among the peaks, rather than to leave their work to be tucked away on a high shelf unread?[28]

From this perspective, the virtue of the genre is its ability to seize readers' attention; several examples of these philological and philosophical essays, written specifically to argue a point to a broader audience, are included or referenced in Liang Zhangju's (1775–1849) *Zhiyi conghua* (Collected words on regulated essays).[29] In addition to these studies, we find serious philosophical deliberations and political provocations articulated in *shiwen* form by a range of well-known Ming and Qing figures.[30]

Of particular interest are *shiwen* that cross the bounds of literary genre in their focus on individual subjectivity, claiming to offer deeper insight into the thoughts and moods of a range of characters from dramatic works such as *Xixiang ji* (The western chamber), as well as ordinary people who happen to have been mentioned in passing in the classical canon. As numerous scholars have suggested in recent years, these essays cannot all be dismissed as mere whimsical writings; the category of "writing for amusement" (*youxi zhi bi*) was broad enough to include subtle reflections on a person's state of mind as well as joke essays remarkable primarily for their silliness.[31] In many cases, these essays find close kin in the "small topic" works that drew selectively on the Classics and the Four Books in such a way as to require an unusual level of creativity on the author's part.[32] In composing a "small topic" essay one might be expected to convey the concerns of a woman whose weaving does not find customers, or inquire into the intersubjectivity of the gaze between young lovers who do not have recourse to a matchmaker, as we will see in more detail in chapter 2.

From writing that expressed the innermost thoughts of the best-known characters from the theater, or those who had bit parts in the classical canon, it turned out to be a short step to making use of the *shiwen* form for letters to one's family, or, in the case of Qu Jingchun (1507–69), as a mode of autobiographical writing (discussed in more detail in chapter 5).[33] Scholars of Tang poetry have a long tradition of considering the regulated verse genre (*lüshi*) as a literary phenomenon that goes well beyond its use in the civil examinations of that dynasty. To the extent that scholarship on *shiwen* has in contrast tended to confine itself within the walls of the examination compound, it seems that a greater consciousness of the narrowness of the field delimited by the phrase "examination essay" is in order.

"Eight-legged essay" (*bagu wen*), the name now used most frequently by modern scholars and most familiar to general readers, appears surprisingly late in the development of the genre. This term originally referred to essays written in response to a single type of examination topic that seemed to lend itself formally to a particular kind of symmetrical approach. Later it was popularized by Gu Yanwu and the authors of the *Mingshi* (History of the Ming) to cover essays written on the full range of topics drawn from the Classics and the Four Books.[34] Since the term "eight-legged essay" was rarely (if ever) used before the seventeenth-century epistemic shift in discourse on examination prose, its popularity in the Qing must be understood in conjunction with the newly critical approach to the genre characteristic of that period. As we have seen, this negative cast to the term only intensified in the early twentieth century, and "eight-legged essay" continues to carry a great deal of that baggage to this day.

By emphasizing questions of form, "eight-legged essay" clearly distinguishes the essays in question from policy essays; in this way, it is more precise than "examination essay." Unfortunately, most "eight-legged" essays did not have eight legs as they are ordinarily understood (four pairs of simply matched lines). More significantly, as we will see in detail in chapter 3, many had little of the extreme symmetry this term implies. It is worth pointing out here that the only official stipulation governing the format in which these essays were written was a limit on length; there was never an explicit requirement that an essay include parallel legs, and some did without them entirely. In reifying a single formal characteristic found only in some essays to characterize the genre as a whole, the term "eight-legged essay" conditions readers to think of these works merely in terms of manipulation of components to fit a given "grid," rather than as texts with their own organic coherence that may display a range of formal features in a variety of formats.

Other phrases, such as "essays on the Four Books" (*sishu wen*) and "explanations of the Classics" (*jingyi*), do have a well-defined meaning in the Ming and Qing contexts but lose that generic specificity in English translation. *Zhiyi* (制義) comes into common use in Qing official texts and can be translated variously as "essays written to imperial order," "regulated essays," and "formulated exegesis." The term *zhiyi* (制藝), "regulated arts," provides a homophonous alternative that stresses the aesthetic rather than the ideological qualities of the essays.

The most nuanced name for these essays in general use at the time was *shiwen*, translated by Pierre-Henri Durand as "prose moderne" and by Andrew Plaks as "the prose of our time." Huang Qiang identifies *shiwen*

as by far the most commonly used term in unofficial contexts throughout the Ming and Qing, highlighting its negative connotations.[35] At the
same time, it is important to note that this genre was defended precisely
insofar as it could be understood to be "contemporary," "timely," or
"modern" (*shi*) by Yuan Hongdao, Li Zhi, and Dai Mingshi (1653–1713):
for these and other advocates *shiwen* (and the related term *shiyi*, "modern
arts") was in fact a positive designation.[36]

Numerous commentators emphasize that dominant styles changed
with each new examination cycle—one providing a cycle-by-cycle
breakdown of changes from the 1670s through the 1710s—an intense
focus on the newest styles (*xinyang*) on a seasonal basis that reminds one
of Barthes's study of Parisian fashion.[37] Specific changes that occurred
by cycle could subsequently be organized into broader narratives that
attempted to impose order on the kaleidoscope of changing styles that
was complicated by factional allegiances and regional variations.[38] In
particular, the genre's concern for timeliness meant that changes in essay
styles could link to broader political and cultural change, a phenomenon
that modern scholars have recently begun to emphasize.[39]

The fact that *shiwen* was the term widely used by critics and advocates alike to capture this sensitivity to the zeitgeist seems to constitute a
recommendation with both heft and balance; their disagreements were
not centered on the nature of the genre, nor on the appropriateness of
the name, but on the extent to which this characteristic timeliness was
to be valued or critiqued. It is also clear that more than any other term
in use in the Ming and Qing, *shiwen* includes a sense of a broader field
of discourse, a practice in relation to its social and cultural context, that
goes beyond the papers written and graded in examination compounds.
It is telling that Kai-wing Chow and Alexander Woodside, two scholars
who have drawn on the early modern paradigm originated by historians
of Europe, present the civil service examination system as integral to the
early modern paradigm, whether that system functions in close conjunction with the market in cultural products or as a crucial innovation in
meritocratic and bureaucratic order that would inspire European reformers in the eighteenth and nineteenth centuries.[40] Indeed, the complicated
dialectic that develops between *shiwen* and *guwen* (classical prose) in the
Ming and early Qing reminds us of the *querelle des anciens et des modernes*
that played a central role in French literature of the early modern period.

In both cases, advocates of the "new" or "contemporary" ranged themselves against writers and critics who insisted on locating the source of literary and intellectual inspiration in the distant past. Timeliness is consistently identified as a key aspect of this self-consciously modern genre, whether understood in terms of stylishness (*shimao*) or ephemerality. For these reasons, I have decided to refer to these essays primarily as *shiwen* and to the genre as modern prose.

Zeng Xi Was Fond of Jujubes

Let us begin with an example. The following essay, by the noted member of the Jingling School Tan Yuanchun (1586–1637), inquires into Zengzi's unwillingness to eat jujubes, which Mencius attempted to explain to Gongsun Chou.[41] Lines that read as parallel are in italics.

Zeng Xi was fond of jujubes

[Mencius] takes that which is distinctive to explain unbearability (*buren*); his intention can be imagined. Now Zengzi felt the loss of his parent to be unbearable, and was particularly moved by the food that his parent liked to eat; that being so, an explanation in terms of commonality and distinctiveness serves to enlighten Gongsun Chou but does not fully explain Zengzi.

Now the heart of the filial child has aspects that are not knowable to those of later generations; even among contemporaries, *the heart of the filial child has aspects that are not knowable to those who are not close.* The reasons for this are based in "unbearability"; as for the thing that is unbearable, the time at which it is unbearable, and the reasons for its unbearability, there is none who knows them.

Even such a small thing as a jujube, Zeng Xi happened to like to eat it; when Zeng Xi died, Zengzi saw jujubes and was saddened by them. *People noticed that he did not eat them, and thought it was simply that he found it unbearable.* Reaching Mencius's time, *the fact that Zengzi found it unbearable was still passed on, but people thought it was simply a question of not eating.*

Starting from this and imagining further, one can know the desolateness of his condition; should one insist on understanding it in more depth, there is no means by which the cause of his desolateness can be determined. So then is it to be sought in questions of relative deliciousness and whether to eat or not?

As for the question about minced meat, how shallow Gongsun Chou was!

Mencius replied to him with shallow words only, saying:

Now, jujubes of course are not as good as minced meat, but minced meat is a liking shared among many, and jujubes are liked distinctively; it is in their distinctiveness that Zengzi found sadness. You know the taboo on names, certainly? What difference is there between personal name and family name, that only the personal name is taboo, if not the distinctiveness of the personal name? *Tabooing the personal name is a feeling shared by all sons; not eating jujubes is a feeling specific to Zengzi. The feeling of all sons is based not on similarity but on the distinctiveness of one person from another; this is how there is one root.*[42] *Zengzi's specific feeling is based not on similarity but on distinctiveness; this is how intentions are nourished.*[43] Zengzi is a true filial son.

Alas, Mencius's words are clear on Zengzi's reasons for eating minced meat and not jujubes, but he did not speak about the reasons that Zengzi found this unbearable; so unbearableness had something about it that could not be grasped and explained by people of those days.

Now does unbearableness have sound, color, smell, or taste? *In some cases one is touched by something and is moved, but one can be moved even in the absence of physical touch; in some cases one is touched by seeing something that is distinctive, but one can* also *be touched by seeing something that is shared.* Sadness comes and one then cries; how could there be a constant rule? Even Zengzi did not know why he felt it to be unbearable, how could another person know? This is not something that can be spoken of with "people who focus on eating and drinking."[44]

Perhaps the single most obvious feature of this essay, when compared with the original *Mencius* passage on which it is based, is Tan Yuanchun's interest in moving beyond Mencius's explanation of Zengzi's behavior to explore the question of *unbearableness* in more depth. Weaving in references to no fewer than three other relevant passages in the *Mencius*, Tan suggests that he has something to add that could not be "grasped and explained" in Mencius's time. Where Mencius neatly solves Gongsun Chou's problem by demonstrating the key role of distinctiveness, Tan opens the question up again by arguing that the feeling of unbearableness has a deeper emotional logic to it that cannot be fully accounted for, even by the individual who experiences it directly.

In his comments to this essay in the canonical *Qinding sishu wen* (Imperially authorized essays on the Four Books), Fang Bao (1668–1749) writes that Tan takes a stand outside the topic, without missing what is crucial within the topic—"To like 'overturning judgments' originally is not orthodox. But there is in fact an argument here that puts forward something not put forward by his predecessors, and suffices to move and excite the reader, so the essay cannot be constrained to a conventional approach."[45] Going beyond the text by distinguishing Mencius's response as adequate to Gongsun Chou but not adequate to Zengzi, and then venturing to explore the question of what kind of response might be adequate to Zengzi's feelings, the essay takes us far from the certainty and fidelity that we may expect from the genre. It insists on raising difficult questions and is content to end on a note of indeterminacy.

The forward movement of this argument is clear throughout, despite the inclusion of parallel passages, and the parallelism is careful but not identical. A parallel set in the *qijiang* (initiation of discourse) is separated by the phrase "even among contemporaries," while the two elements in the next parallel set are separated by the phrase "reaching Mencius's time." Although the separation of parallel elements in a set is not unusual, especially after the Wanli period, Tan adds a historicist twist by working the two different eras in question—Zengzi's lifetime, and Mencius's—in through these instances of separation in proper chronological order. This progression foreshadows Tan's eventual claim to move beyond the limited perspectives of these earlier eras.

The next set, comprising the third and fourth legs, picks up on the inadequacy of Mencius's explanation hinted at in the first paragraph and suggests that the how and why of unbearability will be Tan's focus: the fourth line includes an additional *ruhe* in two places where the third line had none, and we find syncopation rather than separation. Finally, a parallel set in the conclusion includes an additional "also" to jar the match and emphasize the point that one can be moved by something shared as well as by something distinctive. Here the essay ends by undercutting the very argument that Mencius has made and that Tan is supposed to be advancing. In chapter 3, we will see from a range of substantially bolder formal experiments that parallelism is far from an immutable rule in modern prose. Even in this more typical case, it is clear that parallel correspondences are used to propel the argument, not simply to reiterate or restate claims inherent in the source material.

In addition to advancing a logical argument, the formal qualities of this essay also allow the reader to imagine the feelings of the people who are spoken for. As Liu Dakui (1698–1779) writes of modern prose, "its aim is not only to convey the meaning of the ancients, but also to illustrate their spirit"; this spirit (*shen*) is in fact more important than the reasoned content presented (*li*).[46] Writing in the twentieth century, Qian Zhongshu likewise emphasizes the emotional resonances in essays like Tan Yuanchun's:

> I believe that if you really want to understand Confucius and Mencius's feelings and the events in their lives, then look for them in the best eight-legged essays of the Ming and Qing, where they are able to come to life. The Han and Song commentaries and Tao Shizheng's Qing-dynasty "Confucius Alive" are nothing in comparison. It is the eight-legged essays that are skilled at embodying experiences and marvelous in imagination; in this they are like *zaju* and *chuanqi* drama.[47]

Tan's essay speaks of Zengzi's grief, and in turn of individual feeling as an aspect of human nature more generally. Taking a different approach, essay writers could "borrow" topics to produce moving representations of specifically contemporary suffering by relating it thematically to the assigned passage, as in the case of Qiu Yi's use of a topic from the *Great Learning*, "Men are partial where they feel sorrow and compassion," to lament social conditions in the waning years of the Ming in convincing detail.[48]

Inevitably, when understood in terms of the classic polarity between *shi* 實 (real, concrete, full) and *xu* (potential, imaginary, empty), "logical argument" and "moral philosophy" fall under the former, and questions of "spirit" and "tone"—aesthetic and emotional force—are seen to belong to the latter.[49] According to Jiao Xun (1763–1820), "Essay topics have two aspects, potential and realized. The realized aspect takes the logic as the method; the potential aspect takes the spirit as the method."[50] Although it is true that modern prose could be dismissed as "empty" in the negative sense, this term also has interesting positive resonances: as mentioned previously, when contrasted with "reality" or "concreteness," *xu* can be understood in three different ways that go beyond mere emptiness. It stands for generality and abstraction; it designates a creative potential that can result in something new; and it allows one direct access to sensations unfiltered through rational discourse. Andrew Plaks has written of the key significance of the first of these three readings to the examination essay: the ability to condense and abstract an argument at certain points in the text, while balancing that abstraction with a wealth of concrete detail elsewhere, allows the author to generalize and make use of indirection in the development of the argument.[51] In this book I explore instead the second and third aspects of *xu*, which refer to specifically aesthetic dimensions of the term: the imaginative and potential rather than the already realized and the focus on sensation rather than on pure reason.[52]

These contrasts also work to mark a distinction between what is commonly accepted by everyone (basic moral precepts) and what is unique to each individual (the formal means chosen to voice one's argument). Yuan Renlin writes in the early eighteenth century that "things and their logic are the same for everyone but the tone of voice [with which one expresses those things] is unique to each person."[53] Indeed, the most popular genre of romantic fiction in the Ming and Qing—*caizi jiaren*— links the idea of distinctive literary talent or genius (*cai*) directly to examination success. Through this accomplishment, a hero proves to be an appropriate match for a beauty.[54] Although talent could manifest itself in a wide variety of other fields, from painting to poetry, there was for most Ming and Qing readers no doubt that literary genius could be found in modern prose as well: an essay written by Tang Xianzu as a teenager is praised in the following terms: "One foot of cloth makes a quilt to cover the nine provinces, truly original genius (*qicai*)."[55] Over the course of the Ming and Qing, there is a growing sense among critics and supporters alike that modern prose constituted a distinctive aesthetic tradition, one where essays could be judged against their predecessors and successors rather than merely dismissed as transparent vehicles of ideology or instruments through which wealth and power could be gained. Modern prose was an arena in which literary talent could be legitimately employed. From parallelism to prosopopoeia to the construction of the self, the following chapters inquire into the forms through which a substantial part of Ming-Qing imaginative cultural production took place.

Shiwen as/against *Wen*

The *shiwen* form is unmistakably central to both written production and arguments about the literary in Ming and Qing China, and not just because it constituted the better part of most students' instruction in writing.[56] Many critics identified the modern prose essay as a particular triumph of Ming dynasty writing, a worthy successor to genres such as the rhapsody of the Han, poetry of the Tang, prose or songs of the Song, and drama of the Yuan, and some influential and iconoclastic writers went so far as to rank the essay as one of the highest accomplishments in Chinese literature.[57] Indeed, for people as radically different in outlook and approach as Yuan Hongdao and Ruan Yuan (1764–1849), modern prose could serve as a key example to substantiate their broader claims about *wen* as such. Writing in the late Ming, Yuan puts his emphasis on the timeliness of *shiwen*: "Those who criticize [modern prose] do not even understand that there is such a thing as timeliness (*shi*); how could they understand what is literature (*wen*)?"[58] Ruan Yuan, writing from a very different perspective more than two centuries later, emphasizes these essays' potential to transcend their moment in time, making room for *shiwen* or "essays on the Four Books" in his definition of *wen*, which depends heavily on the use of parallelism and attention to tonal variation. For Ruan, these formal qualities of the essays bring them closer to the true lineage of the literary (*wen zhi zhengtong*) than much of what is conventionally referred to as "classical prose" in the Ming and Qing.[59] Although each critic seizes on a different aspect of *shiwen* to champion, both assume that the genre demonstrates the relevance of that particular quality to a more general definition of *wen*.

Shiwen had a close relationship with the texts that appeared in Ming and Qing collected works (classical prose and poetry) and with other genres that became central to the field of premodern Chinese literature defined by twentieth-century scholars. Terms and concepts in common use in modern prose criticism form the foundation of the structural analysis that becomes typical in the fiction and drama criticism of this period, and *shiwen* are noticeable as sources of thematic and formal inspiration in the works themselves.[60] Whether criticized for extending its pernicious influence to an entire dramatic genre or praised for bringing a new level of coherence and organization to writing for the stage, modern prose was widely understood to have a close connection to the theater.[61] As we will see in more detail in chapter 3, archaic or classical prose (*guwen*) was closely linked to examination writing as early as the Northern Song; even poetry could not escape, with numerous critics highlighting analogies between the genres and appropriating techniques of *shiwen* criticism to better understand regulated verse.[62]

Conversely, modern prose maintains a strong interest in integrating aspects of other genres into a single text. Jiao Xun's claim that *shiwen* "can contain a multitude of genres: talent for history, a poet's brush, and the logical argument of treatises" is just one example of a common tendency.[63] Often the exchange between the essay and other genres was dialectic: Qian Zhongshu notes the effect Tang Xianzu's *Mudan ting* (Peony pavilion) had on students preparing for the examinations, but Tang himself was writing well-received *shiwen* long before he began writing the plays that he is now best known for.[64]

In this context, it comes as no surprise that Zhou Zuoren could claim that eight-legged essays "are the crystallization of Chinese literature—no, one can simply and more boldly say Chinese culture."[65] My own sense is that few individual essays can approach vernacular works such as *Peony Pavilion* and *Jin Ping Mei* in their riotous and unapologetic appropriation of other texts and traditions. But where vernacular fiction and drama often borrow from other genres in the key of parody or pastiche, with a resulting emphasis on specific quotations from other works, modern prose essays tend to weave borrowed techniques and attitudes into a subtler, more cohesive fabric. In this book, I focus particularly on the following points of contact between modern prose and other genres: interest in the question of literary voice, and representative speech more generally (chapters 1 and 4); attention to narrative structure and textual organization (chapter 3); and the creation of the distinctive individual through writing that claims to be expressive (chapters 4 and 5).

Despite the debts contracted between the modern prose essay and other literary genres individually and the clear significance of *shiwen* criticism in sparking analytical discourse on literary form more generally, modern anthologies of Ming and Qing literary criticism generally exclude discussions of *shiwen* aesthetics, even by writers and critics well known for their contributions to other fields. This exclusion has led a range of scholars of premodern literature to underestimate how much of the critical tradition has survived.[66] In fact, a substantial amount of *shiwen* criticism is extant and has recently begun to be reprinted or excerpted in modern scholarly works.

Together with *shiwen* themselves, these works of criticism are the primary sources on which this book is based. They run the gamut from sophisticated aesthetic treatises to records of casual conversation to instruction manuals that provided intermediate students with the nuts-and-bolts technical skills to produce acceptable essays. I note only four outstanding examples out of the dozens that are extant. Wu Zhiwang's *Juye zhiyan* (Loose words on the examination métier), first published in 1588, begins by developing a lengthy and systematic analysis of *wen* that rivals any work published since *Wenxin diaolong* (The literary mind and the carving of dragons). Yuan Huang's *Youyi shu wengui* (Literary guidelines from the School for Taking One's Ease in the Arts) and *Youyi shu xu wengui* (1602), are if anything even more valuable: treasure troves of writings by a range of Ming critics on examination prose, including Yuan's own detailed analysis of specific essays, running to a total of more than 400,000 characters. In *Loose Words* and *Literary Guidelines*, we hear from authorities on modern prose style and significant figures in the classical prose tradition, as well as from late Ming luminaries such as Yuan Zongdao, Dong Qichang, and playwright Wang Heng. Tang Biao's *Dushu zuowen pu* (Manual for reading and literary composition, 1699) served as an inspiration for Angelo Zottoli's nineteenth-century study of Chinese prose. It has been overlooked by more recent scholars of premodern literature because of its relative inaccessibility, but it contains a wealth of insights into prose aesthetics in their broader literary context and is widely quoted by later critics.[67] Finally, Liang Zhangju's nineteenth-century *Collected Words on Regulated Essays* stands as somewhat of an exception: the most readily available of these works, it is modeled on the *shihua* genre of poetry criticism, and the literary criticism that it contains—extended quotes from earlier critics, and Liang's own assessments—is mixed in with a variety of other examination-related anecdotes.[68]

The standard modern anthologies of Ming and Qing literature and literary theory do not generally feel a need to explain their choice to exclude these and other texts related to *shiwen* aesthetics; to get a justification for their selective approach we need to look elsewhere. Typical is Jin Kemu's rationale for the study of the eight-legged essay: even as an advocate, relatively speaking, he argues that modern prose is a cultural phenomenon (*wenhua xianxiang*) and as such should be included in literary history (*wenxue shi*), which is not to be confused with the more narrowly defined study of aesthetically distinctive "literary works" (*wenxue zuopin*) in which, it is implied, the eight-legged essay would find no place.[69] Indeed, although Gong Duqing, Andrew Plaks, and Pierre-Henri Durand have carefully delineated a sophisticated generic ideal type of *shiwen*, and Huang Qiang, David Rolston, and Stephen Roddy have investigated the connections between *shiwen* and other genres, the field of Chinese literary studies as a whole has continued to keep *shiwen* at an arm's length. There is much work still to be done to understand the place of modern prose in the literary tradition and the discourses of *shiwen* aesthetics in the genealogy of Chinese literary criticism.

For some *shiwen* advocates, the problem is our failure to recognize that modern prose has the same range of aesthetic quality as any literary genre: examples of brilliant writing are there if only we would open our eyes to them. As Zhu Jian reminds us in his preface to Liang Zhangju's *Collected Words*, to characterize the examination essay genre with reference only to its worst examples is to take the part for the whole.[70] Durand captures this dynamic well, noting both that one would expect some notable successes over these centuries of practice on a national scale and that for many the challenges of the form would have been too much, leading them to transform "the flowers of this required rhetoric into bouquets of nettles."[71]

Huang Qiang's groundbreaking work on the relationship between *shiwen* and other literary genres elaborates on this point in detail. Rather than reiterating a distinction between examination essays on one hand and literature on the other, Huang argues for a division of the essay genre itself into two categories: instrumental essays written solely to achieve worldly aims and "realm of the imagination" (*jingjie*) essays concerned with exploring aesthetic, moral, and scholarly questions.[72] In demonstrating the range and diversity characteristic of modern prose as a genre, Huang makes an important contribution, but he insists on a coherent unity within each of the two categories among author's motivation, attitude toward the scholarly tradition, interest in creative argument, and inclination to employ specific literary techniques. This argument is not always convincing. Leaving aside the question of authorial motivation, we may note that essays that take a rigid approach to parallelism may in fact feature startlingly original insights, essays with startlingly original insights may not be as serious in their scholarship, essays that are not serious in their scholarship may in fact be quite innovative in their form, and so on. Here I would like to take a different approach to the question of the literariness of *shiwen* by inquiring into the rhetorical construction of *wen* and *shiwen* as mutually defining categories in the Ming and Qing.

To the extent that literature is considered as literature, *shiwen* may seem to constitute an exterior boundary; a discursive field of anthologies and a tradition of aesthetic criticism is marked by their exclusion. Modern prose is one element of the frame through which the literary is perceived, whether that frame is sharply demarcated or consists of a graded zone of transition.[73] Yet we find many references to *wen* in Ming and Qing texts and titles that turn out, when looked at more closely, to refer specifically to *shiwen*.[74] Here I highlight the intriguing overlaps between one of the key texts in the *shiwen* critical tradition, Dong Qichang (1555–1636)'s *Wenjue jiuze* (Nine instructions on literary writing), and the "Pingwen" (Evaluating literary writing) chapter in the third volume of his collection *Huachan shi suibi* (Random writings from Zen Painting Studio). These two texts serve as powerful evidence of the imbrication of *wen* and *shiwen* in the Ming and Qing.

One contrast between these two sources is immediately evident: *Random Writings from Zen Painting Studio*, which foregrounds lengthy discussions of painting and calligraphy in its early chapters and more random remarks on literature and Buddhism in later chapters, appears in the *Siku quanshu* (Complete library of four treasuries), is readily available in reprint editions, and is included in a variety of Qing and modern collectanea. *Nine Instructions on Literary Writing*, on the other hand, is not so easy to find. The relative scarcity of extant *Nine Instructions* editions is particularly striking because it had been one of the more frequently cited texts in discussions of literary technique in the examination context from the late Ming onward, circulating in a variety of reprint editions and under several different names.[75] The orientation of the two texts also seems rather different. The "Evaluating Literary Writing" chapter appears to be a collection of casual remarks on literary writing generally, whereas *Nine Instructions* is a more systematic explanation of a set of related techniques for composing *shiwen*. *Nine Instructions* shows a greater interest in correctness than the more casual "Evaluating Literary Writing" chapter, and we are not surprised to find text of the *Nine Instructions* punctuated, while the version of the *Random Writings from Zen Painting Studio* reproduced in the *Complete Library* lacks punctuation.[76] These characteristics fit with a general stereotype of what examination writing pedagogy might be, as distinct from the more aesthetically inclined, less instrumental *wen* composed by an elite artist and calligrapher at his or her leisure. In Pierre Bourdieu's distinction, *Nine Instructions* would be a means for acquiring educational capital narrowly defined, while *Random Writings* is a work whose consumption demonstrates a certain level of (inherited) cultural capital.[77]

On closer investigation, however, we notice significant similarities between the two texts, including substantial sections that are identical word-for-word. It should also be pointed out that the *Complete Library*'s compilers' remarks on *Random Writings* specifically note Dong's skill in the modern prose essay and highlight the "Evaluating Literary Writing" chapter as an example of his approach.[78] At the same time, we should note that *Nine Instructions* enthusiastically picks up on some of the more challenging and provocative comments about literary writing from the "Evaluating Literary Writing" chapter and develops them further. *Shiwen* lurk within Dong's discussion of "pure literature," just as sophisticated questions of literary technique are addressed in detail in his handbook for essay writing.

This imbrication of discourses on *wen* and *shiwen* turns out not to have been an isolated case: it is likely that Dong's remarks on literary writing came first and the instructions second, but in the case of a manual compiled by Gui Youguang (1507–71), one of the best-known Ming writers of literary prose, we see a similar process in reverse. Gui's *Juye qieyao gujin wenze* (Key literary principles old and new for examination writing), published in 1572, was later abstracted, recopied, and published under the more "literary" title *Zhenchuan xiansheng du guwen fa* (Mr. Gui's method of reading classical prose) in 1734. In this "second" edition, all the individual example texts are removed, as well as almost all references to the examination métier (*juye*), to make the work seem more generally applicable.[79]

To what extent is the category of *wen* in the Ming and Qing ordinarily, if not always, haunted by *shiwen*, a genre that not only appears as ghostly other or inferior mockery of "literary prose" but also reveals its fundamental and problematic core? Kai-wing Chow notes a persistent suppression of economic concerns in discourses on literati writing and publication in the early modern period.[80] A similar dynamic is clearly at work when texts and collections that deal primarily with the technical aspects of writing *shiwen* tend to identify themselves in broad terms as discussions of *wen* (yet manage to find their way into the hands of eager candidates perfecting their examination essay writing nonetheless). At the same time, it is difficult to escape the realization that the primary prose alternative to *shiwen* in the Ming and Qing, *guwen* (classical prose), is itself implicated in the essay from its earliest moments in the Northern Song down through each substantial paradigm shift in essay writing over the following centuries.[81]

When we broaden our perspective to consider not only literary writing but Ming-Qing cultural production and reproduction more generally, in which the literary is articulated to questions of ethics, ideology, practice, identity, and intentionality as the least element in the triad *lide, ligong,* and *liyan,* we find that literature narrowly conceived as a conscious aesthetic practice is often condemned on precisely the same grounds that modern prose was. Writing that is produced with an idea of the literary as such in mind is thought inevitably to tend toward formalism and inauthenticity, a critique that has a substantial lineage.[82] It is not just that most educated men spent as much time writing *shiwen* as any other kind of writing, but also that the very condemnations of modern prose as a genre tend to mirror critiques of literary writing more generally. Critics insist that a true author does not make a name through attention to stylistic detail but from sensibility, clarity of moral vision, or depth of feeling, which find *natural* expression through literary means that are categorically subordinate to the ends that they express. David Nivison writes of this tendency that it "has had the effect of making literary criticism in China a variety of moral philosophy."[83]

In this sense, *shiwen*—in their emphasis on working from a dense and complicated body of conventions and wrestling with the dynamics of speaking in a constructed voice—turn out to constitute not the excluded other, exterior to the literary canon, but the very epitome of literariness as such, the clearest instance of a problematic that lurks at the core of the literary endeavor. As Liu Dakui puts it: "Now literary composition is the finest among the arts, and eight-legged modern prose is the finest of the fine."[84] Zeng Yizhuan (1590–1644) poses the following questions: why should literati write, out of all the other things they could do? And of all types of writing—including magicians' texts, novels, and actors' songs—why examination essays? *Shiwen* are simultaneously the finest example of the literary arts and the least valid element in this category whose validity itself is always subject to question.[85] In these cases, the dispositions and techniques of modern prose constitute a framework that organizes the category of the literary from the inside as much as they do a frame that defines it from the outside by negation.

One could say for this reason alone that the *shiwen* genre is fundamental to conceptions and articulations of the literary in Ming and Qing China. The only critic who can in good faith exile *shiwen* from the category of the literary is one who begins from the position that literature as such, as a distinct end toward which an author works, should not in fact exist.[86] Indeed, historically speaking, criticism of modern prose does not arise in isolation but constitutes an integral part of a more general skeptical attitude toward literary culture—and "literariness" itself—in the seventeenth century. This attitude was manifested as often in attacks on the practice of "writing for exchange" (*yingchou*) or attention to stylistic detail (*ziju*) as it was in the better-known criticisms of the eight-legged essay and the "huckster scholarship" of the Ming.[87]

In the end, the question of whether we categorize the modern prose essay as literature or not is less significant than the realization that the relation of *shiwen* to *wen* is in important ways analogous to the relation of *wen* to the sphere of aesthetic, ethical, and political action broadly defined. Even as more *wen* is produced in the Ming and Qing in the form of *shiwen* than any other genre, however difficult writers may have found this fact to accept, most political and ethical acts in this same period are constituted by words, as Zhang Xuecheng points out; and these are often words in writing.[88]

Innovation and Imitation

> Producing a new play is like reading modern prose: what is wonderful is hearing what one has never yet heard, and seeing what one has never yet seen.
>
> —Li Yu, *Xianqing ouji*

Although one tends to think of *shiwen* as exercises in reproducing truths found in the standard Song dynasty commentaries to the Classics, the claims of orthodoxy were frequently undercut in practice, even in those essays composed in the examination compound. Striking a tone familiar from a wealth of works dealing with examination writings, Jiao Xun sharply criticizes writers who "just borrow the mouths of the Sages and Worthies" to put forward the teachings of Laozi, Zhuangzi, and the Buddha in their essays; scholars often interpret comments along these lines as evidence of the philosophical conservatism of the examination regime.[89] But Jiao also offers the following praise to the many essays that show off what in his view are appropriate workings of the literary imagination: "As for those essays that manage the broad and level, but have deep reflection; and those that are situated in the ordinary, but give rise to challenging words (*weiyan*): some resemble the work of the philosophers Zhuangzi, Liezi, Shen Buhai, Han Feizi, Deng Xi, and Gongsun Long."[90] This appreciation for "challenging words" is apparent in even the most canonical essay anthologies: when Fang Bao was commissioned to compile the *Imperially Authorized Essays on the Four Books*, he made sure to exclude those essays that followed the commentaries too closely and failed to add anything significant to them. In fact, many of the evaluative comments in this canonical collection are particularly favorable to interpretations that differ from those found in the Cheng-Zhu commentaries.[91] A century later, Liang Zhangju devotes three volumes of his encyclopedic nineteenth-century work on the modern prose essay, *Collected Words on Regulated Essays*, solely to the discussion of essays that either supplemented or outright challenged canonical interpretations.[92]

Examiners occasionally went so far as to show a sense of humor about these challenges: when a candidate used earlier commentaries rather than Song commentaries to ground his interpretation in an essay graded by the famous scholar Ji Yun (1724–1805), the latter wrote in the margin: "You use this to scare the old guy, but the old guy is not afraid."[93] Although the significance of the examination system as a means of ideological reproduction cannot be ignored, we must note at the same time that examiners not infrequently chose topics that gave candidates a chance to articulate political critiques with contemporary relevance, and perceptive candidates made the most of those opportunities.[94] My aim in this book is not, however, primarily to show that *shiwen* could present intriguing and original arguments but rather to investigate the means by which such content could be presented to great effect—the aesthetics of the genre.

In considering the politics of power in early modern China, scholars have tended to focus on ideological reproduction and critical difference in a narrow sense, with particular attention to the extent to which a specified interpretive framework is deployed or contested by examination candidates in their essays. Questions of style have often been overlooked on the simple assumption that the "formalism" of *shiwen* meant that even when there might be disputes of philosophical or philological significance, no meaningful aesthetic variation could exist. But as we will see in detail in the following chapters, it is precisely through the "emptiness" (*xu*) of imaginative aesthetic variation that solid critical difference often finds its beginning. The task here is to remind ourselves of the range and room for originality in a genre that is known primarily for its formal restrictions. We may begin with the question of how comprehensive and consistent the effects of these supposed restrictions were, in fact. As Huang Qiang notes of the hundreds of essays collected in the canonical *Imperially Authorized Essays on the Four Books*, "if you want to find a typical eight-legged essay among them, it will be a difficult task."[95] This is due to the range of possibilities explored by the writers that Fang Bao felt best represented the genre and to the historicity and heterogeneity even of the very conventions that the most innovative writers worked in turn to take their distance from.[96]

Scholars who have investigated the formation of the *shiwen* genre in detail generally conclude that certain key elements of the genre appear already—separately and in combination—in certain examination essays of the Song dynasty, and that these elements continued to play an important role in Yuan dynasty examination essays.[97] At the same time, most agree with Gu Yanwu that what we generally think of as the eight-legged essay in its most complete form—*poti* (topic-breaker) and *chengti* (topic-receiver) as introductory elements, with the main body of the essay dominated by three or four parallel sets—takes shape in the Chenghua reign (1465–87) and is epitomized by the work of Wang Ao (1450–1524).[98]

Writing two centuries later, Wang Fuzhi (1619–92) presents a critique of Wang Ao of a type that will ring familiar to readers of premodern literary criticism: Wang Ao represents a mastery of the genre so complete that the examination essay is closed off as an area for future innovation. His perfection becomes a tie that binds all writers from that point forward, giving them walls along which they can feel their way, with the result that later essays sound as if they came from one mouth alone.[99] Wang Fuzhi is exaggerating for effect here, but the sense that Wang

Ao—who worked as associate examiner and chief examiner several times after his own examination success—is perhaps the single person most responsible for the stylistic parameters within which later candidates write is one that is shared by most subsequent critics.[100]

Modern scholars generally echo this assessment of Wang Ao's significance. No work of scholarship in Chinese would be complete without an explanation of his central place in the canon, and scholars writing in English have tended to highlight two of his essays in particular as formal epitomes of the eight-legged essay: "When kindred spirits come from afar" and "If the people have plenty, their prince will not be left to want alone." These essays, like others by Wang Ao that are regularly cited, represent a kind of ideal type, with a strict parallel order in each of the four main sections and an initiation of discourse (*qijiang*) and conclusion that are easily identifiable.[101] It was no doubt the clarity and coherence of Wang Ao's approach that made it possible for so many later candidates to imitate his distinctive voice.

Yet the story is more complicated than this account might suggest. First, essays marked by extremely strict parallelism appear already in the early decades of the Ming, more than half a century before Wang Ao earned his *jinshi* degree.[102] Second, what is characteristic of Wang Ao's essays is not simply the strict parallelism pioneered by earlier writers but an involution of parallel practice that adds a layer of complexity, such that segments of the text that are parallel at one level are not parallel at another and vice versa, an innovation that is of comparable importance to the essay form as the invention of counterpoint would be to the development of Western music. As we will see in chapter 3 and the epilogue, involution serves to structure both literary texts and the social dimensions of cultural material production. Here we note only that although Wang Ao makes consistent use of this technique in his essays, he is neither the earliest writer to employ it nor the most extreme in its service.[103]

Finally, and most significantly, the fact that many candidates never strayed beyond the path established for them by Wang Ao does not mean that alternatives did not emerge, just as the many imitations of Du Fu and Li Bai in later dynasties do not prove that innovation in Chinese poetry ended in the Tang. (Painting did not end with Van Gogh's *Café Terrace at Night* either, despite the countless imitations and direct reproductions of that work in a wide variety of media that continue to appear to this day.) Given the immense numbers of examination essays produced in the Ming and Qing, it would be surprising indeed if many essay authors did not look to one of the most successful examination candidates for stylistic inspiration. Here it is important to remember Zhu Jian's admonition not to characterize the whole genre by the work of those writers who had the least skill or imagination.[104] In fact, even as Wang Fuzhi was complaining that the essay genre consisted of nothing but copies of Wang Ao, his contemporary Gu Yanwu emphasized the radical variability characteristic of this genre, claiming that essay styles change from exam session to exam session and that writers of his era did not even know what an eight-legged essay really was.[105]

The selective view of *shiwen* resulting from excessive emphasis on Wang Ao can be well understood by analogy: suppose our familiarity with the canon of Western classical music were limited to the Brandenburg concertos and the *Well-Tempered Clavier*. If we were to assume on this basis alone that the music of Mozart (Gui Youguang), Beethoven (Tang Shunzhi), and Wagner (Ai Nanying), not to mention Schoenberg (Fang Bao), must not only be difficult to distinguish one from another but also represent no real difference in approach or technique from the work of Bach, we would not have much ground to object to anyone who might call our judgment into question. As we will see in chapter 3, the "perfection" of Wang Ao's parallelism and those most influenced by him was one approach that was always available to candidates from the mid-Ming onward, but it was not invariably the approach those candidates chose to make use of.[106] Indeed, it was not even the case that a single person would always choose to write in the same style.[107] As we have seen previously, commentators who took modern prose seriously frequently emphasized the extent to which the genre changed over time; freshness and originality were often noted.[108]

With tens of thousands of modern prose essays written each year, there is no doubt that any notable innovation that was seen to succeed found many imitators, but this fact speaks primarily to the sheer numbers of essays produced, not to an inability on anyone's part to innovate.[109] As we will see in more detail in chapter 5, incentives to innovation in many cases match up well against the impulse to imitate successful essays from past cycles that we tend to imagine as dominant.

The stylistic differences that resulted from these incentives were in some cases extreme enough that an essay written in all seriousness by a skilled author could be taken by some readers as a joke.[110] Given the widespread distribution of essays that met with success, and differing comfort levels with and abilities to reproduce on one hand and create on the other, a feedback system of nearly fractal complexity appears. For every rule we can formulate about the development of the essay form, there is not only an exception but often a category of exceptions, and then exceptions to that category of exceptions, appearing in quick succession by examination cycle.

Stylistic change occurs at many different levels: changes in essay length as a whole and changes in the length of certain constituent parts; omission of components that had previously been standard and the introduction of new ones; inclusion of vocabulary and concepts previously considered unacceptable and the avoidance of those that had previously been the norm; more or less attention to questions of sound, especially tone distribution and rhyme; varying levels of strictness about references beyond the cited topic; and perhaps most striking, substantial differences in approach to the stylistic feature that has been taken as characteristic of the examination essay, parallelism, which will be discussed in chapter 3.[111] Even the terms used for the different parts of the essay were in constant flux, with many of the key words we are now accustomed to use in discussing essay structure dating only from the early to mid-Qing—indeed, even the term "eight-legged essay" itself.[112]

It is no accident that the term *shimao* can refer to fashionable examination writing as well as to fashionable clothing in the Ming and Qing.[113] As Dorothy Ko has shown, the insistent Western discourse on Qing China as a realm without fashion serves to figure the system more generally as basically changeless;[114] similarly the repeated characterizations of *shiwen* style as repetitive and unoriginal, aiming only at the faithful mimesis of the words of the Sages at best and mere imitation of past successful essays at worst, refuse to acknowledge the dynamism of the examination field and contribute to a broader sense of a society's "failure" to develop. My hope is that this introduction, and the close readings of essays in the chapters to follow, can help articulate a more nuanced understanding of the significance of *shiwen* in the Ming and Qing.

Chapter Summaries

I begin in chapter 1 with the trope of representative speech, central to the single most influential attempt to define Ming-Qing examination writing, a chapter on the examination system in the *History of the Ming* composed at the end of the seventeenth century, which remarks that the authors of these essays "spoke in the voices of the ancients in writing them (*dai guren yuqi weizhi*)."[115] This trope, which is now more often rephrased as "speaking for the Sages and Worthies" (*dai shengxian liyan*), although convincing to modern scholars, admits of significant objections. The first objection may be understood as historicist. It turns out that there is no evidence for "speaking for the Sages and Worthies" as the defining principle of the genre before the late seventeenth century. Despite the centrality of representative speech to later understandings of *shiwen*, it seems to have been understood as only one among a group of literary techniques well into the seventeenth century. Second, the place of this representative speech (*daiyan*) in the structure of the essay is not as simple or clearcut as is often suggested, as essays often move fluidly in and out of the representative mode, sometimes within a single sentence.

To address these complexities, chapter 1 constructs a genealogy of the concept of representative speech—its transformation over the course of the sixteenth through eighteenth centuries from a stylistic technique used tactically in essays on topics for which it was thought to be particularly appropriate, to an ideological structure with a reach broad enough to fold even those essays that clearly did not make use of it in under its auspices. Of particular interest is the way in which this focus on the concept of literary voice clarifies the trope of representation as a field of struggle, in which questions of agency and control are foregrounded: candidates were expected to speak *as* the Sages and Worthies even as they said things the Sages and Worthies themselves never said. Similarly, the idea of voice as an integration of content and form figures the tension between ideological reproduction aimed at class allegiance and the stylistic differentiation that proves to be the basis on which one candidate could be selected over another. In this sense, chapter 1 attempts to do justice to both the discourse and the literary practice of representative speech.

The figure of representative speech leads us into a broader analysis of *shiwen* aesthetics and politics. Style is a conundrum. Why should it be important? If it is so important, why is there so little direct prescriptive control over it? Chapter 2 inquires into the stylistic range characteristic of the genre, finding significant aesthetic variation that led in turn to ideological variation: Wang Yangming, the *Zhuangzi*, and Chan Buddhist approaches were integral to modern prose style by the end of the sixteenth century and, despite harsh criticism from ministers and outsider literati alike, remained significant well into the Qing. Examiners drove this stylistic variation as much as candidates and critics did; although boasting openly of their own importance was impossible, it was clear that examiners at the various levels maintained a control over the standards for evaluations that ministers and rulers could not. "Speaking for the Sages and Worthies" in this way articulates a class that joins candidate and examiner even as it divides them: a class that is productive, rather than defined by consumption, and focused on the aesthetics of a literary field, with its own ethos distinct from classical scholarship. The author is not just speaking for oneself among one's friends and (limited) social networks but also speaking on behalf of a broader group that sets rules for itself. Such rule-setting on aesthetic terms, although reminiscent of the formation of the bourgeois identity in Europe, is rather different in this case. The individual is constituted not just as a consumer of literary commodities but also as a representative agent; the literati class as a whole mediates between ruler and society more generally.

Much of the scholarly energy spent on the question of parallelism—the second key element in the *History of the Ming* definition of the essay genre—has been devoted to the question of how early one can find precedents for Ming and Qing uses of this mode of structural organization. Chapter 3 works in a different direction, asking first, how consistently dominant parallel writing actually was in Ming and Qing modern prose; second, how parallelism worked; and third, what its implications were. It turns out that parallelism functions not as an obvious one-to-one correspondence between strings of words but as a complex principle of reading and writing evident at a range of levels of textual generality and abstraction. With the introduction of what I call *involutionary parallelism* in the late fifteenth century, for example, essays could be constructed out of textual elements that matched as parallel when read in isolation, but at another level failed to match as one would have expected; at the same time, passages that seem at first to be loose prose could turn out eventually to constitute one part of a higher-level pairing. At the generic level, it becomes clear that the "classical" or "archaic" prose (*guwen*) against which examination writing was often contrasted could itself appear as a coherent conceptual category only as the converse of "modern" prose (*shiwen*), a relationship that can be traced back to roots of the modern prose essay in the eleventh century.

Parallelism was not always neat in its correspondences. Although some candidates treated it as a simple rule to be observed strictly, better writers often saw it as a site of struggle where authors could strive to throw readers off balance to a greater or lesser degree. On this basis, chapter 3 also inquires into the work of the reader, who becomes aware of parallelism only in and through time, as it would not be immediately present to the eye except in the simplest of cases. You may not know how you want to parse the essay in structural terms until you have read the whole; there may be provisional parsings abandoned along the way. When there are alternations of loose and parallel prose, or nested parallels, different readers can disagree about how exactly parallelism manifests itself in the essay—or even whether it does.

The late Ming is a magical moment for scholars of drama, casual prose, and vernacular fiction, as well as cultural production more generally. This efflorescence is often attributed—explicitly or implicitly—to the rapid development of the market economy in the sixteenth and early seventeenth centuries, although there are also less materialist accounts grounded in weariness with standard cultural and ideological forms or the decadence of a dynasty sensing its days are numbered. In none of these explanatory paradigms does the examination system play a positive role. But it must be noted that many of the sixteenth- and seventeenth-century writers conventionally understood to be most creative or iconoclastic, from Li Zhi to Li Yu (1610–80), saw value in *shiwen*. Chapter 4 examines this apparent paradox from two different angles: first, the valorization of a distinctive individual self, able to act with natural spontaneity, in *shiwen* as well as in critical commentary; and second, the frequent, even obsessive use of the first-person voice in these essays in ways that recall free indirect discourse in the modern Western novel. Literary scholars have drawn intriguing parallels between the articulation of individual subjectivity in the late Ming and early Qing on one hand and early modern Europe on the other, particularly in the novel, with special attention to the role of silver and the market. This chapter suggests that the intense subjectivity characteristic of the late Ming moment, influential well into the Qing, draws inspiration from the examination system as much as from the market; its voice comes as much from *shiwen* as it does from the novel.

The concept of cultural capital, so important to cultural analysis that works within the early modern paradigm, depends on a discursive system of names in which simple recognition is too often privileged over actual engagement with the aesthetic work. Chapter 5 begins from a different scenario of reading in which a text is considered strictly on its own terms, without reference to the place of its author in a broader scholarly or social hierarchy. In the ideal case, Ming and Qing examiners read essays without knowing the names of the candidates who had written them. Although practically speaking there were exceptions due to corrupt behavior on the part of candidates, examiners, and other staff in the examination compound, it is nonetheless likely that most essays read at the provincial and metropolitan levels were subject to blind assessment. Under these circumstances, I argue, the ability to write distinctively became even more significant, not only for the candidates themselves, but also for the examiners, who hoped to find a way to distinguish among the candidates. The stereotypical understanding of *shiwen* as the epitome of conformity is far too simple. What is even more significant is the extent to which the exam system grounds itself on discernible difference between individuals, and the consequences of this bureaucratic insistence. Generally speaking, what we see is appearance of the natural authentic voice as a fetish, playing a role of similar significance in the examination system to that played by commodity fetishism in the capitalist market. Both fetishisms ultimately function to cover over the crucial significance of labor—literary *work*—but they do so in different ways. This work is not a simple post hoc mimesis or expression of a preexisting essence but a process of subject formation.

The epilogue takes a step back to consider the modern prose essay in a broader world-historical context. I suggest that current approaches to the history of global literary production would benefit from further consideration of the imbrication between literary and material economies. For example, what role does the practice of literary examination as a systematic means of administrative recruitment play in the formation of a substantial, well-organized, and stable market for the world's silver? What are the effects of the "industrious revolution" that we see in Chinese literary writing of the fifteenth and sixteenth centuries? In conclusion, I suggest that although the dynamics through which a literary sphere argues for its autonomy from social constraints are similar whether those constraints are imagined primarily as market demands, state incentives, or a combination of the two, the resulting aesthetics do differ between systems in which value formed through consumption is privileged and those in which emphasis is placed instead on the production of a distinctive yet representative voice.

CHAPTER ONE

Voice

An Ideology of Technique

Shiwen (modern prose essays) speak for the Sages and Worthies: this proposition has reigned uncontested in critical and scholarly discourse for three centuries as a defining characteristic of the genre. Representative speech (*daiyan*) as a *performative* project is crucial to Qing and later understandings of examination writing for critics and advocates alike. While Yuan Mei (1716–98) argues that modern prose authors are just like actors mouthing another's words and miming emotions they themselves do not feel, Guan Shiming (1738–98) praises the genre for its ability to invest logical argument with live emotion, exclaiming "how much better even would Zhu Xi's commentaries on the Classics have been if the modern prose form had been available then for his use!"[1] Indeed, although critics of *shiwen* have often fixed on the trope of "speaking for the Sages and Worthies" as an ideological constraint, it is notable that the quality that is aimed at in this project turns out to be authenticity of tone (*kouqi*) more often than purity of content or strict adherence to formal standards. In Li Guangdi's (1642–1718) words, "If the tone is wrong, the reasoning will all be wrong."[2]

In an intriguing essay by Chen Nieheng (1700 *jinshi*) on the topic "While it was yet twanging, he laid the instrument aside, and rose," we actually go a step beyond language: Chen does not speak for Confucius, as we may expect, nor does he speak for Dian, Confucius's disciple, who has yet to begin speaking at the moment he sets aside the zither. Instead, Chen's essay (included in the appendix to this volume) concentrates on the sound of the zither, or more precisely, the aftertones that fade away as the instrument is set aside:

Dian was focused on rising in respect, but the zither still
seemed to have something to say . . .
*The meaning at first is not in the strings, but between meaning
and not meaning, the lingering sound still stirs;*
*The string has already left the hand, but at the bounds of what is
not hand and not string, the echoing sigh still circles.*[3]

In an approach that foreshadows Yuan Renlin's eighteenth-century explanation of the "empty words" so crucial to examination prose—"their
meaning is none other than the material force (*qi* 氣) they articulate"—
this essay takes the concept of tone of voice past its ordinary limits to
highlight not ethics or metaphysics but the aesthetic, whether understood in the original definition of the term as the rejoinder that sensuous experience could pose to rational thought within a philosophical
framework, or in the extended understandings that would appear later
in eighteenth-century Europe, involving a sense of fluent spontaneity,
sublime distance, or purposiveness without purpose.[4] Qian Zhongshu
and Pierre-Henri Durand have both noted interesting parallels between
shiwen and European rhetorical traditions in which the written text is
charged specifically with giving its readers a sense of the voices of figures
from the past.[5] What I want to emphasize in this chapter is not merely
the relevance of representative voice as a specific rhetorical technique
but also the significance of the concept of voice as integral to the basic
ground of the aesthetic.

The central problematic of the aesthetic in early modern Europe
consists in the attempt to articulate the personal and the universal
through a concept of taste. Kant begins from the following difficulty: we
refuse to agree that something is beautiful on the basis of reasoned argument alone; we insist on seeing the object in question with our own eyes.
Once we have done so, however, any statement about the object's beauty
that we may make constitutes a judgment that claims to go beyond individual experience and represent the potential experience of others. "And
yet, if we then call the object beautiful, we believe we have a universal
voice, and lay claim to the agreement of everyone, whereas any private
sensation would decide solely for the observer himself and his liking." As
we will see over the course of this chapter and later in chapter 4, distinctions between "universal" and "private" are never straightforward; what
is particularly significant in this context, however, is Kant's focus on the

concept of voice: he goes on to assert that "we can see, at this point, that nothing is postulated in a judgment of taste except such a *universal voice* about a liking unmediated by concepts."[6] This postulated voice—this idea that one could assume to speak for others on questions of taste—initiates the field of the aesthetic in modern Europe. In the introduction, I suggested that the discourse of *xu* ("emptiness" or "the imaginary") in the Ming and Qing has significant commonalities with the aesthetic. As we will see in this chapter, representative speech is characteristically *xu* in two ways—in its emphasis on the imagination, and in its focus on tone in addition to (even over and above) logical content—indicating, like Kant's universal voice, a close connection to the aesthetic.

The question of voice in modern prose is, however, quite complicated. It is not just that the "person" spoken for is not always Confucius or Mencius or even necessarily a person, rather than, say, a zither. There was never a formal requirement that candidates write in another's voice; indeed, representative speech existed as a regular practice for two centuries before any critic thought to address it in detail. A majority of essays make use of the technique but many do not; not infrequently, it is actually unclear whether an essay or part of an essay is meant to be understood as the words of a Sage or Worthy or those of the author. This chapter inquires into the phenomenon of representative speech, asking the following questions. How characteristic is it? How does it work? When does it shift from implicit practice to an explicitly articulated condition of writing, and why?

I aim to emphasize the ways the trope of representation unites formal qualities with questions of power and its distribution that may ordinarily be thought of as more properly political. The work of Pierre Bourdieu has been immensely influential in recent scholarship on early modern China, with the concept of "cultural capital" inspiring notable interest. I suggest that writing modern prose is not merely a type of investment but also a kind of representation, an act that itself constitutes subjectivity through struggle and contestation. Rather than begin from questions of aesthetic value and the accumulation and circulation of cultural capital—concepts derived from and ultimately beholden to a specific historical narrative of the development of the capitalist market economy—this chapter aims to account for the significance of the examination system on different grounds, focusing on the aesthetics and politics of speaking for others.

How to Represent

The formulation that has gained the widest currency among modern scholars is *dai shengxian li yan* (speaking on behalf of the Sages and Worthies), but there were a variety of alternatives used over the course of the Qing, many of which seem to focus more closely on the concreteness of the words spoken. The *History of the Ming* explains the technique as *dai guren yuqi* (representing the voice of the ancients), for example, and Liu Dakui writes of *dai shengxian zhi kouyu* (representing the speech of the Sages and Worthies).[7] What these alternatives all have in common is the trope of representation (*dai*), in the abstract sense of "standing for" someone and in the more concrete sense of re-presenting something— it is the genius of this trope to in most cases leave indeterminate the question of whether the representation ultimately is of persons or of the language itself, of a distinctive discursive mode.[8]

It should be noted that in no case can an essay be characterized as representative speech from start to finish: the "speaking for" portion of the essay generally begins with the *qijiang* (initiation of discourse) and often includes the parallel sections. The two introductory elements (*poti*, "topic-breaker" and *chengti*, "topic-receiver"), on the other hand, and the conclusion (if there was one) were generally written as "assertive creation" (*duanzuo*) and were ordinarily understood as the unmediated voice of the author. And even in the *qijiang* and parallel sections, things could become tricky. Although in many essays representative speech is demarcated quite clearly, in others it is not so obvious.[9] The speech represented may be that of multiple characters in dialogue or conversation. Representative speech may arrive "late" or leave "early," constituting a kind of flourish within a single *gu* rather than the main content of the text, or the essay may alternate between assertive creation and representative speech.[10] Acknowledged authorities in the field from Wang Ao (1450–1524) to Fang Bao (1668–1749) have well-known essays that clearly do not speak for a Sage or Worthy at all.[11] As a result, in essays that begin the *qijiang* with a phrase that does not specifically identify the sentences to follow as the words of a different speaker and do not make use of the first person at any point, it would be just as easy to argue that the essay is assertive speech throughout rather than representative speech. Finally, there were several essay subgenres in which representative speech was simply not used.[12]

Furthermore, we cannot overlook the fact that although critics reading retrospectively identify isolated uses of this technique as far back as the Southern Song with great specificity, they are not able to point to a single moment at which speaking for others was institutionalized as an aesthetic standard prior to the late seventeenth-century composition of the *History of the Ming*.

For these reasons, it becomes particularly important to understand how writers and readers in the Ming and Qing distinguished representative speech from other styles of writing in concrete terms. The first text to treat the question of representative speech in detail is Dong Qichang's late Ming *Nine Instructions*, mentioned in the introduction. Because Qing accounts of examination essay writing put decisive emphasis on representation of speech, one might expect that it would also be prominently featured in *Nine Instructions*, but it comes only fifth out of nine techniques, following analyses of the guest–host relationship (*bin*), turning (*zhuan*), reversing (*fan*), and twisting (*wo* 斡). This raises the possibility that prior to the seventeenth century, the trope of representation may be understood primarily in technical terms as one aspect of characterization, rather than as the justification grounding and circumscribing the examination essay as a genre that it would later become.

The discussion of *dai* in *Nine Instructions* begins in what we now would consider to be conventional style, suggesting that one's writing cannot aspire to excellence if it is solely "one's own argument" (*zishuo*): "'Representing' means the following: to speak on the topic based on my [thoughts] would only be my own argument. Therefore I also represent the speech of the author of that time and representatively write what he has in mind, which is called accessing the inexhaustible source."[13] This seems rather straightforward. Things get more complicated when Dong starts to cite specific examples and the reader begins to wonder what kinds of inexhaustible sources are being accessed. First, Dong mentions the pigeon in the *Zhuangzi* who is quoted as saying: "I take flight with effort and make it to the elm or sandalwood; sometimes I don't reach it and am forced to the ground. What point is there in going 90,000 *li* to the south?" The next example cites a nameless Yan general whose city is besieged by Qi; he kills himself rather than surrender to Qi or return to Yan, either of which might have him executed. According to the *Shiji* (Historical records) account, cited in *Nine Instructions*, he ends with the words, "I would rather kill myself than be killed by another."[14] The narrowmindedness of the pigeon and the valor of a military man caught between unacceptable alternatives are conveyed quite clearly, but these are not, perhaps, what we might ordinarily think of as ideal examples of "speaking for the Sages and Worthies." Instead, the examples that Dong selects give us a broader and more nuanced sense of what representative speech may consist of.

Next we find Confucius, as represented by Su Xun (1009–66) in his essay "Discourse on the Changes" (*Yilun*). This Confucius is rather more sly than one might expect: having established proper social order with the Rites, which clearly delineate social roles and the relations between them, he worries that the people will not maintain respect for an order that is grounded merely on the understandable; there must be an element of mystification to make it sacred. He hits on yarrow stalk divination as an ideal basis for this mystification, because it combines what is knowable (the division of the stalks into groups of four) with what is not (the exact number of stalks in each group when the forty-nine are first separated into two groups). Although *Nine Instructions* gives only the quote attributed to the Sage, I include the full conclusion of Su Xun's essay to give a sense of the context:

> The Sage said: "[Yarrow stalk divination], in which heaven and humans share, is the Way; the Way has in it the means to extend my teachings." Thereupon he made the *Changes*, mystifying the eyes and ears of all under heaven, and his Way was in consequence respected and not abandoned. This is how the Sage used his skill to hold the hearts and minds of all under heaven and transmit his Way into the infinite.[15]

We are not to understand that the Sage is necessarily addressing another here; the words may represent a type of monologue imagined by Su Xun. These words are not what the Sage is recorded as having said but what Su Xun can imagine him saying, quite possibly only to himself, and perhaps not even out loud.

This point about representation is made much more explicit in the *Wenzheng* (Evidence of the literary), an examination preparation manual most likely dating from the nineteenth century, which follows up and expands on the points made in *Nine Instructions*. In several examples drawn from the *Mencius*, the trope of representation is defined entirely in terms of imagined speech, not words that were actually ever uttered by

the person for whom Mencius is speaking. The first example referenced
is *Mencius* 1B.1; the passage in question consists in part of the following:

> Now suppose you were having a musical performance here, and when the
> people heard the sound of your bells and drums and the notes of your
> pipes and flutes they all with aching heads and knitted brows said to one
> another, "In being fond of music, why does our King bring us to such
> straits that fathers and sons do not see each other, and brothers, wives and
> children are parted and scattered?" . . . On the other hand, suppose you
> were having a musical performance here, and when the people heard the
> sound of your bells and drums and the notes of your pipes and flutes they
> all looked pleased and said to one another, "Our King must be in good
> health, otherwise how could he have music performed?"[16]

Another example comes from *Mencius* 1A.7: "Should someone say to you,
'I am strong enough to lift a hundred *chün* but not a feather; I have eyes
that can see the tip of a fine hair but not a cartload of firewood,' would
you accept the truth of that statement?"[17] In these cases, it is not only
that the "speaker" being spoken for is not sagely—the examples include
the ordinary people and someone who is supposed to be addressing King
Hui of Liang—but that the speech in question is purely hypothetical.
The ordinary people did not, in fact, say "Our king must be in good
health," and presumably no one would be foolish enough to say to the
king, "I can pick up a hundred *jun* but not one feather."

The significance of this *hypothetical* quality of represented speech is
clearest in an example drawn from *Mencius* 2B.8: "'Is it true,' someone
asked Mencius, 'that you encouraged Ch'i to march on Yen?' 'No. When
Shen T'ung asked me, "Is it all right to march on Yen?" I answered, "Yes."
And they marched on Yen. Had he asked, "Who has the right to march
on Yen?" I would have answered, "A Heaven-appointed officer has the
right to do so."'"[18] Shen Tong did not ask who had the right to march on
Yen; Mencius tells us how he would have responded if Shen Tong had
asked. Instead of the actual words of the Sages and Worthies, then, representative speech as seen in *Nine Instructions* and *Evidence of the Literary*
allows for a broad range of possible speakers and suggests that the specific
words in question do not need to have historical truth value.

Confirmation that the significance of representative speech as technique lies in part in the *exclusion* of the actual words of the Sages and
Worthies comes from an interesting source: a forged essay attributed to

Su Zhe (1039–1112) in the Qing collection *Examination Essays by One Hundred and Twenty Famous Masters*. As Huang Qiang has shown in detail, this "essay" on the topic of Mencius's floodlike material force (*haoran zhi qi*) is actually an edited version of notes on the *Mencius* that Su Zhe drew up for his own use. To transform these notes into a modern prose essay, the unknown editor's primary action was to remove all direct quotes drawn from the text of the *Mencius* and the *Analects*.[19]

Gui Youguang's examination essay on the topic "The Master, when he entered the grand temple," is a good example of this imaginative supplementation of the historical record in actual practice. It addresses a passage from the *Analects* in which someone challenges Confucius's authority on ritual on the basis of his questions at the grand temple. The original text and commentary explain Confucius's insistent questions as an expression of his humble and diligent attitude, noting that he did know the rituals that he was asking about. Gui goes a step further to imagine—counterfactually—some remarks that Confucius could have made under those circumstances (instead of asking the questions he did ask) to demonstrate how rude and inappropriate those alternatives would have been: "I knew that!" and "Yes, you happen to be right."[20] In this essay we see Confucius not "as he was," but *as he could have been*, behaving in this fashion merely to prove the writer's rhetorical point.

For its part, *Nine Instructions* cites a particularly involved example of representative speech in an essay attributed to sixteenth-century writer Shao Guijie. In response to "Tao Ying asked," a topic taken from *Mencius* 7A.35, this *shiwen* stages representation as a form of double identification: the examination candidate speaks for Mencius, who in turn imagines himself speaking for Shun. "To stand in Shun's place is to understand his heart. He must have been about to say: 'At court, feelings are weighty and the law is weightier, and at the time one is hard-pressed by the inability to decide. By the seaside, the realm is light and family is weighty, and the law fades in its inability to apply.'"[21] It is not only that Shun never says these words—it is imagined in the essay that he was on the point of saying them—but also that the original *Mencius* never explicitly makes the claim that we can understand Shun by standing in his place. The validity of that assumption is taken for granted in the original passage and becomes a subject of discussion only through the essay's representation of Mencius.

Considered as a whole, this essay manifests two further interesting aspects of representative speech: (1) the first half of the essay represents Tao Ying's speech, only to be followed by a shift to Mencius's voice; and (2) the fact that this first half is meant to represent Tao Ying does not become entirely clear until after Tao Ying has finished speaking, at which point the author marks the transition with following words: "This definitely was Tao Ying's point. Mencius thereupon instructed him, saying . . ." Unlike the relatively straightforward examples of representative speech provided so far, this essay begins from the possibility of simple representation and proceeds to intensify and complicate it, leaving readers uncertain at times about *whose* voice, exactly, we are listening to.

The explanation of representation found in the *Nine Instructions* entry starts from the conventional idea that representation involves accessing and giving voice to a meaning that originally belongs to another, which fits nicely with the trope of the essay writer as actor that would be articulated by critics as diverse as You Tong (1618–1704), Yuan Mei, and Jiao Xun. But after the variety of examples given, the emphasis shifts in the concluding sentences of Dong's discussion to suggest that a more accurate analogy is that the writer is manipulating figures on stage—putting words in their mouths. The item ends with the following words: "All literary composition is an empty frame. As with marionettes on stage, the control is one's hands; if it is not firmly fixed as if dead, then it will truly be a piece of writing."[22] Returning to the examples cited previously, it is clear that their "representationality" consists precisely in the author's skill at imagining words that have not been said; he is putting words in the mouths of the people he claims to speak for. Indeed, even though the *shiwen* author may claim to give voice to the ideals of the Sages, it is hard to avoid the conclusion that at the same time he is appropriating an image of the Sage and writing a script for that image; in other words, speaking through that Sage's mouth, rather than providing the mouth through which the Sage can speak.

Tang Xianzu, known to his contemporaries for his essays as much as his work for the stage, introduces the Sage's voice in one of his essays with the following words: "I think that what he meant to say was . . ." The idea that this could be merely an empty form becomes less tenable when we learn that on being asked his advice on preparing for the examinations, he supposedly said, "Read my plays."[23] Similarly, Gui Youguang writes of a technique that he calls "riding emptiness and setting up meaning," giving as an example Su Xun's essay "Discourse on the Spring and Autumn Annals" (*Chunqiu lun*): "At that time, Confucius's intention in writing the Spring and Autumn Annals was not necessarily like this; [Su Xun's argument] is a case of riding emptiness and oneself putting forward a new meaning."[24] More than two centuries later, Jiao Xun notes with exasperation that "even the teachings of Laozi, Zhuangzi, and the Buddha, and the decorative tendencies of the men of letters—none of these cannot be included in [modern prose]. [Candidates] just borrow the mouths of the Sages and Worthies to speak them."[25] One begins to wonder if the discourse of "speaking for the Sages and Worthies" as a valorized form of "speaking for" that becomes so prominent over the course of the Qing might be not a simple description of the exam writing process but an occasion for critics to weigh in on whether examination candidates should think of themselves as puppetmasters and playwrights or as mere actors.

A Genealogy of Representation

Given that modern scholars frequently use the trope of "speaking for the Sages and Worthies" to characterize the Ming examination essay as well as those written under the Qing, one question seems worth asking: how far back can we trace the use of terms such as *dai shengxian liyan* and, more generally, the idea of representation? The discussion of the examination system in the *History of the Ming* mentions "writing [essays] by representing the voices of the Ancients" (*dai guren yuqi weizhi*), but this description dates only from the late seventeenth century, as does Dai Mingshi's reference to "imagining the intention of the Sages and speaking out on their behalf" (*xiangxiang shengren zhi yi dai wei liyan*).[26] Some decades later, Fang Bao writes of "representing the words of the Sages and Worthies" (*dai shengren xianren zhi yan*) in his memorial proposing the canonical examination essay collection *Imperially Authorized Essays on the Four Books*.[27] *Dai shengxian liyan* itself begins to show up regularly in a wide range of eighteenth-century texts concerning the literature produced by the examination system.[28] But this phrase does not appear in the edicts establishing the Ming civil service examination system in the fourteenth century, and it seems to be absent from early to mid-Ming analyses of examination writing as well.[29] Indeed, the term *dai* is used only in a negative sense in Qiu Jun's fifteenth-century proposal to reform examination practice, referring not to a practice of speaking for the Sages and Worthies but to illegitimate usurpations of candidates' voices by overenthusiastic examiners on one hand and illegal schemes to ghost-write candidates' essays on the other.[30]

Critics of the *shiwen* genre in the Ming dynasty have many tempting targets: faddishness, heterodoxy, ignorance of the Classics in favor of "classic" essays, and focus on mere technique and surface brilliance, among others. They are not, on the whole, much concerned with the phenomenon of representative speech. Early to mid-Ming specialists in *shiwen* technique likewise see speech that is presented in the voice of a Sage or Worthy as merely one part of a broader project in effective characterization. Mao Kun's mid-sixteenth-century *Lunwen size* (Discussion of prose: four points), for example, specifically mentions the importance of keeping Confucius's and Mencius's voices clearly separate in one's essay writing, but he explains this as correct "recognition of the topic" (*renti*) rather than noting it as a quality of represented speech.[31] Similarly, neither Gui Youguang's much longer *Key Literary Principles for Examination Writing Old and New*, a compilation of 150 texts grouped under the headings of several dozen stylistic principles, nor Yuan Huang's encyclopedic *Literary Guidelines* mentions *daiyan* even when discussing closely related techniques.[32] Dong Qichang's contemporary Wu Zhiwang (1552–1629) does not identify representation as one of the twenty crucial aspects of *wen*, and he includes only one brief comment by another writer on this question in the expanded edition of *Loose Words*.[33] The noted critic Lü Liuliang (1629–83) does not mention *dai* in his *Lü Wancun xiansheng lunwen huichao* (Lü Wancun's collected remarks on literary writing), and as late as 1695, the examination preparation manual *Xuehai jinliang* (A guide to the sea of knowledge) defines *dai* as just one of forty techniques used in modern prose writing, saying of *dai* merely that to use the Sage or Worthy's voice in the second or third parallel section of an essay is a way to give the writing new meaning.[34]

How is it that by the beginning of the eighteenth century, representative speech has acquired stand-alone significance in critical discourse on examination writing, a significance it would retain over the course of the Qing dynasty and down to the present day? It is not only that representative speech appears as a crucial element in the formal definition of the genre in works as authoritative as the *History of the Ming* and *Imperially Authorized Essays*, but also that remarks on the technique were retroactively added into some earlier texts in the form of margin comments and supplementary material by eighteenth-century critics.[35] Why did a technique that had been in continuous but not universal use since the fourteenth century suddenly become a locus of theoretical interest in the seventeenth, whether technical in the case of Dong Qichang or more specifically ideological in the writers and critics who followed him? How does this technique shift from a kind of last resort for those writers who feel the need to add a twist to their argument to a defining characteristic of composition generally? As numerous scholars have pointed out, isolated examples of speaking in another's voice can be found in examination writing dating back to the Song, as well as in other literary genres.[36] This technique is regularly used throughout the Ming; what is new in the seventeenth century is its explicit articulation as a description with normative force, on the basis of several centuries of essay-writing practice in which this technique has come to constitute an important component. How could a formal approach that in a significant minority of essays was not actually used, and in many more is difficult to distinguish with any degree of certainty, come to stand as a defining characteristic for the genre as a whole?

It is possible that one reason was the late Ming heightened interest in drama, an interest that led to new levels of critical attention to and theoretical analysis of writing for the stage. From Ni Yuanlu (1593–1644) to Yuan Mei, Jiao Xun, and Liu Shipei, critics have often paired plays with *shiwen* as literary works in which the author creates fictional dialogue.[37] *Shiwen* that took quotes from famous plays as their topics capitalized on this perceived similarity to win over audiences that might not have willingly consumed works based on the Four Books. Authors of some plays attempted in return to realize the moral lessons supposed to be characteristic of the essays in longer dramatic forms.[38] From a rather different perspective, You Tong harshly criticizes modern prose as a means of selecting officials in part because he sees it as too close to theater. Ironically, he is now better known for an essay composed on a topic selected from *The Western Chamber*.[39]

In the late Ming in particular, a distinct interest in establishing conceptual ties between dramatic works and *shiwen* is signaled by the questionable assertion that the Yuan dynasty included aria writing as part of the civil service examination process. The best known of several instances comes in Zang Maoxun's 1616 prefaces to his *Yuanqu xuan* (A selection of Yuan drama), in which he slyly advances this claim by raising it and saying that he will not disagree with it. But Zang makes no mention of the concept of representative speech in these prefaces, which is especially striking given his investment in reinterpreting the *zaju* genre with reference to the civil service examinations, which Patricia Sieber has analyzed in detail.[40] Similarly, Li Yu would draw an analogy from the novel *The Water Margin* rather than from modern prose when explaining the technique of speaking for others in drama.[41] It is not until Wu Qiao (1611–95) that we find a successor to Ni Yuanlu's comment clearly articulating drama to modern prose through the concept of representing another's speech (*dai taren shuohua*).[42] As Huang Qiang points out, perhaps the most interesting question is not the exact extent to which drama and *shiwen* overlapped but why certain seventeenth-century critics become so interested in arguing this point. He concludes that there was a concerted effort by drama advocates to move the genre up the aesthetic ladder, and asserting kinship to the more respectable examination essay was a useful tactic in this regard.[43]

I suggest that beyond the question of similarities in technique between specific genres, the trope of representation becomes a central site of contestation in late Ming and early Qing struggles that are political as much as aesthetic. The question of whom an educated individual is representing when he composes an essay that may include a central portion where he speaks in the voice of another has a variety of answers, none of them simple.[44] The widespread practice of assigning small topic questions at the local and provincial levels limited to a mere fragment, sometimes as few as one or two characters of the original passage, broadened the range of individuals for whom the candidate might be expected to speak; because essays on small topics were in most cases not meant to go beyond the bounds of the specific phrase selected as a topic, candidates could find themselves asked to write not in the voice of the Sage but in that of a less worthy character.[45] The early nineteenth-century author of *Diankan ji* (Notes on punctuating and grading) writes with some degree of exasperation about small topic essays in which authors are assigned to represent "joking interaction," "quibbling between men and women," "women's chatter," "the wrath of a tyrant," and even "the self-justifications of a mediocre ruler" and end by doing a job that is far too convincing. He concludes that a few such texts teach cleverness, but most of them impair the formation of good judgment and as such must be used as teaching material only with great care.[46] Jiao Xun is similarly wary of these kinds of topics, suggesting that candidates should use *duanzuo* (assertive creation) rather than representative speech when assigned to write about figures like Yang Huo and Zang Cang, presumably to avoid personally speaking *for* problematic individuals; better to speak *about* them instead.[47]

Representation of characters who are not Sages or Worthies can be found in large topic essays as well. Mao Kun gives voice to the Five Hegemons in "Follow no crooked policy in making embankments" and Tang Shunzhi (1507–60) speaks for Zimo in "Zimo holds a medium between these."[48] Even in situations where most candidates would choose to write in the voice of a Sage or Worthy, exceptions were possible, as in Shang Lu's early fifteenth-century essay on the topic "The Master said, 'Small indeed was the capacity of Guan Zhong'" and Wu Hong's Qianlong-era essay on the topic of "Zizhang asked about employment as an official." The latter is of particular interest in that the selection of this topic suggests that the answer be presented either from Confucius's or Zizhang's point of view, but the author makes it clear that he is writing from a contemporary perspective throughout, with repeated references to the "nation" (*guojia*) and the civil service examination system as a means of selecting talented administrators.[49] Ironically, the most controversial essays could be those that fulfilled the expectation they speak for Confucius and Mencius but did so in such a way as to challenge accepted norms of the Cheng-Zhu interpretive tradition, as pointed out by Jiao Xun in the quote earlier in this chapter. By presenting what are clearly one's own arguments in the voice of a Sage or Worthy, a practice well known and regularly denounced by the Wanli era as *lingjia* ("riding roughshod" or "riding high"), a candidate challenges the state's interpretive authority over its own declared ideological basis.[50]

Dong Qichang's explanation of representative speech maintains a broad focus, explicitly acknowledging the fact that candidates were often asked to write in the voice of less than sagely characters. At the same time, he emphasizes the creativity and latitude that is expected of an essay's author. When representationality begins its transition from one technique among others to the defining characteristic of the genre, however, a different set of concerns comes into play. Zhang Shichun (1575–1644) and Ai Nanying (1583–1646), for example, highlight the ideal of speech that is representative of the Sages and Worthies to critique early seventeenth-century trends in essay writing. Instead of the positive challenge set by Dong (the writer must take control) these critics present the challenge in negative terms—the writer must refrain from using language that is not suitable. In a preface to a collection that does not hesitate to point out shortcomings in the works included, Ai writes, "If one wants to make examination essay texts sufficient to completely represent the meaning of the Sages and Worthies (*dai shengxian zhi zhi*) . . . that would be difficult."[51] Ai and Zhang argue against "alley" (*lixiang*) language and "alley" teachers as unfit to represent the words of the Sages and Worthies (*dai shengxian zhi yan*).[52] As members of the Yuzhang Society, these two men built on certain concerns expressed by their predecessors not only to criticize what they saw as literary excesses of the Wanli period but also to argue with renewed insistence for the crucial social and political significance of these disputes over *shiwen* style.[53] As the best-known anthologist of the late Ming (indeed, together with Fang Bao one of the two most influential *shiwen* anthologists of any period), Ai had an especially powerful impact; his interest in constraining candidates' writing by reminding them of their role as representatives was echoed by a range of commentators in the Qing.[54]

Ai and Zhang's contemporary, Ni Yuanlu, takes a similar tack, arguing that this task of representation was originally set for the literati by imperial authority.[55] In the broadest possible sense, Ni is correct, in that the examination system was established as an integral part of the state, and a hermeneutic approach to the classical canon was defined as the grounds on which candidates would be examined. The key misrecognition occurs when this idea of an imperial mandate to interpret is joined with Zhang and Ai's insistence that one cannot stray beyond certain aesthetic parameters in this interpretive project because it is literally representative of the Sages in the most concrete possible sense: candidates are not only speaking for but also speaking *as* the Sages and Worthies. This can be seen as the moment at which representation shifts decisively from a literary technique selected by authors into a response to a supposed state mandate that necessarily carries political implications. Ni in particular was no stranger to the real-world stakes involved in representative speech: he spoke in defense of the Donglin Academy in memorials to the Chongzhen emperor at a crucial moment, and once his view won out, wrote on behalf of that same emperor in honor of the Donglin Academy, condensing into a single incident two very different vectors of representation.[56]

It is no coincidence that these immensely productive misrecognitions should come when debates over modern prose style had become a key means of organizing factions for political competition within the state as well as in society more generally.[57] Writing in the early nineteenth century, Zheng Haoruo argued that the increasingly sharp distinctions drawn between literary factions in the late Ming led to significant increases in the publication of essay collections; the relationship between factionalism and literary style, mediated through these collections, became especially noticeable in the case of the Donglin Academy and the Renewal Society (*Fushe*).[58] Although criticisms of popular trends in *shiwen* composition could be heard regularly from the middle of the sixteenth century, these were at first merely lamentations of a general decline in standards. It was not until the early decades of the seventeenth century that problematic approaches to questions of style could be reliably blamed on one or another clearly identifiable faction. As far as we know, at no point in the Ming was there an official statement that candidates must write in the voice of a Sage or Worthy. Representative speech was a literary technique that candidates could and did make use of as early as the Song and increasingly into the first half of the Ming. It is acknowledged explicitly as such around the turn of the seventeenth century; it is then adopted as a means of political and ideological critique in the late Ming by a variety of critics, some of whom never held official position. It is referenced as a defining characteristic of the genre in an official context for the first time only at the turn of the eighteenth century and comes to be widely accepted and officially endorsed as such only by the mid-eighteenth century.

Rather than a universal given, demanded by the ruler or the minister of Rites acting on his behalf, the conception of modern prose as a representation (*dai*) of the words of the Sages and Worthies emerges as an explicit norm only over the course of several centuries. Although common by the time the compilers of the *History of the Ming* formulated it in the words that have served to characterize *shiwen* to this day, it functions not so much as a stylistic precondition but as a story that literati in and out of office begin to tell themselves about the examination system, and a dramatically oversimplified story at that, which raises the question: why?

The increasing tendency over the seventeenth century—from Ai Nanying to the authors of the *History of the Ming*—to emphasize representative speech in *shiwen*, together with that genre's commitment to parallelism, as a means of demarcating the Ming examination essay from its Song (and Yuan) predecessors, was not a neutral description but an attempt to establish representation as such as the primary locus of aesthetic value within the *shiwen* genre. It designates the civil service examination system as not just an arena for competition between individuals for wealth and power but also an occasion for those individuals to speak for and take a stand for others.

The ideological character of this claim becomes clear when we examine the actual practice of essays that claim to faithfully represent the voices of the ancients. Realistically speaking, the tone of voice (*kouqi*) in essays that claim to speak for the Sages and Worthies is generally quite different from the canonical texts from which the essay topics are drawn. This difference appeared most strikingly to critics at the time in form of inappropriate word choice: disapproval of "unsagely" sounding language, whether of terms drawn from Buddhist and Daoist texts or expressions that were excessively colloquial, becomes increasingly common from the middle of the sixteenth century forward.[59] Writing in the early Qing, Lu Longji argues against using colloquial language from Cheng-Zhu lectures and commentaries and excessively obscure language from the Classics in order to be as pure and comprehensible as possible. But he himself serves as a prime example of the difficulty of controlling one's voice when he breaks into an extremely vernacular style precisely in the clause attempting to specify the correct approach to canonical language, claiming, "The writing of the Six Classics was at that time spoken aloud in front of one."[60]

Disputes over which individual words might be acceptable were one thing. But seventeenth-century critic Lü Liuliang makes a more significant point: if one really aimed to imitate Zhou dynasty diction word for word, "I fear that at that time there was no such manner of speaking in lengthy parallels."[61] This objection poses a direct challenge to the concept of representative speech that depends on a specific tone of voice. Although there are many shorter instances of parallelism in the Four Books, and (with the exception of the *Analects*) some medium-length instances as well, there is very little that resembles the lengthy parallel lines that develop as part of the involutionary approach in the mid-fifteenth century and continue to play a central role in later trends such as the "use of archaic prose to write modern prose." This contrast between the canonical texts and Ming and Qing attempts to represent them could ordinarily be glossed over because a single essay did not usually employ both representative speech and recorded speech (quoted directly from the Classic itself), but in the rare cases where this does happen, the difference between them is unmistakable. In Zhang Yuan's essay on the topic "Killing a man with a stick and with a sword," the speech that claims to represent Mencius is much closer in style to the assertive speech portion of the essay—the voice of the essay's Ming dynasty author—than it is to the words quoted from the *Mencius*.[62] In Xue Yingqi's essay "Ci, you think, I suppose, that I am one who learns many things and keeps them in memory," the contrast between the use of *yu* (Confucius's reference to himself in the first person, included once in the essay) and *wu* (Xue's reference to Confucius in the first person when speaking for him throughout the rest of the essay) is quite striking.[63]

Furthermore, as mentioned earlier in this chapter, the line between representative speech and assertive creation is not always simple to draw. Representative speech may appear where it is not conventionally expected to appear, or it may be absent where expected to be present. There are a variety of expressions that can be used to begin the *qijiang*. Some of these expressions can be used only if the essay is representing another's speech, but there are many commonly used alternatives that do not make it clear whether the body of the speech is to be taken as representation or assertion.[64] *Ruoyue* (As [the Sage] would have said . . .) and *changwei* (I have once thought . . .), for example, make it clear that representative speech is on the point of beginning; *qie* or *qiefu* (Now . . .), on the other hand, leave the question of who is speaking open. If the "identity" of the speaker is not clearly marked in the *qijiang* or at some later point, or through the use of first-person pronouns or personal names, the only way to be certain is to consider the content of the essay, and even this does not necessarily yield a definitive answer. For this reason, although many essays distinguish clearly between representation and assertion, a substantial proportion are finally ambiguous and can be understood to include representative speech with confidence only if we begin with the assumption that represented speech is a specific requirement rather than one choice—although the most common—from among several alternative conventions. This is even before we take into account creative approaches like that found in Chen Nieheng's essay, in which a musical instrument speaks! As suggested by this example, such experimentation is not limited to the late Ming: Shang Yanliu notes in the Qing a general tendency to be more flexible with representative speech in practice, even as the discourse of representative speech becomes narrower and more predictable.[65]

The standard model represents only one approach to the essay form: other approaches include the *duanzuo ti* and *jishi ti*, in which candidates wrote in their own voices throughout, whether to put forward an argument or provide a narrative; and the *wenda ti* and *lianzhang ti*, in which multiple voices could be heard.[66] Even when an essay did not make use of an alternate format, there was no guarantee that the "represented speech" of the Sage would arrive at the expected time or that it would continue without interruption for the duration of the parallel legs of the essay.[67] What are the implications of these shifts in person and voice, whether occurring in the transitions from one section of an essay to the next or as abruptly as sentence to sentence, or even clause to clause? We will return to this question in detail from a different perspective—the construction of subjectivity—in chapter 4.

One begins to suspect that the discourse of "speaking for the Sages and Worthies" as a valorized form of "speaking for" that becomes so prominent over the course of the Qing was not a neutral characterization of *shiwen* nor a founding criterion from which the genre had developed over the course of two dynasties, but a composite formation of two other discursive moves that constitute a kind of oblique dialectic. First was a rearguard action aimed at convincing examination candidates they should think of themselves not as puppetmasters or playwrights but as mere actors. Second, given the careful negotiations over the power to offer interpretations of the Classics between the Qing court and the bureaucracy, was a claim for the moral authority of examination candidates—and literati more generally—that depends in part on precisely this "mere actor" status, akin to the dynamic James Scott identifies in his reading of spirit possession as an occasion for resistance.[68]

The fact that the significant *shiwen* subgenres that did not involve this "speaking for" are invariably overlooked in broad characterizations of the genre does not call the significance of representative speech into question, but rather clarifies the ideological dimensions of the link asserted between *shiwen* and the concept of representation. The reason *dai shengxian liyan* appears and persists is not simply that it serves one side or another in any particular contest for power within the examination field, but that it articulates the terms on which these contests were held and insists that the examination system is a key arena in which they are to be resolved.

The seriousness with which candidates, examiners, and high-ranking officials alike took the representative writing understood to be characteristic of the examination essay is evident in the formation of schools and "literary groups" such as the Donglin Academy and the Renewal Society that had the aim of influencing examination standards and advancing specific political goals. It also appears in the selection of specific topics by examiners that lent themselves to a discussion of current affairs, in the use of model *shiwen* collections and commentary to make intellectual and political points, in the careful attention the state devoted to monitoring these tendencies and even to analyzing the examination papers after the grading process, and finally the solicitation of candidates' opinions on the structure and conduct of the examinations in the policy questions section.[69]

The tendency to represent, or perhaps to be representative, can be found among examiners as well, all of whom were once candidates. Stories of an examiner's unconventional preferences in one exam cycle setting candidates in the years to come to work tailoring their approaches to meet new standards come as no surprise, but examiners and critics alike followed general trends in literate culture as often as they anticipated or initiated them.[70] By the mid-Qing it was common practice for examiners to make use of the policy section of the examination to ask candidates for their opinion on potential changes in structure, emphasis, and interpretive approach, a development that endows the exam system as a whole with a striking degree of reflexivity.[71] In the case of the two most controversial and far-reaching developments in Ming and Qing intellectual culture—the challenges posed by Wang Yangming and his followers in the sixteenth century and the "evidential scholarship" (*kaozheng*) of the eighteenth century—approaches that were strongly critical of the ideological infrastructure on which the examination system was supposedly based found their way into the essays and the questions posed in the decades following their rise to popularity in more general educated discourse.[72] Similarly, a broad surge of interest in the pedagogy of poetic technique in the early to mid-eighteenth century, measured by an increase in annotated anthologies and other related publications, did not follow but rather preceded the restoration of poetry composition as an item on the examinations after centuries of its absence.[73]

Generally speaking, representation constitutes one aspect of the mediation that literati—particularly literati who serve in the bureaucracy—perform between ruler and ruled. The discourse of "speaking for the Sages and Worthies" attempts to set the terms on which educated individuals can be selected for this task. More specifically, representation becomes a crucial trope when it is understood as struggle between autonomy and subordination, because it figures the tension between ideological reproduction (which aims to ensure the allegiance of the class as a whole) and stylistic differentiation (used to choose one candidate rather than another), as we will see in more detail later in this book. At the same time, as the politics of representation is manifested primarily in aesthetic terms, it becomes clear that ideology and style cannot ultimately be disentangled. In the next chapter, we look into more general questions of individual and class agency that took shape through the examination aesthetic.

CHAPTER TWO

Representative Style

In the first month of 1532, Minister of Rites Xia Yan memorialized against examination candidates' use of difficult language and bizarre word choice to cover up for shallow reasoning and limited vision. The memorial was approved by the Jiajing emperor, suggesting that he shared the minister's concern over flashy language and expected examiners to rein in candidates who aimed to impress by pushing the stylistic envelope.[1] In the third month of that year, the Jiajing emperor adopted Xia's wording and proclaimed, "Literary style is connected to the fate of the realm. In recent years candidates' essays have been difficult and tricky, truly harming governance. This year we will work to pick elegant essays, and will not accept the bizarre (*qipi*)."[2] Despite this warning, the twenty-two-year-old Lin Daqin composed an essay at that year's palace examination session that was strikingly unusual. One examiner exclaimed, "Really strange!" on reading it, and another concluded that it was well constructed even though it broke with convention; they ranked it third, and the emperor subsequently revised the list to rank it first.[3]

Under the circumstances, one can only imagine how much weight candidates in the next cycle would put on the Ministry of Rites proclamation in October 1533 that "all writing must be elegant and clear, without excessive ornament, risking the strange, or making use of difficult words."[4] It comes as no surprise that the Jiajing emperor's stated aim, to reduce the emphasis on literary technique, was not realized; despite his attempts at reform, the tendencies that he criticized were back in full force by 1540, if they had ever diminished in the first place.[5] The only surprise would be that his words had even a temporary effect. Liang Zhangju's short history of candidates who broke the rules by writing about all five Classics in one essay (rather than selecting just one) and were rewarded for it—in one case, the offender was allowed to skip

the metropolitan examination and receive an appointment directly—
suggests that strategically flouting expectations and even, in some cases,
the stated regulations could pay off.[6]

Although the general mood under the Qing is usually thought to have
become substantially more attentive to the claims of orthodoxy across
a wide range of fields and, as a result, less tolerant of experimentation
than the late Ming, questions that allowed for responses to focus on
aesthetic concerns rather than or in addition to moral issues continued to
provide examination candidates with significant room for innovation.[7]
Hu Renyu, *zhuangyuan* (first-place finisher) in 1694, makes a point of
exploiting this latitude at several levels in his essay on the topic "Dian,
what are your wishes?" in which he is asked to address Confucius's choice
of Dian's aim (bathing in a stream with companions and chanting poetry
on the way home) over the more conventional and serious aspirations of
three other disciples.

By selecting a passage in which Confucius affirms the pleasures of
bathing in a stream and singing, rather than political projects such as
governing a state or serving as a ritual attendant, the examiners invite
candidates to take the aesthetic seriously, and Hu Renyu responds. At
the most concrete structural level, his essay poses significant challenges.
Once we finish the relatively standard opening paragraphs, we find that
the essay consists of only two sets of legs, not four; the second set can
barely said to be parallel at all. These two parallel sections struggle to
maintain their dominance in the overall structure of the essay in the face
of an extended transition section between the two, as well as a striking
concluding section. (A complete translation of this essay appears in the
appendix to this book.)

The content of the argument is as challenging as its form. In the *qijiang* (initiation of discourse), Hu presents a strong critique of contingent
dependency that has a distinctly Buddhist flavor: "The serious efforts undertaken in one's past were empty even though real, why? Because they
depended on something. The past-times of those days, although empty,
turned out to be real, why? Because they did not depend on anything."
This theme is developed in more detail in the first set of parallel lines.
The second set of parallel lines directly challenges the orthodox assessment of Dian as "wild" (*kuang*) even as it evokes an image of a person
who takes pleasure in what circumstances afford him, which reminds

us more of the Seven Sages of the Bamboo Grove than of the Sages and Worthies Hu Renyu has supposedly been asked to speak for. Finally, the essay's summation takes direct issue with the standard Cheng-Zhu interpretation of the passage, an interpretation that is dismissed without ceremony as what "some have argued"; Hu goes on to suggest that what is necessary here is not a rational explanation of Confucius's reasons for siding with Dian but an appreciation of his approving sigh, an "empty word" (*xuzi*) that is best understood in aesthetic terms.

This essay won Hu Renyu first place in the Jiangnan provincial examination of 1681, and for its "novel tone," it was reprinted in Fang Bao's *Imperially Authorized Essays on the Four Books*, sponsored by the Qianlong emperor. Han Tan (1637–1704), the 1673 *zhuangyuan* who was known as one of the leading essayists of the early Qing, praised Hu's summation as "getting the key point" of this particularly challenging passage. Liang Zhangju, compiler of *Collected Words on Regulated Essays*, seconds Han's approval, adding a note on his own appreciation of the rest of the essay.[8] The inclusion of an essay like this in what would turn out to be the single most canonical collection of examination essays of the Ming and Qing, and the approval it won from contemporaries and later critics, suggests that there is more room in *shiwen* for stylistic and ideological diversity than we might expect and furthermore that essays that can be understood to bring forth aesthetic aspects of a proposed topic may be allowed greater latitude than those dealing with more straightforward "moral" questions. Recent scholarship has conclusively established the fundamentally contested nature of the examination system in its politics of power and its ideological dynamics.[9] But there has been less attention to questions of aesthetics: the specific forms through which the voices raised in contestation took shape.

Chapter 1 looked closely at the transformation of one literary technique among many into a norm with political and ethical force; this chapter examines the imbrication of style and politics, and of aesthetics and ideology, more generally. Why is style so important that the Jiajing emperor could claim that "literary forms are connected to the fate of the realm," a statement that echoes Cao Pi's assertion in *Dianlun* (Classic discourses) that "literature is a central project in the management of a state," but seems to cry out for a more detailed explanation?[10] For Cao Pi, literature was a realm of positive possibility, the arena in which a state, through the achievements of its individual writers, can obtain a fame that will last without end. In the Ming and Qing, such optimism is in shorter supply: as the editors of the *Complete Library of Four Treasuries* write in their comment on the *Imperially Authorized Essays on the Four Books*, the only examination essay collection from the Ming and Qing deemed worthy to be included in their project, "Literary forms become twisted and the habits of the literati go bad; the habits of the literati go bad, and the fate of the nation follows."[11] In the late Ming, Huang Hongxian suggests that the solution lies in the specifics of literary tone—"In order to correct literary forms, one must set the literati's style aright"—and offers six concrete prescriptions to that effect.[12] The truth that must have seemed unnecessary to spell out for these later writers would be that while Cao Pi could imagine literary excellence in terms of a handful of the most talented writers representing his rule to later generations, the literary forms in question in the Ming and Qing were the primary means by which the government would be staffed and through which the human resources to meet all of its immediate challenges must be identified.

It is almost a commonplace that preparation for and participation in the examinations is the vocation of the literati (*shiren zhi ye*), as Feng Ban puts it.[13] The importance of this formulation should not be overlooked: the vocation of the literati is not primarily to serve as officials but to prepare to take the test that might qualify them to serve as officials, prepare others to take this same test, grade the test papers, supervise the administration of the test, and even take it upon themselves to write comments to and arrange for the publication of passing and failing essays. Perhaps that description misses some of the importance of the test preparation and test taking process? To put John Dewey's famous remark on education to a slightly different use, what if participation in the examination system turns out not to be mere preparation for one's vocation but in large part a vocation in and of itself?[14] As we have seen in the introduction, the examination system was a fundamental social fact and one of the major tasks of the bureaucracy. For every person who served as a formally appointed official in the bureaucracies of the Ming and Qing, dozens worked in various capacities related to the examination system as teachers, editors, critics, and graders. How do the aesthetic politics of modern prose work in turn to define the literati as a social group, even a class? What are the particular effects of a focus on *representation*, whether implicit or explicit?

Benjamin Elman has suggested that the format of the examinations in the Ming and Qing should be thought of as the product of a prolonged struggle between the Cheng-Zhu "Study of the Way" (*Daoxue*) and belles-lettres, a struggle that has been wrongly understood to have resulted in a definitive victory for the philosophical tradition. He sees the success of *Daoxue* in the examination regime as "incomplete," concluding, "Unless we can fully appreciate the literati ardor for *wen*, we will never really understand why literary style loomed so large in medieval and late imperial civil examinations."[15] More concretely, Huang Qiang sees the *shiwen* form itself as a dynamic compromise between forces that championed the use of regulated verse and rhapsodies to select officials and those that advocated for essays limited to interpreting the meaning of the Classics.[16] Whether approving or critical in tone, there is no shortage of claims from the early 1500s on that modern prose has assumed the status of a separate field (*biejing*), in which literary force (*wenshi*) and form (*tige*) constitute more important concerns than moral metaphysics (*yili*) and which is no longer subordinate to classical scholarship or the accepted literary genres.[17] In 1843, Yang Wensun wrote that "the rules have become even more fine and the forms more complete, there have been famous specialists in each generation, and the essay collection imprints could sweat oxen and fill rooms to the rafters, establishing a new category (*bie li yi men*) beyond Classics, history, philosophers, and collections . . . one could take inquiry into examination essays alone as one's task."[18] Even for ideologues as committed as Zhang Shichun and Lü Liuliang, the necessity of avoiding vulgarity (*su*)—a question of aesthetics—has assumed a central place among the tasks that the modern prose writer is charged with.[19]

Beginning from this point, this chapter inquires into the investment in style characteristic not just of individual writers and literary groups but of the system as a whole. What is the nature of this commitment as realized in bureaucratic practice, rather than merely subscribed to as an abstract article of faith? Under these circumstances, how could direct challenge to articulated standards be sustained and even appreciated by the examination regime? One approach to this last question can be found in chapter 5, which addresses the production of distinctive individual *authors* through the competitive dynamics of a system characterized by extreme selectivity. This chapter focuses instead on the nature of the standards and the question of who has the authority to articulate them. I argue that the aesthetic—as much as if not more so than ideology simply defined—is a key arena for contestation of and over authority, as well as for the imagination of the literati as a class.

Standards and Transgressions

In his reflections on the origins of modern prose, Zhou Zuoren highlights the importance of parallelism in ordinary usage, such as couplets hung on doorframes, as well as the similarities between the logic of the topic-breaking first line and popular pastimes such as lantern riddles, and stakes out a claim that seems at first rather surprising: "If [the logic of the lantern riddle] is brought to a relatively high level, it turns into the key mechanism of the eight-legged essay topic-breaker (*poti*); for this reason, I believe that the creation of the eight-legged essay is due primarily to tendencies among the people, and not solely to the efforts of some emperor who happened to champion the eight-legged essay."[20] Although the process may not be as straightforward as Zhou suggests (with couplets growing naturally out of paired characters or expressions, and the lengthy parallel lines characteristic of modern prose resulting naturally from couplets), even the imperial edicts reestablishing the civil service examination system at the beginning of the Ming show that the definition of the examination essay as we now understand the genre is not in the end the province of the emperor or the Ministry of Rites.

It is clear from the historical record that the Hongwu and Yongle emperors took great care to specify the texts and associated commentaries that examination topics would be drawn from, as well as the concrete logistics of examination management. But questions of style received much less attention, with two early edicts merely repeating Yuan dynasty stipulations of 1313 that writing be "clear" and "not stuck in old forms," stipulations that had originally constituted an attempt to shift the emphasis in the examinations *away* from literary skill.[21] The contrast between this reticence on concrete questions of essay format and the detail with which questions such as who is eligible to take the examinations, the exact trail that the completed papers should follow through the various offices in the compound, and what kind of servant each examiner could bring with him (illiterate) are addressed is striking.[22]

As we have seen in the first chapter, the phrase "speaking for the Sages and Worthies," which would become central to the presentation of the examination system three centuries later in the *History of the Ming*, does not appear in early Ming edicts and regulations; neither did any hint of a requirement of parallel composition.[23] It seems likely that the instruction not to be "stuck in old forms" was aimed in part against precisely those forms that had appeared already in the Song and would only become more firmly rooted and more systematically employed in the Ming and Qing, such as the *poti* opening and the use of parallelism as a structuring principle.[24] What the first Ming emperor aimed to accomplish, then, was to take the restoration of an examination system that had fallen into some disarray in the chaotic years of dynastic change as an opportunity to call for a return to simpler styles of writing. From his annoyance at the "empty writings" he received as a result, it seems that restoring the institution in all its logistical complexity was easier than controlling the stylistic development of the texts it produced.[25]

Indeed, despite the careful attention that emperors and ministers paid to the essays produced in the examinations, it becomes clear from their complaints about unsatisfactory conduct that their direct power over examination questions and answers was strictly limited in practice: the 1392 stipulation that essays should include a "great exposition" (*dajiang*) among other formal components was disregarded almost from the moment it was instituted.[26] Conversely, the Kangxi emperor prohibited the use of "concluding summaries" (*dajie*) in 1720, and this ban was reiterated under the Qianlong emperor in 1746, but essays with such summaries continued to appear.[27] Successive ministers of Rites endured a history of frustration of their attempts to constrain candidates to orthodox approaches and conventional aesthetics, and other officials at the highest level in the bureaucracy were not necessarily any more effective at setting a stylistic tone. The powerful Grand Secretary Zhang Juzheng (1525–82) was suspected of having successfully pulled strings on behalf of his second and third sons when they sat for the exams in 1577 and 1580, but when it came to influencing aesthetic trends more generally, the results of his efforts (including composing model essays) were temporary at best.[28]

The Qianlong emperor is a particularly instructive case. There is ample evidence of his fussiness and willingness to intervene in the examination process, but even at the palace examination the ruler would read (or have read to him) only a sampling of the essays produced. When we look more closely at the cases where the Qianlong emperor did intervene to affect the assessment of essays, he seems to have been motivated as much to break up conspiracies to collude as he was to establish or enforce stylistic standards.[29] This suggests that the role of the emperor and the minister of Rites in matters of examination style is primarily negative and reactive. Even then, those at the highest level may not have the courage of their convictions, with the result that the essay form developed and changed over the years with a fair degree of autonomy relative to the court and high-level officials.

Recently scholars have argued convincingly that the late Ming saw a period of unusual intellectual openness in the field of examination writing as in other areas of cultural production, linked to the rapid development of the publishing industry as well as broader social and economic trends.[30] How can we best understand the interaction between this ideological contestation and the aesthetics of the essay form? As the introduction suggests and chapter 3 will show in more detail, the fifteenth century saw a wide variety of approaches to the examination essay form, with involuted parallel structures enjoying particular attention from the Chenghua reign period (1465–87) forward. In the early decades of the sixteenth century, this approach was further complemented by a turn that Fang Bao represents as "using classical prose to write modern prose" (*yi guwen wei shiwen*); Tang Shunzhi and Gui Youguang would become two of the best-known exemplars.[31]

For many mid-Ming writers, finding stylistic inspiration outside of the Four Books and the Five Classics was not a problem; the idea of appropriating Sima Qian's narrative verve to write essays that joined "the Classics and the Histories" was well accepted by the middle of the sixteenth century. By this point, candidates in search of newer stylistic resources had moved on to prose masters of the Tang and Song, and the more adventurous did not shy away from Daoist texts (especially the *Zhuangzi*) and even Buddhist sutras.[32] As early as 1520, He Jingming's curriculum for the students that he supervised as Shaanxi education commissioner included selections from the *Zhuangzi* and the works of Qu Yuan and Yang Xiong.[33] For Gu Yanwu, writing a century after the fact, the final straw comes in 1568, when one of the model essays provided to examination candidates included the word *zhen* (truth) in the *poti*: the boundaries of orthodox discourse in the examination context were becoming difficult to mark with any degree of certainty. As Gu points out, this term appears nowhere in the Classics or the Four Books and is strongly associated with Daoist texts from its earliest appearance. The *Shuowen jiezi* (Explication of written characters) even provides as its primary definition "an immortal's transformation in shape and ascension to heaven." Confucius himself appears as a character in the "Old Fisherman" chapter of the *Zhuangzi* and asks about *zhen*, only to find out how much he still has to learn. As Gu goes on to note, the early association of *zhen* with Daoism would have been heightened from the Song onward, when the commonly used Daoist term *xuan* (abstruse, mystery) became taboo due to its use as part of an imperial reign name; *zhen* was regularly substituted for *xuan* in the titles of religious Daoist texts.[34]

There was more to come. Gu also notes Ai Nanying's claim that the first instance of Chan language appears in an examination essay in 1577 and quotes at length from Minister of Rites Feng Qi's memorial of 1601.[35] This memorial, an overview of heterodoxy involving Li Zhi, explains how canonical terms are appropriated to introduce Buddhist teachings into examination essays.

> [Candidates] take the real and make it empty, and take the empty and make it real; they take the ethical code (*mingjiao*) as fetters, and moral standards as superfluous; they take unrestrained words and abstract discussions to be marvelous, and reckless disregard for the rules and sweeping away distinctions between right and wrong and between what is honorable and what is shameful as open-minded and grand. They take remarks in Buddhist texts that somewhat resemble discussions of the mind and human nature and sneak them into the words of the Sages; they take instances of words such as "empty" and "non-existing" in the Sages' canon and forcibly interpret them according to Chan Buddhist meanings.[36]

With some hyperbole, Gu writes that in the final decades of the Ming, there was no candidate who did not make use of Buddhist and Daoist texts in his examination essays.[37]

Although Gu Yanwu overstates the case, the nineteenth-century scholar Liang Zhangju as well as a range of scholars working more recently have provided ample documentation of the "heterodoxy" characteristic of the examination field more generally in this period.[38] But the struggle for the linguistic and conceptual purity of the examination essay did not begin in the Wanli era. Worries at the ministerial level about the uses of "heterodox doctrine"—including the *Zhuangzi* and *Liezi*—as sources of aesthetic inspiration in examination essays date back to at least the 1530s.[39] At the provincial level, terms such as *kong* (emptiness; Sanskrit *śūnyatā*), *ding* (settled focus; Sanskrit *samādhi*), and *hui* (wisdom; Sanskrit *prajñā*) were banned as early as the 1489 Shuntian session in an attempt to keep Chan interpretations out of the examination halls.[40]

These worries were not groundless. A wide range of Buddhist and Daoist expressions begin to appear in examination essays no later than the Chenghua reign period and become increasingly common in the early sixteenth century.[41] In many cases, these terms were not mere flourishes but central to the argument advanced in the essay.[42] And while we may not be surprised to learn that innovative late Ming essayists such as Yang Qiyuan (1547–99) and Tan Yuanchun wrote commentaries on the *Zhuangzi*, Gui Youguang, one of the leading stylists of the preceding generation, also put together commentaries on the *Zhuangzi* and the *Daode jing*, cited Tao Yuanming's "Guiqulai ci" (Homeward bound) as "an example of natural and unrestrained writing" that would help examination candidates transcend the vulgar in their own work, and did not shrink from citing Lu Xiangshan and directly referencing the *Zhuangzi* in his own essays.[43] Given that many examples of similar usage can be found in the canonical *Imperially Authorized Essays*, it seems that there is more than a grain of truth to Gu Yanwu's claim. Use of Daoist and Buddhist texts was evident over much of the course of the Ming dynasty, increasingly popular from the Wanli period forward, and continued to be widely accepted by critical authorities in the Qing.[44]

What is notable is the degree to which these influences were defended on aesthetic grounds. The late Ming author and critic Zhang Shichun, although severe in his disapproval of "the empty fantasies of Laozi and Zhuangzi," also allows that writers who fail to take account of the subtleties of these texts can end up with vulgar arguments such as those made by "rotten alley scholars," which can win temporary enthusiasm due to their superficial resemblance to the Sages' true teachings.[45] Although these "rotten alley scholars" may approximate the ideological content of the Sages' words, their failure to take into account those words' aesthetic refinement dooms them to vulgarity. Writing in the generation after Gu Yanwu, well-known *shiwen* anthologist Yu Changcheng argues similarly at the turn of the eighteenth century that it is appropriate to make use of texts like the *Zhuangzi* and the Surangama Sutra as sources of aesthetic inspiration, even though that inspiration must be grounded in the basic morality of the Cheng-Zhu commentaries.[46]

What we see forming over the course of the Ming and early Qing is a sense that the very conception of modern prose as a sphere of action implies that imposing exhaustively uniform aesthetic standards is necessarily wrong. Where something approaching the Kantian categorical imperative would not be automatically problematic in putting the Way into practice in moral terms, it is precisely the tendency toward universalization of successful aesthetic choices that critics (and even some supporters) find disturbing about the examination system. Despite his harsh words for examination essays that make use of Buddhist and Daoist philosophical approaches, Gu Yanwu argues that "Literary writing has no set format (*dingge*). Setting up a format and then writing [to match that format] results in writing that is not worth speaking of."[47] The echoes of this assertion can be heard decades later in Zhang Taikai's distinction between the content and form of well-written essays: "Each topic has a given logic to it, but the writing [that expresses that logic] has no given form," a formulation that Gao Dang subsequently integrates into his more lengthy discussion of essay dynamics at the end of the Qianlong era.[48] Even when Liu Dakui makes the claim that *shiwen* writers cannot add anything to the meaning of the Sages, or subtract anything from it, he goes on to emphasize that one can be inspired by the spirit, sound, rhythm, and structural intricacy of master prose stylists to take the content of the topic and run with it.[49] The Qing critic Ye Xie writes of literature more generally that although there is no such thing as individual morality (*yijia zhi dao*), there are distinctive individual literary styles (*yijia zhi wen*); this works as a call for the stylistic autonomy of "pure literature" and, as we will see in the last chapter, turns out to be a crucial presupposition for the smooth functioning of the examination system as a selective regime.[50]

The significance of questions of style and technique, however, is that they do not stay limited to their specified arena but constitute a home base from which challenging attitudes can move out into related realms.

Here we can return to Feng Qi's 1601 memorial for an explanation of the
implications of this process:

> Since literary writing began to flourish, literati habits of writing have
> become increasingly uninhibited; they begin by being fed up with the
> ordinary and tend toward the trivial and wasteful; they do not stop at the
> trivial and wasteful, but gradually swarm after the new and unusual; they
> do not stop at the new and unusual, but gradually take interest in the
> bizarre and eccentric. At first, they planted their flags close to the various
> philosophers, but now they brandish their axes on behalf of Laozi and the
> Buddha, turning their backs on Confucius and Mencius and destroying
> Cheng and Zhu; it is only the language of the *Zhuangzi* and India that
> they honor and strive after.[51]

Such challenges could come in a wide variety of forms. Wang Ao does
not hesitate to swat away the standard Cheng-Zhu commentary dismis-
sively in his essay on "The wife of the prince of a state"; Tang Shunzhi
takes Mencius's critique of a passage in the *Classic of History* as inspiration to make a more general argument about liberties of interpretation
and breadth of source material. Noted late Ming iconoclast Li Zhi was
inspired by the essay form to write a book of personal reflections—the
Shuoshu (An explanation of the Four Books)—that he claims to have
been most pleased with of all his works.[52] In some cases, rejection of the
standard interpretation of the original text, through repetition, could
itself acquire a certain authority in the examination field.[53] In other cases,
we see authors investing great effort into creatively reconciling Cheng-
Zhu commentaries with the original texts as Ming and Qing scholars
later came to understand them, showing that perceived differences
between text and commentary could open the door to more subtle and
nuanced means of distinguishing oneself from the received tradition.[54]

More conservative critics, with a less imaginative view of what is appropriate in literary writing, may have had the clearest understanding of
the difficulties involved in separating different stylistic languages from
the intellectual paradigms associated with them. Candidates begin by
attempting to distinguish themselves with creative vocabulary choices,
new approaches to essay structure, and a wider range of aesthetic references in the late fifteenth century, but the circle of acceptable texts seems
to widen inexorably. By a certain point—the exact date seems to depend

on how skeptical one is about the way of the world—novelty eventually could no longer be isolated as "merely aesthetic."

Certainly aesthetic innovation seems difficult to separate from ideological challenges when the twenty-year-old Tang Shunzhi writes an essay on the topic "I beg to ask the steps of that process" for the metropolitan examination, in which he makes it as clear as possible that he is not merely adding formal flourishes but integrating "heterodox" approaches directly into his argument.[55] Tang takes a passage from the *Analects* that is foundational to Zhu Xi's (1130–1200) approach—an explanation of the phrase *keji fuli* (to subdue oneself and return to the rites)—and interpolates a scene from the *Zhuangzi* right into it. "In the past, Yan Yuan asked Confucius about benevolence (*ren*) and received instruction on subduing oneself and returning to the rites. I imagine that Yan Yuan's will to seek benevolence was fixed through fasting of the mind (*xinzhai*), and the distinction between principle and desire was silently understood from Confucius's instruction."[56] "Fasting of the mind" clearly refers to a passage in the *Zhuangzi* that—not coincidentally—also happens to be a conversation between Yan Yuan and Confucius. In this conversation, Yan Yuan explains to Confucius that he aims to instruct the young ruler of Wei, and he proposes, among other tactics, to conform to the appropriate rituals and make use of the rhetoric of antiquity. Confucius (as imagined by the *Zhuangzi*) insists that this will not accomplish his goal and suggests "fasting of the mind" as the best approach. Yan Yuan asks what this "fasting of the mind" would consist of, and Confucius replies:

> Confucius said, "Make your will one! Don't listen with your ears, listen with your mind. No, don't listen with your mind, but listen with your spirit. Listening stops with the ears, the mind stops with recognition, but spirit is empty and waits on all things. The Way gathers in emptiness alone. Emptiness is the fasting of the mind."
>
> Yen Hui [Yan Yuan] said, "Before I heard this, I was certain that I was Hui. But now that I have heard it, there is no more Hui. Can this be called emptiness?"[57]

When read in the context of Zhu Xi's appropriation of the Cheng brothers' interpretations of the classical canon, the full extent of Tang's mischief becomes evident: it was precisely to restrain Cheng Yi's presumed inclination toward Buddhist and Daoist approaches that Zhu Xi had foregrounded *keji fuli* as an active struggle to realize the Way that is both complementary and superior to the more meditative practice advocated by Cheng.[58] In response, Tang sends the informed reader right back to the *Zhuangzi*—and not to any other point in the text but the exact moment at which Confucius instructs Yan Yuan in the fine points of emptiness.

It is not just writers critical of modern prose trends who recognize a tendency for aesthetic innovation to lead to changes in approach to related fields; some advocates do as well. Gao Dang writes in *Lunwen jichao* (Collected transcriptions of discourses on literature) that "the more innovative (*qi*) [writing] gets . . . the more an author must develop new thinking (*biezhan xinsi*)."[59] Similarly, Yuan Cuijun writes that in the Ming and early Qing, the best writers innovated in beauty and style, but this has been exhausted, and now (beginning with Li Guangdi, and continuing on through Fang Bao, among others) the focus is on moral philosophy (including challenges to Zhu Xi's readings of the original texts) and philological research, in which standing out (*zhuoyue*) is also possible.[60] The line between form and content is itself a formal choice that is regularly subject to negotiation; it is one that changes according to one's historical perspective, as we have seen in the previous chapter.

Representation and Autonomy

So who is in control? How could the strict stylistic norms characteristic of the late fifteenth century develop in the absence of specific directives from above? Conversely, how was it possible for aesthetic innovation in the early sixteenth century along the lines of "using classical prose to write modern prose" to move within decades to specifically ideological challenges to the approved commentaries on which the whole system was supposed to be based, challenges that continue to resonate within the system even as exterior vehicles for critique (such as literary societies) are suppressed in the seventeenth and eighteenth centuries?

Even as the discourse of representative speech was beginning to take shape and acquire a specifically political relevance, we find new attention to the question of who should set the aesthetic agenda and to the relationship between examiners and candidates. Writing in the late Ming, Ai Nanying tells a compelling tale of decline. Previously, in the fifteenth and early sixteenth centuries, there was harmony between public opinion (*yulun*) and the examiners' standards: examiners selected essays that turned out to be generally well thought of, and the reading public approved of essays selected by examiners. By the time Ai himself is writing, however, there is a divergence, and force is required to coerce the acceptance of examiners' selections, evidence for him of a "realm without the Way." In the long run, Ai claims—in an argument that resonates in its vehemence with his famous examination essay on the topic "The people are the most important element in a nation"—that this authority based on brute force must lose out to authority based on virtue.[61] In another, somewhat more temperate late Ming preface, Xu Shipu (1608–58) gives a sense of how this shift might happen: with examiners failing at their job, those outside the government are stepping in to fill the vacuum by publishing preparation manuals and annotated essay collections and by forming literary societies that cross clan and village boundaries.[62]

In his path-breaking account of the complicated relationship between the publishing market and ideological contestation in the Wanli period and later, Kai-wing Chow writes of a group of literary professionals (*shishang*) who did precisely this, "[promoting] models of literary excellence that were at odds with the official standard. Through editing critical anthologies of examination essays, they expressed dissatisfaction and criticism of the selection of examination candidates and consequently intervened in the awarding of political offices through mobilizing public opinion of the examinees and the organizational power of professional critics."[63] Although the examination hierarchy centered on Beijing, by the late Ming these critics were most active in Jiangnan, evidence of "a general expansion of the literary public sphere that was outside kinship and the imperial government."[64] Examination essays were the subject of constant public attention: critics who prided themselves on their distance from the examination bureaucracy printed collections of essays that failed with explanations of how they should have passed, as well as collections of essays that passed in which every perceived fault was highlighted and the case was more than occasionally made that the candidate in question should have failed.

Although certain *shishang* clearly wielded great influence as publishers, authors of innovative commentaries, and organizers of literary societies in the late Ming, distinctive commentaries and activist literary societies begin to come into their own only in the last decades of

the sixteenth century: "new studies" commentaries inspired by Wang
Yangming appear in large numbers only in the 1590s.[65] Yet challenges to
orthodox Cheng-Zhu approaches actually began decades earlier, as noted
previously in this chapter, drawing complaints in the Jiajing era. By the
1560s, these challenges appeared even in the model essays compiled by
the examiners themselves, which were meant to serve as standard and
inspiration. Late Ming commentators excused their own unorthodox
interpretations in some cases by making explicit reference to the fact
that certain examiners had accepted these approaches in previous exam
cycles.[66]

Many of these tendencies continued in the Qing despite the suppression of literary societies and repeated (though less successful) attempts
to ban the publication of examination essay collections.[67] What this
suggests is that although literary society activities and their publications were key means through which aesthetic challenges and intellectual provocations were advanced in the late Ming—and we may note
that advocates of representative speech such as Ai, Zhang, and Ni were
particularly active in this field—these nonstate organizations played just
one part in a broader contest over the politics of appropriate essay form.
It is also important to note that although challenges to the standards
endorsed by examiners could come from critics who openly advocated
Wang Yangming's approach to the Classics as an alternative to Cheng-
Zhu orthodoxy, the status quo could be subject to criticism from the
opposite direction as well. More conservative critics like Ai Nanying
scolded examiners for their excessively tolerant approach to essays
inspired by Wang Yangming and those that went so far as to borrow
terms and concepts from Buddhist and Daoist texts.[68]

In this connection, Su Xiangfeng's harsh critique of the state of *wen*
in the late Ming and early Qing, advanced in his preface to the *Jiagui
ji* (Collected examination essays from 1624 through 1643), is intriguing.
He attributes the "three great faults" in literati approaches to writing to
"three bad habits" of literary composition, which are in turn blamed on
the "three poisonous seeds," transmitted by identifiable groups of people.
The last of these is "wielders of the brush," that is, professional annota-
tors and commentators whose works are available on the open market.
The second to last is fathers, older brothers, and teachers, who should
know better but lead the younger generation astray instead. In the first

position, credited by implication with the greatest degree of influence, are the examiners at all levels.[69] Indeed, as early as the fifteenth century, one-time Minister of Rites Qiu Jun (1421–95) had already suggested that examiners bore the greatest responsibility for problematic tendencies in examination writing.[70]

For most modern scholars, the crucial opposition that constitutes the examination system has tended to be between literatus and the examination regime, or between literati as a class and the state. It is difficult to get beyond the image of the candidate struggling to please a judgmental monolith that comprises faceless graders, higher-level officials in the Ministry of Rites, and ultimately the emperor. Our attention is often called to the antagonism and marked difference in status between candidates and examiners not only in scholarly works that attempt to understand how the situation of candidates as a category of individuals changes over time but also in more personal accounts, such as Ai Nanying's preface to his own works, which contrasts the physical and psychological torments that hopeful participants experienced with the comparatively comfortable circumstances he understood the examiners to find themselves in, and Pu Songling's imaginative "Seven Likenesses of a Candidate."[71] Under these circumstances, it is hard to imagine how challenges to aesthetic conventions and ideological standards could come from anywhere but outside the system.[72]

But serious conversation about how examinations should be conducted and what they should value was not restricted to critics excluded from the system. Unsurprisingly, the extent of the practical power to innovate that examiners would have is never stated outright in imperial edicts establishing or reforming the examination system.[73] Yet contemporary critics often highlighted the differences in approach and the potential for tension between the official position of the minister of Rites and the practice of actual examiners, as well as provincial education commissioners in the late Ming. For example, Yuan Zhongdao draws a distinction between officials who have the authority to ban certain stylistic provocations and those who in most cases are actually doing the work of selection and welcome these provocations.[74] It is likely that with the exception of the most extreme cases of perceived *lèse-majesté*, examiners at all levels of the system came to wield decisive power in the selection of topics, the specific formulation of types of questions, and the evaluation of the

essays produced in response and could further influence the development of the examination field by publishing model essays they wrote and
candidates' essays with their comments attached.[75]

The clearest example of the lead taken by provincial and lower-level
examiners comes in the invention and elaboration of the "small topic"
(*xiaoti*) exam questions. These questions originated as a means of reducing duplication between essays in an exam cycle and replication of
essays from past years by radically increasing the possible number of
questions—in other words, as a technique for increasing examiners' ability to differentiate among individual candidates. Small topic questions
forced candidates to focus only on specific phrases or even individual
words from the classical canon, without making excessive reference to
the surrounding context.[76] Examiners had a distinct interest in reducing copying: if passed candidates were later found to have copied essays
from an essay anthology, their examiners would be punished.[77] In a later
development, combined questions were introduced, juxtaposing words
or phrases from different passages in the canon and requiring candidates
to address the two in a unified and coherent fashion.[78]

The harsh criticism of small topic questions by commentators on
the exam system hints at the significance of the changes they inspired.
Writing in the decades after these questions began to appear, Minister of
Rites Qiu Jun paints a dismal picture:

> In the time of the dynastic founder, all examination topics drew from the
> larger principles and organization of the Classics and the Four Books, and
> dealt with morality and governance. . . . But in recent years, the
> examiners have set themselves to challenging the candidates, using what
> the candidates do not know to show off the examiners' own ability. In the
> first session questions drawn from the Classics and the Four Books the
> examiners invariably seek out the obscure and strange, forcibly cutting
> sentences up, fragmenting the text of the Classics, joining together what
> should not be joined together and cutting what should not be cut. This
> leaves the students nothing to rely on, and they put effort into areas
> where they should not, while neglecting the most important sections.[79]

I have shown in detail elsewhere how the small topic format allows space
for—even necessitates, in some cases—a creative approach to the examination essay.[80] I mention here only briefly a Qing dynasty essay on "There is a
beautiful jade here," drawn from a passage in the *Analects* in which Zigong
compares the Master's virtue to a jade and asks whether he will consider

"selling" the "jade." Confucius responds that he will sell it, of course, he is merely waiting for the right buyer. Zhu Xi's commentary unsurprisingly emphasizes Confucius's determination to serve only the right ruler—expressed through his willingness to wait for a buyer, rather than seek one—and it would be hard to argue that this is not the main point of this brief exchange.[81] Because the small topic essay cannot go beyond the confines of the specifically cited topic, however, this essay cannot touch on that point. To the consternation of the modern annotator, the essay ignores Confucius's response and focuses strictly on making the best statement of Zigong's case.[82] Essays such as this one form a good argument for the small topic approach: not only do they force the candidates to do more than simply repeat the standard glosses of the overall passage in question, they require candidates to come up with an interesting argument based on a very small fragment of text, encouraging depth of analysis. This essay consists partly of a virtuoso display of mastery of the geography of jade production in early China, and it goes beyond this to remind the reader at several points that although jade in its natural state serves as a nice metaphor for the virtuous person who would benefit his ruler and his people by participating in government, worked jade functions equally in metonymic fashion to index political and ritual power. While Zhu Xi gets the obvious point of this passage as a whole—do not commit yourself to serve just anyone, wait for the right ruler, who makes his rightness clear in part through his manner of approaching you to request your assistance—it could well be argued that our anonymous author's miniature dissertation on the political implications of jades in early China makes our understanding of the original text considerably richer.

When we read Wang Fuzhi's criticism of small topic questions, which he assumes appeared for the first time in the late Ming, subsequent to the widespread popularization of Wang Yangming's new approaches to the canon, his reaction may at first seem overwrought. What does it matter if the topic is a mere phrase selected from a broader argument if candidates have trained for years to memorize the texts and questions and will immediately be able to locate the phrase in its original context?[83] But when the practice of small topics is accompanied by an understanding that one is not to "connect above" or "connect below," intellectual fragmentation of the original arguments becomes a fundamental condition under which the exam essays are produced. The single clear wrong answer is to parrot a conventional interpretation of the argument based on a larger section of the text. When one compares the different treatments resulting from longer or shorter selections of the original text that appear even among big topic essays, the significance of the small topic restrictions becomes especially clear.[84]

Gong Duqing points out that Wang Fuzhi's chronology is mistaken: Wang believes that the small topic questions arose in the Wanli era, whereas in fact small topic questions first appeared over a century earlier and were quite common even before Wang Yangming was old enough to participate in the examination system. But like Wang Fuzhi, Gong sees a close link between small topic questions and Wang Yangming's new learning; it is just that the arrow of causation is reversed. The pervasive use of small topic questions is as important as—if not more important than—the sixteenth-century lecturing movement (*jiangxue*) in opening up a new arena for critical reconsideration of the received interpretations of the Classics. Small topics brought new challenges on the grounds of meaning and interpretation by "fragmenting" the canonical texts and gave candidates particular leeway to substitute their own conclusions for those they were meant to be representing.[85] On a smaller scale, Jiao Xun attributes a newly serious interest in philology at the regional level in the late eighteenth century to a set of particularly difficult small topic questions posed by an education commissioner assigned to Jiangsu in 1774–75.[86]

In Qiu Jun's critique, the emphasis is placed on inappropriate cutting or fragmentation of the text, but passing mention is given to "joining together what should not be joined" as a related issue. Lu Longji is more detailed on this question, using tropes of carpentry to argue that "authors have no choice but to use techniques of drilling and forcing together to create the text." What the small topic requires is a renewed focus on the craft of putting a coherent essay together, with candidates judged by their ability to order their responses and make convincing connections between separate fragments of texts, rather than simply reproducing an ideological take from a single passage.[87] The aesthetic is not merely one of coherent arrangement but also one of literary inventiveness, as we can see from a comment from the early eighteenth century that gives a sense of how these essays could be judged first and foremost on formal terms: "The small topic essays of our dynasty make *xuzi* into *shizi*, forcefully breaking more ground, and far succeeding over those of the Ming dynasty."[88] This treatment of *xu* elements as if they were *shi* (實) can best be understood as a new focus on the formal features of the original text as the subject of discourse, under certain conditions and to some extent replacing the ethical content that previously would have been seen to constitute the most solid, "real," aspect of the text. The innovation in question format that was the small topic question called forth innovative essays in response.

The invention of the small topic question led to a radical shift in writing and evaluating examination essays and corresponding transformations in the relationship between the ideological and the aesthetic in the examination sphere. But no individual steps forward to take credit for this innovation. It was not a policy articulated from above, nor a reform inspired by a critic of the system, but a strategy adopted by examiners in provincial and local examinations on an ad hoc basis that quickly spread to become an unspoken norm. Notice was soon taken at the highest levels, and an imperial edict in 1441 specifically banned the use of small topic questions.[89] Like many other high-level attempts to control the development of examination aesthetics, this edict met with no success— small topic questions only proliferated in number and type in response.[90] For at least one fifteenth-century critic, a crucial aspect of the small topic phenomenon was the use of these questions by examiners to assert an inappropriate degree of autonomy: to put aside the original meaning of the texts and make "their own points" instead.[91]

The belated and grudging official acceptance of these types of questions in 1738, some three centuries after they first became common, reminds us not only of the limitations in the power of the central authorities overseeing the examination system but also of the sometimes radical disjunction between the prescribed conduct of the examinations and actual practice.[92] This disjunction opens up a space in which unwritten precedent and shifting standards of evaluation constitute a noticeable degree of autonomy in the system. Generally speaking, the "rules" governing the essay were not so much handed down from above as they were generated within the examination bureaucracy and, increasingly over the course of the Ming dynasty, in negotiations among members of that bureaucracy, educational officials such as provincial educational commissioners, and independent tastemakers in the publishing world.

The independent critics did not depend primarily on examination success to gain status; indeed, in some cases they succeeded at the highest level examinations only quite late in life if at all.[93]

In this context, even standards that have been ordinarily taken as nearly immutable—such as parallelism, the arrangement of the component parts of the essay, and writing in the voice of the Sages and Worthies—turn out to be less fixed criteria than questions of style to which different answers can be given depending on the examination cycle. From our perspective, as suggested in the introduction, rather than thinking of the examination arena as a space for reiterating ideological truths and reproducing unchanging standard literary forms, something like the "fashion system" imagined by Roland Barthes would be closer to the mark.[94] Indeed, the term *shimao*, still used today to denote the popular and fashionable, was applied to modern prose already in the late Ming.[95]

Modern scholars' focus on the disagreements between critics and examiners in the late Ming and again at the height of the Qing movement for Han Learning calls our attention to moments at which the imperial project of ideological reproduction encountered open and sustained resistance. But struggles for control over the examination process and its broader social significance were not limited to these periods: they were rather endemic throughout the Ming and Qing. In addition to open conflict motivated by ideological considerations or personal grievances about the selection of one candidate rather than another, in which critics and publishers find themselves in opposition to "the state" broadly conceived, the history of the examination system is marked by a subtle but persistent structural tension between examiners on one hand and the court and supervising Ministry of Rites on the other.[96] The division here is between individuals who actually participated in grading exams and those who merely proclaimed the standards by which grading was supposed to be conducted. When approached from this perspective, the majority of examiners may find themselves identifying with critics writing from outside the system, rather than with the highest levels of the bureaucracy. But unlike critics, who anticipate financial benefit from making their positions clear and have little to worry about in terms of retribution, examiners in the system had little to gain and a great deal to lose by leaving a record of their disagreements with the minister of Rites or the ruler. As we might expect from reading the work of Michel de

Certeau and James Scott, these more persistent differences are expressed explicitly and discursively not nearly as often as they are in terms of practice.[97] The creation of a wide range of small topic question types, and the persistent use of these topics in spite of direct imperial instructions to stop, are only the most striking examples of this kind of "dissent through practice."

Writing in the final decades of the Ming, Xu Shipu tells us a story about how civilized the examination field was before the Wanli era: there were no traveling literati, no private editions, and no literary societies beyond village level. Like the ideal society imagined in the *Daode jing* (80), people stayed in their place and never even traveled to the next village (despite hearing their dogs and roosters).[98] As a nostalgic recollection of a time when examination preparation was a cottage industry rather than a national market, this narrative seems complete only insofar as we forget that the examination regime constituted one of the primary motivations for travel and interaction beyond one's hometown from the earliest years of the Ming all the way to the twentieth century. Similarly, the aesthetic and ideological contestation so evident in the late Ming is not so much unprecedented as it is unprecedentedly explicit and surprisingly profitable.[99] The outside critics who become so dominant in the late sixteenth century are late arrivals to a tug-of-war that has gone on with more subtlety for decades. The conflict flares out into the open now in part because the rapidly expanding publishing market needs names and personalities to establish the value of the intellectual goods for sale, and benefits from conflict and confrontation. By contrast, officials within the system ordinarily advance their own interests and stylistic innovations not through outright advocacy but—more safely—through their own unadvertised practice.

Imagination of a Class

If the modern prose author is best conceived of not primarily as a cultural capitalist, a speculator in words and value like the writer of occasional prose, but as a representative agent (as I suggested in the introduction and chapter 1) and as a producer writing for other producers (as we will see in later chapters and in the epilogue), then even as the essay represents the individual, the individual represents a broader group, one that we may tentatively refer to as a class.[100] To what extent can this class be understood as constituted of groups and individuals who participate in a broader conversation about aesthetics, even though the differentials in power between different positionalities in this conversation can be quite marked? Whom is the candidate speaking *to* when he speaks for the Sages and Worthies?

As we saw previously, Su Xiangfeng is highly critical of the problematic tendencies that examiners encourage among candidates. He is even more concerned about the autonomy, even circularity he sees in the examination field, which appears to allow no provision for correction from the outside. "Examiners select from the literati, and literati in turn become examiners, back and forth like waves blown by the wind, knowing no end, this is the poisonous seed transmitted by those who select officials."[101] This worry over the potential for feedback loops intensified in the late Ming, as we see in Ai Nanying's broad condemnation and Li Tingji's comments more narrowly focused on education commissioners. But if we return to Qiu Jun and Xia Yan, the ministers of Rites quoted earlier in this chapter, we find related concerns articulated in the fifteenth and sixteenth centuries. Qiu argues that if candidates are expected by examiners to produce a certain (problematic) kind of writing, once those candidates themselves become examiners they will expect the same kind of writing from future candidates. Xia notes in 1532 that candidate essays were being printed as models for future exams, rather than model essays composed for that purpose alone by examiners, and he proposes that if this practice continues, examiners should at least be certain to add corrections to all such essays before they are published to check the spread of inappropriate stylistic tendencies.[102]

For critics of modern prose, the inauthenticity of speaking for another, rather than for oneself, is matched by the problem of writing for another on a topic that the other has provided. But what if that other for whom one writes is also, in some sense, oneself? Let us turn to Zhou Zuoren's intriguing description of how essays were read aloud:

> When [Chinese people of earlier generations] read those essays, I imagine everyone can still remember their demeanor: nodding and shaking their heads, almost as if they were listening to Mei Lanfang sing opera. Some might ask on seeing one doing this, "Humming his way through a modern prose essay (*shiwen*) as rotten as mud, how can he be this happy?" I know that he is intoxicated by music . . . he hears only his own clear tones ringing in his ears, and it is as if he were in a theater.[103]

I suggest that this essay reader chanting to himself, who appears in a range of texts over the centuries, can serve as a key figure to better understand literati as a class in the Ming and Qing, as constituted through the examination system.

The civil service examination system may be thought of as an arena in which literati represent themselves as a class to the upper reaches of the state, but also as one where the educated class (examiners, critics, amateur scholars, and others) undertakes a massive (and, it must be acknowledged, sometimes repetitive) project of representation to itself. Here we can remember Ni Yuanlu's representational work from the previous chapter, in which he writes first on behalf of the Donglin Academy to the ruler and then writes on behalf of the ruler, about the Donglin Academy, to an audience that is literate society in general. This work could also be understood in negative terms, depending on the circumstances. Qiu Jun argues that examiners should make only minor edits to the model essays they print and distribute; to go any further in improving the successful candidates' work would be to substitute their writing for that of the candidates (*dai juzi zuo*).[104]

In this sense, the *shiwen* genre, which began as a representation of the individual to the state and a process of ideological reproduction among those individuals, acquires not only the sense of representing the literati *as a class* to the state but further, the function of representing literati class *as a class* to itself. Writing (and reading!) exam essays is what literati *do*, the vocation of the literati (*shiren zhi ye*), as noted previously in this chapter.[105] The content is about what literati are supposed to *be*. Practically speaking, essay writing went some way toward serving this purpose in the Song, but the explicit articulation of *dai* as fundamental to examination discourse now locates authority not primarily in the logic of the argument but in a form of identification best understood as aesthetic, the object of which can be a Sage or Worthy. (I return to this identification process in more detail in chapter 4.) "Speaking for the Sages and Worthies," then, is a question not just of conveying their intention but also of creating a form appropriate to that intention. The class as a whole, which the individual speaker is standing in for, is defined in part through that form.

The simultaneity of the examination experience was a powerful means for imagining community among candidates along the lines of the simultaneous newspaper reading that Benedict Anderson understands to assist in the imagination of the nation.[106] To the regular rhythm of the examination cycle, around which entire industries were arranged, we may add the experience of serving now as playwright for, now as performer of, the same Sages and Worthies (among other characters) that all other candidates are. Anderson argues of the novel with multiple narrative strands and the newspaper that "these forms provided the technical means for 're-presenting' the *kind* of imagined community that is the nation."[107] More than a "technical" means, we can see the commitment to representative speech as a specifically *aesthetic* means through which a class identity is imagined.[108] As Guan Shiming argues, speaking for the sages is superior to commentary because it is a type of identification rather than objectification—affective as much as logical in that it involves both embodiment and critical appropriation. By explicitly foregrounding the aesthetic dimension, the work of literati in the Qing, and retrospectively the Ming, is distinguished from that of earlier examination regimes.

We have seen from Su Xiangfeng a distinct skepticism about the possibility that an autonomous group can control its own negative tendencies. Similarly, Gu Xianzheng laments the freedom that his late Ming contemporaries have to draw from Buddhist and Daoist texts, the *Shanhai jing* (Classic of mountains and rivers), and even vernacular fiction, writing only about what they are inclined to. He concludes that with "no constraints from within in the form of standard commentaries, and no worries about the fetters of rules and regulations from the outside," the task of the essay writer has become easy.[109] Indeed, what greater freedom can there be than speaking freely to oneself in exactly the manner that one chooses? But how can this finding of radical autonomy be reconciled with the tropes of stale imitation and reproduction that become more and more common in criticism of the essay form beginning in the late Ming? Gu Yanwu's critique of the "set format" holds that if only candidates had the freedom to write without restraint, outstanding talents would appear.[110] Are there constraints or not?

This seeming paradox is strikingly reminiscent of Kant's account of genius, with its insistence that genius can be "followed" but not "imitated," with the similar apparently contradictory dynamic of free choice in aesthetic matters that turns out nonetheless to accord with certain universals.[111] In terms more familiar to Chinese literary criticism, this resembles the internalization of *fa* (method, technique), to the point that one is no longer conscious of one's mastery. This dynamic, so characteristic of writers' concept of their own literary work in Ming and Qing China, provides a useful way to understand the transformation of the literati as a class under the examination system and its associated typical production.[112] Individuals give themselves the aesthetic law by internalizing it and then freely conforming to it as an ideal for writing specific texts; educated individuals as a class select the aesthetic standards for their own assessment. This class has set itself certain rules, including attention to questions of representative address and parallelism, in those of its writings that will be submitted to the state for consideration. Although rank within the class is often determined by the ability to break the rules appropriately, the basic fact of membership in the class is determined by a conscious awareness and mastery of those rules in the first place.

Although this process may also remind us of Terry Eagleton's account of the bourgeoisie giving itself the law through the aesthetic in Britain and Western Europe, the bifurcation between aesthetic production and consumption that modern Western theorists tend to rely on cannot accommodate the undeniable social importance of the examination regime.[113] In Bourdieu's study of nineteenth- and twentieth-century France, for example, aesthetic production constitutes the means by which a small number of people take positions in the subfield of restricted production that allow them to make a living. Aesthetic consumption is a much broader phenomenon, a type of secondary capital market—in which the gains that a family or group has made in material capital may be reproduced, elaborated, and maintained. The famous writer or commentator who finds a career for himself in the late Ming publishing market appears quite similar to what Bourdieu is talking about;[114] name-brand critics and commentators seem to be writing for their audiences and not necessarily so much for other producers.

But in the Ming and Qing, it is clear that these audiences themselves are also producers, in that they take part in ordinary exchange of writings central to literate society (*yingchou*) and take the civil service examinations (in many cases, repeatedly). At the same time, we recall that a group like the *shishang* could emerge over the course of the late Ming only as a *supplement* to the system that has already developed, centered on the exam system, in which producers write for producers. Literary "excellence" in Ming and Qing China is not merely a means of reproducing social status but a method of acquiring it in the first place, and aesthetic production is not the province of a few professionals, but rather—no less than aesthetic consumption—a prerequisite for membership in the class of literate people.[115] The characteristic dynamic in which producers write for other producers (rather than for readers, who only consume) does not serve to define an exclusive avant-garde, as Bourdieu finds to be the case in Western Europe, but sets the outermost boundaries of the class as a whole. Although a broader and less professionally specific mode of aesthetic production could be imagined to herald a social order in which oppressive relations have vanished altogether, as in Marx's utopian conception of the arts in a communist society, this broader mode of production could also, as we see here, serve as one of the foundations of a different but no less thorough system of class-based social domination.[116]

What does it mean for the classes of producers and consumers of written texts to be so nearly coextensive? Rather than focusing on the question of judgment through aesthetic consumption and the associated assessment of aesthetic value, as so much European theorization of the aesthetic does, discourses on literary aesthetics in the Ming and Qing are concerned primarily with the problem of aesthetic production. It is as if the primary emphasis of Kant's *Critique of Judgment* were in fact genius, rather than taste.[117] The focus shifts from the work of art as an isolated object with an inherent or acquired aesthetic value to the voice of the producer, a determinate relationship between the producer and his or her work. When Ming and Qing authors use *dai* to single out pieces in their collected works that were written to be published under another person's name, the "substitution" referred to is a complicated phenomenon: not only labor that will be compensated but also a kind of ventriloquism, in which the ghostwriter is ultimately putting words in the mouth of the person who hires him, as we saw in the previous chapter, and finally, an impersonation that is a form of identification, as we will see in more detail in the fourth chapter of this book.[118] Explanations of representative (*dai*) speech that begin from the model of cultural capital catch only the first of these three aspects, precisely because of their emphasis on value rather than voice (I return to this question in chapter 5 and the epilogue). The writings of Dong Qichang, Ai Nanying, and many other critics from the late Ming onward suggest a more complicated understanding of the "representation" that is taking place when "speaking for the Sages and Worthies." *Dai* is not a straightforward process of reproducing an already given text in different words, but an arena where questions of agency, control, and identity are foregrounded instead of being swept under the rug. These questions may never have definitive and generally persuasive answers, but the fact that they are being asked is quite significant.

Ming and Qing critics of the examination system often argue that more weight should be given to policy questions and less to the "formal-istic" modern prose essays on the Four Books, and indeed both major reforms in the Qing shift emphasis in precisely this fashion—the down-grading of *shiwen* in favor of *lun* in the Kangxi era, which was soon reversed, and in favor of *lun* and *celun* in the early twentieth century, which lasted a mere three years before the system was abandoned.[119] Even as representative speech is conceived of as central to *shiwen*, despite the many examples where that approach is ignored or not even applicable, this genre—composed in response to prompts taken from the Four Books—takes on outsized importance in the examination framework because its insistence on the relevance of form allows significantly more potential for aesthetic "free play" and differentiation among candidates. Elman writes, "Both the needs of Ming and Ch'ing imperial ortho-doxy and the acute cultural sensibilities of educated men were met and compromised in the examination regime. It was not a one-way impe-rial hegemony based simply on political or social power. Nor was it an autonomous field of literati authority."[120] This is a balanced assessment of the system as a whole; what should be added is that this "compromise" is both dynamic and uneven, in that specific areas in the system lend themselves to hegemonic control while others enjoy relative autonomy. Policy essays were too directly political in their applicability to social and administrative questions of the moment, and as a result they seemed to place more explicit constraint on the candidates, making it more difficult for examiners to differentiate between one essay and another. *Shiwen*, by contrast, were judged as much on *how* a given position was presented as they were on the content of that position. From the beginnings of systematic discourse on the aesthetic in Western Europe, the potential the aesthetic has to serve as a ground of innovation and destabilization comes precisely from its claim to take its distance from ideological ques-tions. A similar dynamic is at work in the Ming and Qing.

To return to Hu Renyu's essay: Confucius has asked four of his disciples, if you were to be taken seriously by a ruler, what would you like to do? Three earnestly present the equivalent of policy essays, and Confucius merely smiles in response. Dian offers us an aesthetic experience that makes a point about dependency. Confucius sighs in appreciation, but Hu refuses to assimilate this sigh to a consistent ideological system—rather, it is the material force of Confucius's deeply felt reaction that is its meaning (*yi*), in Yuan Renlin's formulation.

Open ideological confrontations within the examination system erupt periodically; the first two chapters of this book have focused on the stylistic and discursive infrastructure that makes these open debates on intellectual orthodoxy possible and even necessary—an infrastructure that is best understood as simultaneously aesthetic and ideological. Beneath battles over the correct interpretation of difficult passages in the Classics and the appropriate scholarly approach to such passages, we find over the course of the Ming and early Qing the development and refinement of new means of articulating literati identity as a class; and as we shall see later in this book, a profound real-world test of received notions of creativity, authenticity, and authority that would have ripple effects far beyond the examination system itself.

CHAPTER THREE

Measures and Matches

If there is one formal trait for which we think we know *shiwen*, it is parallelism: a thudding echo line by line that comes with deadening regularity, symbolizing in its inevitable consistency the inability of the essay writer, burdened with the task of mimicking the ancients, to come up with an original and unique line of argument. Indeed, writing at the end of the seventeenth century, the authors of the *History of the Ming* identify writing in parallel sentences as one of the two key formal characteristics of the modern prose examination essay.[1] The continuing prominence of parallelism in critical discourses on and popular imaginations of examination writing can also be seen in the persistence of the evocative yet only occasionally accurate name by which the genre is generally known, the "eight-legged essay." Despite a broad recognition among modern scholars that the essay could have four, six, or even ten legs, its bipedal and symmetrical nature has not been subject to question in any consistent fashion.[2] This chapter takes parallelism not as an a priori, nor as a settled conclusion that marks the end of productive inquiry into the essay form, but as a problem that repays further investigation. What does it mean when we identify two sentences or sections of an essay as "parallel"? What is the significance of the work done by authors and readers to end with this result? What may we be overlooking in our haste to define the modern prose essay form primarily on this basis?

Parallelism has long been considered central to Chinese poetry, and more recently has also been emphasized in the study of other genres, such as long vernacular fiction and drama. In these contexts, it is often understood as the concrete expression of an underlying worldview or cosmology that aims at symmetry and balance between or among multiple terms that may well be thought of as metaphysical, rather than as specifically aesthetic.[3] In discourse on literary prose, however, parallelism

is not accepted as a given as it was in poetry, nor as an overarching organizing principle as it was in fiction. Rather, it is taken to be the subject
of an unresolved debate around which the tradition takes shape, as in
the case of Han Yu's reaction against the prose styles characteristic of the
Six Dynasties and debates over the distinction between literary writing
and "plain writing."[4] This question only becomes more problematic in
examination writing from the late eleventh century onward: although
prose masters of the Song such as Ouyang Xiu (1007–72), Wang Anshi
(1021–86), and Su Shi (1037–1101) are known primarily for their classical
prose, we can see evidence of parallel style in examination essays already
in the Song.[5] *Shiwen* of the Ming and Qing extend this principle far
beyond regulated verse and Six Dynasties parallel prose (*pianti wen*):
instead of five characters followed by five characters in parallel, or seven
characters followed by seven in parallel, typical in poetic composition, or
the four-six rhythm characteristic of parallel prose in the style of the Six
Dynasties, modern prose lines could run to dozens of characters.[6] Indeed,
although Chu Quan's late fifteenth-century essay "On this account, the
exemplary man does not wait till he sees things, to be cautious," made
up largely of two almost exactly parallel wings each over 100 characters
in length, is an extreme example, essays with parallel sections not much
shorter than this are not uncommon.[7]

Matches between characters or groups of characters across two parallel stretches of text can be semantic, syntactic, or phonetic; in essay
criticism of the Ming and Qing key distinctions are drawn between
imaginary and real (*xu/shi*), active and passive (*dong/jing*), and even tone
and oblique tone (*ping/ze*). Elements of contrast consisting of concrete
differences that can be subsumed at a higher level of abstraction when
presented in parallel form—for example, large against small (size), positive versus negative (value), past and present (time), first and third person
(voice), and so on—are particularly useful building blocks.

What are we to do, then, with Tang Shunzhi's famous early
sixteenth-century essay on wrestling with tigers, "Feng Fu of Jin"? In my
translation of this essay, included in the appendix, I use italics to highlight the brief parallel portions; the rest of the essay is "loose" (*san*) or
"single-file" (*danhang*) prose, without any clear matches or doubling. On
the face of it, this essay cannot be thought of as predominantly parallel;
the parallel portions constitute less than a sixth of the whole, a figure

that would not be out of place in many classical prose essays. Even more striking than the scarcity of parallel wording is its full integration into the flow of the narrative, and Tang's apparently casual attitude toward its placement. Examiners looking for four instances of parallel matches would be able to find them in this essay. But to call this an "eight-legged essay," as if these brief eight stretches of parallel wording define the structure of the text in any fundamental way, would be rather difficult to justify.

Indeed, when we compare this essay to a canonical work of classical prose, Han Yu's "Yuan dao" (Tracing the Way), the point becomes even clearer: although classical prose is often contrasted with modern prose as an ordered sequence of singular (not parallel) sentences heading in a single rhetorical direction, and Han Yu is generally acknowledged as the epitome of a classical prose author, the proportion of parallel sequences in "Tracing the Way"—well over a third—is markedly higher than in "Feng Fu of Jin."[8]

What does it mean for us not to find parallelism where we would expect it in Tang's essay? Let us turn to two key sentences midway through, at the moment of highest tension:

> So the crowd's tactics were *exhausted,*
> and the crowd's minds were *also frightened and uneasy and*
> *there was nothing to be done*

> 於是眾人之技窮
> 而眾人之心亦且惶惶然無可奈何矣

Due to the imbalance between the words in italics, these lines do not form a parallel match. They easily could have, however, if they had been written somewhat differently:

> So the crowd's tactics were *exhausted,*
> and the crowd's minds were *apprehensive*

Given that these lines, central to Tang's essay, could be much more fully parallel with a slight adjustment, this "failure" to match must have been received as a stylistic choice. If this "failure" had been considered a mere mistake, this essay likely would not have been preserved, let alone reprinted. But if we suppose that writing against parallelism is a deliberate choice, what are the likely effects, intended and unintended? This question is taken up in more detail later in this chapter. At this point, I highlight only the fact that by setting up a potential parallel and then choosing to overrun it by modifying "minds" with nine characters compared with one only modifying "tactics," Tang calls the reader's attention to the psychological state of the crowd in particularly striking fashion.[9]

Although Tang's essay is an extreme case, we will see that writing against the parallel grain is not so rare among *shiwen* by well-known stylists of the Ming and Qing. Conversely, we find frequent criticism of lines that match too well not only from writers who were skeptical of the value of modern prose but also from a wide variety of writers who took the genre quite seriously. The phrase *hezhang zhi bing* (the "praying hands fault") was a favorite critical term for excessively symmetrical parallelism: probably already a cliché by the time Tang Xianzu used it in the sixteenth century, it continues to appear regularly in essay criticism well into the nineteenth.[10] Writing in the seventeenth century, He Zhuo (1661–1722) praises an essay that does not balance two parts as "getting rid of the old two-wing setup," and an eighteenth-century critic claims that "In writing one must get rid of the traces of parallelism; those with conviction are not willing to follow the vulgar in looking up and down."[11] Gu Dashao (1576–?) puts it even more strongly: too much parallelism in an essay is like a person who has no animating spirit and is nothing but an expressionless zombie; one remedy for this is to leaven the parallel passages with stretches of single-line prose.[12] Even Li Guangdi (1642–1718), one of the foremost Qing authorities on modern prose style, who praises Wang Ao's perfectly matched parallelism as the epitome of the genre, also argues for the unique value of lines that seem to match but do not (*sidui budui*).[13] The modern scholar Huang Qiang goes so far as to identify a rigid adherence to the rules of parallelism as one characteristic of poor quality essays.[14]

Other commentators insist on historicizing parallelism: Gu Yanwu sees the "eight-legged" form taking shape in 1487, but remaining dominant for only a few decades, whereas Zhu Jian's preface to *Collected Words* sees more emphasis on parallelism in the Yongzheng and Qianlong periods than earlier or later in the Qing.[15] As Ji Yun comments later in the eighteenth century, simply following the given parallel structure of the topic is not enough. If the topic itself seems to resolve easily into parallel sections for essay treatment, the writer must work against the grain to complicate it in some way. To substantiate this point, Liang Zhangju notes several early nineteenth-century exam sessions where all essays that relied on straightforward divisions of the topic into parallel sections did not pass.[16] For these writers, parallel matching (*dui*) is not a basic, immutable requirement but one more quality of modern prose that is valued differently at different historical moments.

Individual authors could also show striking variability in their approaches to this question in different essays. Ai Nanying's "The people are the most important element in a nation" is often seen as less than perfect in its parallelism; in fact, this essay is better understood as fundamentally "loose" or "single-file" in its structure, akin to essays by Tang Shunzhi and Wan Guoqin, among others discussed later in this chapter. In "To the mind belongs the office of thinking; by thinking it gets the right view of things," by contrast, Ai makes much more extensive use of strict parallelism to organize his essay.[17] Going back over 100 years to the mid-fifteenth century, we see a similar range in the essays of Luo Lun (1431–78), including the relatively straightforward parallelism in "The Duke Ai asked Zai Wo about the altars of the spirits of the land," and the significantly more complex essay on the topic "Long ago, a former king appointed its ruler to preside over the sacrifices to the eastern Meng," which Fang Bao finds to anticipate the work of writers in centuries to follow.[18] Finally, in the case of Fang Bao himself, we can compare the relatively strict "'All the day active and vigilant'—continually, as the time passes and requires, does he act" with the much less evenly balanced "The Master was wishing Qidiao Kai to enter on official employment," discussed later in this chapter.[19]

If parallel style is to some extent contingent rather than essential, and even when expected in some form could be overdone, we begin to understand how one mid-Qing commentator could write that "Loose or non-parallel (*sanxing*) prose was not originally the standard form for examination essays. But if one is able to express [the Sage's meaning] through discourse (*yilun*) and use one's own shuttle and loom, it is indeed not impossible."[20] Another, several decades later, wrote that "In any essay, four parallel elements (*bi*) are acceptable, two large parallel elements are acceptable, three large parallel elements are also acceptable, even not using parallel elements and writing purely in loose prose has nothing unacceptable about it."[21] Already in the late Ming we find praise of *liushui* (flowing water) as a writing technique that can overcome excessive parallelism. It is not that flowing water does not occasionally eddy and swirl back on itself, but it never loses its determining force and overall direction.[22]

This chapter begins from the apparent contradiction between the accepted definition of the "eight-legged essay" in terms of its symmetry on one hand and highly successful nonconforming essays by writers like Tang Shunzhi on the other, and aims to build on existing scholarship in two ways. As I have suggested here and will show in more detail later, the claim that parallelism was a basic requirement, to which each essay had to conform through the use of a prescribed set of techniques, is problematic. This chapter works instead from the concrete construction of parallel sets in specific essays to argue that rather than a natural manifestation in words of a mentality that sees little change over the centuries, parallelism in the modern prose essay is better understood as a discourse with its own specific history, a distinct mode of writerly and readerly labor, and even a site of struggle. Michel de Certeau writes of surveys of routes walked in the city that "transform action into legibility, but in doing so [cause] a way of being in the world to be forgotten."[23] My aim in emphasizing the *work* of parallelism is to attempt a partial reversal of this kind of transformation, which is also too common in writing on *shiwen*. Challenging the conventional understanding of the essay—one that invests too heavily in an overly simple idea of what it means for two things to be "parallel"—not only results in a more nuanced understanding of the *shiwen* genre, particularly in its relation to classical prose, but also raises more general questions about involutionary dynamics and the social construction of equivalency that have broader comparative implications.

How Modern Prose Parallelism Works

As a formal principle of literary composition, parallelism manifests itself in a wide range of scales and levels of abstraction, from word choice to number of words, from the structure of individual clauses to the thematics of paragraphs.[24] Tang Shunzhi's essay on Feng Fu is striking in its deviation from our expectations; at this point it may be useful to look at a more typical example of a parallel set, drawn from Xu Fuyuan's (1535–1604) essay on the topic "Is our Master for the ruler of Wei?" which references the martyrs Bo Yi and Shu Qi, famous for their unwillingness to compromise their standards for the sake of gaining power:

> If one were to cause Yi, say, to go against his father's orders and
> Qi, say, to be contrary to heavenly morals;
>> even if one were to seize the realm and become a feudal
>> lord, he could not have one day of peace over the officials
>> and people.

假令夷也違父命而齊也悖天倫
　雖竊國為諸侯不可一日安於臣民之上.

> Now it is only since Bo succeeded as a son and Shu succeeded
> as a younger brother;
>> that therefore they discarded the realm like a worn-out
>> sandal and could exist nobly between heaven and earth.

夫惟伯遜其為子而叔遜其為弟
　故棄國如敝蹝可以浩然存於天地之間.[25]

We notice immediately several points at which the parallelism is less then perfectly symmetrical: although "as a son" and "as a younger brother" are perfect matches within the second line, they match imperfectly with "go against his father's orders" and "be contrary and without morals," their counterparts in the first line. This disjunction results necessarily from the difference between *ye* (preceding these clauses in the first line) and *sui* 遂 (preceding these clauses in the second line): whether understood as a mere pause, with phonetic value only, or as an explicit marker of topic, *ye* delays the arrival of the verb in question by a beat. On the other hand, *sui* itself is a verb, and what follows is its object. Reading the first half of each line out loud makes this rhythmic mismatch clear; if we remember that excessive symmetry itself is often seen as problematic, however, it seems likely that these mismatches are deliberate.

Somewhat more subtle is the contrast between the two actions taken—*qieguo wei zhuhou* and *qiguo wei bixi*—in that the grammatical structure is quite similar: $V_1 N_1 V_2 N_2$, with *wei* as the second verb in both cases.[26] Noting in passing the niceness of pairing feudal lords with worn-out sandals as a match, our attention is called to the question of tone: both syllables of *zhuhou* are even in tone, whereas *bi* and *xi* are both oblique.[27] Sound plays an important role in the composition and consumption of *shiwen*; we frequently encounter individuals reading essays aloud or chanting them repeatedly. The question of the sounds of the individual words that make up an essay is a particularly productive point to explore the interaction of difference and similarity within the parallel sets, since the best matched parallel lines tend to exhibit tonal variation that often seems quite deliberate, as had been the case in regulated verse for centuries.[28]

Prompted to take tones into consideration, we return to the framing elements of these two lines, which at first seemed to constitute very straightforward parallels: "If one were to . . ." and "Now it is only since . . ." at the beginning; "even if one were to seize" and "therefore they discarded," at the hinge of the line; and "over" and "between" at the end all seem to work much more smoothly as parallel elements than the other parts of the two lines. But these elements require a closer look. Starting from the end of the lines, we notice not only the obvious semantic difference between *shang* and *jian* but also that the former is oblique in tone and the latter even. Moving back, we notice the same tonal difference between *sui* 雖 and *gu*, except with the terms reversed—*sui* is even and *gu* is oblique. At the beginning of the line, *jialing* is oblique-oblique, and *fuwei* is even-even. As far as the frame goes (including the feudal lords and worn-out shoes for good measure), the first line begins obliquely, goes even at the hinge, and ends on an oblique note; the second line begins evenly, goes oblique at the hinge, and ends on an even note.

This is not to say that parallel lines need to be mirror or nearly mirror images of each other, tonally speaking. Just as musical counterpoint expects that the two voices will move in synchrony at points and diverge at others, the tonal profiles of the lines may coincide at some points and differ at others in what seems to be random fashion.[29] It is rather to say that at those moments where the symmetry seems most striking in semantic and grammatical terms, we should not be surprised to find highly marked contrasts, tonally speaking. In this case, the tonal contrast returns us to the overall difference in mood between the two lines. The first sets up a problematic hypothetical, which the second resolves with a statement of things as they are that meets our expectations; somewhat akin to the statement of a musical theme first in a minor and then a major key. With this contrast in mood, the parallel set condenses the original topic into its essence: a question about whether Confucius would offer his support to the ruler of Wei—a problematic hypothetical—and the answer that he would in fact not.

What we have also seen in the lines from Xu Fuyuan's essay is something that could be understood as a kind of syntactic syncopation: with the "failed" match of *sui* with *ye*, the verb lands in a different place in the line. Even more common than this approach is a simple syncopation resulting from the addition of a single word to a sentence, usually a *xuzi* (empty word), ordinarily to the second of two otherwise parallel lines. Syncopation can contribute to the liveliness of the voice without calling the overall parallel structure of the lines in question, reminding us that the "spirit" added by *xu* elements in writing can be quite specific and small-scale.[30] Syncopation can also add rhetorical force to an argument by emphasizing an unexpected turn in the second line of a parallel set, as in the following lines from an essay by Yang Qiyuan: "That which nourishes literati who are focused on the Way and serves as evidence of one's studies, is emoluments. That which distracts the minds that aim at the Way and serves as a burden on one's studies, is *also* emoluments." The added character "also" serves to mark the unexpected turn from praise to critique of emoluments.[31]

Syncopation in and of itself does not take us too far away from the strictest parallel balance, resembling *chenzi* (padding words) in *ci* lyrics. But it opens the door to the kind of more varied and substantial play with balance and imbalance that we saw in "There was a man named Feng Fu of Jin" at the beginning of this chapter. Gui Youguang, for example, allows apparent parallels to run away from him in "The men in former times in the matters of ceremony and music," but he also carries surplus characters forward or backward across clauses, yielding lines that are equal in length when taken as a whole but whose individual clauses are not in balance.[32]

Equally tricky are semantic cross-overs, in which the number of characters may remain the same but the meaning is "carried." In "Ziqin asked Zigong," Gui Youguang writes that

> Ziqin used the vision of a conventional person to seek
>   Confucius's mind . . .
> Zigong used the depth of observing feeling to put forth his
>   own views . . .[33]

The obvious initial match here is between the "vision of a conventional person" and "the depth of observing feeling," based on their positions in the respective lines. But when the reader reaches the end of the relevant clause in the second line, it becomes clear that "his own views" (*zide zhi jian*) is also a contrasting and even clearer match with "the vision of a conventional person" (*changren zhi jian*). At the same time, we are left with the intriguing match of Zigong's views against Confucius's mind. Tang Shunzhi, among others, is a master of even more complicated crosses of this type, as in his essay on the topic "Ji Lu asked about serving the spirits of the dead."[34] Further complexity could ensue from an approach inspired by linked-verse poetry, in which each leg refers to the preceding leg and to the next leg, cutting across the divides between individual parallel sets.[35]

Dong Qichang makes a point of arguing for these kinds of shifts in his ninth "word of instruction," *li* 離 (displacement): "Writing's strongest taboo is simple parallelism; it values criss-crossing (*cuozong*) its forces. What is dispersed (*san*) it can bring together and what is together it can disperse. Displacement is dispersal."[36] The logics of displacement—carrying and crossing—find their fullest expression in a larger scale structuring of the essay that I define as *involutionary parallelism*. In this type of parallel structure, which I suggest is as characteristic of the modern prose essay as the more usual epithet "eight-legged," the principle of symmetry is expanded across entire paragraphs, yet at the same time folded back against itself. As Qi Gong has pointed out, a shorter parallel passage within one *gu* in a set did not necessarily need to match the corresponding shorter parallel passage in the otherwise matching second *gu* in a set. He does not make much of this, merely implying that the rule of parallelism was not always strictly observed; other modern scholars also tend to gloss over this phenomenon.[37] But this involution of the principle of parallel resemblance is not mere relaxation of that principle. Rather, it intensifies the essay's structural complexity, with significant consequences for the reader's identification of that parallelism during the reading process.

I begin with a relatively simple example. Wang Ao's essay "When good government prevails in a state, language may be lofty and bold, and actions the same" has a two-leaf structure in which the leaves are not simply parallel to each other but organized as follows:

A₁   Now when it comes to speaking, the exemplary person (*junzi*)
        indeed is right at times to be silent, but when a state has the
        Way, there is no reason to rely on silence; therefore when there

is a principle that should be articulated, it must be articulated; direct criticism and remonstrances at court are examples of frank discussions of what is right that do not yield.

B_1 As for affairs of benefit and harm, there are those that all others do not dare to speak of, and only [the exemplary person] speaks of them;

B_2 As for things subtle and latent, there are those that all others cannot speak of, and only [the exemplary person] speaks of them.

C_1 Whether reporting in private to the ruler or speaking in public to others, all are set off by loyalty and correctness, the speech is straightforward not in order to win one a reputation, but rather straightforward because the times allow it.

A_2 When it comes to action, there is no time when the exemplary person is right to lower himself, and when a state has the Way, there is no need to depend on lowering oneself, therefore when there is a just action that should be taken, it must be taken; grasping the Way [against] jealousy and evil consists of expansive movements of material force that do not recoil.

D_1 When it is not just, not one grain does one give others, nor does one take from others.

D_2 When it is just, one takes no notice of criticism by a single clan, nor does one take notice of criticism by the realm as a whole.

C_2 Whether it is serving one's ruler, or maintaining one's own self, all are nobly upholding justice, the action's aim is not to distinguish oneself, but rather is straightforward because the Way requires it.[38]

When reading through this type of essay, what seems at first to be loose prose (A_1), followed by a short parallel section, followed by more loose prose (C_1), turns out to be parallel at a higher level when the second leaf is read and a match provided. And it is precisely the part that forms a parallel within the first leaf (B_1B_2) that does *not* find a corresponding parallel in the second leaf, because D_1D_2 has a different structure. In other words, the provisional distinction between parallel and nonparallel that the reader has drawn on reading the first leaf (up until the words "because the times allow it") is inverted once the second leaf is read.[39]

Wang Ao is particularly known for this type of complex nested multi-level essay—one commentator notes in response to another essay of his that the *gu* structure "transforms and exchanges, showing complex unevenness"—but many other authors excelled as well.[40] One of the most complex examples of this style likely precedes Wang Ao's examination triumph by at least several years: "When the Son of Heaven visited the princes, it was called a tour of inspection" by Dong Yue (1431–1502, 1469 *jinshi*).[41] This essay (translated in full in the appendix) consists primarily of a two-leaf parallel section made up of as many as seventy-three separate elements; given the many different types of resonances throughout, we may better understand it as a multidimensional weave rather than simply two parallel threads. If, as before, we assign a letter to each individual prose unit, allowing subscripts to mark parallels, we end up with the following breakdown.

$$A_1B_1C_1B_2C_2 \quad D_1E_1E_2F_1G_1F_2G_2 \quad H_1I_1J_1K_1K_2 \quad L_1M_1N_1O_1P_1Q_1R_1 \quad S_1T_1 \quad S_2T_2 \quad S_3T_3T_4 \quad U_1V_1W_1X_1$$

$$A_2B_1Y_1B_2Y_2 \quad D_2Z_1Z_2Z_3\Delta\Phi\Delta\Phi \quad H_2I_2J_2\Gamma\Gamma \quad L_2M_2N_2O_2P_2Q_2R_2 \quad S_1\Lambda_1\Pi \quad S_2\Lambda_2\Pi \quad S_3\Lambda_3\Pi_4 \quad U_2V_2W_2X_2$$

At this point, we are forced to acknowledge the tremendous amount of literary labor that writing extended involutionary prose requires. My choice of involution as a trope for this mode of essay production refers not just to the concrete arrangement of the words on the page but ultimately to a broader social paradigm proposed to explain the dynamics of labor and economic change across a wide span of the early modern world. I return to this question in the epilogue, noting for now that the idea of involution in economic history always implies a judgment on the productivity of investing one's work in one arena rather than another.

What about the work expected of the reader? Looking at this schematization of Dong's essay, it is hard to believe that, as one commentator writes, "[although] as one hundred odd sentences long it is read as a single sentence." At the surface level, however, the essay wears this complexity surprisingly lightly: we can see from a glance at the original essay (included with the translation) that it is possible to skim through it without consciously attending to each complicated similarity the author uses to hold it together. It is when one asks how the parallelism in the essay is meant to work that things become much more difficult. What I would like to dwell on here for a moment is the difference between the end result of a thorough reading (and possible rereading or two) of the essay on one hand and the provisional estimates constructed by the reader (and subsequently adjusted) during the reading process. In the case of Wang Ao's essay quoted in part above, we can identify two moments of transition that have disruptive potential: the transition from B_1 to B_2, where one wonders whether an A_2 will arrive; and the transition from C_1 to A_2, where one realizes that A_2 arrives after all. In the case of

Dong Yue's essay, the complexity comes in enough layers that it becomes a difficult task even to figure out how many different moments of transition are likely to throw the reader into confusion. When sketched out schematically, with a single symbol standing for a clause or group of clauses that belong together, the pattern becomes much clearer. But for the reader encountering such a text for the first time, without the benefit of line breaks or punctuation, this bird's-eye view of the whole is something that can be acquired only gradually through trial and error over the course of the reading process. And as de Certeau reminds us, it is all too easy to forget the processes through which a bird's-eye view is produced once we have that view before us.[42]

When Dong Qichang and other critics abjure simple parallelism, the effect is not in most cases to abandon matches altogether but to locate parallel effects as relative qualities that shift over the course of reading the essay. What was not parallel becomes one part of a larger parallel, what was parallel is now no longer: this is not a question of essential qualities as much as it is the experience of moving across distinctions between binary polarities. From one perspective, the essay is a textual surface creased by folds in which the reader resembles an ant walking over creased fabric or a person hiking in a mountain range; from another perspective, a device structured around swinging hinges.[43] The bird's-eye view from which these qualities are finally fixed in place acquires its certainty only after a reading is complete, and may require multiple readings to reach full resolution. The designation of any part of an essay as parallel is the result of a *reading process*, a negotiation between and among authors, readers, and commentators. I return to this question in more detail later in this chapter; first, however, we need to get a better sense of the generic implications and the broader moral and aesthetic valences of *ou* (parallel) against *san* (loose or dispersed) and, relatedly, *ou* (even in number) against *qi* (odd in number, and also odd in style).

Prose Odd and Even

Up to this point, we have focused on formal matching or failure to match, deeming a section of text parallel (*ou*) or loose (*san*). This distinction turns out to resonate at the generic level as well, where modern prose and classical prose, *shiwen* and *guwen*, are distinguished along analogous lines. Yu Changcheng sees two sides to Wang Anshi's essay writing in the Song, one that looks forward to the Ming and Qing examination essay, and one that looks backward to an ideal of classical prose, marked partly by a contrast between focus on an assigned topic on one hand and expression of one's own views (*jijian*) on the other, but even more so by the oddness or evenness of the writing itself. "Now odd and even match together to make up heaven and earth, the standard and the altered rise and fall to make up the old and the new . . . things all come in pairs, and *wen* is no different."[44] In discussions of literary genre and prose style, classical prose is ordinarily posed against examination writing. One of the earliest references to *guwen* as a prose style—rather than as written characters that were literally archaic, or as literature of the ancients more generally—appears in Ouyang Xiu's "Ji jiuben Hanwen hou" (Noted after an old edition of the works of Han Yu). In this influential note, Ouyang Xiu contrasts the modern prose he had to master to win the *jinshi* degree against these inspirational writings of Han Yu, to which he returned whenever he had time to spare.[45] Although Ouyang Xiu was not the first to praise Han Yu's writings, he was crucial to the initiation of a discourse of classical prose as a literary category in which those writings would play a central role.[46]

Well established by the twelfth century, this discourse would continue into the early twentieth; the proposed contrast with the *shiwen* genre plays a crucial role throughout. Ruan Yuan writes that "Ming writers called the work of Eight Masters of the Tang and Song 'classical prose' on account of its difference from essays on the Four Books."[47] Even among many writers who aimed to show how the two genres should not be viewed as radically separate, the distinction between them holds, whether as a balanced polarity between *ou* and *san*: "It is not that classical prose completely lacks parallelism, but the single-line prose sections are more numerous; it is not that modern prose completely lacks single-line prose, but the parallel sections are more numerous."[48] Or the rather less balanced relationship between a source of inspiration and the derivative genre it can be used to improve, as in this comment in the introductory section of a Ming anthology of classical prose: "this collection is specifically for the purpose of providing material for exam competition"—a reasoning that gets taken up in Qing imperial collections of classical prose prefaces.[49] This latter distinction is ordinarily a value judgment, one that is echoed by many modern scholars.[50]

Yet the logical priority of *guwen* did not go entirely unquestioned, nor did the possibility of conclusively distinguishing between classical and modern prose. According to a 1628 preface to *Mingshi wenzong* (Literary greats known to the world): "Today, everyone's classical prose (*guwen*) is actually modern prose (*shiwen*). Not only today, but even as early as in the Song, when they began examinations that were called classical prose, it was also today's modern prose."[51] Some Qing critics picked up on this challenge: Fang Bao argued that the best examples of modern prose could be considered classical prose; Liu Dakui identified the examination essay as "one genre of classical prose." Yao Nai recalls that at the age of twenty, when he asked Liu Dakui about how to distinguish one's examination writings from the vulgar, Liu merely smiled and said nothing. Later, on reading modern prose masters like Tang Shunzhi and Gui Youguang, Yao suddenly got it, exclaiming to himself: "This is also classical prose! How could they be considered two different paths?" At another point, Yao follows Fang Bao's argument that quality writing is classical prose no matter the genre, and all other writing is "modern prose."[52] Rather than a descriptive approach, Huang Zongxi and Dai Mingshi take a prescriptive approach to this same question, arguing that treating classical prose and modern prose as radically distinct actually led to a decline in the quality of both types of writing.[53]

Taking a slightly different perspective, Wang Yangming seems to allow for the possibility of distinguishing the two types but presents classical prose as the *result* of modern prose, rather than its antecedent. He writes in a 1506 preface to a reprint edition of *Wenzhang guifan* (Models for literary composition) that just as we could have the Classics as a distinct category of texts only after the Philosophers started to appear, "since the practice of examination writing began, there has been what is called classical prose."[54] Ai Nanying makes a similar argument in the late Ming, and as Bao Shichen puts it two centuries later, "once there was the term 'modern prose' in the Song dynasty, 'classical prose' was distinguished against it, what is wrong with that?"[55] Indeed, Ouyang Xiu's definition of classical prose as a distinct mode of writing in the eleventh century cannot be understood apart from his advocacy of that mode as a means for the reform of examination writing when he served as examiner.[56]

Historically speaking, the dependency of the category of classical prose on modern prose and the institution of the examination system is clear: the recognized masters of classical prose style in the fifteenth through nineteenth centuries were also all recognized *shiwen* masters and were almost without exception successful at the very highest levels of the civil service examinations.⁵⁷ Looking back at the earliest canons of classical prose from the eleventh and twelfth centuries, we see evidence that the anthologies of that era, which defined the basic parameters of the genre for centuries to come, appeared as study guides for the civil service examinations of that period. In some cases these anthologies included contemporary examination essays as well as the works of earlier masters like Han Yu.⁵⁸ The sharp rise in prose collection publication in the mid-Ming parallels developments in the broader economy that raise demand for classical prose written for the occasion and, more significantly, a renewed interest in classical prose as a means to improve one's modern prose essays.⁵⁹ Mao Kun, the influential editor of *Tang Song ba da jia wenchao* (Compilation of the writings of the Eight Great Masters of the Tang and Song), was another contemporary who excelled at *shiwen* while taking the genre seriously as a sphere in which literary technique could not be neglected.

In retrospect, critics like Fang Bao referred to this development as "using classical prose to write modern prose" (*yi guwen wei shiwen*).⁶⁰ But instead of thinking of classical prose as a separate tradition in its own right that could be appropriated to liven up examination writing, we may want to consider this moment as an occasion for *shiwen* to further consolidate the "classical prose" category that we still work with today, first by treating texts that were generally understood as representative of classical prose as a distinct and separate source of technical inspiration, and second, by developing the binary opposition through which classical prose would be approached well into the twentieth century.

Formally speaking, the tie between modern prose and classical prose is just as marked: even the most strictly parallel eight-legged essay includes introductory elements in nonparallel prose (*poti, chengti,* and *qijiang*) and most include at least one transitional or concluding section (*chuti, guojie,* or *shoujie*). Although these sections of the essay could include short parallel passages, as a general rule they tended not to emphasize parallelism, leading Jiao Xun and Liu Shipei to compare the parallel sections of the essay to opera arias and the introductory, transitional, and concluding prose to recitative.⁶¹

Classical prose—thought of as prose that is loose—was also often hidden in plain sight in the parallel sections themselves, as numerous commentators have suggested.[62] Zhang Zhongxing explains: "If you look only at, for example, the first half of an initial pair of legs in what is called an 'eight-legged essay,' it would be loose prose of the Eight Masters of Tang and Song. But then when you look further at the second half of that initial pair, even though that too is loose prose it matches the first half at every point, is this transformation into *Literary Selections* style not just marvelous?"[63] For example, consider a passage from "Learning without thought is labor lost," by Gu Qing (1460–1528), which makes use of devices typical of classical prose writing to lead us through a multi-step argument:

> Learning is practicing things, broadening one's cultivation in order to increase one's knowledge, reflecting on traces in order to make oneself more useful; who could abandon learning? Now [the object of] learning is things. Things must be controlled by a logic; this logic is present in the mind, and the office of the mind is none other than thought. If one does not think then one cannot penetrate the subtle; thus learning necessarily depends on thinking in order to harmonize with the ultimate logic. Otherwise, study and memorization will merely be hard work to no purpose, playing with things and not exhausting their logic; tried and true methods, although effective, will merely be slavishly followed, and not actually experienced. The subtleties of metaphysics will end in ignorance and confusion; how could one hope that they would spread throughout?[64]

Having read this passage, we are not surprised to learn that Wang Ao, head examiner for the session where Gu Qing won his *jinshi*, likened his writing to that of Su Shi. Yet this argument, unlike most similarly lengthy passages of classical prose, is followed by its nearly perfect parallel match.[65]

As early as the twelfth century, critics complained of a distorting effect specific to parallel argumentation: if there is only one substantial point to account for in the topic, the candidate has to divide it in two for balance.[66] In a different context, Stephen Owen has written that *The Literary Mind and the Carving of Dragons* can be understood in part as a product of a discourse machine that generates problematic statements by the systematic operation of parallel logic, statements that must then be recuperated by the author.[67] Instead of a machine internal to the text that automatically generates parallel correspondences that may go beyond the author's original intent, Wei Xi (1624–81) sees the examination system enforcing genre as a social construct, coercing candidates toward that same end: "when you are finished with your argument, you then have to force yourself to create another argument to balance it."[68] Other writers, such as Tang Biao, reframe this supposed aesthetic flaw as a technical challenge and provide a range of means by which the writer can rise to the occasion.[69] Given that parallels at a higher level of abstraction and sophistication are often privileged over more concrete and obvious parallels, one might wonder what level of reflexivity and referentiality these parallel distinctions might reach. Perhaps it will come as no surprise that within the field of examination writing, parallelism itself finds a parallel, even as the modern prose essay finds itself a generic counterpart.

Thinking back to the contrasts drawn between *shiwen* and *guwen* noted earlier, a theme becomes evident. Conceptually, as well, modern prose as a genre seems to conjure up classical prose through its very requirement of an other as balance; this tendency is as clearly marked in literary criticism of the period as it is in the structure of examination essays themselves. See, for example, Bao Shichen's comment on the differences between the two genres of prose:

> Classical prose speaks entirely of one's own meaning and
>   therefore values the ability to set foot on the real;
> Eight-legged essays represent the meaning of others and there-
>   fore value the ability to lead into the imaginary.
> Classical prose—although it may be a short piece—will
>   exhaust one's own meaning and therefore its shifts and
>   changes come in many transformations; its architecture is
>   wide and steep;
> An eight-legged essay—although it may be lengthy in
>   format—will accommodate the mood of the topic and
>   therefore its inquiry will have few comings and goings; its
>   architecture is narrow and low.[70]

It is no accident that this articulation of the distinction between modern and classical prose itself takes on the parallel form that is supposed to be typical of a modern prose *gu*; this commitment to parallelism can have a distinctly productive aspect. The very mode of modern prose argumentation—argumentation that is assumed to be structured in a specifically parallel format—calls for a particular kind of binary analysis in

Table 1: Zhou Zuoren's View of the Generic Space of Chinese Prose

| | | Content | |
		sagely morality	emotions
Form	formalist	Examination essays	Six Dynasties prose
	balanced	Tongcheng classical prose	(New Literature)

which similarity is found within difference and difference is articulated within similarity. When Wang Yangming claims that "since the practice of examination writing began, there has been what is called classical prose," he is making an argument that holds analytically as well as it does historically. We may be justified in concluding that should there be no generic counterpart to modern prose, one would have to be invented to provide a balance. To be more precise, a specific aspect of the classical prose tradition invented in the Song to reform the examination writing of that era would be appropriated to constitute the Ming and Qing examination essay's other as well.

This generative logic does not immediately cease to operate with the abolition of the examination system. Writing in the Republican era, Zhou Zuoren adds an iteration, making a similar argument about the historical logic behind the appearance of the New Literature (*xin wenxue*). Given that *shiwen* emphasize form and take Sagely morality as content, Tongcheng-style classical prose balances form with moral content, and Six Dynasties parallel prose (*pianti wen*) emphasizes form and takes the emotions as content, there is necessarily space for a type of literature that takes form and content equally seriously (unlike *shiwen* and Six Dynasties prose) and does not take Sagely morality as its content but emotions (unlike *shiwen* and classical prose). This generic space is waiting to be occupied by the New Literature yet to come fully into its own, opposed to Six Dynasties prose in terms of form and to Tongcheng classical prose in terms of content, but doubly opposed to the examination essay on the axes of form and content alike (table 1).[71] Here Zhou Zuoren conceives of the operations of this parallel "discourse machine" as positively (rather than problematically) productive.

Off Balance

The preceding account attempts to supplement the overwhelming emphasis on parallel writing that has dominated scholarship on the civil service examination essay. By incorporating loose prose as an element in a balanced literary presentation, the conventional style one expects to encounter in specific parts of the essay, however, this account reproduces the allegiance to parallelism at a more abstract remove.[72] This contrast between parallelism and loose prose fits into a series of contrasts that are themselves in balance: short and long, relaxed and tight, straightforward and twisting, smooth forward movement and countercurrent, and so on. As several modern prose critics put it, "in the use of sentences, parallel and non-parallel mutually engender."[73]

This focus on the essay as an architectonic whole, assumed to be more or less immediately apprehensible in its balanced entirety, has important resonances with legible maps of the city and the world as imagined by Michel de Certeau, which have forgotten the specific recorded journeys on which their construction ultimately depends.[74] If instead we heed the many stories of essays whose structure (and aesthetic value) becomes clear to the examiner or critic only on a second or third reading and may even require a supernatural prompt, the presumption of immediate legibility seems less justified.[75] It is important to remember as well that modern editions of essay collections, which include punctuation, and in some cases line breaks or divisions of the essay into clearly marked sections, present a rather different reading experience from the original essay—a single block of text with no demarcation into parts other than the very semantic, syntactic, and stylistic characteristics of the written words themselves. Earlier in this chapter, we saw the potential that moments of transition in complex involuted essays had to disrupt the reading process. In the essays discussed previously, this disruption is eventually recuperated: returning to Wang Ao's essay "When good government prevails in a state, language may be lofty and bold, and actions the same," for example, the eventual appearance of unit C_2 comes as no surprise, fully restoring the parallel balance one might have questioned earlier in the reading process. In this section, we look at essays whose disruptiveness cannot be so easily contained.

Modern scholars often ignore moments out of balance in individual essays or see them simply as unintended or insignificant lapses on the part of the author; some do note these moments of "deviation" from the supposed norm but inquire into neither the reasons for their appearance nor their effect on the reader. At best they are explained as moments where "practice" does not fully express "literary spirit," or as evidence that even in the case of the eight-legged essay, content can win out over form through its sheer inert resistance to being shaped.[76] I suggest that a different approach is warranted.

Writing in the early eighteenth century, Fang Bao singles out the Longqing and Wanli periods (1567–1620) as the height of literary innovation—in good and bad senses—an assessment that finds some agreement among more recent scholars.[77] Gong Duqing, for example, concludes that by the Wanli reign period, deviation from the norm had become the new norm.[78] Yet while the late Ming may have seen particularly frequent challenges to the standard definition of the essay that we continue to use today—eight parallel legs—we can see from the works of Tang Shunzhi, Hu Ding (1556 *jinshi*), and others that alternatives to the standard (in particular, variations on the norm of parallelism) began to appear within decades of that standard's fullest articulation in the late fifteenth century.[79] Should we assume that there was at least some point before which essays could be safely counted on not to have degenerated into nonstandard forms, we may be surprised to find counterexamples by writers like Luo Lun (1431–78) and Xue Xuan (1389–1464) with prominent nonparallel sections.[80]

On the other hand, should we imagine that the stylistic experimentation of the late Ming was chastened—in the field of modern prose as in so many other types of cultural production—by the establishment of a new Qing order? Well-regarded essays from the early Qing, such as Han Tan's "It is said in the *Book of Poetry*, 'He measured out and commenced his marvellous tower'" and Fang Bao's "The Master was wishing Qidiao Kai to enter on official employment" make it clear that experimentation continued through the end of the seventeenth century and into the eighteenth. Han's essay is particularly striking in its disregard for conventional standards of parallelism: in the central two sections, there are no significant parallel elements. The essay as a whole reads as a notably unconstrained example of classical prose argumentation.[81] Suddenly, Tang Shunzhi's essay on Feng Fu and the tiger seems less like an outlier and more like a trendsetter.

Essays that make unusually extensive use of out-of-balance prose fall into three broad types. On the face of it, the most striking essays might as well be pieces of classical prose, organized around a single line of narrative or argument. In addition to essays by Tang Shunzhi and Hu Ding already cited, we can highlight Wan Guoqin's "How greatly filial was Shun!" as an example. As in the case of Feng Fu and the tiger, a few short clauses that happen to be parallel adorn the substantive paragraphs, and the rest is straight classical prose. The commentator writes that in going beyond the "conventional form" of examination writing, this essay gives one a marvelous view.[82] A second category of essay reduces concrete instances of parallelism to a minimum but maintains a high degree of parallelism at the conceptual level, as in Feng Yuanyang's "Therefore having such great virtue, it could not but be that he should obtain the throne," structured around the terms *tian* and *de*; Han's "It is said in the *Book of Poetry*, 'He measured out and commenced his marvellous tower,'" which contrasts the labored writing of literary types with ordinary people's spontaneous outpourings of song; and an essay by Zhu Shixiu that centers on a parallel between temporal variety (of forces old and new), and geographical variety (of forces in the different states).[83]

As striking as these essays are, and as powerful their challenge to conventional understandings of *shiwen* as fettered by an unvarying commitment to a specifically formalist parallelism, my focus here is actually on a third type, where lack of balance is not necessarily openly flaunted from the start, but appears as a surprise, whether in the form of a sudden twist, or a slowly developing sense that things are not as they seem. The essay "Recompense injury with justice," by Qian Youwei (1550 *jinshi*) represents a fairly subtle example of this kind of twist. In the midst of a complicated involuted parallel structure, the reader suddenly encounters a parallel prose clause that should by rights be loose instead, since it corresponds to a loose clause in the preceding paragraph. Where readers would expect to find a sentence that is loose in and of itself but by virtue of this very looseness is parallel at a distance to the corresponding sentence in the previous paragraph, they find instead a sentence that is parallel in and of itself but does not parallel the relevant part of the preceding paragraph.[84]

Fang Bao's essay "The Master was wishing Qidiao Kai to enter on official employment" is a good example of a more directly challenging use of this approach. It includes several substantial parallel elements, but they are presented in such a way as to thoroughly frustrate the reader's expectations; I include the *ruti* (entrance into the topic) and first parallel set here. The problems begin when the opening of the first parallel set ("The Master's view of Kai") seems to match the opening of the preceding *ruti*, rather than simply foreshadowing the second half of the set. They continue with an unusual detour between the first and second parallel lines due to the insertion of an extra clause, further throwing the reader off.

> *The Master's choice of official service* as the task to set Qidiao Kai means that the learning of my party is not solely for the sake of gaining attention and admiration. Rather if there should be something that can be applied, then it will not be useless to the world.
>
> *The Master's view of Kai* was—himself—that he had gotten it, but Kai then said, "I cannot believe this." Oh! Kai lacked faith in himself, but the Master's faith in Kai was indeed secure!
>
> Now the allocation of talent was already thus; *the Master's command to Kai* indeed had that which could be believed, but the inclination was not yet clear; when Kai said that he lacked faith, he in fact had his reasons for finding it difficult to believe!

The three italicized phrases of the preceding selection are particularly likely to lead one astray on a first read-through. Having encountered the first one in what eventually turns out to be the *ruti*, and then encountering its close match at the beginning of the first line of what turns out to be the first "parallel set," the reader's impulse may be to take these two instances (incorrectly) as the beginning of the first and second line of the first parallel set, respectively. The third phrase, "the Master's command to Kai," calls this interpretation into question, but trouble arises again at the end of this line, when it becomes clear that "now the allocation of talent was already thus" has no earlier or later parallel. It turns out that despite the apparent matches hinted at by these three phrases, this part of the essay is read most easily as loose prose. The second and third parallel sets that follow are not quite so unusual, but as with the first they continue to undercut the reader just at the moments when he or she expects to have located the parallel passage. It is a relief to reach the concluding portion of the essay and realize that one will no longer be teased with apparent parallels that refuse to properly coalesce.[85]

Tang Shunzhi's "To give entire credit to the *Book of History*" is an even more challenging work: as Fang Bao points out, the content of the essay is as strikingly imaginative as the work of Ouyang Xiu and Su Shi, ending with the bold assertion that "If scholars can begin from words [of the original text] and bring the text together with their minds, examining the traces and using rational principles to decide on their validity, then every book in the world is of use to me." Formally speaking, this essay also provokes the reader. As is the case in his "Feng Fu of Jin," the few short parallels within individual sentences play no substantial structural role. What is particularly worth noting is the truly bizarre match between the phrases "There is no time to distinguish others" (*Ta gu wei xia bian ye*) and "The rest cannot be trusted" (*Ta gu wei zu xin ye*). These two clauses are nearly perfect grammatical parallels, but in violation of all conventions of parallelism, the first comes at the beginning of a section and the second comes at the end of that same section, rather than at the beginning of the next.[86] It is hard to explain this as anything other than a deliberate attempt to toy with readers trying to figure out how to understand the essay as a sequence of well-defined parallel sets rather than a rush of loose prose. Fang Zhou's essay "Let me return! Let me return!" takes a different approach. Although loose prose predominates in the first half, a single parallel set of moderate length suddenly appears in the middle, only to yield again to loose prose for the remainder of the essay.[87]

It is hard to overstate the effect of these jarring shifts on the reader. Unlike regulated verse, in which each line is the same length; or *ci* poetry, in which line length varies in accordance with a tune with which the reader is most likely already familiar; or even parallel prose in Six Dynasties style, which appears in periods of four and six characters, modern prose has no fixed line length. Consequently, parallel structures large and small play a key role in speeding the reading process by allowing readers to segment the text efficiently. Essays that offer apparent parallels only to undercut them make the reading unexpectedly rough and irregular, in many cases requiring a second or even third read-through for the essay to make sense.

If the convention against which such essays contrasted themselves had been merely simple plodding parallelism, with two nearly identical legs followed by two more nearly identical legs, and so on, reading them would have been challenging enough. Given the widespread popularity of complicated nested, involutionary parallel structures from the 1470s onward, figuring out how the different levels of parallelism were to be articulated in an essay becomes even more difficult. Different editors and commentators do not always agree on how to break an essay up into sections, even disagreeing as to whether a section in question is meant to be a "parallel" leg or a nonparallel transition such as a *chuti* or *guojie*.[88] When confronted with a complex essay, the reader may be inclined to an early assessment of it as a work in loose prose that merely feints in the direction of parallelism or, on the other hand, as an essay that should be involutionary but may end by dissolving into loose prose. These choices ultimately represent a difference in degree rather than a difference in kind.

In one sense, extended involuted parallels can be said to make room for essays that consist of a single extended classical prose sequence that in the end turns out *not* to be mirrored. "Straightforward" essays like Tang's "Feng Fu of Jin" and Wan's "How greatly filial was Shun!" could be read from this perspective as overly lengthy initial leaves that happen to be missing their second and corresponding leaf. If in the involuted essays what seems as though it would be loose turns out to be parallel, in both the "straightforward" and "out of balance" cases, what one thought would eventually be part of a parallel set turns out not to have a match. Of particular interest in this regard are essays that present a carefully worked-out set of involuted parallels, followed by a passage that seems at first to represent a third, matching, line to the preceding parallel complex, only to fall apart into nothing other than loose prose at the end.[89] In these cases, the reader has been carefully (mis)led to discover parallelism hidden in what seemed to be loose prose and, once that parallelism has been accepted as an organizing principle, to realize ultimately that its applicability is not as extensive as it had at one point seemed.

The Work of Reading and Writing

As we have seen previously, Wei Xi took exception to the necessity of "creating" a second line of argument to match the one already articulated, phrase by phrase and word by word, to produce a parallel passage.[90] But the match is not always so exact, and the parallelism deliberately not so clear, which means the writer is often tasked with marking off the division into sections clearly enough that any confusion on the reader's part is merely temporary and intriguing rather than permanent and disqualifying. The author of *Huayang jijin* (A collection of patterned embroidery), a nineteenth-century writing manual, notes the need for a striking opening to *gu* (sections) that is like a mountain peak suddenly breaking through clouds, suggesting that although there were many essays—indeed, a majority in most periods—where the transitions from one pair of *gu* to the next seem self-evident, reminders that this structure is a product of authorial work and contingent on readerly interpretation are never far from hand.[91]

The interpretive labor required of readers to understand essays as texts organized on principles of parallelism has already been mentioned. Noting the "unprecedentedly long strings of characters that compose the parallel lines (often numbering as many as 20, 30, or even 50 at a stretch)," Andrew Plaks matches his remark that eight-legged essay composition was "a kind of virtuoso performance" with the observation that reading such essays constitutes "a feat of concentration."[92] As Yu Changcheng commented of the essays of Gui Youguang and Jin Sheng: "What seems to be loose prose when you first look at it reveals itself as transformed *gu* technique only on careful reflection."[93] Once the complexities of involuted parallelism and the potential that what one thought would be parallel is not in fact so are factored in, this feat becomes all the more notable.

Here it is worth considering one of François Cheng's claims for the uses of parallelism for an author who aims at complex poetry. "He can disrupt ordinary syntax, while at the same time making himself understood. When a line appears bizarre or incomprehensible, the other line, identical in structure, comes to dissipate the obscurity and show the hidden intention of the poet."[94] This statement applies equally to difficult lines in *shiwen* that are followed sooner or later by exact or nearly exact matches; each line on its own may be ambiguous, but read in succession both become clear. Where parallelism breaks down, this assistance vanishes right at the moment the reader expects to rely on it. In that case, the bizarre or incomprehensible must suddenly be reckoned with on its own terms alone.

For weaker readers, the challenge could be too much. It is not likely that all of the many candidates who complained of examiners' failure to grasp the nuances of their prose were mistaken. At the same time, it is worth noting that the stronger and more skilled the reader, the greater the sudden force of the author's decision to go against parallel expectations. Rather than the sense of confused wonder or gradually increasing frustration characteristic of the reader feeling his or her way through step by step, possibly rereading an essay of only moderate complexity once or twice to figure out what has happened, structurally speaking, the experienced reader will be anticipating the parallel to come only to realize in a flash midway through that the expected echo will never arrive.[95]

Would it seem that the intended audience of many of these essays, the examiners and other skilled and experienced readers, might not have made as heavy work of essay reading as modern readers? Surely detecting the *gu* structure of these texts would have been easier, even automatic, for those who had been writing and reading essays from childhood? Here I cite two types of evidence that make the work of the Ming and Qing reader clear: first, the figure of the essay whose value is recognized only on a second or third reading, or even in a dream, mentioned previously; and second, the sense that an examiner had read only as far in an essay as he had punctuated it. From Ai Nanying's perspective, whether an examiner happens to have passed his eyes over the essay as a whole is not the key question; it counts as reading only if the examiner has left visible traces of his engagement with the structure of the essay throughout.[96]

Indeed, the very complexity of what might have seemed like a simple task—determining where the parallel sections of an essay are located—is echoed in the complicated relationship between two terms used to reference these sections: *gu* and *bi*. These terms seem at first straightforward: two *gu* put together form a single *bi*; there are a total of eight *gu* in the most conventional essays. From this perspective, each *gu* constitutes a singular unit that has a counterpart, whereas each *bi* consists of two equal parts. Yet immediately we run into trouble: one alternative term for *bagu wen* is *babi*, not the *sibi* that we might have expected.[97]

This approach to *bi*—reading it in some cases as referring to a single component part of a parallel set rather than to that set in its entirety, or in other words, as the equivalent of what we have been understanding as *gu*—appears in casual references to the genre as *babi* and in careful analyses of essay structure. Writing of Li Dongyang's essay "From Yao and Shun down to Tang," Fang Bao praises its naturalness, its mastery of archaic style, and its division into "three *bi* evenly arranged." The *bi* that Fang Bao refers to here do not each contain a parallel, but taken together manifest parallels among themselves.[98] Similarly, one preparation manual lists the parallel components of an essay as the first *bi*, second *bi*, third *bi*, all the way up to the eighth *bi*. Gao Dang defines the relationship between *bi* and *gu* as follows: "The first and second *bi* are called the initial *gu*" and "the third and fourth *bi* are called the middle *gu*."[99] Finally, when excerpts from essays are quoted, we frequently see a single parallel set referred to as "two short *bi*," "two small *bi*," "middle two *bi*," "last two *bi*," and we also find the first part of a parallel set is referred to as the "leading *bi*," and the second part of that same set as the "responding *bi*." In all of these cases the individual *bi*'s status as one element out of two in a pair is clear.[100] Where originally *gu* seemed to represent a singular element that could be combined with its match to form an inherently plural *bi*, we find now not only doubling within *gu*—most obviously in essays that make use of involuted parallelism—but also treatment of *bi* as individual components that form a pair (or even a set of three) only when taken together.

Although certain modern scholars do argue for a clear and systematic hierarchical distinction between *gu* and *bi* in theory, there is significant variability—even occasional self-contradiction—in their uses of these terms in practice.[101] One of the few to address these apparent contradictions directly, Li Xu, struggles valiantly to explain the seeming confusion between *gu* and *bi* away as just one more instance of the illogicalities of language; it does not help matters that the difference between singular and plural is not necessarily marked in literary or modern Chinese.[102] Rather than glossing over or dismissing these irregularities, it may be more productive to see the apparent contradictions in the work of Ming and Qing critics and modern scholars alike as symptomatic of the unsettled and dynamic aspects of this type of "parallel" writing.

Unlike Six Dynasties parallel prose, which promises a basic rhythm of units of four and six characters throughout, *shiwen* always have the potential to call regularity into question. Although lengthy stretches of loose prose are the most obvious means of confounding expectations of parallel regularity, tactics such as carried words and phrases and cross-overs also challenge the reader by suggesting that the object of expectations will appear at a certain point in the text, only to have it turn up elsewhere, deferring or rushing the sense of closure. With the involution of the parallel form that begins in the mid-fifteenth century, the question of what size unit of the text the reader is focusing on becomes crucially important. In isolation, a paragraph may seem to constitute a nicely parallel set of two *gu*, but when read from the perspective of the essay as a whole, that paragraph turns out to be the moment at which a larger *gu* framing fails to match its apparent parallel. Indeed, as we saw in the discussion of Wang Ao's "When good government prevails in a state," the embedded *gu* can suggest at a certain moment in the reading process that the larger frame in which it is embedded is not parallel.

Rather than referring us invariably to clearly defined textual units, then, *gu* and *bi* can be thought more generally to indicate framing operations undertaken by writer and reader—attempts to highlight specific parts of texts as areas that have the potential to be more or less strictly parallel. As functions that mediate between the construction of individual sentences and the essay as a whole, and between readings of any given passage as single or multiple, they are not fixed qualities but creative and interpretive processes that may be more or less automatic and self-evident depending on the essay, and indeed may be imposed differently by different readers.[103]

To the extent that it is productive to distinguish between *gu* and *bi*, the determining attribute should not be length or location at a higher or lower level of a fixed organizational hierarchy of the text, but their different approaches to answering the question, asked about any aspect of the text: "Is it one or two?" I have resisted the straightforward adaptation of market metaphors to explain the workings of the examination field—(economic) capital cannot be simply adopted as a figure to explain the functioning of aesthetic regimes, and the concept of cultural capital obscures as much as it illuminates—but it is worth pointing out that the term *gu* is used both for the legs of the eight-legged essay and for the shares that make up the formalized joint business enterprises that become increasingly common over the course of the Ming and Qing. Although the formal splitting characteristic of the essay operates on a different logic from that of the market, it is similarly generative.[104] *Bi*, on the other hand, represents a bringing together in comparative perspective; in Gui Youguang's words, "As for *bi*, it is to take that thing and compare it to this thing."[105] Ultimately, in a genre that is assumed to take parallelism as a basic convention, the decision to identify a given passage as a *gu*, a *bi*, or neither says less about some objective doubleness found in the text than it does about the expectations the reader brings to that passage and his or her preferred interpretation of the passage in light of those expectations. Such an identification is not simply a recognition but rather a declaration that a particular mode of reading should be employed here.

Measuring Up

Toward the beginning of this chapter, I quoted Gao Dang to the effect that "if one is able to express [the Sage's meaning] through discourse and use one's own shuttle and loom," explicit and concrete parallelism is not an absolute requirement in the examination essay.[106] Gao goes on to say that nonparallel prose nonetheless follows some of the basic principles of parallel writing, and he concludes with an assessment that rings familiar: "Literary writing has no fixed format (*ge*), but it does have specific techniques (*fa*), and it also has an underlying logic (*li*)."[107] If, for this critic, what we usually understand as parallelism that is concrete (matching words and phrases, with only minimal deviations for effect) is merely a "fixed format," and more general principles of organization such as opening and closing, direct statements and counterstatements, foreshadowing and referring back are "specific techniques," what would the "underlying logic" of parallelism be, such that it can be found even in writing that is generally thought not to be parallel? For example, Cui Xuegu cites an example from an essay in which Chen Chunyu matches one stretch that is 6 words long with one that is 140 words long.[108] Similarly, a commentary to one essay in the *Imperially Authorized Essays* remarks that there are "clearly two parallel stretches of text, but they are different lengths, causing people not to notice the match," and Tang Biao notes that it is fine to have matches that are uneven in length (*cenci*).[109] Writing about parallelism in texts more generally, Bao Shichen highlights examples of "parallel meaning presented in phrases that are not parallel."[110] Here we find parallelism displaced from the formal level to the conceptual level and even a hint of how parallelism could be understood as *ideology*.

We have seen that inquiry into parallelism as technique provides an opportunity to reflect on questions of similarity and difference at a range of levels in *shiwen* texts, from tonal inflection to grammatical function to the movement of allegory.[111] In the process, it becomes possible to think of the equivalency implied in parallelism not in terms of simple recognition of an objective characteristic of the text but as a project or work in progress. Equivalency between A and B may be silently assumed, it may be formally postulated, or it may be asserted with great effort, but there is no guarantee it will be recognized or accepted, nor that it necessarily reflects some objective reality. As Jack Amariglio and Antonio Callari have shown, for example, Marx's analysis of exchange value in capitalist economies depends on commodity fetishism precisely as a social practice that makes commensurate exchange conceptually possible. Exchange value is conceived of in terms of a standardized socially necessary labor time for the production of a commodity to ensure the possibility of equivalent exchange, even though in practice exchange in these economies involves a trading of unequal quantities of actual labor time.[112]

Indeed, the problem of commensurability and balance in the economic sphere had preoccupied Chinese thinkers with particular intensity from the middle of the Song, with regular discussions of how best to maintain balance in market exchange through equilibrium between different types of currency.[113] As I have argued elsewhere, the literary field centered on the examination system in Ming and Qing China, although imbricated with a flourishing market economy, cannot be reduced to a mere shadow or epiphenomenon of that economy. Rather, we find that substantial portions of that economy depend directly on the examination institution.[114] No matter whether we agree with Hill Gates that it is best to model a "tributary mode of production" as separate from a "petty-capitalist mode of production" during this period, one question is hard to overlook: is there a commensurate exchange typical of the literary field as distinct from the market economy, and if so, what issues of equivalency does it raise?[115] How could these issues be resolved to the relative satisfaction of participants in the early modern examination complex? How does the logic of *gu* in the text relate to the logic of *gu* in the market?

Beginning at the less prestigious edges of the culture industry, we are on relatively recognizable ground: books are written, edited, printed, and sold as commodities in large numbers. One step in finds us in the world of *maiwen wei sheng* (writing for a living), where writers create unique or

customized texts for payment, from business and personal letters to peti-
tions on up to biographies and grave inscriptions. Here, too, things seem
rather familiar: these writers can be understood as artisans or as skilled
professionals; their products, though unique, are still exchanged for
cash. Once we enter the *yingchou* (literature of social exchange) sphere,
however, the rules of the market economy do not seem as directly applicable, and even the substitution of cultural capital for cash as an explanatory principle raises significant methodological problems.[116] By the time
we arrive at the examination compound, ready to spend three days in
desperate competition to be noticed, the lively market in commodities
outside the compound walls, though clearly related in some fashion, is
nonetheless a world apart, operating on rules that no longer apply inside
the gates. The crucial form of investment here is of personal effort—
hours of energy and attention spent in preparation long before the day
itself, as well as focus in the moment—and the key question is whether
one's efforts will meet with any commensurate return.

In the cautionary words of one preface writer: "skill does not necessarily mean success, success does not necessarily mean skill. This is fate; it
cannot be understood through ordinary reason."[117] If it is in fact the case
that each bit of intellectual effort spent on poetry means one bit of effort
less spent on the examination métier, as argued in a story from *Zhaoshi
bei* (The cup that illuminates the world), does it necessarily follow that
each bit of effort spent on examination preparation will bring a candidate one step closer to success?[118] Yuan Huang seems to think so when he
suggests to examination candidates that they create a form on which they
can mark off which hours of each day were spent in productive preparation.[119] Discourses of commensurability pervade popular representations
of examination success, whether in fiction or in morality works, such as
the ledgers of merit and demerit. Such commensurate exchange came in
two closely related versions: the accumulation of merit could result in
success for the virtuous candidate, but improper cash exchanges could
likewise ensure that corrupt people passed.[120]

Highly motivated students might well have kept their ledgers and
schedules close at hand to keep track of their time spent and their merit
accounts and would have turned from these calculations back to careful
study of reference works such as the *Shenglü qimeng* (An introduction to
the rules of rhyme), which pair individual zi and sets of zi with concep-

tual matches that are tonal opposites, or the *Ziyan bianyong* (A manual for wording) and *Pianzi leibian* (A collection of matching words in categories), resources for *huanzi fa* (exchange of one character or phrase for another).[121] These matching *zi* and sets of *zi* are the fundamental units out of which longer parallel passages could be built up.[122] The talismanic power of sets of *zi* can be seen in the popularity of the "X words of instruction" (X *zijue*) genre, where the value of X could be anywhere from one to forty: in addition to Dong Qichang's *Nine Instructions*, also known as "Huating jiuzi jue" (Huating's instructions in nine words), no fewer than a dozen similar sets aimed at examination candidates were in circulation in the late Ming and Qing dynasties.[123] Time spent and progress made in learning texts could be denominated in *zi*: the total number of *zi* in the Classics were generally known, and the number of days necessary to master them could be calculated by setting a fixed number of *zi* of text that each student could be expected to learn in a single day. Bao Shichen counts the number of *zi* in individual passages in the classical canon to calculate the differing rates of "speed" in different sections.[124] Even the cells that candidates were assigned in the examination compounds were designated by characters taken from the *Qianzi wen* (Classic of a thousand characters).[125]

Student associations from the Jiajing period on often called themselves Xiyin hui (Cherishing time societies) to emphasize their careful management of time, and word-cherishing societies (Xizi hui) followed suit.[126] In a previous discussion of these word-cherishing societies, I suggested that "as the conceptual tool that allows one to establish relations of equivalence between different passages of text, [*zi*] is the literary symbol of the potential for commensurate exchange that was a necessary article of faith for any wholehearted participant in the civil service examination system; as such, the insistent attribution of value to written characters . . . for educated individuals in Ming and Qing China is not unlike the constitutive role that commodity fetishism plays in the formation of the bourgeois subject."[127] Commensurability is an article of faith, and the parallelism of sets of *zi* can be one sign of that faith.

For word-cherishing associations in the Qing, respectfully burning scraps of paper with writing on them is a key moment of exchange, grounding the equivalence of two registers—textual and ethical—whose interconvertibility is not at all self-evident. In the examination system, the key moment of matching takes place when the candidate is identified as the person behind the code name. This moment turns out to be doubly complex in that it joins two different questions of equivalence that ultimately work according to different logics. If for the participant the question is whether success is commensurable with effort—can one be obtained through the expenditure of the other?—the system will be preoccupied instead with the question of whether the person matches his writing—can one candidate be reliably distinguished from others? Equivalence was a key concern in examination administration at the most concrete level in that essays copied out for distribution to the examiners were subject to a careful check to ensure no errors were introduced and no alterations made. More generally, the question of whether the candidate "matches" his writing is not just a question of exam security but a more fundamental issue on which the whole system is premised.[128] As we will see in more detail in chapter 5, however, the commensurability between writing and individual serves not a broader regime of exchange between items of standardized value, but a regime of selection of distinctive individuals. The writing belongs to the writer precisely to the extent that it can be differentiated from the writings of others.

My aim here has not been to deny the popularity of parallel structures over the course of the Ming and Qing but to historicize the specific parallel standard ordinarily thought to define the examination essay a priori. I see this standard instead as a contingent development, one that enjoyed an aesthetic dominance less complete than many have supposed, and was subject to challenge within decades of its first articulation. In some cases, critics could even disagree over which lines in an essay were meant to match and which were not. By the end of the fifteenth century, one could say that as a general rule, an examination essay including six or eight nearly perfectly parallel legs was a safe choice. But as Lü Liuliang points out, there are many other possibilities:

> Some are parallel and some are single-line, some are completely orderly and some are loose and scattered, some hide a small parallel passage within a longer loose section, some have uneven lengths within parallel lines. Some are like a rush of water straight down, but in fact the parallel matches are finely worked and people are left unaware; some are parallel passages to the end, but in the rise and fall, opening and closing resemble a single *gu*. If one looks at how people write, how can there be a single fixed technique?[129]

As noted in the introduction, the degree to which standards and expectations varied geographically and temporally meant that a generically "safe" choice was, under many circumstances, considerably less likely to yield success than other approaches might. As we will see in more detail in the next two chapters, the competitive dynamics of the examination system as a whole were such that future generations of candidates who aspired to pass at the highest level or make a name for themselves as masters of the modern prose genre saw conventional forms not as literal models for their own work but as stylistic givens to work off of or against.

CHAPTER FOUR

The Examined Subject

The late Ming has long been identified as a high point in literary and cultural originality, whether that originality is understood in terms of a romantic idea of the author as genius or as a fascination with individual subjectivity and distinctiveness in taste. There are intriguing parallels with the articulation of individual subjectivity in early modern Europe—from Renaissance self-fashioning to the rise of the novel—in conjunction with increased social mobility, the new importance of women's writing, and the intensification of the market economy.[1] The examination system has a material cultural significance rivaling that of the market in Ming and Qing China—though narrower in social scope, its demands are commensurately more sharply focused on the literary culture whose boundaries it plays a crucial role in delineating. How might these demands relate to the original subjectivities that flowered in the late Ming and continued to play a central role in drama and fiction of the Qing?

It might seem strange to think of civil service examination writing in terms of self-articulation, given that conceptions of the self tend to imply interiority, individuality, and agency, qualities generally thought to come in short supply in essays written on a set theme that claim to speak for others, and whose formal conventions "saddened the private mind" of even so successful a candidate as Wu Kuan, the 1472 *zhuangyuan*.[2] From Ai Nanying's seventeenth-century suggestion that classical prose might constitute a kind of interiority to the examination essay and Wang Yuan's assertion decades later that the former is a spontaneous expression of the self and the latter is trammeled by others, to Jiao Xun's mid-Qing formulation of examination essays as "topic-based" where classical philosophical argumentation was "self-based," it is a short step through the trope of representation to Bao Shichen's understanding of classical prose as speaking one's own meaning and examination writing as speaking for others, and Yuan Mei's likening of essay writers to actors playing parts on stage.[3]

Although modern scholars have for the most part found this articulation convincing—it is rare to encounter a discussion of the eight-legged essay that does not reference the trope of "speaking for the Sages and Worthies"—we saw in chapter 1 that the history and practice of representative speech is complex and rife with motivated discourse, raising more questions about agency than it could hope to answer. Taking a hermeneutical perspective, Huang Qiang makes the point that the meaning found in modern prose written to speak for the Sages and Worthies "did not only occasionally go beyond the bounds of the 'Sages and Worthies' intentions, but was invariably located in a situation beyond the bounds of those intentions; understanding and interpretation is not a process by which the 'original meaning of the Sages and Worthies' is reconstructed, it is rather always a creative process."[4] Indeed, Wu Zhiwang argued four centuries earlier that the figure of representative speech is a pretext: "Speaking for the Sages and Worthies is nothing more than explaining moral philosophy clearly, and moral philosophy is what my mind naturally has; it is nothing more than speaking of the affairs of the world, and the affairs of the world are what my body has itself experienced."[5] In this connection, the insistent use of explicit first-person references characteristic of *shiwen*, far exceeding the norm in other genres of literary prose or poetry, appears particularly significant. To give one example, Zhu Xie's (1535 *jinshi*) essay on the topic "Virtue is not left to stand alone. He who practices it will have neighbors," has a total of sixteen mentions of *wu* and *wo* in an essay under 450 characters in length.[6] Who is speaking through this profusion of "I"s?

At the same time, we cannot overlook the social function of the examination essay: although one might think—insofar as the author seems to attempt to speak in the voice of the Sages—of the words contained in a typical examination essay as "belonging" to another, the examination system makes them belong to their immediate author in a very specific and concrete way. The writer of the examination essay should pass or fail—should be differentiated from other candidates—on the basis of these words alone. This question is addressed in detail in chapter 5.

Finally, we must note the surprising praise for *shiwen* by individuals usually identified as characteristic representatives of the late Ming moment, such as Yuan Hongdao and Li Zhi, as well as the genre's importance to somewhat earlier advocates of authenticity in writing such as Tang Shunzhi, who gained great fame for the originality of his modern prose.[7] Li Zhi not only argued for the value of *shiwen* as an outstanding genre by which the Ming could be known to later dynasties—a claim we might be tempted to dismiss from a modern perspective as a contrarian flourish, intended to irritate rather than to clarify—he went on to say that of his own writings he was proudest of *An Explanation of the Four Books*, a volume of reflections inspired by the *shiwen* form written at home for his own personal interest.[8] Similarly, Ai Nanying explains the publication of his modern prose essays as a means to "preserve the feeling of a friend who knows one's true self" (*yi cun zhiji zhi gan*).[9] This commitment to individual distinctiveness even finds its way into Bao Shichen's recommendations for teaching essay composition: students should be allowed to learn from the models that they themselves find inspirational, rather than from ones chosen for them by their fathers and teachers.[10] It is precisely from this perspective—the struggle to mark out a distinctive self through literary means—that this chapter aims to reassess the relationship between the examination system and the development of literary subjectivity. What does it mean to write oneself into a text addressed primarily to others who also write?

Self

The narrow, "selfish" version of the self, linked conceptually to profit or advantage rather than right or appropriate behavior, has a long tradition in Chinese philosophical thought as the antagonist against which the individual who aims at moral excellence must struggle; Zhu Xi's particular emphasis on *keji fuli* (restraining oneself and returning to the rites) is the most prominent example.[11] What we find in discourses on classical prose in the Ming and Qing, in contrast to Zhu Xi's approach, is a self—*ji*—that is not selfish in a negative sense but *authentic*. From the seventeenth century forward, the authenticity of this self's words is often guaranteed precisely by their contrast to the words spoken for another that are supposed to make up the modern prose essay. Wu Qiao (1611–95) argues that all writing from the Classics on down "naturally speaks the author's own intention" (*zishuo jiyi*); Yuan plays are the first to "speak for other people," and eight-legged essays do the same.[12] Liu Dakui draws a more nuanced distinction between the two genres, but it relies on a similar difference between the writer's self and others: "In writing classical prose, it is necessary only for one's own spirit (*ziji jingshen*) to dominate; in writing modern prose, it is necessary for one's own spirit to reach an accommodation with the spirit of the Sages and Worthies."[13]

The ideal self attributed primarily to classical prose is an inexhaustible resource that knits together natural, unselfconscious flow on one hand and distinctiveness on the other. Its fullest and best-known articulation is found in the emphasis on naturalness put forward by the late Ming Gong'an School and other associated critics: Yuan Hongdao comments on literary excellence generally that "innovation and originality in literature has no fixed form. All that is necessary is to put forward what no one else can put forward, and when the techniques for writing sentences, words, and compositions flow out one after another from one's own heart (*cong ziji xiongzhong liuchu*), this is true innovation and originality."[14]

Unlike the Qing stylists mentioned previously, however, members of the Gong'an School did not necessarily construct this authentic self in opposition to the modern prose essay. Yuan Hongdao's defense of modern prose has been noted in the introduction; here I highlight his younger brother Yuan Zhongdao's remarks on the examination essay: "Although the modern arts (*shiyi*) are said to be a minor craft, there are also examples of these essays that consist of expression from one's natural disposition (*shu zi xingling*) and not from what one has seen or heard."[15] Yuan Zhongdao proceeds to cite the key phrase from his older brother's discussion of literary excellence, "*cong xiongzhong liuchu.*" Similarly, the Yuan brothers' close associate Dong Qichang makes a point in *Juye beilei* (Examination flowerbuds) to emphasize the individual mind of the writer, referring to it frequently in arguing that if one relies on one's own inspiration (*zijia xingling*), it is not necessary to rely on others.[16]

Wu Zhiwang, who obtained the *jinshi* degree in the same class as Dong Qichang, wrote on this topic in more detail in *Loose Words on the Examination Métier* (1588). "It is always said of writing that it is as brilliant as if there was divine assistance. It is not that there is divine assistance: [writing] is realized through one's own spirit (*zijia shen*) and there are aspects of it that are so without one knowing how they come to be so."

From this perspective, the assigned topic is merely the pretext for one's writing: "There is already a completely finished text in my own mind, and I simply borrow the topic to manifest it; this is what our predecessors referred to as 'the topic is made use of by me, I am not controlled by the topic.'"[17] As Gong Duqing has pointed out, the renowned author and critic Wang Shizhen (1526–90) plays a crucial role as chief examiner in the 1589 metropolitan session, placing the startlingly original Tao Wangling (1562–1609) first and passing Dong Qichang and Wu Zhiwang.[18] His influence on the latter is suggested by the title *Loose Words on the Examination Métier*, clearly modeled on Wang's *Yiyuan zhiyan* (Loose words on the field of the arts). But if Wang encouraged literary innovation and unique styles in this one session, there was a far less well-known sixteenth-century writer who had a more fundamental and lasting influence on the discourse of individual subjectivity and naturalness.

Decades before Yuan Hongdao and Yuan Zhongdao called for writing that would connect one's authentic interior with the larger social world, and a full generation before Li Zhi would champion the "child-like mind," we find Qu Jingchun (1507–69; 1544 *jinshi*) presenting a similar argument in "Mr. Qu Kunhu's Remarks on Literary Writing." Qu notes the importance of "one's own true spirit" (*ziji zhen jingshen*) to successful modern prose, writing of *shiwen* that

> Writing must begin from one's internal thoughts and feelings and flow forth. At first it will seem difficult, but it will naturally get easier (*ziyi*), as extreme familiarity itself can (*zineng*) produce skill. Today's youth focus on reading over poor quality modern prose essays, thinking they will obtain literary technique; is it possible that knowing that I have the ultimate treasure that can be obtained without going in search of it, [I] instead make use of the voices of others as resources to eke out a living? It is truly pitiful. And when they get a topic, they invariably take old writings as models, at first thinking that they will save themselves effort, but not knowing that they soil their eyes and ears, and dizzy their mind and intent; their own original spirit (*zijia benlai lingxing*) is sealed up and not able to show through; even if they are able to produce writing in this fashion, it will be shallow and mediocre, not worth looking at.[19]

Although Qu allows for practice to develop one's unique voice, the potential is there from the start; the concept of an interior origin of literary inspiration and the insistent use of *zi* (自) as a modifier establish a clear emphasis on autonomous literary selfhood. The importance of this statement as a touchstone in the discourse on *shiwen* composition is hard to overstate: it is regularly quoted in anthologies and instruction manuals from the Wanli period down through the nineteenth century.[20]

We find this emphasis on the natural expression of thoughts and feelings in Qu's *shiwen* as well. In an essay on the topic "The richest fruit of benevolence," he takes a line that at first seems to match the immediately preceding parallel set off in a different direction—as we gradually fall out of line with the earlier parallel passages, the unselfconscious movement of hands and feet begins in response to music. As it becomes clear that we are no longer in step with the preceding passages and find ourselves swept into a stretch of loose prose, this movement is attributed to a self-in-itself *zai wo zhe*, even as the self-conscious "I" (*wu*) cannot gain awareness of it (*bu de zizhi ye*).[21] Foregrounding a self that is not self-conscious as the appropriate object of the modern prose essay would remain immensely influential through the late Ming and well into the Qing.[22]

Qu goes so far as to see *shiwen* as a vehicle for autobiography. "One day I happened to catch sight of the flowing water and the movement of the breeze in the mountains, and suddenly had the thought of all things attaining their place. On that day I wrote on 'In regard to the aged, to give them rest' borrowing this topic in order to focus entirely on describing the things in my heart, following the tendencies of those things in every particular."[23] After giving two other examples of *shiwen* written on topics "borrowed" to express his feelings, Qu concludes, "Now what I encountered in moving about, what I saw with my own eyes, my feelings of happiness and sadness, pains taken over things that were difficult to manage; as soon as I allegorized these in writing, although I did indeed intentionally arrange the words, there was always something that was so without my knowing how it could be so, outside of the written words and language itself."[24] Clearly for Qu modern prose could serve to express one's "own" feelings, and the proper essence of those feelings emerges naturally even though the composition process is highly intentional. Indeed, in a trope that is well suited to writing aimed at other writers (rather than mere readers), the writing process plays a crucial part in the *production* of the self, even as that self ultimately transcends the constraints of language.

The locus of the natural self that is so highly valued here is interior, found in the mind (*xin*), as we see in two other essays by Qu. "The path," from the opening passage of the *Doctrine of the Mean*, demonstrates a preoccupation with the individual mind that is a level more intense than the commentary on this passage, which refers more generally to things one knows that others do not. The concluding sentence of the essay goes as far as to refer explicitly to Wang Yangming's "Learning of the Mind" (*xinxue*) as well as to Daoist meditation practices.[25] Similarly, "King Wu did not slight the near" mentions *xin* repeatedly, despite the fact that this concept appears nowhere in the associated commentary, nor in the original passage. What brings the diversity of all under heaven together as one is not *li* (moral logic) in general, but "the moral logic of my own mind."[26]

As we have seen, this approach found sympathetic ears among *shiwen* stylists like Wu and Dong, as well as prominent late Ming literary figures such as Yuan Hongdao and Li Zhi. Could it survive the transition from Ming to Qing? As mentioned in the introduction, the dynastic transition was accompanied by an epistemic shift in discourse on literary work in general, which is often characterized as a conservative turn: by 1700, criticism of the decadent styles of late Ming men of letters, as well as their "huckster scholarship" and their factional politics, was common. But although this epistemic shift had direct implications for critical discourse on the modern prose essay as a genre, it had fewer practical effects on the writing and reading of these essays in the Qing than one might have thought. When it came to the evaluation of individual essays, even so canonical a figure as Fang Bao, compiler of the *Imperially Authorized Essays*, highlights a literary originality that is closely linked to interior subjectivity, writing approvingly of examination essays of the late Ming that authors "focused on originality and distinctiveness" and "borrowed the topics as pretexts to express all that they wanted in their own hearts (*xiongzhong*) to say."[27] He backs up this general assessment with praise for specific individual essays: of the essay by Tan Yuanchun in which he says he can imitate Confucius's greatness, Fang writes, "Observing things and examining processes are all dredged up from the mind, this is not a case of merely begging for inspiration from old paper"; of an essay by Jin Sheng, "The significance is completely attained in the mind, the words necessarily themselves (*ji*) come out, opening a cavern in the eight-legged essay that must be opened."[28]

Here I consider two seventeenth-century examples in a little more detail. In a striking essay on the following passage from the *Analects*:

"It is by the *Odes* that the mind is aroused. It is by the *Rules of Propriety* that the character is established. It is from *Music* that the finish is received," Zhang Yongqi (1652 *jinshi*) wrestles with the question of how to adequately represent the relationship between "natural" impulses and conscious learning. His three-stage formulation builds on the original text and the standard commentary to narrate a self-conscious first person, sensible of his inadequacy—"If one's own natural character cannot be relied upon, is it not the case that what can be relied upon must be gotten through study?" This individual is led through an awakening to moral reflection by the *Book of Poetry*, to formation by means of the *Rites*, and ultimately an ease with one's "realized" character and a concurrent release from conscious striving by the *Music*: "not knowing that it is like this and yet it is like this; this is the result of the *Music*."[29] The "I" (*wu*) that appears in the introductory section of the essay and in the first leg dealing with the *Book of Poetry* represents an individual questing for knowledge and reflecting on moral questions. First-person references are absent from the second leg. In the third and final leg, the "missing" first person is replaced with invocations of natural action: the virtues of music are explained as follows: "The individual who understands it does not depend on emotional response but is nevertheless naturally in motion (*zidong*), does not depend on support but nevertheless self-strengthens (*ziqiang*)."[30] This shift in emphasis from the self-conscious "I" to a higher unselfconscious stage of individual realization is all the more noticeable as it was precisely the point where the commentary did not allow for "naturally" bringing one's efforts to an end that Zhang marks off with the self-conscious *wu* in the first parallel set.

Han Tan's essay on the topic "It is said in the *Book of Poetry*, 'He measured out and commenced his marvellous tower'"—mentioned in chapter 3 for its challenges to conventional notions of parallel form— makes a similar case for spontaneity. The essay notes early on the standard interpretation of poetry as articulating one's *zhi* (intent or will). The question arises, however: why in particular an ode to the marvelous tower and in such detail? If the ode to this tower were taken as a product of an author (*zuozhe*), one would have no reason for surprise, as the form of literature produced by authors is characterized by its beautiful and extravagant language, concealing some subtle point (*weiyi*) the author wants to make. But as we learn in the next-to-last paragraph, the ode to the marvelous tower is different: it dates from an age when even ordinary people were skilled in literary matters and refined in expression, and when those people saw the marvelous tower, they "spontaneously described (*zixie*) their sincere loyalty and love." As Fang Bao points out in his comment, Han Tan presents this passage to us from a poet's point of view; in addition, he goes beyond the assigned passage to bring the ordinary people into the essay as authors themselves. This calculated transgression of the bounds of the topic allows him to foreground their voices by referring to the following sentences from the original text: "And yet the people rejoiced to do the work, calling the tower 'the marvellous tower,' calling the pond 'the marvellous pond.'"[31]

In his imagination of this poem from a writer's perspective, Han Tan runs into a paradox; it is precisely his expansion on and gloss of the original that ends as the writerly product of the kind of author he critiques. How to escape this trap of conscious intentionality? In the final paragraph, Han notes (in the voice of Mencius) the natural and spontaneous deepening of the ordinary people's feelings (*qing zishen*) and goes on to end the essay in highly original fashion by restaging the moment at which Mencius quotes their words from the *Book of Poetry* and leaving it at that.[32] The last word in the essay, which would ordinarily belong to the author, in this case is not a highly worked phrase of the essayist but the "natural" outpouring of the unnamed subjects of King Wen of Zhou. Rather than mediated representative speech, the final lines claim to bypass not only Han Tan but also Mencius in their direct access to the Classic. For contemporary readers, the abruptness of this ending, with no attempt to frame or otherwise recuperate the quoted original, would have stood out as a striking and unusual attempt to resolve the paradox of "unselfconscious" literary composition.

Even as Qu Jingchun anticipates the late Ming interest in a natural and autonomous literary self in the most minute detail, and Fang Bao subsequently gives this interest a canonical seal of approval in the early eighteenth century, we realize that Qu's interest in subjectivity and interiority not only resonates with the essays of his mid-sixteenth-century contemporaries, such as Gui Youguang and Hu Ding, but also finds precedents among writers of the late fifteenth and the early sixteenth centuries from Wang Ao and Tang Yin to Tang Shunzhi.[33] Wang Ao writes that

> Writing is not a mere craft; it is rooted in my mind and expressed in words, and cannot be done falsely. . . . If you merely use modern prose to write modern prose, and do not use "myself" to write modern prose (*yi wo wei shiwen*), you will go back and forth and end up only with some phrases from old essays; you will never open up a new world or create a new forge, and although you may exhaust your efforts, you will never stand out from others.[34]

Tang Shunzhi remarks, "If one truly has a mind that acts for one's own self (*you wei ji zhi xin*), then examination essays also naturally can lead to correct learning through words."[35] This sense of a distinctive individual self plays a role in Tang Shunzhi's essay on the topic "[Guan Zhong] united and rectified the whole kingdom," which makes use of the self (*ji*) to connect the dots between the assigned passage and "I beg to ask about the steps of that process" (also from the *Analects*), where active pursuit of benevolence is identified in the commentary as "one's own duty." Tang also makes use of this self (*ji*) to imply a contrast between the two passages, as Guan Zhong's "own duty" is defined differently from but not necessarily in conflict with benevolence.[36]

Another essay, for which "I beg to ask about the steps of that process" was the assigned topic, was mentioned already in chapter 2. Tang builds on the original passage's assertion that benevolence comes from the self, and not from others, with a movement from the interior out, emphasizing the self as resource. "The mind in truth controls vision and hearing . . . what is said and what is done is controlled by the mind."[37] Similarly, when given the topic "Formerly, when King Tai dwelt in Bin," where the original text and the standard commentary merely present the king as being asked to choose between courses of action, without raising any question of interiority, Tang brings up the necessity of *reflexive* inquiry in the first sentence: "The Great Worthy presented two plans for action and thereby charged the ruler with examining himself." As the essay unfolds, the king is asked to reflect on himself and his own mind to decide whether he should abandon his ancestral lands.[38]

It is perhaps not surprising that this interest in reflexive interiority accompanies a particular emphasis on complex and involuted parallelism of the type discussed in chapter 3. Indeed, I suggest that the preoccupation with the dynamics of individual subjectivity characteristic of the late Ming develops in part through the complex structures of the modern prose essay, of which Wang Ao and Tang Shunzhi's works are only the best-known examples. These structures are clearly evident by 1500 and firmly established as a characteristic quality of *shiwen* no later than 1550. I now turn to look at these prose structures in more detail, with particular emphasis on the role of the first person.

The I That Writes and the "I" That Is Written Of

As we have seen in chapter 1, the discourse of representative speech that becomes central to the definition of modern prose continually draws our attention back to the question: who is speaking? Commentators on the Chinese novel begin to highlight the eyes through which scenes are seen and the mouths through which they are narrated in the early seventeenth century. By the middle of the eighteenth century, identifying an individual character (or characters) as an allegorical third-person representation of the authorial self was common in longer vernacular fiction. The stability of this allegory in vernacular fiction is maintained in part by the firm distinction between a seemingly objective narrative voice on one hand and the direct quotation of individual characters' speech on the other; moves to call this boundary into question are rare. As a result, scholars who examine the autobiographical aspects of long vernacular fiction tend to locate autobiographical qualities in the substance of the lives of the characters, rather than in the narrative voice itself.[39]

One rare and striking moment of ambiguous voice in the vernacular tradition comes in the opening section of *Honglou meng* (Dream of the red chamber), which seems to break with generic convention so sharply in this regard that some scholars have suggested that this part of the first chapter is actually a preface that was mistakenly copied into the main text. For two early twentieth-century critics familiar with *shiwen*, however, this opening passage is easy to explain with reference to the concept of representative speech. The section of the first chapter in which the author speaks for himself is equivalent to the essay's opening lines; the author has not yet begun to "speak for the Stone," just as a *shiwen* author would ordinarily wait at least until the *qijiang* (initiation of discourse) section to begin "speaking for the Sages and Worthies."[40]

Indeed, although critics writing on vernacular fiction drew substantially on traditions of *shiwen* commentary, there is, generally speaking, a crucial difference between the genres in their treatment of the distinction between narrative and personal voices. In an essay, the phenomenon of representative speech is often complex and subject to differences in interpretation. Unlike in vernacular fiction, it is often surprisingly difficult to determine "who is speaking" at a given moment in the modern prose essay, with the result that commentators and scholars may disagree not only on who is being spoken for in an essay—if anyone—but even at which moment(s) that represented voice emerges distinctly from the narrative.[41] In some cases, the only clue to shifts in voice can be found in the use of a different name for one of the characters addressed or discussed.[42] It is for this reason that the ambiguity of voice in the opening chapter of *Dream of the Red Chamber* lends itself to a reading in terms of *shiwen* aesthetics.

The sixteenth-century prose critic Mao Kun notes the distinctions between different types of *shiwen* that require different narrative strategies in his work "Discussion of prose: four points," and indeed, in one of Mao's own essays, the question of who is speaking turns out to make an urgent claim on the reader's attention.[43] This is the case even though the topic, "When the villagers drank wine," is quite straightforward and does not seem to invite any uncertainty of voice. The first parallel section runs as follows:

> If those who walk with canes have not gone out, and I precede
>   them, the exemplary person would consider that arrogant.
> If those who walk with canes have gone out, and I follow
>   them, the exemplary person would consider that to be
>   appropriate.

Working from the basic assumption that modern prose essays more often than not speak in another's voice once the preliminary topic-breaker and topic-receiver sections have concluded, we may feel confident at this point that this is a clear-cut example of representative speech, and that the "I" (*wo*) who is speaking here is Confucius, but the next line calls that certainty into question by referring to him in the third person: "Only Confucius did not limit himself to this; he did not dare to chat idly at formal meals, and remained within the bounds of respectful conduct."[44] The "I" that we thought was Confucius, it turns out, may well refer to the narrator of the essay instead. One may assume that this kind of abrupt shift would have the useful effect of startling awake an examiner who might have begun to nod off as he skimmed through the thirtieth essay of the evening, but this kind of challenge to one's expectations of the identity and consistency of the first-person voice has broader implications as well.

Such shifts can take the form of a relay from person to person, and from age to age, in a mood that is simultaneously aspirational and conditional. In an essay on the topic "As to the system of hereditary salaries," by Cui Xian (1478–1541), for example, Mencius speaks in the first person as *wu* in place of Duke Wen of Teng, who in modeling himself on previous rulers would inspire future rulers to model themselves on him.[45] As Zhang Taikai notes, one must establish one's own self on the Sages' and Worthies' ground, seeing their events with one's own eyes, and "embody forth a measure of the spirit."[46] Indeed, the passage "At fifteen I had my mind bent on learning" inspired more than one essay author to take direct issue with Cheng Yi's claim that Confucius was not speaking concretely about his own experience but rather outlining a program for later students. As one of these authors, Gui Youguang makes the identification between the Sage and us explicit through the use of *wu*, emphasizing the process by which we are to imagine ourselves acting as Confucius did: "Now the world respects the Sage too highly, and takes him to have absolute virtue in the world, and does not know that it is his diligence without cease that is our own task (*wuren zhi shi*)."[47] Jiao Xun is clearly influenced by this approach when he turns Cheng Yi's critique of readers "enmired" in fixed interpretations against the standard Cheng-Zhu commentaries themselves to argue that certain uses of *wu* in the *Analects* should not be understood as merely referring to Confucius but should apply more generally.[48]

Given the reverence with which the Sages are supposed to be treated, this identification can verge at times on the grandiose, as when Tan Yuanchun concludes an essay with the following line: "Like this, I subsume the great virtue and the little virtue under [it], and thereby can imitate the greatness of Confucius."[49] This move is especially powerful when the writer takes a stand against an interpretation of the original text that has been advanced in the standard commentaries. On the question of what "the licentious sounds of Zheng" mentioned in the *Analects* consist of, the Ming writer Qian Zhenguang criticizes Zhu Xi's interpretation, writing that "The airs of the fifteen states are all complete; why do I say to 'banish the sounds of Zheng'?" Spoken as if it consisted of the words of Confucius himself, Qian's rejoinder to Zhu Xi hits with particular force.[50]

Based on this variety of uses, we may want to think of *wu* in Ming and Qing *shiwen* not only as a designator of person in grammatical terms but also as a mode of normative agency, marking a particular type of identification. Noted authors such as Wang Yangming and Gui Youguang did not hesitate in their essays to provide *wu* with parallel matches that are clearly functioning as verbs: "to feel, be moved" (*gan*), and "to preserve" (*cun*).[51] In this sense, the essay writer who makes a point of speaking as "I" is in the process of articulating an identification akin to the transformation of the subject that Lacan finds to be characteristic of the "mirror-phase" of young children, which "situates the instance of the *ego*, before its social determination, in a fictional direction," aimed at an image whose autonomy and self-consistency can be aspired to.[52]

In the case of a student or candidate writing an examination essay, of course, we are dealing not with an ego that has yet to be socially determined but with an ego in search of social recognition. Just as significantly, interest is located not in an image but in a *voice*: by speaking as *wu*, one postulates a self that can be aspired to.[53] It is precisely in this identification through voice that Guan Shiming finds the modern prose essay to be superior to commentaries, which mark the original text off as an other.[54] This self is not presocial and prelinguistic but constituted in and through language. A return to the distinction drawn between vernacular narrative and *shiwen* at the beginning of this chapter makes this point concrete: although David Rolston draws parallels between the "practice of imaginative identification" characteristic of *shiwen* and the writing of fiction and drama that are at one level very convincing, the relationship between the authorial voice and the imagined voices of individual characters is ultimately rather different in the two genres.[55] The "self-representation" as metaphor that Martin Huang finds pervasive in Qing novels like *The Scholars*, for example, is directly analogous to the phenomenon that Lacan discusses, in that the novel creates an image of an individual with whom the author identifies allegorically.[56] In *shiwen*, by contrast, we have the *voice* of the author developed with and against the voice(s) of the Sages, Worthies, and other characters.

As we have seen in chapter 1, this concern with voice centers primarily on *xuzi* (empty words), which "are entrusted with the spirit and transmit the voice (*yuqi*)."[57] Unlike ordinary nouns and other *shizi*, which are given the task of conveying logic and moral content (*yili*), *xuzi* operate in the realm of aesthetics, making the writer's brush lively, whether considered in terms of form or in terms of affect.[58] It should be noted that the category of *xuzi* has two different interpretations, corresponding to more or less material understandings of the aesthetic. On one hand are words that represent the formless as opposed to concrete reality, indicating in this instance a capacity for abstract imagination; and on the other hand are characters that merely represent sound—the "emptiest of empty words" in Yuan Renlin's phrasing, whose meaning is none other than the material force that they express.[59] In contrast to fully realized things, these words represent potential and imagination; in contrast to the logical faculties, they represent a more direct bodily response.

Given the importance of identification through a process of speaking, it comes as no surprise to find Mao Kun emphasizing the importance of *xuzi yan* (key empty words) as a means of properly representing the Sages and Worthies in his "Discussion of Prose." Like the grommets anchoring a 100-foot sail, *xuzi* function as privileged points of cathexis for transmitting textual energy.[60] Among these "empty words" are not only exclamations but even the pronouns *wu* and *wo*, which can serve in *shiwen* as grammatically appropriate parallel elements to verbs, time words, and even function words such as *ze*, and at the same time as key points in a relay of identification.[61] The figure of apostrophe is understood to address another, to call it to presence in the text; given their imaginative potential, we may say that these first-person pronouns are used in modern prose in large part as an apostrophe to the self.

In Mao Kun's essay, the shift that causes the reader to retroactively identify the author (rather than Confucius) as the speaker takes place over the transition from the first parallel section to the second, leaving little doubt of the effect intended by the author. In other essays, similarly disorienting shifts in voice appear within individual sentences, thereby challenging the reader to work a little harder. Wang Yangming's essay on "The determined scholar and the benevolent person" takes a sharp turn as early as the *chengti*, introducing the first person much sooner than expected and immediately complicating things further by throwing the referent of that first person into question. "Now determined scholars and benevolent people all have fixed authority over their minds and are not deluded by selfishness; for this reason, when [such] people encounter the moment between life and death, I (*wu*) see them seek only not to be ashamed in their consciences, and what worries are there for my body (*wushen*)?"[62] It seems that this reading cannot be right—it makes no sense for the speaker's body to be in danger in this context. There are two possible ways to resolve this difficulty. First, at some point the sentence in question transitions from representing the speaker's own words to imagining the speech of the determined scholars and benevolent people, in which case we could translate it as follows: "I see them seek only not to be ashamed in their consciences: 'And as for *my body*, what worries are there?'" Although we may not be satisfied with this interpretation, it raises an important issue: the sense that *wu* is often, if not ordinarily, an indicator at some level of *quoted speech*, even in the absence of other such indicators. This brings us back to the discourse of representative speech discussed in chapter 1 and hints at the further complications that appear in the practice of that speech to be addressed later in this chapter.

I have shown elsewhere that the *wu* that appears in classical prose of the Ming and Qing often lends itself to translation as the relatively impersonal "one" in a way that other first-person references do not.[63] Indeed, a second possibility is to take this *wu* in the modern prose essay not as a literal first-person pronoun but as a reference to the individual in the abstract, which can be translated in more generalized terms as "personal" or "own" when it modifies the noun that follows, as Andrew Plaks does in his translation of another essay from this same period.[64] In this case, the sentence would read: "I see them seek only not to be ashamed in their consciences; what worries are there for [their] *own bodies*?" When we continue through Wang Yangming's essay and find lines such as "They take *wuxin* as significant, and *wushen* as insignificant," this approach seems to be justified, as "They take their own minds as significant and their own bodies as insignificant," reads more smoothly than "They take their 'my mind' as significant and their 'my body' as insignificant."[65] Either way, there is a certain discomfort; neither the awkwardness of the second choice nor the deceptive smoothness of the first choice seems fully adequate to the original.

Should we assume that potentially disorienting flourishes like this are characteristic only of challengers to the ideological status quo like Wang Yangming, we will be disappointed. The ultimately canonical Wang

Ao includes the following lines in his much-anthologized late fifteenth-century essay on the topic "If the people have plenty, their prince will not be left to want alone":

> I know (*wuzhi*) that
> What is stored in the commoners' houses, the ruler can get all
>   of it [if necessary], it does not need to be kept in the palace
>   storehouse and only then be considered my wealth (*wucai*).
> What is accumulated in the fields, the ruler can use all of it [if
>   necessary], it does not need to be piled up in granaries and
>   only then be considered my possession (*wuyou*).[66]

It seems that the first-person possessive "my" at the end of each of these sentences cannot refer back to the speaker ("I") but must rather refer to the ruler who first appears in the third person midway through. I have translated these lines literally to make the roughness of this shift as evident as possible; other scholars have chosen different approaches that convey a coherent meaning more smoothly. Ching-I Tu, for example, renders the phrase in question as a direct quote from the ruler:

> I know that
> what was kept in the common households would all be avail-
>   able to the ruler, without being hoarded in the treasury to
>   enable the ruler to claim, "This is my wealth";
> what is stored in the farm and the fields would all be accessible
>   to the ruler, without its being accumulated in the vaults to
>   enable the ruler to claim, "These are my possessions."[67]

Benjamin Elman, on the other hand, silently changes the problematic first-person reference to the third person:

> I know that
> The ruler could have everything if it were stored in village
>   households, with no need to hoard it in his treasury as his
>   goods.
> The ruler could use everything if it were placed in the
>   fields, with no need to accumulate it in his vaults as his
>   possessions.[68]

Again we see a choice between direct discourse—marking off the problematic clause as a quote—on one hand, and indirect discourse, converting the problematic first-person reference to the third person, on the other. Again, each choice loses something in translation or removes something that the translator deems superfluous in the original. But this essay, which was written as a model and has remained one of the single best-known examples of the genre through the Ming and Qing, makes it clear that this effect—this apparently superfluous introduction of the first person—is no accident. It is rather a deliberate stylistic choice. It should be evident that converting the second *wu* in each sentence into a third-person possessive indicator such as *qi* (其) would remove any hint of ambiguity; a similar substitution would also have made Wang Yangming's essay substantially easier to read. Ambiguity that could so easily be avoided clearly has a distinct significance.

It is my argument that given the careful attention accorded these essays by their authors, graders, and broader reading publics, the insistence on challenging the reader cannot be explained away but must be examined in more detail. Indeed, although these examples are particularly stark, once we start looking it becomes clear that sudden shifts between third and first person are quite common. Essays in which the identity of the first person speaking is ambiguous for at least some portion of the text did not suffer for this quality at the hands of examination officials or anthology editors.

We find a virtuoso example of this shifting in Gu Xiancheng, "It requires a perfectly benevolent prince to be able, with a great country, to serve a small one":

> Mencius said:
> What is prized in relations with neighbors is none other than forgetting about it when an imbalance in force favors me (*wo*), and following along with it when an imbalance in force favors another. The king asks about the way [to accomplish this]? Your servant will try to outline it, and the king can make a choice. Now there are many peoples and countries in the world, so there is a way to deal with large countries that neighbor me, and a way to deal with small countries that neighbor me.
> How can the large relate to the small? People who are benevolent have gotten the way. The benevolent person says: "If I (*wu*) angrily set myself against a small neighboring country, then I can show my might and cause resentment, but if the aim is to make my virtue evident and I harbor treacherous thoughts, this is the wrong plan." For this reason, in their service to another, the preference is to cause the world to judge me as afraid, and fail to show respect, rather than

to cause the world to judge me as violent, and incur the
calamity of disorder. Of those who carried out this way in
the past, I find two individuals in particular: Tang, who
served Ge, and King Wen, who served Kunyi.[69]

Gu's Mencius begins with a first-person identification with the ruler
("when an imbalance in force favors me"), transitions to a reported
dialogue with the ruler in which he uses a standard third-person reference ("your servant") that can be understood as a humble first-person
reference to Mencius himself, and returns to first-person identification
with the ruler ("countries that neighbor me") at the close of the *qijiang*.
The first long parallel section then quotes benevolent people speaking of
themselves in the first person, returns to referring to them in the third
person when the quote ends ("their service to another"), but suddenly
shifts back to a first-person reference ("cause the world to judge me
as afraid"), a shift similar to those we have seen in essays by Wang
Yangming and Wang Ao. Just as we are recovering from this back-and-
forth with the benevolent people, Gu suddenly introduces a *wu* that, for
the first time in the essay, unquestionably refers to Mencius ("Of those
who carried out this way in the past, I find . . .").

   Although there are countless essays in which a straightforward indicator of representative speech—for example, *yiwei*, "what he meant to say
was"—is followed by a succession of "I" references, each of which points
readers unequivocally to the persona the essay's author has assumed,
shifts and slippages between first and third person (and back again) are
common across a range of stylistic and temporal boundaries. One is
tempted to wonder whether these specific shifts may be as characteristic
of the *shiwen* genre as the more abstract category of representative speech
under whose sign they so often appear. For every clearly motivated use of
the first-person pronoun, as in Zhang Jiang's "If the mind does not feel
complacency in the conduct," where *wu* is clearly required in one parallel
section to make it clear that Gaozi is presenting us with his understanding of Mencius's argument and is dispensed with in the following parallel
section when it is no longer needed, we encounter another case where the
first-person reference seems to represent a kind of problematic surplus
of voice, making the passage more complicated than it needs to be, as
we have seen in the selection from Gu Xiancheng's essay.[70] Although
this instance of excess is particularly noticeable, it is clear that in many

shiwen there are uses of *wu* that are rhetorical and stylistic choices rather than strictly semantically necessary.[71]

It becomes evident that the identity of the voices speaking in any given essay has the potential to be of an order of complexity greater than is generally assumed. Indeed, although one could do a careful study of specific problematic essays, weighing the evidence for who is speaking at what point in the text, my aim here is not to argue whom these essays are *really* speaking for but to ask how and when do first-person references emerge from the text and to what effect? Given the centrality that the question of voice comes to assume in definitions of the modern prose essay as a genre, as we saw in chapter 1, these questions cannot be dismissed as a side issue.

Here we can return to Qu Jingchun's remarks and focus on one sentence in particular: "Today's youth focus on reading over poor quality essays, thinking they will obtain literary technique; is it possible that knowing that I have the ultimate treasure that can be obtained without going in search of it, [I] instead make use of the voices of others as resources to eke out a living? This would be truly pitiful." At the key moment in this critique of students who are willing to give up their distinctive voices, Qu steps forward in the first person to highlight his own imagination of the student's position. Individual creativity is articulated as a concept precisely through this disruptive emergence of the "I" voice. I have suggested that first-person pronouns in modern prose call a subject to presence in the text, willing that self into being in the manner of apostrophe. As J. Douglas Kneale reminds us, apostrophe properly understood involves a sudden turn; it is the sudden and surprising uses of *wu* in modern prose essays that best fit this trope.[72] At the same time, the privilege granted moments of address and representation as the most suitable spaces for this first person to appear reminds us of the significant differences between the modern prose aesthetics of production and other aesthetics that focus primarily on moments of consumption and connoisseurship. I return to this point in the epilogue.

Shifting Discourse

The apparent lack of fit between the first-person pronoun and the context in which it appears poses a problem for the translator: how to render such a sentence in English? In the least striking cases, where *wu* or *wo* seem to come out of nowhere but are not necessarily in contradiction with the context—the sentence or *gu* taken as a whole—the possibilities are to mark these pronouns as direct speech of the author or to generalize them as "one" or "an individual."[73] When the potential for dissonance shades into positive contradiction, however, a little more work is necessary. The clause in question must either be reimagined as the direct speech of another individual—not the author—or be reframed as an indirect summary of what that person would say, with the reference to him or her changed from first person to third person. In the example given previously, Tu chooses the first alternative and Elman the second.

To the student of narrative voice in fiction, this contrast will seem familiar. It is the same choice one faces in trying to explain what is happening in free indirect discourse (*style indirect libre*), a mode poised between direct discourse (quotation of the character's actual words) and indirect discourse (narrator's summary presentation of what the character has said), crucial to the work of authors as varied as Jane Austen and Virginia Woolf. For some critics of modern European and American fiction, this is a choice best not made: they identify free indirect discourse as a special "dual-voiced" mode in which the narrator's voice and the voice of the character represented are so closely imbricated as to be inseparable. Others emphasize not duality but the unmarked shifts between one voice and another.[74]

The similarity between the shifts in voice in Ming and Qing *shiwen* and free indirect discourse in European fiction is that both turn on the substitution of pronouns; the important difference is in the nature of that substitution. Free indirect discourse replaces first-person pronouns with third-person pronouns in its references to the character whose speech is represented. In these essays, by contrast, third-person pronouns are replaced by *wu* or *wo*; alternatively, first-person pronouns are added in places where they are not in fact necessary to a coherent reading of the text. A difference in effect follows from these different trajectories of substitution. Where free indirect discourse presents the reader with an impersonal narrator who gains privileged access to the thoughts and speech habits of a character, the introduction of *wu* and *wo* into sentences where they are unexpected or unnecessary allows a distinctly individual voice to come forward and lay claim to what is supposed to be preestablished canonical discourse.

Studies of free indirect discourse in fiction written in Western languages tend to focus on three formal characteristics: the use of tense, person, and "syntactic features with emotive function," such as interjections and exclamatory sentences.[75] Since verbal tense in literary Chinese is not differentiated as finely as it is in most European languages, for the most part tense cannot be used to contribute to shifts in perspective. But in addition to the play with person that we have already seen, we find the use of *xuzi* with "emotive function" clearly identified as a key element of modern prose voice, particularly representative speech. At the right moment—see, for example, the "Alas!" in Tan Yuanchun's essay on jujubes translated in the introduction—a well-placed "emptiest of empty words" can hint at, or even clearly signal, the transition from one voice to another.

Speaking more generally, specialists on free indirect discourse have often made use of the trope of representation to characterize the relationship between narrator and character; alternative terms for free indirect discourse include "represented discourse" and "represented speech and thought."[76] Given these commonalities, it is clear that although scholars have tended to understand free indirect discourse in Chinese fiction as a twentieth-century development with no local precedent, the intensified focus on characters' "mental and emotional life" that Dorrit Cohn finds typical of free indirect discourse in European fiction is matched in the dynamic and shifting trains of thought we see represented in the *shiwen* genre in the Ming and Qing.[77]

Indeed, although many *shiwen* clearly and unmistakably mark off the distinction between representative speech and assertive speech, and sustain it so thoroughly throughout the rest of the essay that the effect is closer to direct discourse, this distinction is often harder to draw with confidence, as we saw in chapter 1; under these circumstances, it becomes possible for the uncertainties and ambiguities that are typical of the free indirect discourse seen in Austen, Flaubert, and even Joyce to constitute a regular feature of representative speech in *shiwen* no later than the end of the fifteenth century.

Because tense cannot play the same complicating role in the articulation of voices in *shiwen* that it does in novels written in European languages, the significance of the first-person pronoun to these essays is that much more evident. Without unanticipated interjections of *wu* or *wo*, the reader would in many cases have no reason to wonder who might be speaking.[78] Because the reader of Chinese literary prose had long been required to decide whether a given clause or sentence was direct or indirect discourse based on fewer grammatical cues than would be the case in modern Chinese or Western writing, the skillful use of personal pronouns is crucial to establishing any middle voice between direct and indirect discourse or any dual voice that seems to bring the two modes together. Where does this distinctive use of first-person pronouns come from? Given that *wu* can be used in literary Chinese writing more generally in a relatively impersonal fashion—similar to the use of "one" rather than "I" in English—can we trace a genealogy of the more challenging aspect it can take on in modern prose, the eruption, so to speak, of a more personal voice at unexpected moments?

Let us return to Wang Yangming's essay "The determined scholar and the benevolent person," and take a look at this parallel:

> Now when at moments of difficulty [they] avoid getting
>   involved, then they are able to put their bodies (*qishen*) at
>   ease, but cannot put their hearts (*qixin*) at ease . . .
> Now when there are wrongs and [I] go with the flow, then my
>   life (*wusheng*) is kept whole, but my benevolence (*wuren*) is
>   lost . . .[79]

Unlike the examples discussed earlier, this parallel section is easy to grasp: the first half clearly deals exclusively with others, and the second half deals exclusively with the self. This technique—clear alternation between third-person and first-person references, with the line break or the break between *gu* marking the transition in unmistakable fashion—is commonly found in essays of the Ming and Qing, including those by such well-known stylists as Tang Shunzhi, Gui Youguang, and He Zhuo.[80]

The reasons for this technique's popularity are quite straightforward. Although parallelism is an aesthetic standard of defining importance to *shiwen* as a genre, variation within the parallel framework is generally considered superior to simple repetition, as we saw in chapter 3; this parallel section from Wang Yangming's essay reads in far more lively and forceful fashion with the introduction of *wu* to modify "life" and "benevolence" than if the second half had simply repeated the third-person usage from above with "they are able to keep their lives (*qisheng*) whole, but their benevolence (*qiren*) is lost." At the same time, this kind of shift demonstrates a confident grasp of the dynamics of the "guest-host relationship" that Dong Qichang argues is central to modern prose style.[81] In this case, the third-person "guest" is appropriately succeeded by the first-person "host," with the result that the complicated mode of normative agency that we understand as a first-person reference is not the authority grounding the "parallel" speech that issues from it but appears as a stylistic *effect* of that very speech.

As we saw in chapter 3, the very literary mode—classical prose—that is most regularly contrasted against the examination essay in its ability to give authentic voice to the individual's thoughts and feelings in fact owes its definition to modern prose. When Ai Nanying writes that classical prose and the examination métier (*zhijuye zhi dao*) relate to each other as exterior and interior, we are reminded of an aspect of the twentieth-century Western critique of the metaphysics of presence in which the concept of interiority is no longer understood as a quality essentially opposed to an exterior but reframed as a type of space provisionally captured by a fold of a defining surface, a reflexive turning of that surface around on itself.[82] In the Song Cheng-Zhu tradition as well, reflexivity is often expressed through a paradoxical turning inward. In *shiwen*, however, it is more frequently evoked through shifts between first- and third-person presentation that are fundamentally linked to the trope of parallelism. We may understand the parallel turn as akin to this fold, not necessarily in the spatial sense but in the construction of identity though a process of doubling or a layering. This holds true in the generation of opposed writing styles, one of which is privileged as more authentic, and in the emergence of the first person as an effect of a quest for a style that is dynamic even in its balance.

George Saintsbury writes of Richardson's intense focus on the individual's sentiments in the eighteenth-century British novel: "Where are we to find a probable human being, worked out to the same degree, before?"[83] In the shuttling back and forth, the iterated exploration of this *wu* position, we find an analogous "working out" in the examination essay. Shifts to and from *wu* are not unprecedented in Chinese literary prose, but here they are extended more broadly than ever before and in such a way as to become an easily recognizable marker of the genre. Fu Zhanheng (1608–60) writes of examination essays that generally speaking, they "take the straight and curve it to the point of exhaustion"; working from Dong Qichang's fine-grained analysis of the principles of similarity and difference and the dynamics of change and repetition in modern prose, we can categorize shifts between first and third person that fall into an expected rhythm of sorts as an alternation between "guest" and "host" (*bin/zhu*) elements.[84] But Dong puts even more emphasis on shifts that are less expected and have more potential to disturb the reader, such as "twisting," "turning," and "reversing." These less-expected shifts turn out to have profound implications for involutionary parallelism in particular.[85]

In chapter 3, we saw the development of involutionary parallelism at the very historical moment that Gu Yanwu identifies as the realization of the eight-legged form. Wang Ao, considered by critics in later generations to represent an epitome of modern prose style, is the single person most closely associated with this involution. Tang Shunzhi, the leading stylist of the next generation, is known for his mastery of involutionary parallelism, even as he pushes its principles to the point of collapse. It is no coincidence that these two writers also compressed the regular shuttle between self and other that had unfolded across lines and paragraphs into the space of the individual line and even the individual phrase, converting the appearance of the first person from the arrival of a host that we know to expect, having already met the guest, into a disorienting turn, a swerve that throws the reader off track.[86]

Even as some essays destabilize our assessments of what it means to be parallel, others put identity itself into play by internalizing shifts that appeared between lines into the lines themselves. I noted previously that *wu* works as a kind of apostrophe to the self; here we return to the point that such a call to the self often works best as a sudden turn or shift in discourse.

Earlier in this chapter, I drew a distinction between *shiwen* of the Ming and Qing and Chinese vernacular fiction of that era on the basis of the careful separation between narrator's voice and the voices of individual characters in fictional works. But this rule has its exceptions. Had George Saintsbury the chance to read *Dream of the Red Chamber*, for example, he doubtless would have exclaimed at the degree to which the main characters in that eighteenth-century Chinese novel were "worked out" as well. Here I return to the question of the *zhiji*—the friend who knows your true self, whose feelings Ai Nanying claimed to preserve in his modern prose essay collection—with a close look at a brief passage from chapter 32 of the novel, in which Lin Daiyu has just overheard Baoyu declare a measure of his feelings for her.

> On hearing these words, Daiyu unconsciously felt alarm, happiness, sadness, and frustration.
>
> *What there was to be happy about:*
>
> Indeed, [my] own vision was not wrong, previously [I] recognized him as a soulmate (*zhiji*), and indeed he is a soulmate.
>
> *What there was to be alarmed about:*
>
> He praises me with his own private thoughts in front of another, his warmth and closeness do not in fact avoid suspicion.
>
> *What there was to be frustrated about:*
>
> Since you are my soulmate, I naturally can be your soulmate; since you and I see each other as soulmates, what necessity is there for talk of "gold and jade"? Since there is talk of "gold and jade," you and I ought to have it, and what need is there for a Baochai to come along?
>
> *What there was to be sad about:*
>
> [My] parents died young; even if we have an oath inscribed in our hearts and carved on our bones, there is no one to speak on my behalf. Furthermore, these days I always feel shaken in my thoughts, the sickness is already gradually in the process of completion; the doctors in addition say that my material force is weak and my blood insufficient, fearing it is a symptom of extreme exhaustion. Even though I am your soulmate, I am afraid I cannot last long; even if you are my soulmate, what can be done about my ill-fate?
>
> Thinking to this point, she could not restrain her tears from falling.[87]

In Haun Saussy's consideration of the possibility of free indirect discourse in *The Dream of the Red Chamber*, he suggests that this passage is more complex than directly reported speech. Indeed, as was the case in the essays by Wang Yangming and Wang Ao discussed earlier, converting this passage into directly reported speech loses something in the process. Instead, Saussy reads this passage as akin to a commentary explaining the reasons for the four emotions Daiyu is experiencing. He also highlights its use of elements of classical prose rather than the ordinary vernacular used in conversation in the novel and asks, "Did Daiyu think in the language of classical essay-writing?"[88]

I would like to make a more specific claim: Daiyu's train of thought here constitutes a particularly deft appropriation not just of any type of literary language but of the tropes and structure of *shiwen* in particular. The gradual unfolding of a train of thought through a process that can be understood in terms of a beginning (I was right in my recognition of him), development (I have reason to be alarmed about his expression of feeling), sudden turn (why are you and I not the destined soulmates?), and closing (after all, our fate is not to be together), fits the *qi-cheng-zhuan-he* structure of the modern prose essay quite nicely. It is not just the indeterminacy of voice at key moments that reminds us of free indirect discourse but also the balance between first and third person in the first two sections of the passage, and even that sudden turn to second-person address—apostrophe—in the third part, that give us a strong sense of the kind of imagined voice typical of *shiwen*.[89] Like Ai Nanying's modern prose essays, this passage is able to *cun zhiji zhi gan*, "preserve the feeling of a friend who knows one's true self."

The clearest difference from *shiwen* style is found in this passage's use of vernacular vocabulary like *de*, *zhe*, and *ni*, but even on this point the force of its compelling similarity to modern prose writing can be detected: in one of the eighteenth-century manuscript copies of *Dream of the Red Chamber*, the copyist mistranscribes (and in some cases subsequently corrects) a range of *xuzi* in this passage: exclamations, grammatical particles, and in one case, a pronoun.[90] Each mistaken transcription shifts the language used in this passage away from vernacular speech and toward modern prose style. The attraction of the *shiwen* mode of writing in the context of this passage is such that the copyist repeatedly finds it necessary to override his or her automatic inclinations and consciously steer the copied text back in a more vernacular direction.

In the case of *shiwen* written on noncanonical topics, such as lines taken from *The Western Chamber*, we see modern prose writing serving with notable effectiveness to represent words thought by fictional characters, but never spoken aloud. (The cover illustration includes an example of one such essay.)[91] It turns out that the tactics that make up representative speech can be used to imaginatively represent what characters in fictional texts think but do not say aloud just as easily as they work to represent what the Sages and Worthies thought but did not say. *Shiwen* excel specifically in the representation of processes of thought, in tracing the dynamics of a character's inner life. It is ironic indeed that one of the most appealing characteristics of one of China's best-known novels shares so much with a genre that we have been taught to overlook.

What we seem to see in the sixteenth-century uses of *ziji* and *xin* in the modern prose field is a reimagination of a distinctive and confident self (ego) in terms that had previously been negatively characterized.[92] This private self becomes crucially important across the range of vernacular literature in the late Ming and Qing. But is this distinctive self merely rhetoric in the case of the examination essay? Perhaps one could interpret the appropriation of words such as *ziji* and *sixin* in positive terms by champions of classical prose, dramatic productions, and novels in the late Ming and Qing as an attempt to transvalue the ethics endorsed by the examination system and expose its hypocrisy and bad faith in the process. After all, Wu Kuan did write that the restrictions of the examination essay form make his "private mind" (*sixin*) unhappy, alluding to a poem by Han Yu in which privacy (or even selfishness) begins to be reconceived as a literary value even as it remains unacceptable as a moral value.[93] Ai Nanying's well-known essay on the topic "To the mind belongs the office of thinking" sets up a split between *wu* and *xin*, defining the very "mind" whose potential for reflexive inquiry Tang Shunzhi emphasized as itself requiring proper guidance. Where Mencius (like Tang) conceives of *xin* as that aspect of a person that generates moral action through reflection (among other faculties), Ai presents *xin* as an object to be controlled through reflection. "And through reflection to cause my mind to fulfill its duties is none other than the means by which I am skilled at governing [my] mind."[94] Material force, which Mencius insists must arise as naturally as a growing plant, in Ai's understanding is steered by *li*. Through a similar dualism Ai removes the agency from the mind and locates it nowhere else than in the *wu* ("I") in whose voice the majority of the essay is written.[95]

Yet Wang Ao writes that after studying the significance behind the words of the Sages, one "manifests the true opinions in one's own heart in writing." Gu Yanwu draws a distinction between the central part of the essay that can be presented as if it were the words of the Sages and Worthies, and the introduction and conclusion in which writers "themselves present their views." Zhang Xuecheng writes in the eighteenth century that "although examination [candidates] speak for the Sages and Worthies, they also express what they themselves found there." These comments remind us of the extent to which the concepts of "self-presentation" and "self-expression" are constituted and reiterated in part in specific contrast to discourses and practices of representative speech *and* of the fact that they nonetheless continue to be imagined as normative components of the examination essay.[96] Indeed, as Lu Longji points out, and as we have seen in this chapter, the "new meaning" produced by the essay author cannot always be clearly distinguished from the Sage's intent, whether in its placement in the essay or in the contours of the voice with which it is articulated.[97]

When we look more closely, this self turns out to play a fundamental role in the conceptualization of the examination process. Already in the Northern Song, Sima Guang (1019–86) contrasts the appropriate approach, in which candidates base themselves on the classics and use their own intention (*jiyi*) to decide among the various commentary traditions and philosophical schools, against the wrong approach, in which candidates who do not remember the fundamental significance of the commentaries use their own intention to drill into the text to produce strained interpretations.[98] For Sima Guang, and indeed for Zhu Xi, "one's own intention" is the pivot point determining the correctness of an individual interpretation of the canonical text.[99] A similar phrase appears in Cheng Duanli's (1271–1345) family instructions, and the *Yuanshi* (History of the Yuan) later explains that Chinese examination candidates used the Cheng-Zhu commentaries and "concluded with their own intention."[100] This self continues to be of crucial importance through the Ming and Qing, often poised in balance with the Sages and Worthies, marking off the individual as distinct and different.[101] In the fifteenth century, we see a reference to "their own intentions" (*jiyi*) of the examiners and educational commissioners creating small topic questions, an activity that, as we found in chapter 2, foregrounds the question of the legitimate agency of the individual.[102] A century later, we may note Gu Xiancheng's discussion of individual styles grounded on the distinction between a self (*ji*)—with certain inherent strengths, weaknesses, and tendencies—and other people.[103] Clearly, the concept of this self lends itself to talk about differentiation and inherent uniqueness.

To argue that the examination system is merely the inert ground against which a lively new voice can distinguish itself only through a radical break would be to overlook the ways in which the practice of that voice manifests itself as a *consequence* of the examination essay form, as well as the extent to which the very idea of a distinctive individual voice functions as a bureaucratic requirement within the examination system. The next chapter addresses this question: how does the very formulation of "one's own words" as a description of uniquely authentic writing relate to institutional attempts to adequately differentiate between individual candidates on the basis of their writing?

CHAPTER FIVE

Anonymity and Identity

One of the most consistent norms in modern prose writing is that individuals who appear in the original texts, whether Sages and Worthies or scoundrels, are not referred to by name in the opening sentence of the essay. Although proper names are never explicitly prohibited from appearing in the sentence that "breaks the topic," we quickly realize that characters will not be called by their names until later, if at all. Yet this is not a case of true anonymity, as there are specific epithets used to refer to Confucius, Mencius, and so on; examination preparation manuals include exhaustive lists of them.[1] The coding that hides the identities of the essay authors during the grading process, by contrast, is much more thoroughgoing and consequential, constituting a basic condition under which the genre must be read. This chapter inquires into the relationship between candidates' anonymity on the one hand, and the drive to establish oneself as a distinctive individual through literary means on the other. Crucial to this attempt is a concept of creativity and originality, expressed in writing from the period most often as *qi*. Standing out as original in this way depended on a firm grasp of writing as a type of work—work that both advocated for and disciplined the writing self.

The idea of the individual as knowable through his or her writing has a long history in Chinese literature, but the introduction of a civil service examination system with an anonymous grading regime put this idea repeatedly to the test and provided it with a regular and recurring set of social consequences. Although occasional doubts were expressed about the possibility of truly knowing an author through anonymous writing alone, we find a variety of writers ready to argue that examination essays are an effective, even superior means for demonstrating one's uniqueness.[2] Indeed, of the many critiques of the examination system, those focusing on the illegitimate transmission of candidates' identities far outnumber any concerns about whether anonymity might be a generally desirable aim. This approach to literary creativity is grounded not on a concept of aesthetic value that arises in conjunction with the development of the market economy, as was the case in early modern Europe, but on a belief in the authenticity of literary voice, as each writer addresses an audience that is composed of writers.

The Implications of Anonymity

The anonymity of the examination essay calls into question the terms on which the aesthetic is usually understood, whether in Ming and Qing discourses of literary value or more recent Western theorizations of the category of the aesthetic. This is an anonymity that holds only temporarily, but it is key to the purpose of the essay and is closely linked to the extreme individuation that can be seen in many *shiwen* in ways that are only superficially paradoxical. Although there are exceptions at other levels, extreme care was taken on the provincial and metropolitan examinations, the crucial middle and upper levels in the system, to ensure that candidate identities remained hidden while their essays were assessed. Each essay was assigned an identification code and was recopied by examination scribes to remove potential hints to identity in a candidate's handwriting, folding of pages, and other secret signs, and the examiners were sequestered during the assessment process. The instant in which the concealed name is revealed was a moment of high drama, but only as a means of translating an assessment that had already been made into its very substantial effects. At the moment of judgment, the examiners are meant to be ignorant of the specific social location of the individual in question.[3]

No less important, ultimately, than the concealment of the name of the writer is the lack of a paratext—usually a preface written by a better-known author—to anchor the essay in a social network at the moment it is first judged.[4] The contrast with poetry, a great deal of which is occasional and rarely appears in collected form without a preface, is striking, and that with classical prose even more so. From Han Yu forward, classical prose is increasingly identified as the mode in which prefaces themselves are to be written, and the majority of classical prose writings preserved from the Ming and Qing are either biographical accounts or prefaces.

Whether preface, account, or inscription, classical prose works are not merely located in a social context but focus their energies primarily on elaborating and solidifying the structure of that context. The absence of these indicators during the bulk of the examination and grading process requires the essay to speak for its author even as its author was thought to be speaking for someone else.[5]

As noted in the introduction, many *shiwen* were either first created or substantially reworked outside of the examination compound, and when those essays that actually were "examination essays" in the fullest sense were published in collected form and began to circulate on the market, they often acquired a classical prose preface that would locate the author within the broader cultural field with at least some specificity.[6] Many other essays were never anonymous in the first place. But given the dominance of examination success as telos and trope, it would be a mistake to discount either the formal or the practical significance of anonymity to the genre.[7]

It is perhaps self-evident that an examination situation with high social stakes will face the challenge of test-takers trying to make use of forbidden or questionable tactics to gain an advantage. The tactics employed in the Ming and Qing fall into four broad categories, only one of which poses true problems for the discourse of anonymity. Candidates could purchase or copy prewritten essays and attempt to smuggle them into the examination compound in the hopes that one or more would contain useful passages. They could attempt to get a sense of what the topics would be in advance to have more time to prepare their own essays, which could be brought in or (more safely) memorized. They could hire more experienced test-takers to stand in for them or rely on others taking the exam at the same time. Finally, they could attempt to use some aspect of the examination essay to signal their identity to a (hopefully) favorably disposed examiner.[8] These types of cheating were problematic from the standpoint of impartial examiners who hoped to identify the "best" candidates, but it is only the last one that actually reintroduces the specific social identity of the candidate in question as a factor in the assessment of the essay.

We can certainly understand this last technique as a social phenomenon—the Qianlong emperor in particular made every effort to counter its effects—but probably one whose successes were relatively few and far between.[9] It may be more useful to think of the discourse surrounding this kind of technique as an index of its second nature as a kind of powerful fantasy, analogous to the wealth of stories of supernatural reward or retribution in the examination compounds.[10] The narratives of candidates meeting with their just deserts (whether divine assistance in writing their essays in return for accumulated good deeds, or failure, illness, or worse as a result of past misdeeds) assert a logic of commensurate return that many failed candidates might otherwise have felt was all too lacking, as we have seen in chapter 3. Similarly, the idea of candidates successfully communicating their names to examiners who were expected not to know them may have been too intriguing to let go of, even if the number of verifiable cases was quite small. Absent further evidence, it seems likely that with certain exceptions (such as the palace examination, where one's calligraphy could provide a key to one's identity) and occasional failures (collusion), anonymity can be understood as the rule of the civil service examination system.[11]

To get a better sense of the challenge that systematized anonymity might pose to conventional approaches to the question of aesthetic value, we may look a little more carefully at the importance of recognizable names to processes of textual evaluation. Stanley Fish's provocative critique of blind peer review provides a useful clarification of what may be at stake when the names of cultural producers are concealed: he argues that the significance of a text cannot be fully understood without reference to the intellectual context in which it is written, with a privileged place accorded previous writings by that same author.[12] Although the particular moment for which Fish's essay was originally written has long passed, and double-blind peer review remains the standard for scholarly journals, the rhetorical basis his argument takes as its foundation is quite revealing. Fish is profoundly concerned with policing the property rights of those authors who could in some way begin to qualify as "founders of discursivity" in Foucault's understanding.[13] The problem with anonymous review is that it diminishes the standing of these authoritative individuals by forcing journal editors and reviewers to take an essay by an unknown on Wordsworth as seriously as one by Geoffrey Hartman; although Fish does not use the term, his objection is to the failure of anonymous review to take the scholarly or professional capital of the producer into full account at the moment the product is first evaluated. Here an analogy to Gui Youguang and Ai Nanying suggests itself: although both were immensely respected as modern prose writers by their peers, Gui succeeded in obtaining the *jinshi* degree only late in life, and Ai never did. We have good reason to expect that their quests for examination success would have had more directly satisfying results if examination essays were submitted for official assessment with their authors' names attached.[14]

In objecting to the institutional failure to pay appropriate tribute to the extensive scholarly or cultural capital accumulated by certain individuals, I would suggest, Fish shows his affiliation with a structure of cultural (and aesthetic) production that is quite familiar in the modern West: only the few produce, while the many consume.[15] Although this dynamic is fundamental to the for-profit publishing market from the late Ming onward, the realm of literature written for exchange (*yingchou*) functions on somewhat different terms.[16] Even this contrast, between a system in which producers and consumers are as segregated as is practical on one hand, and one where differences between individual cultural production are differences in degree rather than in kind, pales before the reality of the examination cell, where producers write for the eyes of other producers, coming as close to modern blind peer review as any system of aesthetic production and evaluation over the course of human history.

Although blind peer review has won an important place in modern scholarship, it is considered much less significant in the processes of aesthetic production, consumption, and evaluation. The example of orchestras that have candidates audition behind a screen to conceal their identities is the exception that proves the rule; the successful candidate comes out from behind the screen once actual performances before paying audiences begin. This brings us to the importance of names and naming in the modern Western aesthetic and to their even more central position in twentieth-century sociological critiques of the aesthetic. I have argued elsewhere that proper names are crucial to Pierre Bourdieu's investigative tactics and to the theoretical constructs he develops to interpret his results. By means of the questionnaire, aesthetic experience is too often reduced to the recognition (or willingness to fake recognition) of items on a list of names—in some cases, names of cultural producers, in other cases, names of cultural products. Although Bourdieu does supplement the recognition of names with inquiries into the appropriate topics for aesthetic representation (what can be an appropriately aesthetic subject for a photograph?) and the interviewees' self-conception of their ease in the different places on the aesthetic hierarchy, it is noteworthy that his surveys do not include any occasions for actual aesthetic encounters.[17] Instead of asking his subjects to listen to a specific piece of music or read a particular text, Bourdieu resorts to name recognition or to general second-order formulations about music and the visual arts. The differences between this "position taking"—these scenes of display and confirmation of cultural capital—and the process by which an anonymous examination essay is evaluated are striking. To the extent that names serve not only as indicators of a certain aesthetic content, but come to supplant the content itself, "aesthetic" discourse as described by Bourdieu is more a manipulation of names as fungible tokens than an engagement with the deeper significance for which these tokens stand. To earn and spend capital, you do not need to know what it represents (stands for ultimately), only what it can be exchanged for.

The complete substitution of names for content is a bleak picture indeed, but without names, how can aesthetic production and evaluation be governed and managed? In the examination context, the individual is represented by the essay submitted, rather than by the name attached to that essay, and the primary element in evaluation is not an instantaneous recognition but a reading process that is a form of labor. It is not that the examiner's assessment of the essay is not relational: his interpretation will have reference to past essays on similar topics or making use of similar techniques. It is certainly possible for him to integrate the essay into a system of names, by likening it to the work of a past master or currently popular stylist. Indeed, candidates could use their answers to the policy questions in particular to signal affiliation with one or another scholarly approach or political faction, and there is clear evidence that this kind of signaling could take place in examination essays on the Four Books as well.[18] But this identification of a particular affiliation, or more generally, an interpretive stance, is in each case *subsequent* to a reading and analysis of the essay—it is an interpretation of a text, rather than recognition of a name—just as the assessment of the individual candidate's worth is subsequent to and dependent on the reading of his essay.

Anonymity of the candidates to be assessed thus has a significant drawback from a bureaucratic perspective. To the extent that equity is ensured by the suppression of candidate names, which could index existing structures of social power in a very meaningful way, examiners are required to find an alternate means of selecting one candidate over another. Even as each candidate hoped to be able to stand out through his writing, each set of examiners wished for a standard by which individual candidates could be differentiated from one another on the basis of their writing.[19] As the problem of candidates writing similar responses transformed resemblance between two authors from a stylistic flaw into a bureaucratic headache—how to choose the handful of "best" candidates from a much larger group if the submitted essays cannot be so differentiated, and how to avoid passing a candidate who presents another's essay from a previous exam cycle as his own—examiners developed a variety of approaches to move candidates away from reliance on successful past essays (readily available in handcopied and printed anthologies by the late fifteenth century) and force them to write in styles that were more clearly distinctive.[20]

As far as possible, then, the examination system abstracts the individual candidate from his social context, forcing him to produce written answers based on what he has brought in with him, whether in the form of learned techniques and texts committed to memory or materials concealed on his person.[21] Despite every attempt of families and literary societies to convert the exam into a process of collective production—through establishing family schools or the publication of literary society essay collections (*sheguo*), or even by hiring famous writers to produce a set of essays for a group of candidates in the family to memorize in advance, among other tactics—the fundamental unit is the individual.[22] In a letter to a friend, Jiao Xun compares examination essays with certain types of classical prose as follows: "The use of examination writing is for the single individual; the use of literature of social exchange is for its one occasion."[23] The emphasis on the bounded individual at work in the exam compound is particularly striking given the tendency in some recent scholarship to question the significance of the individual in central aspects of Ming and Qing cultural production.[24] Indeed, the very idea of the civil service examination system grows out of a denial of social links as a crucial component of governance and attempts to limit the focus to an individual defined with the absolute minimum of reference to his family or factional ties. However compromised this idea may have been in practice, we may say that for elite men in early modern China, there were few experiences of lonely individualism that could compare to the days spent locked in the examination compound.

"Individual Style"

As noted in chapter 2, the clarity with which imperial edicts attempted to mark out the boundaries of acceptable ideology in the early decades of the Ming—by identifying a set of orthodox commentaries to be adhered to in writing one's essay—is matched by a startling silence on questions of style. Writing in the seventeenth century, Ye Xie reminds us that "there is such a thing as oneself establishing a distinctive oeuvre (*zi cheng yijia zhi yan*) in literature, but not when it comes to the Way," and Yu Changcheng writes approvingly of an essay by Tang Shunzhi that "the style is marvelously innovative (*qi*), and the reasoning is orthodox."[25] Dong Qichang writes, "Speaking of examination essays, even though there are words of the Sages and Worthies, how could they not have places waiting for an author to put a particular twist on them?" He advises candidates that "In literary composition one must know what to take and what to leave. What many make dense, I alone make sparse; what many make artful, I alone make awkward; what many make flowery, I alone simplify."[26] Given the many candidates writing in each session each examination year, "I alone" may be counted as a slight exaggeration, but Dong's more general point, that distinctiveness is a primary goal, is clear.

It becomes evident that the best-recognized aspect of the examination system, ideological reproduction, itself already contested with varying degrees of intensity over the Ming and Qing, was from very early on also imbricated with a rather different function, that of aesthetic differentiation. Although ideology and aesthetics, *dao* and *wen*, ultimately cannot be fully separated, it is clear that variation and individuation tended to be more acceptable as long as they could be understood as questions of style, and as we have seen in previous chapters, challenges that were seen to be primarily aesthetic begin several decades before the open ideological clashes of the Wanli era. The literary creativity and individualism for which the late Ming (c. 1550–1650) is regularly celebrated emerges in dialectic fashion from this conflict between literary reproduction and differentiation.[27]

The concept of creating one's own distinctive oeuvre—a phrase that refers back to Sima Qian's postface to the *Historical Records*—is often associated with tropes of standing out in splendid isolation: it is frequently qualified by the modifier *zhuoran*.[28] Usually this distinctive standing out is thought of as typical of classical prose, but the necessity to avoid excessive similarity with the work of other writers is, if anything, more urgent for the examination candidate.[29] We find this emphasis not just in the work of writers who attempt to validate the modern prose essay in a broader context but also in the more instrumental manuals consulted by candidates as they prepared for the examination sessions. As Yuan Huang insists, winning essays "must put forward meaning that other candidates cannot put forward, and must open the mouth that other candidates do not dare to open."[30] This discourse spans the centuries: Fu Xiaqi (1509–94) points out that brilliant writing will allow the candidate to "[stand out] from among ten million and grab the chief examiner's eye"; writing in the seventeenth century, Li Yu highlights the importance of seizing the examiner's attention; and a nineteenth-century critic remarks that "if you want to stand out among the brave troops and seize the enemy's standard first, it is necessary to sweep away loquat husks and put a trademark (*dubiao*) on one's own originality."[31]

Freshness (*xian*) and novelty (*xin* 新) were important values for examination candidates from the mid-Ming on, as they were for late Ming writers like Yuan Hongdao, but interest in uniqueness among modern prose writers is perhaps clearest in the early emphasis on originality (*qi*), which would eventually become one of the cardinal virtues of late Ming literary production.[32] Writing of painting and calligraphy, Katharine Burnett argues that "originality was without question the foremost aesthetic value in seventeenth-century China"; in relating this discourse to its broader cultural context, she supplies a great deal of evidence for the significance of *qi* as a marker of conceptual originality and "an index of the consciously asserted idiosyncratic self" in the literary domain as well.[33] Although *qi* would become dominant in the art world only in the late Ming, and in literary writing generally in the Wanli period, in the examination field this aesthetic quality had begun to constitute a crucial point of contention some decades earlier. As we have seen in chapter 2, struggles over standards of *shiwen* style involve writing that is identified as *qi* as early as the 1530s.

It is no coincidence that *qi* becomes valorized as a key aspect of essay style even as candidates showed new interest in classical prose as a source of inspiration. On a concrete level, as noted in chapter 3, the single-line or "loose" writing thought to be characteristic of classical prose stands as "odd," in contrast to the "even" parallel lines found in modern prose. More abstractly, the "starkly outstanding" nature of an individual author's views advanced in classical prose was seen against the set topics and conventions of examination writing.[34] Within the examination essay, the *poti*, *chengti*, and *dajie* frame elements are for the most part single-line or "odd" prose and are often read as *duanzuo*, the creative voice of the author, whereas the interior parallel sets are often thought to consist of representative speech in the voice of a Sage, Worthy, or other protagonist from the past. Although each of these characterizations is an over-simplification, as we have seen in the rest of this book, and exceptions are legion from the earliest decades of the Ming down to the end of the Qing, the interpretive power and resonance of this discursive structure for writers and critics cannot be ignored.

By the late Ming, it became easy to understand *qi* as a strategy consciously adapted to a competitive environment: "Writing today chases after originality like centipedes on the march."[35] Or as Minister of Rites Li Tingji puts it, writing of examination essays in the Wanli era, everyone "races towards originality": they despise the plain and simple and instead "stride across the boundaries of different spaces, step on their predecessors, and use their writing to become heroes in this world." He goes on to catalog a list of problematic recent trends in examination essay style and concludes, "all of these arise from the liking for originality. How can it be the case that literature is created in order to serve originality?"[36] Jin Sheng's (1589–1645) essay "When the year becomes cold," on the pine and cypress's failure to lose their needles in winter, references this discourse of competitive originality directly, arguing that in the case of the pine and the cypress, it is not that they are actively and intentionally "battling over originality" (*douqi*), their persistence is just the way they naturally are.[37]

Originality that succeeded in one examination cycle soon found imitators. Fang Bao comments that in the process of literary change and adaptation, there are invariably a few authors who descry hints of what is to come; later writers expand greatly in the direction indicated, and eventually a dominant stylistic trend appears.[38] In his more specific assessment of essay style in the Wanli period, Zheng Haoruo argues that Tao Wangling's bracing corrective of problematic tendencies of the time, so distinctive in technique and tone, was itself subsequently transmuted through widespread imitation into "vulgar techniques" and a "vulgar tone."[39]

Even so, *qi* does not lose its status as a standard, despite those who are consciously striving to fake it or mimic it. Lü Liuliang repeatedly privileges originality in his *Collected Remarks on Literary Writing* even as he levels harsh criticism at many other targets in the literary and intellectual world of the late Ming and early Qing. One also gets a sense of the pervasiveness of originality as a standard in the examination system from Shi Chengjin's *Chuanjia bao* (A treasure to be passed down in the family), a work of basic household advice from the early Qing. In addition to reminding candidates to bring stomach medication, avoid staining their exam papers with grease, and make sure not to write nonstandard abbreviated versions of any characters, Shi argues that trying too hard to make your writing original is a bad idea; it is much safer to write the most inoffensive and balanced essay possible and hope to slip through that way. This advice suggests that for every candidate who ground too much ink all at once (the worry: too easy to spill it onto the exam paper), there was probably another who put so much effort into creating a marvelous essay that he ended up with something nearly unreadable instead.[40]

Gong Duqing attributes the dramatic developments in exam essay aesthetics over the course of the sixteenth century largely to the growing market economy and general tendency toward commodification. In this interpretation, innovative and self-consciously literary styles are the textual equivalents of fine silks and high-quality manufactured goods.[41] The frequent use of terms like *shou* to indicate examination success certainly encourages us to understand aesthetic innovation in terms of a market in cultural goods.[42] But competition does not necessarily have to be understood through the metaphor of exchange on an open market; Shang Yanliu and David Rolston, while emphasizing the significance of competition as a motivating force for innovation by *shiwen* writers, avoid taking this extra step.[43] The need to shock examiners who are reading quickly ("looking at flowers from horseback") into paying attention is sufficient to inspire marvelous feats of creativity in prose ("sticking a flower in from horseback").[44] The late Ming writer Chen Longzheng explains that although safe and reassuring writing is fine at the very lowest levels of the examination system, where one's chances of passing are one in two or one in three, once the level of difficulty increases and one's chances are closer to one in fifty, riskier stylistic choices become necessary. "To put aside forty-nine candidates and select me alone, is this possible?"[45] Was it mere coincidence that *Modern Prose on the* Scripture of Hidden Good Deeds includes saving an ant as a deed that might be repaid by winning *zhuangyuan* status?[46]

Fetishism of the Authentic Voice

> When one's nature is different from another's, one's writing is also different. Is that difference not the means by which one's writing is true?
>
> —Mei Zengliang, "*Taiyi zhou shanfang wenji* xu" (22)

> Writing that is original (*qiwen*) comes only from writers who are distinctively original (*qiren*).
>
> —Liang Zhangju, *Collected Words* (*ZYCH* 7/124)

The literary subjectivity often attributed to the late Ming may be understood as the intersection of three specific fields of concern—uniqueness, interiority, and integrity—each with an associated function that operates across the boundaries of categories such as "content," "form," and "social context." These are the contrast function, differentiating one from all others; the depth function, distinguishing surface from interior; and the consistency function, which articulates surface and interior together in a necessary fashion. What is clear is not only the necessity of standing out in writing but also the necessity that such standing out means something important about the individual. How do these functions work in the *shiwen* arena?

Looking backward from the May Fourth era in search of a tradition of writing that valued the authentic individual and could therefore serve as a foundation for a new, "modern" Chinese literature, Zhou Zuoren makes particular note of the concept of "true color" (*bense*), which was forcefully advocated by Tang Shunzhi.[47] Tang is most familiar to us as one of the best-known *shiwen* writers of the sixteenth century, featuring prominently in chapters 2, 3, and 4 of this book. Other authorities on *shiwen* style such as Yuan Huang and Li Guangdi picked up on this emphasis, whether they used Tang's specific term or worded the point somewhat differently. Yuan writes: "I particularly like Tang Shunzhi's remark that 'Since long ago, writers each have their own *bense*.' From this I was enlightened as to the principle of the examinations." According to Tang, writing that lacks *bense* is necessarily inferior; Yuan reiterates this point by arguing that writing that resembles one's *bense* is marvelous no matter what, and writing that does not is invariably corrupt.[48]

But Yuan Huang also makes a slightly different claim, which seems at first as though it might contradict this understanding: he writes that if the mind is a certain way, the writing (*wen*) will also be that way—the writer has no choice in the matter.[49] This theme is picked up in a variety of contexts from the sixteenth century forward, including Yan Shizhang's remark that "Poetry and prose new and old are always able to naturally resemble their authors; the writing in examination essays is even more uninhibited."[50] In the end, however, these two positions are complementary rather than contradictory. The potential issue that arises should an author choose to write in a way that attempts to conceal or disguise his *bense* turns out to have a straightforward solution: the corrupt and inferior writing that inevitably results does tell us something fundamental about the nature of a person who would try to pull this off. In attempting to hide your "true colors," at another level you are revealing them that much more clearly.[51]

The importance of this article of faith to the examination regime cannot be overstated. In a capitalist market system, the phenomenon of commodity fetishism represents value as naturally inhering in commodities themselves, rather than appearing as a result of social processes. The civil service examination system is similarly invested in the necessary authenticity of candidates' essays—the quality of the candidate should be evident from his writing.[52] The ability to grasp this link between writing and author may, however, depend on the skill of the reader. According to Zhang Xuecheng, if you are not able to take in a text at a glance and recognize its author, you are not a good reader.[53] Lou Jian makes use of the abovementioned play between *qi* meaning "odd" (not parallel) and *qi* meaning "originality" to argue that although examination essays rely on the commentaries and adhere to parallel form, readers who are capable can invariably detect "[the author's] originality in his heart, and on reading them will know which are the heroic."[54]

Here we see the depth function in action in the examination essay—a distinctive interior emerges beneath a surface that may seem conventionalized at first.

Does this originality in the text take effort on the part of the author to produce, even as it tasks the reader with the work of detection? The prevailing discourse on classical prose, of course, devalues intentionality and effort on the part of the author. Although modern prose commentators sometimes also privilege writing that comes forth as a natural, effortless flow, the concept of effortful writing leading to a positive transformation of the self, rather than as merely an indication of an inconsistency between an individual's "true color" and his self-presentation, turns out to play a significant part in the discourse on examination writing. Fang Bao, for example, highlights the "return" of the processes of one's mind (*xinshu*) to correctness through *shiwen* writing as self-cultivation; even more important is the effort expended to do justice to one's distinctiveness as an individual.[55] Fu Zhanheng frames individual literary identity as product of writerly skill, motivated by the desire to make one's distinctiveness clear: "Authors (*zuozhe*) are ashamed to lose their 'I' (*wo*), and therefore find a way to make skilled readers recover it, and say 'these are the words of so-and-so'; this is why it is appropriate that modern prose is a hundred times harder than classical prose."[56]

Similarly, Mei Zengliang, whose assertion that individual distinctiveness constitutes authenticity is quoted at the beginning of this section, explains the paradoxical situation in which writers find themselves: the works of the ancients resemble the ancients themselves, while the works of today's writers resemble the works of others. The ancients wrote from feeling, while today's writers write from what they have learned. But this does not mean that one should not study one's predecessors. "[I] study those authors who are similar to me in nature; although this approach begins in falsity, it will eventually yield truth."[57] Mei was one of the more significant members of the Tongcheng School, which was particularly well known for an intertwined lineage of classical and modern prose style. But this approach to *shiwen* writing was not limited to a single school: as mentioned in the previous chapter, Bao Shichen argues that students should have the freedom to choose models that suit their own inclinations and thereby fully develop their own tendencies.[58] In these cases, the literary self is seen to appear to its fullest only as a result of specifically literary work to develop and manifest the author's distinctive nature.

Confucius is said to have remarked, "I transmit but I do not create (*shu er bu zuo*)"; yet the writers who are supposed to give voice to him (and other Sages and Worthies) in *shiwen* think of their work differently.[59] Many insist on using precisely this term—*zuo*—that Confucius avoids to characterize their labor. Dong Qichang scatters references throughout his influential *Nine Instructions*, and in a school manual from the Qing we find the following definition, in which this labor is specifically linked to individual distinctiveness: "Literary composition (*wenzhang*) is making: making means that one creates on the basis of one's own intention (*jiyi zaozuo*)."[60] A century earlier, Wu Zhiwang used analogies drawn from jade-cutting and embroidery to argue the related point that "Literary writing (*wenzi*) is making: making means to create using labor (*gongfu zaozuo*)."[61]

The one who does this work—not just when it results in a fictional masterpiece, but even more so when it produces modern prose—is an author: *zuozhe*.[62] The primary criterion according to which this modern prose *authorship* is assessed is not the quality of the writer's classical scholarship but the distinctive labor on which his writing depends, and the skill with which his inner feelings are expressed: Lu Longji argues that "authors have no choice but to use techniques of drilling and forcing together to create the text" and Su Xiangfeng emphasizes the expression of internal feelings of indignation (*shu suohuai zhi fenji*) as a defining characteristic of an outstanding author of *shiwen*.[63] Examiners who themselves have wrestled with this task judge essays with the muscle memory of their own struggles still fresh.

Autobiography: Speaking for One's Self

In his classic study of Chinese autobiography, Pei-yi Wu notes the infrequency with which authors wrote about themselves using the first person, an approach that he sees gaining wide use only in the late Ming. "Prior to 1560, very few Chinese autobiographers could bring themselves to abandon the posture of the historian and thus to depart from third-person narration."[64] To explain the sudden popularity of autobiographical writing in the late sixteenth and early seventeenth centuries, Wu suggests a causal link to the increasing significance of the theater in late Ming literature and society.[65] Although it is quite possible that writing for the stage served as an inspiration for literati to write their own life scripts, it seems just as likely that the more widespread training in advancing one's cause even while apparently speaking for another so characteristic of *shiwen* played a crucial role. As Wang Heng puts it in the late Ming, "[essay] writing represents my words and simultaneously represents the words of the Sages and Worthies."[66] Although also a playwright, Wang Heng makes this assertion about representative speech in a discussion of techniques of modern prose rather than playwriting. We have seen already how complicated the question of who exactly is speaking can become in the modern prose essay; here my aim is to explore the connections between this complexity and the rise of autobiographical writing in classical prose in the late Ming and Qing that has already been the subject of scholarly attention.

It is worth noting that when Pei-yi Wu and Martin Huang draw a link between autobiography and literati novels, both cite Li Zhi as a key figure in this regard. Given Li Zhi's interest in *shiwen*, this is one more piece of evidence for the significance of modern prose practice as an integral component in the broader project of writing the self.[67] In the case of "Zhuowu lunlüe" (A brief discussion of Li Zhi), Li's 1577 autobiographical narrative, Wu notes that the *lun* genre lends itself to appropriation for autobiographical purposes in that it allows for first-person quotations and allows the author to dispense with other sources.[68] We may add that these two qualities are equally true of *shiwen*, which is often considered to be a special case of the more general *lun* genre. Indeed, the staging of the self as a character who speaks within a narrative frame that provides context, so familiar from examination writing, turns out to be crucial to some of the better-known autobiographical writing in the seventeenth century, such as Fang Yizhi's *Qijie* (Seven solutions) and Zhang Dai's "Self-written Eulogy."[69]

In the first chapter, we noted a dynamic in which an essay writer who makes use of representative speech can be thought of on one hand as a mere actor and on the other as a puppetmaster or ventriloquist, causing the Sages to dance to his will and speak the words he has chosen. To the extent that significant agency resides with the essay writer, he may be understood to appropriate the given topic for use as allegory, to lodge (*jiyu*) his own meaning in the words he writes for another.[70] As Fang Bao

notes of the best writers of the early seventeenth century, "everything
that they wanted in their own hearts to say, they borrowed the topics
in order to express it"; indeed, Fang did not hesitate to make use of the
modern prose essay outside the examination compound to write about
his personal feelings.[71] Yet as hinted at in the first chapter and elaborated
in chapter 4, the distinction between the voices in question—and by
extension, the levels of allegory—is not always simple.

Stephen Greenblatt writes in *Renaissance Self-Fashioning* of the
complicated dialectic relationships between the self and a problematic
other, as well as those between the self and an acknowledged source
of authority in early modern Britain.[72] In the modern prose essay, the
writer is generally expected to speak in convincing fashion on behalf of
a Sage or Worthy—or, in some cases, someone whose moral qualities are
not so uncontroversial—from long ago, and the "other" and "authority"
who remain quite distinct from one another in Greenblatt's account of
Renaissance England turn out to coincide. The sagely authority is in fact
the other with whom the examination writer wrestles as he attempts to
articulate an original individual voice that will speak for that other and
for his own distinctive worth as a candidate. This dynamic takes the
tendency to appropriate the assigned topic for one's "own" use to another
level. We are no longer considering a writer with clear agency making
use of a scrap of text as an opportunity to develop an individual argument but an ongoing process of subjectivity construction, in which the
very potential for agency that may accrue to "the writer" is distinguished
from the represented subjectivity of the Sage.

By regularly working through the practical question of how to create
a voice of one's own, to be more or less distinctly delineated from the
voice of another, the candidate acquires lengthy training in the rhetorical
techniques through which one's subjectivity can be convincingly articulated. Writing in the late Ming on modern prose, Shen Hongtai made
the general claim that "In [essay] writing, 'You' and 'I' must shape each
other (*wen yao er wo xiangxing*)"; a century later, Zhang Taikai identifies
this trope as a writerly technique (*yongbi*), an instance of the "guest-host
relationship" that Dong Qichang found to be central to the structure of
modern prose.[73]

In a discussion of his *bildung* through the examination process,
sixteenth-century writer Qu Jingchun gives us three examples from his

own life in which he wrote *shiwen* to record and explain his thoughts and feelings at a given moment: one mentioned in chapter 4; another in which he uses an essay on the topic "King Wen possessed two of the three parts of the empire, and with those he served the dynasty of Yin" to explain how he dealt with an old enemy who came to his door looking for trouble; and finally an essay on "The marabou is on the dam," concerning his decision to take a concubine. Indeed, the form of Qu's account is that of an autobiography structured around his life experiences with the examination system in its various aspects, beginning when his frustration with the results of his scattered early efforts reaches a crisis point. Inspired by a passage from the *Zhuangzi*, he secludes himself for three months of meditation, at the end of which he returns to society transformed and thoroughly restructures his approach to all aspects of daily life.[74]

The sense that one's writing and one's person are indissolubly linked can be explained through a naive normative conception of good writing as directly expressive of the essence of the individual (in which case art is merely the negative skill of allowing the subject's aesthetic quality to reveal itself unhindered and unaltered). Alternatively, we see in Qu's case a sentimental insistence that the very practice of writing changes the writer, disciplining the body and mind in distinctive and lasting fashion. The aesthetic product in the exam system is ultimately the self, not just the essay. This is not, then, a simple post hoc mimesis of a preexisting essence but rather representation as a process of subject formation. Through the very aesthetic requirements that the literati as a class set themselves over the course of the Ming, it becomes clear to the candidate that standing out as an individual or establishing a distinctive literary oeuvre is not simply a matter of letting one's own words flow forth but a struggle to mark out a space for the writing self in relation to the "I" performed in the main sections of the essay. For all too many theorists of classical prose writing in the Ming and Qing, the writing self and the "I" that is performed must coincide perfectly or the text cannot be considered literary; once the modern prose essay has been definitively and explicitly formulated in terms of "speaking for the Sages and Worthies" in the seventeenth century, it can no longer count as literary. By failing to engage seriously with the challenges posed by the *shiwen* form, these critics end up repeating the simple assertion that literary technique consists of nothing more than getting out of the way of your own intention as it naturally finds its expression in words. This assertion is repeated often enough, and in formulaic enough fashion, that it comes to rival the most thoroughly imitated *shiwen* that it presumes to criticize in its ubiquity.[75] What this approach loses is any sense of the dynamism and flexibility of a personality that is constructed as it constructs.

It comes as no surprise that the golden age of modern prose leads into the "golden age of Chinese autobiography," which in turn was followed by "the steady rise of autobiographical tendencies in the novel," or in slightly different terms, the formation of a new subjectivism and individualism in literary writing.[76] Throughout the seventeenth and eighteenth centuries, prefaces written to introduce the classical prose of other authors also increasingly insist on first-person references that draw resonance from their usage in *shiwen* beginning more than a century earlier and are increasingly likely to reference the writer's own experiences when appropriate.[77] It would be a mistake to deny the possibilities of self-writing in earlier periods in Chinese history, before representative speech became standard practice in examination writing. It would likewise be a mistake to overlook the extension and transformation of these practices, especially in the prose field, once an entire social class had been set to work by the examination system to construct distinctively individual voices in the Ming. This *work*, ultimately, is what has been neglected, whether by approaches to cultural capital inspired by Bourdieu, where labor is crowded out of the picture through an extension of commodity fetishism to the cultural field, or by Ming and Qing discourses of literary authenticity, in which the effort of writing is discounted.

It is not only that examiners and candidates alike did not need to rely on the rapidly growing late Ming market in all sorts of refined commodities to be pushed toward innovation. What is more significant is that the impulses toward originality that began within the examination system, and the related forms through which aspirations to originality were realized, had a substantial effect on the entire literary sphere outside of the examination system as it expands dramatically through the last century of the Ming dynasty. For every publisher motivated to bring an intriguing new text to market and capitalize on its originality, there was an author whose sense of literary creativity takes examination writing as a negative example—what to avoid—*and* as a positive (though often unacknowledged) foundation on which concepts such as literary identity and originality are based. The discursive emphasis on literary originality throughout the many genres and types of writing in the Ming and Qing cannot be fully understood without reference to an examination system that requires of its candidates that they distinguish themselves as individuals primarily through means that are defined as stylistic.

Shiwen in the World: Three Moments

The preceding chapters have examined specific aspects of *shiwen* aesthetics, including voice, parallelism, and the articulation of individual subjectivity. Here I take a broader perspective on the place that modern prose essays of the Ming and Qing occupy in the global history of literary work in the age of mechanical reproduction, a perspective centered on three key dynamics: literate administration, the diligence of readers and writers, and the discourse of involution.

There is a tradition of locating China outside the general flow of world history, from Hegel to Marx to Wittfogel, with effects that linger to the present day. From the Asiatic mode of production to hydraulic civilization to the tributary mode of production, the unusual dominance of the state form as mode of production is a regular theme. More recent disputes about the nature and causes of a "great divergence" between Western Europe and China in the nineteenth century, although less preoccupied with the state itself, have continued to frame this question in terms of a contrast between involution and development.[1]

As a written genre that stands as the very symbol of the bureaucratic order that is thought to dominate a state-centered mode of production, *shiwen* would seem to epitomize one pole of this distinction in literary terms. It is not only that modern prose essays can be understood as a bureaucratic product, but that their form—to the extent that it appears carefully balanced, involutionary rather than evolutionary or revolutionary in development—seems to import the bureaucratic mentality into the structure of the text. If China is "outside the World's History" (in Hegel's words) and in ways that are intimately connected with its supposedly meritocratic process of bureaucratic recruitment, it might seem that the *shiwen* genre would have little to contribute to broader comparative literary and cultural criticism.[2] In this epilogue, I suggest that the opposite is the case; I aim to reintegrate the modern prose essay into global histories of literary work by highlighting its ability to call into question the very terms on which the literary is asserted.

Over the past few decades, historians have challenged the trope of China as autonomous and isolated from the broader world to great effect, in projects ranging from archival research on the place of silver in Chinese society to more general macrohistorical critiques such as *ReORIENT* and *Adam Smith in Beijing*.[3] These scholars focus on the economic strength and dynamism of the Chinese market in the long term, arguing that this economy more than any other has served to propel global development over the past millennium. This new approach to economic history has literary implications. As Ning Ma makes clear in her groundbreaking *Age of Silver*, a more nuanced historical understanding of world market formation allows for a thorough reimagination of the terms on which Franco Moretti refers to the novel as "the first planetary genre." Instead of visualizing branches from a single trunk with roots in Western Europe, Ma details a phenomenon that arises nearly simultaneously in locations that are geographically distinct (China, Spain, Japan, and Britain) but find themselves newly connected through the silver trade.[4]

At first glance, it seems that *shiwen* suffer in contrast to the novel, which benefited greatly from this trade in silver. The modern prose essay was in fact temporarily abandoned in the 1660s as a standard means for selecting officials in the wake of a dynastic change that was tied in part to uncertainty in the global supply and transport of silver. If we take the long view, however, it becomes clear that the modern prose essay is no mere passive recipient of silver shocks but plays an integral, though indirect, part in the initiation and maintenance of that trade on a global scale. Here I suggest that in addition to appreciating the reach of this intensified market in silver, we should pause to consider the orientation of its flow and the reasons the Chinese economy in particular exerts such a strong attractive force in the early modern period, such that one Portuguese author wrote that silver "wanders throughout all the world in its peregrinations before flocking to China, where it remains, as if at its natural center."[5]

Literate Administration

The attraction that inspires this flow of silver stems largely from the size, coherence, and stability of the Chinese economy relative to the rest of the early modern world. These three interrelated qualities cannot be understood in isolation from the Ming-Qing administrative system, staffed on the basis of writing, reading, and selecting *shiwen*. This bureaucratic system allowed an economy of unprecedented scale and demand for silver to develop, and further provided enough stability for that social order to withstand a silver shock and dynastic conquest in quick succession, without measurably reducing the long-term appetite for silver that had become so important to the economies of mining and exporting nations in the Americas, Europe, and elsewhere in Asia. Leaving aside the very real direct material effects of the examination system and its associated industries on the Chinese economy—in the realms of publishing, travel, and education, among others—we may ask: how does this system work to organize and sustain a prosperous social order more generally?[6] How did individuals' and families' investments in the modern prose genre serve as resource for the expansion and ballast for the stabilization of the state?

Modern scholars have answered this question in great historical and sociological detail; the work of Iona Man-Cheong and Alexander Woodside in particular is intriguing for their comparative emphasis.[7] Man-Cheong turns Benedict Anderson's account of the means by which the nation could be imagined against him, demonstrating the usefulness of the synchronized writing and grading of examination essays to the coherent organization of that "Middle Kingdom" against which Anderson had defined his European "imagined communities." Although Man-Cheong does not directly challenge Anderson's use of China as a prime example of a traditional polity organized around a "sacred language," she provides a nuanced explanation of the ways in which Anderson's account of novels with multiple narrative strands and simultaneous newspaper reading as "technical means for 're-presenting' the *kind* of imagined community that is the nation" works equally well for candidates in examination compounds, where "everyone involved did the same task at the same time, mostly physically unseen by each other but *imaginable* to that community."[8] Woodside goes a step further, destabilizing conventional Eurocentric narratives of modernity from a different perspective by teasing out rationalization from capitalism on one hand and industrialization on the other, suggesting in the process that key aspects of the modernity that we have convinced ourselves we see in nineteenth- and twentieth-century Europe and Great Britain derive from careful study of Chinese models.[9] In this view, the civil service examination system is a crucial element in the global history of bureaucratic rationalization, a history in which questions that have only recently begun to arise in Western bureaucracies have a centuries-long history of discussion in the Chinese context.

In the writings of European critics contemporary to some of the essays I have discussed in this book, we see similar understandings, differently expressed. For British writers of the late seventeenth century, as well as in the decades following, there was an evident connection between the literate administrative officials they understood to be typical of China and government that was coherent across wide ranges of geographic and regional variation, stable and long-lasting. The society that could depend on these officials and this government was in consequence prosperous beyond European measure.[10] At a moment of crisis in the union of England and Scotland in 1703, for example, Andrew Fletcher argued that the Chinese civil service system provided an inspiration for any state that "contains divers kingdoms" as a means to extend a cohesive and systematic government to all. Several decades before this, John Webb drew on a range of sources to highlight the stability of the examination system— and the bureaucracy staffed by "Literati" more generally—through the transition from Ming to Qing. William Temple wrote approvingly of the durability of the Chinese "constitution and government" and proposed study of a Chinese model, in which class distinctions are not between "Noble and Plebeian," but between "Learned and Illiterate," to assist in reconstructing the British aristocracy.[11] A meritocratic order that was desirable for its beneficial social effects was fundamentally linked to a literary mode of bureaucratic recruitment, which involved "strict enquiries and questions both of language and learning, and much critic upon the several writings, produced by the several pretenders, and submitted to the examiners."[12]

> At which examinations, as the Doctors of the Chaire in the Universities with us, with much more diligence and rigour nevertheless, and indeed with great severity, they appose and make trial what Proficients those that stand Candidates for preferment are become in their Literature

and Characters of their Language, in the study of which by their books written, not only their Learning, but also the Elegancy of their Speech consisteth.[13]

Although some of their Chinese contemporaries would have denied that *shiwen* could be considered *wen*, it is unlikely that Fletcher, Temple, and Webb—or for that matter, French thinkers such as Turgot and Quesnay—would have hesitated to count the Chinese modern prose essay as literature.[14]

Questions of literary style have been closely connected to distinctive economic paradigms with broad social effects in China as recently as the nineteenth century and as far back as the Han dynasty.[15] I turn to a sixteenth-century modern prose essay by a person whose "several writings" won him the opportunity eventually to play a crucial role in the intensification of silver flow into China: Zhang Juzheng. As Grand Secretary, Zhang was responsible for the Single Whip reform of the late sixteenth century, which stipulated that taxes be paid in silver rather than in kind; in this essay we see an early example of his concern for maximizing the economic strength of the state by encouraging production. Writing on the topic of "There is a great course also for the production of wealth" from the *Daxue* (Great learning), Zhang does not hesitate to bend the original text to his purposes: an ideology of "endless accumulation" of wealth by the state reminiscent of that which Braudel proposes as the beginning of capitalism in the West.[16]

> If [the populace] works diligently (*qin*) by focusing on the
> 　　root, the influx of resources will be inexhaustible;
> If [the ruler] controls use by means of frugality, the outflow of
> 　　resources will be limited.
> When inexhaustible resources supply limited uses:
> Those below will always contribute and those above will always
> 　　be in surplus; even if there is a great crisis in the realm,
> 　　there will naturally be resources in the inner and outer
> 　　palaces to draw on and there will be no shortfall.[17]

Coming at the very end of the *Great Learning*, a text that moves from individual sincerity and commitment through the ordering of one's family to the establishment of virtue throughout the realm, the selected topic is originally part of a section dedicated to benevolent government that takes the interest of the people as its own. For the *Great Learning*, virtue is the source and the material wealth that accumulates in the state is merely derivative. As a result of the ruler's virtue, there will be followers; on the basis of these followers, the state will take territorial shape; this territory will produce material wealth, which then can be used.

Rather than directly confront this paradigm in which material resources are decidedly subsidiary, not to mention the assertion earlier in the passage from the *Great Learning* that a state that emphasizes the accumulation of material wealth will scatter its people (*cai ju ze min san*), Zhang shifts the terms of discourse in the *qijiang* of his essay with two claims: "One gathers followers by means of material wealth" and "the proper administration of wealth is called justice." These claims draw from the following words in the *Yijing* (Book of changes): "How can the ruler gather followers? Through material wealth. The proper administration of that wealth, correct instructions, and prohibitions against wrongdoing by the people constitute justice."[18] Although Zhang would have had no difficulty finding references to material wealth in the Four Books and the Five Classics that echo the *Great Learning*'s assertion that such wealth should be considered secondary, he instead makes a point of citing the rare canonical passage that identifies material wealth as a primary factor in building the state. In the process, he reverses the logical sequence in the original text, where wealth had been identified as the natural result of followers accumulating, rather than as the necessary means of attracting them in the first place.

The assigned topic from the *Great Learning* emphasizes the importance of generosity and a sense of proportion on the part of the ruler, with great states refusing to stoop to squeezing small sums from individual producers, and suggests that officials who steal from the state are less problematic than those who are too exacting toward the people. In striking contrast, Zhang's essay pairs a call for frugality in government with an insistence that the people must be driven (*qu*) to diligence. From generosity as a means to inspire production, we have moved to discipline as a means to reduce waste and, more significantly, to discipline as a means to maximize production.

This concept of diligent labor is of central importance, as the term *qin* (diligent, industrious) appears no fewer than three times in the essay. *Qin* is not a term much used in the Four Books, nor does it appear in the standard commentary to the selection assigned to Zhang as a topic. *Qin* appears prominently, however, in the *Sanzi jing* (Three character classic), a popular instructional text dating from the Southern Song, where diligence is presented as a key virtue of people who study texts, including those preparing for the civil service examinations. After citing several examples of diligent individuals, the *Three Character Classic* concludes with the following words: "Diligence has merit, play yields no advantage. Be forewarned! It is suitable to make the effort."[19] In his essay, Zhang Juzheng takes this diligent reading and writing expected of aspiring examination candidates and applies it as a universal pattern for labor throughout society.

The emphasis on diligent work even—or especially—among members of the dominant classes must certainly have come as a shock to European elites in the early modern period. For some, the idea of social rank that is not merely inherited but primarily earned was attractive for its potential as a corrective to aristocratic idleness. This approach promised to go beyond mere administrative efficacy to reimagine the processes of class reproduction.[20] It sparked the enthusiasm of Robert Burton, who wrote in his *Anatomy of Melancholy* that "Their Lau-Sie, Mandarins, Literati, Licentiates, and such as have raised themselves by their worth, are their noblemen only, thought fit to govern a state."[21] The contrast with British nobility, too many of whom "hawk, hunt, eat, drink, game alone," was unmistakable. Similarly, William Temple concluded, "Honour and respect is no where paid to nobility and riches so much as it is here to virtue and learning . . . every one seeking preferment here only by merit, attributes to it that of other men."[22] Although the eighteenth and nineteenth centuries would see increasingly critical discourses on China taking root, this concept of a bureaucratic administration staffed through competitive selection played a crucial and continuing role in the formation and consolidation of state power in Europe and the United States through the end of the nineteenth century.[23] The broader discourse of class reproduction as pervasive competitive striving that extends across the entire reach of the social canvas has been slower to spread, but at our own particular historical moment has come to feel increasingly powerful.

Diligence and Literature

What does this literary diligence look like, practically speaking? Exhortations to diligence are legion in the Ming and Qing, from general works with nearly universal circulation like the *Three Character Classic* and the *Quanxue wen* (Encouragement of learning) to more specialized works tailored to particular aspects of study, like the *Manual on Reading and Writing*. In his discussion of literary writing, the founder of the Donglin Academy, Gu Xiancheng, remarks that "reading and writing are the most labor-intensive tasks in life"; his advice is to "take pleasure in the work they require."[24] Responses to these exhortations were necessarily mixed. We need only consider the reactions of fictional characters like Baoyu in *Dream of the Red Chamber* and Qu Xianfu in *The Scholars* to get some idea of how calls to diligence could fail to inspire. But an existing copy of the *Manual on Reading and Writing*, rich with note slips pasted in the margins, gives us a sense of the effect the insistence on diligence could have on students who were more open to this type of literary work. The unidentified reader of this copy jotted down notes that range from specific month-by-month plans for a schedule of preparatory meditation to instructions to repeat certain phrases over and over again.[25]

This conjunction of units of time and words was no accident: as we have seen in chapter 3, the Ming and Qing associations dedicated to "cherishing time" and "cherishing written characters" suggest that one crucial aspect of this diligence is the careful management and use of resources available. But the individual written characters were not mere tokens to measure one's progress—they were also the distinctive building blocks of the essays that students learned to produce.

The careful attention to questions of textual structure and the dynamics of rhetoric in *shiwen* led to a new understanding of literary writing in terms of crafts like sewing and carpentry. Rather than flowing forth naturally as *wen*, texts were constructed piece by piece, and those pieces themselves were cut to fit one to another. It is impossible to overstate the importance of the small topic phenomenon in this connection. Once it was acceptable for examiners to cut and join canonical texts to construct a topic, in some cases setting candidates a topic that consisted of a single word alone, how could it not be acceptable for a candidate to approach the writing process in a similar frame of mind?

Given the new attention to the materiality of the literary text implied in this emphasis on words themselves (*zi*), it comes as no surprise that critics in the Ming and Qing begin to supplement accounts of *wen* with discussions of a somewhat different category: *wenzi*. As Wu Zhiwang explains it, "Literary writing (*wenzi*) is making; this making is creation through the use of labor (*gongfu*). Jade becomes a vessel only through carving, embroidery becomes a complete work through organization, and words and deeds become literature only through composition."[26] The idea of literary work as a hands-on craft yields in turn a new sense of the writer as creator, constructor, and fabricator—*zuozhe*—discussed in chapter 5. This individual, who appears only rarely in earlier works of general literary criticism like *Wenfu* (Rhapsody on literature) and *Literary Mind and the Carving of Dragons*, shows up regularly in *shiwen* criticism and eventually in commentaries to Ming-Qing fiction and drama commentary. Indeed, it is *pingdian* commentary—so closely tied to the examination complex—that provides a platform on which to speculate about the author in great detail. Whether interpreting authorial intent or judging the quality of specific word choices, sentence patterns, or paragraph structures, the commentary makes frequent and extended reference to the role of the author as originator and organizer of the text in question. Like the examiner whose careful punctuation and assessment of an essay is aimed at evaluating the person who wrote it, the newly engaged readers of the Ming and Qing freely mark up texts and do not hesitate to leave evidence of their views of the author understood to be behind that text in the process.

It is evident that *wenxue*, the modern term for literature, is no simple replacement for *wen* but a reconceptualization of the category that retains certain elements in a new setting, with new companions. The contents of premodern *wenji* (poetry and classical prose) are, for the most part, well represented among the texts now studied in departments of Chinese literature as *gudai wenxue* (premodern or traditional literature). They are complemented, however, by a range of texts drawn from a different, vernacular canon of novels, short stories, and plays, championed by early twentieth-century intellectuals like Liang Qichao, Hu Shi, and Zheng Zhenduo. But this shift from *wen* to *wenxue*, as sudden as it may seem in normative elite discourse, built on the *longue durée* of changes in literary practice over the course of the Ming and Qing. Ironically, *shiwen*, a genre whose relationship with *wen* had always been fraught and one of the few types of originally excluded writing not subsequently drawn into the new category of *gudai wenxue*, turns out to have played a crucial role in this long-term transformation of written practice. At home in neither the *wenji* of the past nor the academic field of *gudai wenxue* to come, *shiwen* stand nonetheless at the inflection point between the two.

We saw in chapter 1 that claims to similarity between examination writing and dramatic works were advanced by some playwrights and connoisseurs in the late Ming and early Qing as a means to elevate the status of works for the stage. According to Wu Qiao, "If the eight-legged essay is an elegant genre, then *The Western Chamber* and *The Lute* should not be rejected as vulgar, since they similarly speak for other people."[27] Commentators writing on vernacular narratives also frequently made reference to *shiwen* to support their claims for the merits of fiction and the skill of individual authors. In this sense, modern prose opens the door for vernacular fiction and drama to be taken seriously in literary terms. My interest here is not so much in the explicit arguments made for these vernacular genres in the Ming and Qing, but in the everyday practice—the habits of writing and reading—that laid the necessary groundwork for such arguments to suddenly command broad and enthusiastic assent as the Qing was replaced by the Republic.

Once these principles of diligent writing and reading were regularly applied to vernacular narrative and drama in the seventeenth century, it became common in turn to see these genres as an appealing entry point for candidates learning the craft of writing essays. If the questions of narrative structure and voice could also be explored in the vernacular genres, and the stories were more engaging than those found in the classical canon, why not supplement mastery of the Four Books and Five Classics with attentive and interested reading of novels and plays from which these principles could be absorbed more pleasurably?[28]

In this application of specific practices of reading and writing across generic boundaries, what we find is the gradual formation of a new kind of literary field. Although this field is more concrete than the broadest conceptions of *wen*, which subsume nearly all forms of culture under the sign of the pattern, it is significantly more general than any of the specific genres of *wen*, such as regulated verse, rhapsody, song lyric, or travel account, and more comprehensive in scope than conventional collected works (*wenji*). This field allows for aesthetics of appreciation and analyses of form that are not tied to one genre but are appropriate to any piece of writing the reader deems worthy of investing effort into reading seriously. As Huang Qiang suggests, the most suitable term for this more general field is in fact *wenzi*, a category to which even the most exacting critics will allow *shiwen*, and in most cases, plays and novels as well, to belong.[29] When some writers complain about readers who use "*shiwen* eyes" to read classical prose or poetry, what is at stake is that these genres of *wen* too are now being treated as *wenzi*. By the eighteenth century, individual "words and phrases" (*ziju*) vied with more general structural patterns for the attention of literary critics.[30]

The fact that *shiwen* would rarely—and novels, vernacular short stories, and plays never—win inclusion into the *wenji* publication format should not distract us from the fact that over the four centuries between 1500 and 1900, these types of *wenzi* were written, published, and read in ever greater numbers, occupying correspondingly increasing investments of time and energy on the part of the reading public, inspiring commentaries, sequels, and public dispute. In this sense, the formal recognition of vernacular genres as *wenxue* in the early twentieth century, spurred in part by the commonalities seen between these genres and those dominant in the nineteenth- and twentieth-century West, was also a belated acknowledgment of the practical reality that consumption of the texts found in *wenji* had long since been outstripped by attention to *shiwen* and vernacular genres at all levels of literate society. It is no accident that Wenchang, originally the patron saint of the examinations, who eventually added written characters more generally to his portfolio, had by this point extended his authority to cover the entirety of print culture.[31]

I have argued elsewhere that *zi* is particularly well suited to figure the concrete processes of cultural reproduction. As Xu Shen explains it, "'*Wen*' are the roots of all images and things. '*Zi*' means to be fruitful, multiply, and gradually increase."[32] *Wenzi* is a field where diligence in reading and especially writing can be applied without apology. It is also a field suited by its very name to an era in which texts become mechanically reproducible on a large scale, especially when contrasted with *wen* as such. Anxiety about ruining texts by breaking them down into their constituent parts is matched among critics of *shiwen* by an anxiety about uncontrolled reproduction of texts, especially essays, whether by unscrupulous publishers or by candidates who sought to gain an advantage. As Lothar Ledderose has shown, there is a long tradition of modular production of a wide variety of different goods from the earliest periods.[33] The application of this modular approach to literary texts posed a challenge to readers and writers not just of *shiwen* but also of vernacular fiction, as the narrator of *Dream of the Red Chamber* points out in his critique of the scholar-beauty romances that were so popular in the early modern period.[34]

Industry and Involution

The shift in readers' and writers' investment from a strictly limited field referred to as *wen* to the broader and more contentious arena of *wenzi* over the course of the Ming and Qing has intriguing correspondences with the transformation of the word *literature* in eighteenth- and nineteenth-century Europe.[35] In material terms, each of these shifts is closely linked to a rapid expansion in the publishing industry. Conceptually speaking, they represent a new interest in creative and imaginative writing—writing that in a Chinese context could be designated as *xu*—as fiction and drama claim a central place in the category of the literary. Finally, each proposes a certain, though limited, autonomous status for the literary field, as we saw in chapter 2. In these senses, the reinvention of *wenxue* at the turn of the twentieth century as a translation for contemporary Western understandings of "literature" is merely a belated discursive acknowledgment of similarities that had long existed in practice between "literature" and *wenzi*. The parallels break down, however, when we try to read the literary against its broader social contexts.

The story of literary production in Europe is often told as a transition from a type of patronage production in a small community to a modern and relatively autonomous status in which the economic sphere constitutes both a partner and an antagonist.[36] By contrast, in China the market acquires decisive social importance significantly earlier than in Europe (twelfth century CE) but is eclipsed as a dominant structuring force in the lives of cultural producers by the civil service examination system—already well established in the eleventh century and of central importance by the early fifteenth century. In the late sixteenth and early seventeenth centuries—an era whose intensive commercialization and urbanization inspired the "sprouts of capitalism" school of historical research—drama and long vernacular fiction flourish to an unprecedented degree. But the number of people who made a living writing in or publishing these genres would have been orders of magnitude smaller than those making a living from teaching examination preparation, writing preparation manuals, and editing collections of sample essays.[37] Indeed, in almost every case, novelists and playwrights would also have participated in the examination system at least as candidates and in some cases as examiners, critics, or editors of essay collections. In terms of sheer volume of books sold, critics from the 1500s through the early 1900s generally agree that examination preparation materials were among the most popular genres.[38]

If nineteenth-century French poetry finds its primary antagonist in the market, with each poet forced to take a position that places more or less emphasis on publishers' and audiences' demands—in the process also taking a position within the subfield of restricted production that is more or less dominant—writers in Ming and Qing China confront a highly developed commercial publishing market and even more imposing administrative system that ranks educated individuals primarily with specific reference to their aesthetic accomplishment on a series of examinations. It is this examination regime that serves as the ultimate motivation for much of the production, exchange, and consumption that constitute the commercial publishing market. Even more significant, this regime constitutes the ultimate ground of an economy of social obligations expressed in cultural (primarily literary) terms: *yingchou zhi wen*, or the literature of social exchange. It is here, and most emphatically not in Europe or the Americas, that we see a phenomenon that begins to approach a "cultural capital" invested on a large scale to reap returns denominated culturally.

How can we think of the aesthetic in circumstances under which the market—whether more or less capitalist in spirit and practice—is not the single context within which and against which the aesthetic takes shape, but is only one system in society and not necessarily the dominant? How might the aesthetic need to be rethought if literature of significance is produced not only by poets who identify as "legislators" in a metaphysical sense but also by actual administrators (and would-be administrators) who engage in prose and poetry writing? What turns out to be crucial here is not a stark contrast between state and market but the distinction between producers who are writing for other producers, and producers who are writing for mere consumers; or more precisely, the relative significance of these two different modes of literary production in different contexts. We have touched on this distinction already in discussions of speaking in a representative voice, the claims that are made for an authentic self, and writing in the first person. Here I would like to consider it in more general terms.

Writing of early eighteenth-century England, Daniel Defoe imagines authors as just one kind of employee: "The Booksellers are the Master Manufacturers or Employers. The several Writers, Authors, Copyers, Sub-writers, and all other Operators with Pen and Ink are the workmen employed by the said Master Manufacturers."[39] As Bourdieu explains it, the early nineteenth century then marks a moment of relative emancipation for these "employees," as a restricted, semi-autonomous field of cultural production forms within the broader compass of a market denominated in material capital. Most writing is done by professional writers and consumed by readers who do not write for a living. These works are properly understood *not* as vehicles of cultural capital to be invested, but rather as "goods" (*biens*) or resources to be obtained, preserved, displayed, and consumed by members of the bourgeoisie in general as part of a much larger drama of capitalist material production. Under these conditions, literature written by producers primarily for other producers—avant-garde writing—is in material terms only a small-scale negation of the logic of a broader market in which professionals write for consumers.

In Ming and Qing China, however, it is more appropriate to think of texts written for payment (*maiwen wei sheng*) not as the horizon against which all other texts should be judged but as an effective absorption mechanism for surplus literary production capacity that originates in a different arena. This surplus production capacity arises in a literary system that operates on the fundamental principle that producers write first and foremost for other producers. In an essay on the topic "The woman would have excess cloth," Tang Xianzu defends the exchange of surplus cloth and grain on the market as logically secondary to the spontaneous forces of household production but at the same time necessary to maintain that production in balance.[40] Similarly, the core function of literary training in the Ming and Qing was as a means of class reproduction in which producers write first for other members of the producing class—whether as examination candidates writing for examiners, or as men and women writing literature of exchange to establish themselves among their peers. Writing for paying consumers who do not themselves write is not a basic condition under which literary production takes place, but an epiphenomenon that works to keep excess production capacity from becoming a social problem. Writing for other writers, on the other hand, is class work, a means for the reproduction of the literati class as a whole, whether mediated through the examination system, exchanges of poetry and prose, or in some cases profitable sales.

Writers who "sell their writing in order to live," like Defoe's "Operators with Pen and Ink," engage primarily in Marx's C-M-C cycle: they produce commodities to sell in exchange for money, which they then use to purchase the commodities that they themselves need to live, such as food and shelter. In contrast, writers who engage in the literature of social exchange are not selling their writing: they are investing it, with the aim of eventually claiming yields that are also denominated in cultural terms. To give a simple example, writing a preface for another author's collected writings, one has the potential to later request a preface in return from that author or from a third party who happens to be indebted to that author. Although such potential gains could always be converted into cash, that conversion is not necessarily the ultimate aim. If we were to call anything cultural capital—I have written elsewhere of the contradictions inherent in this term as it is usually employed—it is what is at stake in this literary exchange.[41] Invested literary potential aims at returns in that same coin, and a social class of producers is defined in the process. What is particularly important in this context is that there is nothing comparable in Europe or the United States in the nineteenth and twentieth centuries. By this point in the West, literary producers have narrowed to a profession rather than a class; their production is consumed within a market framework as commodities rather than employed as investment vehicles.

What are the social and theoretical implications of an aesthetic that is conceived primarily in terms of investment and production ("genius") rather than consumption ("taste")? The aesthetic in Western Europe, preoccupied with consumption, leads to questions of value, which serve to explain the workings of taste, articulate the concept of the commodity, and make sense of the market economy. In Ming-Qing China, an emphasis on production instead leads to questions of authenticity, with each writer relying on skill and diligence to articulate a distinctive voice, whether formally in the examination compound or informally in the back and forth of literate social exchange. In this context, the more potential a type of cultural product has to define one's class standing, the more thoroughly the *prises de position* through which one imagines the social place of that product are necessarily imbricated in a corresponding investment of labor to realize it.[42] Diligent work is always necessary, even for "cultural capitalists," and the object of that work is not just the text one writes but also the self that writes.

I have used the descriptive word *involutionary* in this book to designate a particular intensification of parallel style that is found primarily in the modern prose essay. Chapter 3 explains involutionary dynamics in the processes of reading and writing texts; the second half of chapter 4 argues that these dynamics elaborate a shifting and complicated literary voice that resembles the free indirect discourse characteristic of the modern novel in important ways. One's "own voice" does not in the end flow out automatically but turns out to be a constructed product like any other, the result of diligent application.

Involution is a charged term, however, that has also played a key role in the work of economists and social historians who wrestle with questions of comparative development and the "great divergence." For most of these scholars, the intensification characteristic of involution defines a form of labor that in its application to limited resources is inherently less productive than it could be. Geertz writes of farmers in Java "driving their terraces, and in fact all their agricultural resources, harder by working them more carefully."[43] It is intriguing that Geertz draws this term, which would become so important in twentieth-century histories of Asian socioeconomic development, not from the work of economists or sociologists but from an essay by Alexander Goldenweiser on the nature of decoration and adornment in the "primitive" work of art:

> But there are also instances where pattern merely sets a limit, a frame, as it were, within which further change is permitted if not invited. . . . The pattern precludes the use of another unit or units, but it is not inimical to play within the unit or units. The inevitable result is progressive complication, a variety within uniformity, virtuosity within monotony. This is *involution*. A parallel instance, in later periods of history, is provided by what is called ornateness in art, as in the late Gothic. The basic forms of art have reached finality, the structural features are fixed beyond variation, inventive originality is exhausted. Still, development goes on. Being hemmed in on all sides by a crystallized pattern, it takes the function of elaborateness.[44]

How interesting that theories of economic development should find themselves beholden, in their representation of the material world, to a trope that originates in the aesthetic assessment of works of art. Can we in fact draw a clear distinction between involution and development in the comparative history of different societies that is not ultimately aesthetic in nature rather than quantitative?

The similarity of Goldenweiser's characterization to critiques of the *shiwen* genre on formal grounds from the seventeenth century to today is striking. From another perspective, when the modern prose essay is considered as social practice, what could be more involutionary, in Geertz's sense, than an ever-increasing number of candidates spending more and more years of their lives in a competitive process tilling textual fields that were inherently fertile yet strictly limited in scope? The literary yield of this year distinguishes itself from the last not primarily by expanding into new source material but by more thoroughly and diligently appropriating the given canon. With ingenuity and effort, one can do more with less, as large topic questions increasingly yield to small topic questions. This process of involution finds its way into the fabric of the modern prose essay, with parallel passages folding back on themselves in patterns that become more and more complex.

As Akira Hayami has suggested, however, the world-historical implications of diligence (*qin*) cannot be dismissed. Making use of this same written character that was so important to Zhang Juzheng, he proposes an "industrious revolution" (*kinben kakumei*) in production that formed a necessary ground for the better-known Industrial Revolution.[45] Similarly, heated debates over the causes of the nineteenth-century "divergence" between China and Europe have made it clear that one scholar's evidence of involution is another's proof of development. Without a bird's-eye perspective that stands outside of history, coming to a definitive assessment of a social process as involution or development could be even more challenging than reading an essay that perpetually tilts out of balance. Finally, as I have suggested here, it is the industrious administration of the Ming and Qing that contributed a necessary condition for the unprecedented early modern flow of silver into China: the unified and prosperous market for silver depended on a bureaucratic infrastructure for its coherence and longevity.

Diligence has transformative potential in the literary sphere as well. The careful involutionary tendencies of fifteenth-century *shiwen* carry within them the seeds of complex and thoroughgoing challenges to the parallel style under whose rule they were supposed to have been written. The contradictions inherent in the imperative that the voices in these essays must be familiar yet distinctive join with this involutionary impulse to give rise to a radically new approach to prose subjectivity. Ultimately, the diligence characteristic of *shiwen* reading and writing is infectious: it spreads to other genres in such a way as to redefine early modern literary practice in China long before the discourse of literature came to be similarly contested.

Four Essays and Their Translations

鏗爾, 舍瑟而作
陳矗恆

瑟有餘聲, 惟其作而舍也。

夫鏗爾者, 非舍瑟之聲耶? 我聞其聲, 而已知其作者之為點矣。

昔四子言志, 次當及點。而點方鼓瑟, 以故後於求、赤。迨夫子有何如之問, 而适會其希矣。夫侍君子之禮, 問更端, 則當坐而起。點之作也, 於禮固然。

然而希則希矣, 瑟猶在御也, 將有事於作焉, 而瑟亦若或告之也。

以為是前音之已收而未收也, 似也但少屬耳。

以為是後音之莫續而猶續也, 似也但加促耳。

意初不在弦, 而有意無意之間, 餘音猶振。

弦已脫於手, 而非手非弦之際, 虛響猶傳。

不宮不商, 律呂幾無可調之處, 蓋鼓之則調, 舍之則不復調也。

何嘄何咩, 性情杳無可傳之實, 蓋鼓之則傳, 舍之則不復傳也。

夫因舍瑟, 斯有鏗爾之音, 而治之以耳者, 早以知肉。聲之不足, 而絲亦改乎其度也。

且因作, 斯有舍瑟之舉, 而治之以目者, 正以覘足。容之有餘, 而手亦應乎其節也。

可以舍而舍, 可以作而作, 其諸寓意於物, 而不留於物者乎。

可以坐而安弦, 可以作而舍瑟, 其諸和之以樂, 而又節以禮者乎。

瑟離於人, 人離於席, 一時之舉止, 居然風雅之遺。瑟將絕而未絕, 人將言而未言, 此際之會心, 已在絲桐之近。迄今緬其流風, 挹其餘韻, 而氣象之雍容, 猶將神往焉, 況於身親其際者哉。

"While it was yet twanging, he laid the instrument aside, and rose"
Chen Nieheng (1700 *jinshi*)

There is residual sound from the zither only because he rose and put it aside.

Now this twang, is it not the sound of putting the zither aside? I hear this sound, and already I know that the one rising is Dian.

When the four disciples spoke of their intentions, the next one to speak should have been Dian. But Dian was at that moment playing the zither, and so he came after Qiu and Chi. Confucius waited to ask Dian about his intentions until he reached a point when the notes were few. Now when in attendance on an exemplary person, it is appropriate to rise when asked a question about something new. Dian's standing up was certainly in accordance with the rites.

Now it is true that the notes were few, but the zither was still being played; Dian was focused on rising in respect, but the zither still seemed to have something to say.

It seems as though the preceding notes have finished but are not yet finished; it is just that the sound is softer;

It seems as though the notes to follow do not continue yet continue; it is just that they are more hurried.

The meaning at first is not in the strings, but between meaning and not meaning, the lingering sound still stirs;

The string has already left the hand, but at the bounds of what is not hand and not string, the echoing sigh still carries.

Neither one or another of the notes of the scale, there is almost no point at which the pitch pipes could keep it in tune; so when playing one keeps it in tune, but when setting it aside one no longer tunes it.

What jawing, what bleating? One's own nature is distant and has no reality to be transmitted; so when playing one transmits it, but when setting the zither aside one no longer transmits it.

Now by setting aside the zither, there is the twanging sound, which is managed by the ear, to sooner know the richness of the sound; the sound does not suffice, and the string also changes to its measure;

By rising, there is the act of putting aside the zither, which is managed by the eye, to properly observe sufficiency; there is ease in his demeanor, and his hand responds already to his restraint.

Being able to put it aside and putting it aside, being able to rise and rising, can the various meanings lodged in the thing not remain in the thing?

Being able to sit and quiet the strings, being able to rise and put the zither aside, these can all be harmonized with music, but are they also disciplined by the rites?

The zither is parted from the person, the person is parted from his seat: an instantaneous action that leaves an elegant legacy to later generations. The zither is about to stop but has not yet stopped, the person is about to speak and has not yet spoken: the meeting of minds at this moment is close to the silk and paulownia. This breeze reaches down to the present day, as does this lingering sound, and their refined and graceful spirit sends the mind wandering; how much more true this must have been for those close by at that time![1]

點, 爾何如
胡任興

隨所遇而志在焉, 聖人之所與也。

夫點志何異乎? 春風沂水之間, 有化機焉。子故用嘆夫點耶?

嘗思人生俯仰甚寬, 而恆鬱鬱焉, 憂志之不遂者何為乎? 異日之經綸, 雖實亦虛, 何也? 以其有待也; 當日之寄託, 雖虛亦實, 何也? 以其無待也。

若點之志足述已。

勳業者, 君相之遇合也, 禹皋伊旦, 當時若無此遭逢, 豈遂湮沒以終老? 天壤甚大, 倘必有所待而後抒懷, 設所如不偶, 將畢生無自見之期矣。

景物者, 達士之功名也。黃農虞夏, 今日豈異此風期, 安見熙皞之難再? 人物依然, 如其無所待而皆快意, 將動與天遊, 任目前皆自得之致矣。

維時點承夫子之問, 鼓瑟方闋, 餘音鏗然, 容止之間, 蕭然自遠。

一若三子之兵農禮樂, 何必不虛? 而乃不欲為其同。

當前之物序人風, 何必不實? 而乃獨自見其異。

彼莫春春服, 正知我時也, 冠者童子, 皆合志人也; 風浴詠歸, 盡酬知具也, 雖各言其志, 而以此思點, 點何如耶?

性情之際, 安往不得? 忽焉而值此時, 忽焉而思此人, 忽焉而娛此境, 任耳目間之取攜, 而生平不盡嘯歌之致。此其氣象, 類不在三代一下也。將點狂也, 不幾於道歟?

宇宙之故, 安在可執? 如必莫春而後為其時, 必童冠而後為其人, 必風浴詠歸而後為其境, 自命曠觀之高致, 而寄情猶域形跡之內, 此其意量, 不過石隱者流也, 將點深也, 不猶之乎淺歟?

論者謂點之志, 與夫子老安少懷之志微有合者, 故亟與之。然而孔子當日, 唯是喟然嘉嘆, 至其所以與者, 終未嘗言其故云。

"Dian, what are your wishes?"
Hu Renyu (1694 *zhuangyuan*)

Going along with what is encountered and one's intent appears there in it, this is what the Sage approved of.

Now how was Dian different? There is a vital transformative element in the spring breezes and the waters of the Yi. Is it for this reason that the Master sighed in response to Dian?

I have thought that one's life is very broad in scope; to constantly be depressed in it and worry that one's intent will not be fulfilled, why behave in this way? *The serious efforts undertaken in one's past were empty even though real, why? Because they depended on something. The past-times of those days, although empty, turned out to be real, why? Because they did not depend on anything.*

An intent like Dian's is worth giving an account of.

Meritorious service is the coming together of ruler and minister: but if Yu, Gao Yao, Yi Yin, and the Duke of Zhou had at that time not had this meeting, how could they have sunk into the mists to grow old and die? The world is extremely large, if there is something on which one necessarily depends and only then can express one's heart, and we suppose that there was no encounter [with this] then they would have had no expectation of making themselves seen in their lifetimes;

The surrounding landscape is the "official career" of realized gentlemen: how could today's scene be different from that of the Yellow Emperor, Shen Nong, Yu, and Xia, how could it be hard for auspicious radiance to reappear? People are still there, if there this is nothing that is depended upon and all are joyous in mood, about to voyage together with Heaven, relying on what is before their eyes all achieve the ultimate in self-possession.

At that time when Dian responded to Confucius's question, the zither was on the point of falling silent, with the aftertones resonating, his demeanor was untrammeled and naturally distant.

As for the military, agricultural, ritual, and musical concerns of the three disciples, why must they not be empty? It is for this reason that he did not want to do the same as they did.

The things present at the time order people's manners, why must they be unreal? It is in this that his difference is seen.

That last month of spring, and the clothing appropriate to it, lets you know my time; the men and boys are the people whose intent matches mine; bathing and enjoying the breeze, and singing on the way home exhausts the completeness of fellow-feeling. Even though each spoke of his intent, and based on this Confucius thought of Dian, what about Dian indeed?

As for the interface of one's nature and things, how can it be unattainable once gone—suddenly one meets with this time, suddenly one thinks of this person, suddenly one takes pleasure in these surroundings—relying on what the ears and eyes take up and not exhausting the ultimate in singing at full voice throughout one's life, this atmosphere is not inferior to the Three Dynasties, so to take Dian as unrestrained and wild is not close to the Way;

The things of this universe, how can they be grasped firmly—if it must be the last month of spring and only then be the right time, if they must be these boys and men and only then be the right people, if it must be bathing, enjoying the breeze, and returning in song and only then be the right surroundings—proclaiming oneself to be the ultimate in lofty and grand vision, while one's feelings are still restricted to traces of form, then one's capacity for intention is no greater than that of hermits, if we take Dian as deep, surely this approach would be shallower?

Some have argued that Dian's intent fits subtly with Confucius's intent to give rest to the aged and treat youth tenderly, and so he praised it. But on that day Confucius only sighed in appreciation; as for the reason why he praised Dian's intent, he never spoke of it.[2]

晉人有馮婦者
唐順之

晉人始則改行以從善, 終則徇人而失己也。

夫改過貴於有終也, 馮婦既己為善士矣, 而猶搏虎焉, 何其不知止哉?
孟子蓋以此為發棠喻也。

若曰: 君子之道, 時行則行, 時止則止。吾謂復為發棠, 猶之馮婦者。
馮婦何如人哉? 彼獸之難搏者莫如虎。晉人有馮婦者, 則善於搏虎
者也。搏者善宜乎負其能而不知返矣?

馮婦則謂: 以勇力自逞, 非所以尚德也, 與猛獸相角, 非所以愛身也。

翻然改其素習之行, 而趨於善士之歸, 馮婦於此, 亦自以為終身不復
搏虎矣。

一日而行於野, 适有虎焉, 而眾人逐之, 虎見人之逐己也, 則負嵎以
張其勢, 人見虎之負嵎也, 則畏縮而不敢攖。攖之且不敢, 而況搏
之也! 於是眾人之技窮, 而眾人之心亦且惶惶然無可奈何矣。

适見馮婦之至也, 趨而迎之。當此之時, 人之與虎相抗者, 其勢誠急,
而其求助於有力者, 其情誠切也。

馮婦於是攘臂下車, 豈不以偶一為之, 於吾未有所損, 而赴其所急,
於人深有所濟乎?

吁, 若馮婦者, 其始之搏虎也, 不知其卒為善士也, 其已為善士也, 不
知其復為搏虎也。然則人之望我復為發棠。亦何異於馮婦之攘臂
下車也哉!

"Feng Fu of Jin"

Tang Shunzhi (1507–60, 1529 *jinshi*)

There was a person from Jin who at first changed his ways and reformed, but finished by submitting to others and losing himself.

Now in correcting one's faults completing the task is valued; Feng Fu had already become a good gentleman, and then again wrestled with a tiger, how could he not have known when to stop? Mencius thus used this as a metaphor for opening the granaries of Tang.

It is as if he said:

It is the way of the exemplary person to act when it is time to act, and stop when it is time to stop. If I called for the granaries of Tang to be opened again, I would be like Feng Fu. What kind of person was Feng Fu? Of the beasts, the most difficult to wrestle is the tiger. There was a person from Jin named Feng Fu who was good at wrestling tigers. Given that he was good at wrestling, was it appropriate to rely on this ability and not know when to turn back?

Feng Fu said: *To use one's bravery and strength to show off is not the way to appreciate virtue, and to lock horns with a savage beast is not the way to preserve one's body.*

He thus completely changed his old habits and hastened to the refuge of the virtuous; at this point Feng Fu himself indeed thought that he would never again wrestle a tiger.

One day, he was traveling in the country and encountered a tiger there, with a crowd of people pursuing it. *When the tiger saw that people were pursuing it, it took advantage of a mountain ravine to make the most of its might; when the people saw the tiger take advantage of the mountain ravine, they recoiled in fear and did not dare provoke it.* Not even daring to provoke it, how could they grapple with it? So the crowd's tactics were exhausted, and the crowd's minds were also anxious and unhappy and there was nothing to be done.

They happened to see Feng Fu's arrival, and hastened to meet him. At this time, in their struggle with the tiger, *the people's might was truly pressed*, and in seeking help from a strong person, *the people's feelings were truly eager.* Feng Fu thereupon bared his shoulder and got down from his carriage; how is it not the case that he was thinking that to do this just once, *will not harm me*, and rushing to their aid, *will greatly help them*?

Alas, the case in question is like that of Feng Fu; he began by wrestling tigers and did not know that he would become a good gentleman; having already become a good gentleman, he did not know that he would again wrestle tigers. And people are looking to me to open the granaries of Tang again; how would this be different from Feng Fu baring his shoulder and getting down from his carriage?[3]

天子适諸侯曰巡狩
董越

時臣述先王有君臣往來之典, 各舉其名而釋其義焉。甚矣! 先王之
時, 君巡狩於臣, 臣述職於君, 一往一來, 皆非無事也。時臣述之以
為其君告, 得無意乎?

昔齊景公欲比先王之遊觀, 而問於晏子, 故晏子述先王之典以告
之。

謂夫

天子以一人之尊而宰制六合, 有土地焉, 不能以獨理, 有人民焉, 不能
以獨治, 諸侯故不容於不建也。然諸侯散處於諸邦, 各限於封守。
歲事, 未必其皆修; 侯度, 未必其皆謹; 而人民之在所統理者, 又
未知其皆至於各安生養否也。使時巡之禮不舉焉, 則奉職者何所
勸, 不職者何所懲, 而王朝式序之典, 寧不幾於廢墜耶? 於是乎必
時适諸侯, 而名之巡狩焉。

巡狩者何? 巡行諸侯所守之土耶, 殆以視其田野孰辟歟, 人民孰安
歟, 侯度職貢孰謹而孰修歟。夫然後黜陟加焉, 賞罰行焉, 而天子
宰制之勸實於是乎見矣, 夫豈無事而空行也哉?

諸侯承一人之命以藩屏一方, 有土地焉, 皆天子所命以分理, 有人民
焉, 皆天子所命以分治, 職業亦不容於不修也。然自茅土既分與明
廷, 而天顏每違於咫尺。雖職貢之勉修, 不敢自必其為修; 侯度之
已謹, 不敢自必其為謹; 而人民之見於統理者, 又未知其果可勉於
勿予禍謫否也。使人覲之禮不修焉, 則有言曷從而敷納, 有功曷從
而明式, 而王朝考績之典, 寧不幾於虛設耶? 於是乎以時朝於天子,
而名之曰述職焉。

述職者何? 述其所受之職也, 殆必陳其田野不敢以不辟, 人民不敢以
不撫, 而侯度職貢不敢以不舉不修。庶幾乎予奪舉焉, 功罪明焉,
而諸侯藩屏之職亦於是乎盡矣, 又豈無事而空行也哉?

吁, 先王巡狩、述職之典如此, 宜晏子述以告景公, 而孟子復引以証宣
王雪宮之為獨樂也。

"When the Son of Heaven visited the princes, it was called a tour of inspection"
Dong Yue (1431–1502, 1469 *jinshi*)

The minister at that time [Yanzi] described the rituals of the Former
  Kings according to which ruler and official visited each other, raising
  each term and explaining its meaning.
How true it is that in the time of the Former Kings, the ruler's tours
  of inspection among the officials, and the officials' reports on their
  duties to the ruler, one going out and the other coming in, were never
  purposeless! Could the description provided by the minister at that
  time to his ruler have been meaningless?
Once Duke Jing of Qi wanted to travel about and observe the sights as
  the Former Kings had, so he asked Yanzi and Yanzi described the
  rituals of the Former Kings to him.
He said:
The Son of Heaven uses the majesty of one person to rule the six directions:
  there is land there, but it cannot be managed by him alone; there are
  people there, but they cannot be governed by him alone; the feudal lords
  would not accept not being established. The feudal lords, however, are
  located in their various realms, and each is limited by his outposts. As for
  the seasonal rituals, it is not necessarily the case that they observe all of
  them; as for the ruler's law, it is not necessarily the case that they follow it
  completely; and as for the people under their management, it is not known
  whether all are secure and flourishing or not. If the ritual of periodic tours
  of inspection is not carried out, how can those who fulfill their duties be
  encouraged, and those who fail to fulfill their duties be punished; would
  the ritual ranking of officials at court then not be practically abandoned?
  For this reason it is necessary to periodically visit the feudal lords, and this
  is called a "tour of inspection."
What is a "tour of inspection"? It is to travel among the lands kept by the
  feudal lords, for no other reason than to observe their fields to see who
  has broken new ground, whose people are secure, who is following the
  ruler's law and who is fulfilling their duties. Then titles can be conferred
  or withdrawn, and rewards and punishments effected, and the power of
  the Son of Heaven to rule is in fact seen through this; how could this be
  purposeless and empty activity?

The feudal lords receive a mandate from one person to protect one area: there is land there, which the Son of Heaven has mandated that they separately manage; there are people there, which the Son of Heaven has mandated that they separately govern; their duties would not admit of not being carried out. Since, however, the fiefdoms have been assigned at court, the Imperial countenance is now distant. Even though one strives to fulfill one's duties, one cannot dare to assume to be seen as dutiful; even though the ruler's law may already be followed, one cannot dare to assume that it will be seen as followed; and as for the people's opinion of their management, it is not known whether they will be successful in their urging "not to punish or reprove us" or not. If the ritual of audiences with the ruler is not practiced, how could those with opinions offer them, and how could those with accomplishments be evaluated on them; would the ritual examination of achievements at court then not exist in name only? For this reason the feudal lords periodically have audiences with the Son of Heaven, and this is called "reporting on their duties."

What is "reporting on their duties"? It is to report on the duties they have been assigned, which is to say that they must make evident the fact that they do not dare not to break new ground in the fields, that they do not dare not to nurture the people, that they do not dare not to carry out the ruler's law and fulfill their duties. So that the powers to grant and deprive are exercised, and merit and blame are clear, and the duty of the feudal lords to protect is also completed through this; how could this be purposeless and empty activity?

Oh! The tours of inspection and reports on duties in the time of the Former Kings had these rules; it is appropriate that Yanzi described them to Duke Jing, and that Mencius drew on this to correct King Xuan's selfish enjoyment of Snow Palace.[4]

NOTES

Abbreviations

JYZY	Wu Zhiwang, ed., *Juye zhiyan* (1599 edition)
LWJC	Gao Dang, ed., *Lunwen jichao*
MWH	*Ming wen hai* (Qing dynasty Hanfen lou edition)
QSJ	*Qinding sishu wen jiaozhu*
ZYCH	Liang Zhangju, ed., *Zhiyi conghua*

Introduction

1 *ZYCH* 13/258.
2 Gui Youguang is particularly known for his ability to set a scene. In his essay on the topic "The Master, when he entered the grand temple," Gui imagines what Confucius could have said instead of asking questions about rituals that he was already familiar with. The results are subtly but unmistakably impolite. *QSJ* 120. For an example of a "mathematical" essay, see Wang Ao's response to the topic "In a great state, where the territory was a hundred *li* square" (*QSJ* 80).
3 See Qian Fu's essay on the topic "Confucius ascended the eastern hill, and Lu appeared to him small" (*QSJ* 82), as well as essays by Li Guangdi and Sun Luoru on the topics "When the year becomes cold" and "King Wu and the Duke of Zhou displayed their various robes" (*ZYCH* 9/150, 11/213). On manure, see *ZYCH* 11/202–3 and Deng, *Qingdai bagu wen*, 168–73.
4 Bao Shichen remarks that eight-legged essays value the ability to "lead into the imaginary (*dao yu xu*)." Bao, *Yizhou shuangji* 2.39b. See also "Guwen xiaopu" item 2; Tao Wangling's comments in *Congxian wenjue neipian*, reprinted in *Xijian Mingren wenhua ershi zhong*, 1303; Yuan Huang, *Youyi shu xu wengui* 2/197; Wu Zhiwang, *Juye zhiyan* (1588 edition) 2.39b–40a; and Gao, "Wenfa jishuo," 14b.
5 Yuan Renlin, preface to *Xuzi shuo*, 1b. On *xu* in literary aesthetics generally, see Chen Jiajun, *Xushi zhangfa xilun*.
6 Kant, *The Critique of Judgement*; Caygill, *Art of Judgement*, esp. 152–60; Eagleton, *The Ideology of the Aesthetic*, 13–17, 75–87.
7 Qian Yong, *Lüyuan conghua* 21.17ab. See also Qian Zhongshu, *Tanyi lu*, 31, 359–60.
8 Zheng Haoruo, among others, has commented on this; as Zhou Yiqing points out, examination essays had been included in the *wenji* of individual authors under the Song, so their exclusion in the Ming and Qing is notable. *Xuehai tang ji* 8.7b, 8.29ab. See also Zhang Zhongxing, "*Shuo bagu* buwei," 61, and Jin Kemu, "Bagu xinlun," 78. *Shiwen* often circulated in stand-alone editions and sometimes were included in individual *wenji* as a supplementary volume. Qian Qianyi's expanded edition of Gui

Youguang's collected works, *Zhenchuan xiansheng ji*, is an unusual case in which essays appear ahead of poetry, as Gui was better known for his essays. In an 1801 edition of Tang Yin's work, by contrast, seventeen of his essays are included only in a supplementary volume that follows a volume on painting (*Liuru jushi quanji*).

9 For example, see Bourdieu, "The Market of Symbolic Goods," and Guillory, *Cultural Capital*.

10 Shang Yanliu sums the situation in the nineteenth and early twentieth centuries up as follows: "collectors did not value essay anthologies, bibliographers did not discuss them, and libraries did not collect them." *Qingdai keju kaoshi shulu*, 244. For translations of essays into Western languages and Japanese, see Tu, "The Chinese Examination Essay"; Alt, "The Eight-Legged Essay"; Lo, "Four Examination Essays"; Durand, "L'homme bon et la montagne"; Guy, "Fang Pao and the *Ch'in-ting Ssu-shu-wen*," 170–75; Plaks, "The Prose of Our Time," 206–17; Elman, *A Cultural History*, 397–407; Ōki Yasushi, *Genbun de tanoshimu*; and Yinghui Wu, "Constructing a Playful Space."

11 For critical examinations of tendencies to represent these other practices as simply "feudal," see Ko, *Cinderella's Sisters*, and Des Forges, "Opium / Leisure / Shanghai." As Rui Magone suggests, by ignoring the eight-legged essay in writing about modern Chinese literature, "we get only half of the story because we fail to see the traditional influences that May Fourth intellectuals were most anxious about." Magone, "The Silence of the Lanes," 344.

12 Zhou suggested that study of the eight-legged essay should be a required course and meet for at least two hours each week. *Zhongguo xin wenxue de yuanliu*, 30, 37, 60–61. See also Huang Qiang, *Bagu wen yu Ming Qing wenxue*, introduction, 6.

13 In a 1942 address, Mao likened eight-legged essays to foot-binding bandages. Mao Zedong, *Oppose the Party "Eight-Legged Essay*," 7–8. As Deng Yunxiang points out, there is an increasing tendency from this point on for criticism of the genre to come from individuals who have no firsthand knowledge of it. *Qingdai bagu wen*, 2.

14 Zhou Zuoren, *Zhongguo xin wenxue de yuanliu*, 37–38; Gong, *Mingdai bagu wen shitan*, introduction, 2–3. On the perceived contrast with women's writing, see Shuen-fu Lin (trans.), "The Chapter Comments," 266, and Ko, *Teachers of the Inner Chambers*, 52.

15 On conservatism in the early Qing, see Zhou Zuoren, *Zhongguo xin wenxue de yuanliu*, 29; Ropp, *Dissent in Early Modern China*, 40; Pei-yi Wu, *The Confucian's Progress*, 235; Chow, "Discourse, Examination, and Local Elite," 185–86.

16 Roddy, *Literati Identity*; Elman, *A Cultural History*, 530–35. You Tong's preface to *Guwen lüshu* (1663) makes it clear this book was assembled specifically to prepare candidates for the reformed version of the exams in effect between 1663 and 1667. From the *Benchao Zhewei sanchang quanti beikao* it seems as though topics for which one might compose *shiwen* did appear in 1666, but only in the second examination session, not the more important first session.

17 Gu, *Rizhi lu jiaozhu* 16/913.

18 See Plaks, "The Prose of Our Time," 206–8; Roddy, *Literati Identity*, 51–58.

19 Yuan, "*Zhu dajia shiwen xu*," 185.

20 Other notable examples include Tang Shunzhi, and the three Yuan brothers, Yuan Zongdao, Yuan Hongdao, and Yuan Zhongdao. Chih-p'ing Chou writes that "It is

surprising and disturbing to some that such wholehearted praise of the eight-legged essay was actually written by the free-spirited Yüan Hung-tao, the same man who championed innate sensibility (*hsing-ling*) and spontaneity in his literary theory." Chih-p'ing Chou, *Yüan Hung-tao and the Kung-an School*, 42–43. Chou explains this contradiction away by arguing that Yuan was blindly reacting against classicist tendencies on the part of previous generations, but as I will show in chapter 4, Yuan's interest in *shiwen* makes more sense on its own terms as part of a broader commitment to literary individualism.

21 Wang Yunxi and Gu Yisheng pass over Li's praise for the modern prose essay in silence in their discussion of "Tongxin shuo." *Zhongguo wenxue piping shi xinbian* 2:150. Zhou Xunchu singles Li's assessment out for criticism in *Zhongguo wenxue piping xiaoshi*, 159–60. For an account of the deletion of Li's praise of modern prose from "Tongxin shuo" quotations in works by other modern scholars, see Huang Qiang, *Bagu wen yu Ming Qing wenxue*, introduction, 4–5.

22 On this question, see also Huang Qiang, *Bagu wen yu Ming Qing wenxue*, 2–8, and Durand, "L'homme bon et la montagne," 230–31.

23 Policy essays responded to specific questions about governance rather than a topic chosen from the Classics. Expectations for the form that they would take and the rhetorical techniques they would make use of were different. For a discussion of policy essays in contrast to essays on the Four Books and Five Classics, see Elman, *A Cultural History*, 425–27, 443–59.

24 *Shiwen* could also be referred to as "writing of the exam rooms" (*changwu zhi wen*) or products of the "exam *métier*" (*juzi ye*). See, for example, *ZYCH* 1/15, 21; Qian Zhonglian, "Tongcheng pai guwen yu shiwen de guanxi wenti," 78–79; Gong, *Mingdai bagu wen shitan*, introduction, 14, and 70, 194, 267, 268, 276, 305, 334, 416.

25 Over the course of one's career as student, candidate, and official, scholar, or teacher, it would not be unusual to compose over a thousand *shiwen*. In the case of Hanlin scholars, for example, it was still necessary to produce passable essays on a regular basis to maintain one's position. Deng, *Qingdai bagu wen*, 46–47. As Deng later argues, the essay should not be known solely as an examination form but also as a means of cultural education and instruction in literary composition (211–12). See also *Xiaoti zhenggu* and Yu Yue, *Yu Yue sishu wen*.

26 Shen Defu, *Wanli yehuo bian* 27/687.

27 *Yinzhi wen zhiyi*.

28 Quoted in *ZYCH* 13/258.

29 *ZYCH* 10/186, 10/194, 13/257–58, 13/263, 14/281, 15/297.

30 Li Zhi writes in his preface to *Fenshu* that his *Shuoshu* (Explanation of the Four Books) took its inspiration from his friends' *shiwen* compositions. Li Zhi, "Zixu," 1; Handler-Spitz, Lee, and Saussy, *A Book to Burn and a Book to Keep (Hidden)*, 4–5. *Shuoshu* apparently no longer exists as a separate work: Zhang Siqi identifies the *Daogu lu* as *Shuoshu*; given its location in *Li Wenling ji*, the supposed date of composition, and its contents, this identification seems likely to be correct. *Bagu wen zonglun bazhong*, 241. See also Huang Qiang, *Bagu wen yu Ming Qing wenxue*, 145–50. For Zhao Nanxing's angry indictment of the literati as a class, see his essay on the topic, "They who shrug up their shoulders, and laugh in a flattering way," *QSJ* 343. On Lü Liuliang, see Chow, "Discourse, Examination, and Local Elite," 185–88, and

Spence, *Treason by the Book*. Zeng Yizhuan's "Zixu *Sishu lunshi*" is included in Huang Zongxi's original *Ming wen hai* (309/3005–6) although not (perhaps understandably) in the more widely available *Siku quanshu* version of the collection.

31 For example, see Yu Yue's remarks in *Yu Yue sishu wen*, 12a, 15b. On the range of essays written "for amusement," see Ōki, *Genbun de tanoshimu*, 9–54; Huang Qiang, *Bagu wen yu Ming Qing wenxue*, 323, 398–415; Huang Qiang and Wang Ying, *Youxi bagu wen yanjiu*; and Yinghui Wu, "Constructing a Playful Space," 503–45. A substantial number of essays written "for amusement" are reprinted in Huang Qiang, *Youxi bagu wen jicheng*; the most important reprint edition of a single premodern collection is Gong, *Yasu cangshu*.

32 Huang Qiang notes similarities between small topic essays and fictional narrative. *Bagu wen yu Ming Qing wenxue*, 398–99.

33 On family letters, see Huang Qiang, *Bagu wen yu Ming Qing wenxue*, 346. Also worthy of note is Zhang Chao's "Bagu shi zixu."

34 Lu Longji, "Lu Jiashu xiansheng lunwen," 2ab; Huang Qiang, *Bagu wen yu Ming Qing wenxue*, 4. Although there are references in Shen Defu's *Wanli yehuo bian* to *babi* and *sigu babi* (23/595, 25/649, 25/650, 27/687), and a single reference to *bagu wenzi* in Ai, "Xu Wang Zigong *Guansheng cao*" (3029), I have yet to find the term *bagu wen* as such in Ming texts. This suggests that as late as the early seventeenth century, *bagu wen* may not have been a fixed term in regular use. For more detail on the relationship between the terms *bagu* and *babi*, see chapter 3.

35 Plaks, "The Prose of Our Time"; Durand, "L'homme bon et la montagne," 231; Huang Qiang, *Bagu wen yu Ming Qing wenxue*, 7.

36 Yuan Hongdao, "*Zhu dajia shiwen* xu," 185; Li Zhi, "Shiwen houxu," 2b–3a and "Tongxin shuo," 2b–3a; Dai Mingshi, "*Xiaoxue lunxuan* xu," 90 and "*Song Songnan zhiyi* xu," 113; Tang Biao, *Dushu zuowen pu* 9.1a; You, "*Jichou zhenfeng* xu"; introductory remarks to *Lianglun lianzhang caifeng ji*, 1a; Jiao, "Shiwen shuo," 154–55. Indeed, modern scholars Zhou Xunchu and Chih-p'ing Chou separately attempt to explain away Li's and Yuan's advocacy of the *shiwen* genre in the same way: as merely an unfortunate side effect of their unthinking commitment to the new in all of its many forms. Zhou Xunchu, *Zhongguo wenxue piping xiaoshi*, 160; Chou, *Yüan Hung-tao*, 42–43.

37 Many essay collections focus on writers who were likely to have been known at the moment of publication rather than on classic favorites. Peterson, *Bitter Gourd*, 47; Shen Junping, *Juye jinliang*, 225; Gao, "Lunwen zatiao," 13b; Cui, *Xuehai jinliang* 2.4ab; ZYCH 2/35–36. As Shang Yanliu points out, this incessant change is the main reason so few essay anthologies survive out of the many that were printed. Shang, *Qingdai keju kaoshi shulu*, 257. Barthes, *The Language of Fashion*, 78.

38 Fang Bao's chronological division of the Ming into sets of reign periods in the "Fanli" (introductory remarks) to *Qinding sishu wen*, each set with its own distinctive essay style, has become convention in the field (Guy, "Fang Pao and the *Ch'in-ting Ssu-shu-wen*," 164–66), but there are a range of alternative periodizations. See, for example, Lü Liuliang, *Lü Wancun xiansheng lunwen huichao*, 3b–4b; ZYCH 1/19, 6/87, 7/121–23, 8/142, 12/233, 234–36; introductory remarks to ZYCH, 7; Zhu Jian's preface to ZYCH, 3; *Xuehai tang ji* juan 8.

39 Gong, *Mingdai bagu wen shitan*, 389–92, and also introduction, 9–10; Huang Qiang, *Bagu wen yu Ming Qing wenxue*, 135; Qi, *Shuo bagu*, 37.

40 Chow, *Publishing, Culture, and Power*; Woodside, *Lost Modernities*. See also Teng, "Chinese Influence on the Western Examination System."

41 *Mengzi*, 116. Andrew Lo has a translation of this essay in "Four Examination Essays," 179–81; my interpretation differs at several points.

42 Referring to *Mengzi*, 41.

43 Referring to *Mengzi*, 57, where Zengzi's treatment of Zengxi is characterized as "nourishing intention" (*yangzhi*) while Zeng Yuan's treatment of Zengzi does not measure up: it is merely "nourishing mouth and body."

44 *QSJ* 640–41. The reference in the final line is to *Mengzi*, 90.

45 *QSJ* 640.

46 Liu Dakui, "*Fang Xiyuan shiwen* xu," 97; "Shiwen lun," 2a. Similarly, Dai Mingshi explains that the task of *shiwen* vis-à-vis the classics is to "depict their spirit (*jingshen*) and resemble their tone (*yuqi*)" in addition to "making manifest their moral philosophy (*yili*)." "*You Ming lichao xiaoti wen xuan* xu," 14. See also Zhang Taikai, *Zhangshi lunwen yuezhi*, 12b–13a.

47 Qian Zhongshu, *Tanyi lu*, 32.

48 Quoted in *ZYCH* 7/129–30.

49 Yuan Renlin notes of *xuzi* that in the teachings of the Sages and Worthies and the writings of scholars, it is *xuzi* that are "entrusted with the spirit (*jingshen*) and transmit the tone of voice (*yuqi*)." Preface to *Xuzi shuo*, 1a. See also Yuan Renlin, *Xuzi shuo*, 35a.

50 Jiao, "Shiwen shuo," 154. See also Zhang Taikai, *Zhangshi lunwen yuezhi*, 10a; Liu, *Lunwen ouji* (1959), 18–19; as well as Gao Dang's margin comments to Mao Kun, "Mao Lumen lunwen size," 1a, and his "Titi leishuo," 2b, and "Wenfa jishuo," 14b. Two centuries earlier, Sun Kuang (1574 *huiyuan*) made use of these characteristic dialectics of reality and imagination to argue that the true meaning of *shiwen* is "not in the content words (*shizi*) of the topic, but rather in the empty words (*xuzi*) of the topic; not in the places where there are words, but rather where there are no words." *JYZY* 2.11b–12a.

51 Plaks, "The Prose of Our Time," 210.

52 On the significance of imagination and creativity in discourses on *xu*, see Chen Jiajun, *Xushi zhangfa xilun*, 189–250. On the role of sensation in *shiwen*, see Lu Longji, "Lu Jiashu lunwen," 4a; Yuan Renlin, preface to *Xuzi shuo*, 1a–2a; see also *Xuzi shuo*, 35a–41b; Zhou Zuoren, "Lun bagu wen," 62–63.

53 Yuan Renlin, *Xuzi shuo*, 37a.

54 Robert Hegel, *The Novel in Seventeenth-Century China*, 175.

55 As early as the fifteenth century, Tang Yin wins the title of "Most romantic genius of Jiangnan" (*Jiangnan diyi fengliu caizi*) largely for his examination essays; Jin Shengtan includes a *shiwen* anthology in his seventeenth-century series of "books of genius." Gong, *Mingdai bagu wen shitan*, 257–58, 277, 439; Jin Shengtan, *Xiaoti caizi shu*. See also Huang Qiang, *Bagu wen yu Ming Qing wenxue*, 388, and Qian Qianyi, *Muzhai youxue ji* 45/447.

56 Huang Qiang argues that the examination essay was the genre subjected to the most intense attention throughout the Ming and Qing. Whether judged by sheer number of writers and readers, time and energy invested, or the level of anxiety the genre could induce, this assertion would be difficult to refute (*Bagu wen yu Ming Qing*

wenxue, introduction, 2–3). Similarly, Zhou Zuoren claims that without a comprehensive knowledge of the eight-legged essay, it would be impossible to understand both premodern and modern Chinese literature ("Lun bagu wen," 60, 62). See also Tu, "Chinese Examination Essay," 394–95; Plaks, "The Prose of Our Time," 216–17.

57 Li Zhi, "Tongxin shuo"; Ai, *Tian yongzi ji* 3.8a, 8.1a and "*Wang Kanghou hebing gao xu*," 3027; Jiao, *Yiyu yuelu* 15.2a and "Shiwen shuo," 155. See also the early Qing preface to Dong Qichang, *Dong Sibai lunwen zongzhi*, and You, "*Jichou zhenfeng xu*," as well as Huang Qiang, *Bagu wen yu Ming Qing wenxue*, 22, 143, 321–22, and Roddy, *Literati Identity*, 49–51.

58 Yuan Hongdao, "*Zhu dajia shiwen* xu" (Li Zhi makes the converse claim in "Shiwen houxu").

59 Ruan, "Shu Liang Zhaoming taizi '*Wenxuan* xu' hou," 106; Roddy, *Literati Identity*, 49–51. Ruan felt strongly enough about the significance of the examination essay genre to set his students at Xuehai tang in the early 1820s the assignment to write on the topic "The origins and development of essays on the Four Books." Five of these student papers were published in *Xuehai tang ji*, followed immediately by Ruan's preface to an encyclopedic reference work, *Sishu wen hua*, that he compiled together with some of these same students (8.1a–52b). Although this work was never published, it did have an influence on Liang Zhangju's *Zhiyi conghua*. See Magone, "Examination Culture and the Non-Commercial Book."

60 Plaks, *The Four Masterworks of the Ming Novel*, 33–34; Plaks, "Terminology and Central Concepts," 120–21; Rolston, "Sources of Traditional Chinese Fiction Criticism," esp. 17–29; Rolston, *Traditional Chinese Fiction and Fiction Commentary*, 17–18; Huang Qiang, *Bagu wen yu Ming Qing wenxue*, 381–426. For a comprehensive assessment of the importance of the eight-legged essay and the examination system as metaphor to several of the best-known works of fiction in the Ming and Qing, see Ge, *The Scholar and the State*. On the significance of the examination regime to the broad range of sixteenth- and seventeenth-century vernacular fiction, see Ye Chuyan, *Mingdai keju yu Ming zhongqi zhi Qing chu tongsu xiaoshuo yanjiu*. The best-known fiction commentator, Jin Shengtan, also published at least one edition of examination essays with commentary, *Xiaoti caizi shu*; see Rolston, "Sources of Traditional Chinese Fiction Criticism," 19, for mention of one (or possibly two) other such collections attributed to Jin Shengtan.

61 Rolston, "Sources of Traditional Chinese Fiction Criticism," 20–21, 23; Huang Qiang, *Bagu wen yu Ming Qing wenxue*, 352–80. The oldest extant edition of *Xixiang ji*, dating to the late fifteenth century, includes *shiwen* based on topics drawn from the script. Yinghui Wu, "Constructing a Playful Space," 511.

62 Yokota Terutoshi, "Hakkobun ni tsuite"; Qian Zhonglian, "Tongcheng pai guwen yu shiwen de guanxi wenti"; *ZYCH* 2/35; Qian Zhongshu, *Tanyi lu*, 242–43; Pauline Yu, "Canon Formation in Late Imperial China," 94, 98–104; Huang Qiang, *Bagu wen yu Ming Qing wenxue*, 463–516; Shang Wei, *Rulin waishi and Cultural Transformation*, 142.

63 Jiao, *Yiyu yuelu* 17.7a. See also Jiang Guolin's discussion of the similarities between the essay and "*ce* in its reference to affairs, *lun* in its rational discussion, *fu* in the breadth of its subject matter, and regulated verse in its strict adherence to patterns of sound" (preface to *ZYCH*, 5), and Bao Shichen's genealogy of the distinctive

strengths of the genre: "the purity of its meaning and cleanliness of its words are grounded in the Classics, the greatness of its views and strength of its perception are brewed in the Histories, the preciseness of its descriptions relies on the Masters, and the vast reach of its waves sources from Belles-lettres." Bao, *Yizhou shuangji* 2.38b–39a.

64 Qian Zhongshu, *Tanyi lu*, 33, 360–62; Rolston, "Sources of Traditional Chinese Fiction Criticism," 2. On Tang's essays, see Des Forges, "Industry and Its Motivations."

65 Zhou Zuoren, "Lun bagu wen," 61–62. Huang Qiang similarly suggests that "of all the premodern Chinese literary genres, the eight-legged essay has the greatest ability to synthesize [a range of generic traditions]." *Bagu wen yu Ming Qing wenxue*, 50.

66 See, for example, Zhou Zuoren, *Zhongguo xin wenxue de yuanliu*, 30, and Roddy, *Literati Identity and Its Fictional Representations*, 51. Even Shen Junping's otherwise encyclopedic study of Ming dynasty examination preparation books, *Juye jinliang*, excludes works that focus on stylistic questions by Gui Youguang, Dong Qichang, and Wu Zhiwang, among others. Given this history of exclusion, the recent publication of modern reprint editions of selected sources for essay criticism such as *Bagu wen zonglun ba zhong* (Eight types of general discussions of eight-legged essays), one volume in the series *Lidai keju wenxian zhengli yu yanjiu congkan*, is particularly interesting. Although such works dramatically improve accessibility to the critical tradition, to the extent that their contents are conceptualized as "documents for research on the examination system," these reprint editions continue to respect and reinforce the distinction between "literary criticism" on one hand and "history of the examinations" on the other. One promising exception in this regard is *Xijian Mingren wenhua ershi zhong* (Twenty rarely-seen texts of prose criticism from the Ming), published in 2016.

67 On the usefulness of this work to Zottoli and Durand, see Durand, "L'homme bon et la montagne," esp. 242.

68 Magone, "Examination Culture and the Non-Commercial Book" is a good introduction to *Zhiyi conghua*.

69 Jin Kemu, "Bagu xinlun," 79.

70 Zhu Jian, preface to *ZYCH*, 3.

71 "N'est-il pas normal en effet qu'une pratique de plusieurs siècles à l'échelle de la nation tout entire ait été marquee par de notables réussites?" In the next paragraph, after detailing the many constraints within which candidates had to work: "Quoi d'étonnant que les sujets moins brillants—la majorité—aient transformé les fleurs de cette rhétorique imposée en bouquets d'orties?" Durand, *Lettrés et pouvoirs*, 80.

72 Huang Qiang, *Bagu wen yu Ming Qing wenxue*, 84–113. Worth noting in this context is the wide range in production values among different types of instructional materials. Cheaply produced manuals highlight efficacy in particular. *Xiaoti jianfeng*, preface, 1a; *Wenjin yingji hexuan*.

73 Zeng Yizhuan, "*Xu Wenjiang zhiyi* xu," 3004; *Xuehai tang ji* 8.7b; You, "*Jichou zhenfeng* xu."

74 See, for example, Huang Qiang, *Bagu wen yu Ming Qing wenxue*, 323–24.

75 In addition to its publication in 1599 as part of the expanded edition of *Juye zhiyan* (under the title "Wenjue jiuze"), in *Youyi shu xu wengui* (1602, as "Sibai Dong xiansheng lunwen"), and in *Lunwen jichao* (as "Huating jiuzi jue"), it also appears in a

1681 printing under the name *Dong Sibai lunwen zongzhi.* Qian Zhongshu notes a *Lunwen jiujue* (also referred to as *Zhijuwen jiufa*) by Dong Qichang that seems likely to be similar if not identical; excerpts appear in the early Qing *Nan Wu jiuhua lu*, in which the author claims to have seen a silk manuscript version of the text written by Dong Qichang himself. Qian Zhongshu, *Tanyi lu*, 360. Gong Duqing includes a reprint in full in *Mingdai bagu wen shitan* (449–54). Other references appear in Zhang Taikai, *Zhangshi lunwen yuezhi*, 12b; throughout other parts of *LWJC*; *ZYCH* 6/88–89; Ouyang Quan, *Diankan ji*, 48b–49b; *Wenzheng* 4.37a; and *Huayang jijin* 3.12a, 3.22a.

76 In at least one case, the *Wenjue jiuze* corrects a quote that is mistaken in the "Pingwen" chapter; in other cases, the *Wenjue jiuze* attempts to clarify potentially confusing statements or attributions.

77 Bourdieu, *Distinction*, 80–96. Note the similarity to Huang Qiang's distinction between instrumental essays and essays that enter a "realm of the imagination." See also Sophie Volpp's discussion of "pedantry" in *Worldly Stage*, 89–128.

78 "*Huachan shi suibi* mulu," 2b.

79 *Xinkan pishi juye qieyao gujin wenze* is at the Beijing University Library; *Zhenchuan xiansheng du guwen fa* is at the National Library in Beijing.

80 Chow, *Publishing, Culture, and Power.*

81 On Song examination writing, see De Weerdt, "Canon Formation and Examination Culture." As Ai Nanying (1583–1646) puts it, "examination essays and classical prose are interior and exterior to each other"; even critics like Huang Zongxi (1610–95) see the two as inseparable. Ai, "*Jin Zhengxi gao* xu," 3032; Huang Zongxi, "*Li Gaotang wenchao* xu," 80. See also Huang Qiang, *Bagu wen yu Ming Qing wenxue*, 86–87. The crowning irony is that the Tongcheng School, with its attempts to disguise its commitment to examination pedagogy as simply interest in classical prose, is only the most extreme example. Chow, "Discourse, Examination, and Local Elite"; Dai Shadi, "Xinhai zhi ji wenlun de chengqian qihou."

82 See, for example, Gu, *Rizhi lu jiaozhu* 19/1060. An important early example of this attitude, thoroughly developed in the Song commentaries, is the comment from the *Analects*, "If there is leftover energy, it can be used to study *wen*" (*Lunyu*, 2). For Tang and Song debates over the proper place of literariness in the examination system, see Bol, "Examinations and Orthodoxies," 32–39. In this connection, it is worth noting the anxiety that Bruce Rusk picks up on in scholarship on the *Shijing* from the Song forward; when this scholarship was inspired by developments in the field of literary criticism, the sources of that inspiration could not be cited explicitly. Rusk, *Critics and Commentators.*

83 Nivison, "Protest against Conventions and Conventions of Protest," 183.

84 Liu Dakui, "*Xu Lishan shiwen* xu," 93–94.

85 Zeng, "*Xu Wenjiang zhiyi* xu," 3004. See also Fang, "*Yang Qianmu wengao* xu," 300–301. Intriguingly, Lü Liuliang finds a positive commonality between *shiwen* on one hand and poetry and classical prose on the other, in that in both words follow from one's inner virtue, rather than from intentional construction. Lü Liuliang, *Lü Wancun xiansheng lunwen*, 8a. Some writers take a matter-of-fact approach to modern prose, including it as "literature" without making a point of arguing the validity of this move. See Jin Xuelian, *Shu'an lunwen bielu*, preface, 5b, 6b, 14b–16b, 20a; Yao, "Xibao xuan yu," 4b.

86 Zhu Xi begins by condemning the examination prose of his era and ends up forced by the logic of his argument to sweep in classical prose in the process. Huang Qiang, *Bagu wen yu Ming Qing wenxue*, 454; De Weerdt, "Canon Formation and Examination Culture," 111–12.

87 Des Forges, "Paratexts, Collected Works"; Yuming He, *Home and the World*; see also Bruce Rusk's mention of early Qing critiques of the "independent-minded and omnivorous" late Ming "commentarial machine." Rusk, *Critics and Commentators*, 86–88.

88 As David Nivison explains, for Zhang, "words, as historical utterances, are themselves events; and events are complexes that always involve words. To keep them separate, he argued, would be to make a metaphysical mistake, which in turn would make it impossible for the reader to apprehend the full significance of either words or events." Nivison, *Life and Thought of Chang Hsüeh-ch'eng*, 225.

89 Jiao, *Yiyu yuelu* 17.7ab. For a concise statement of the conventional wisdom on the ideological restrictions governing modern prose, see Qian Zhongshu, *Tanyi lu*, 353–54.

90 Jiao, "Shiwen shuo," 154.

91 Original introductory remarks to *QSJ*, 1. For example, Fang writes in appreciation of an essay by Jin Sheng (1589–1645) that "this opens a cavern in the eight-legged essay that must be opened," and references the outer chapters of the *Zhuangzi* to praise one of Tang Shunzhi's essays as "spontaneous and unthought joy referring to the transformation of things." *QSJ* 101, 446.

92 *ZYCH* vols. 13, 14, and 15; "I have taken those with sublimely unusual structures and unique insights, which are completely different from past commentators, and have included some here, both in order to supplement the inadequacies of existing commentaries and in order to refresh the eyes and ears of scholars." Introductory remarks to *ZYCH*, 9.

93 *ZYCH* 11/219.

94 See, for example, Elman's discussion of Ai Nanying (Elman, *A Cultural History*, 403–7), and also Huang Qiang, *Bagu wen yu Ming Qing wenxue*, 204–6; Wang Kaifu, *Bagu wen gaishuo*, 195–98; Wu Weifan, *Ming Qing zhiyi jinshuo*, 180–81.

95 Huang Qiang, *Bagu wen yu Ming Qing wenxue*, 111.

96 Shang Yanliu and David Rolston note the need for individual writers to distinguish themselves; in Rolston's words, "the intense competition and the high degree of sophistication in essay criticism over the years would certainly be a good incentive to innovation." Shang, *Qingdai keju kaoshi shulu*, 250; Rolston, "Sources of Traditional Chinese Fiction Criticism," 20.

97 See, for example, *ZYCH* 1/11; Gong, *Mingdai bagu wen shitan*, 145–46; Huang Qiang, *Bagu wen yu Ming Qing wenxue*, 60–83.

98 Gu, *Rizhi lu jiaozhu* 16/919–21; *ZYCH* 1/16; Gong, *Mingdai bagu wen shitan*, 148; Elman, *A Cultural History*, 382.

99 Wang Fuzhi, *Xitang yongri xulun waipian*, 1b.

100 See, for example, Yu Changcheng's comments in *ZYCH* 4/56, the quote from Li Guangdi immediately following in *ZYCH*, and Fang Bao's high praise in *QSJ* 25, 71; the research papers published in *Xuehai tang ji* 8.1a–51b; Elman, *A Cultural History*, 387; Gong, *Mingdai bagu wen shitan*, 242–55.

101 See Ch'en, *Chinese Literature*, 506–8; Tu, "The Chinese Examination Essay," 400–402; Plaks, "The Prose of Our Time"; Elman, *A Cultural History*, 388–91, 397–99; Gong, *Mingdai bagu wen shitan*, 249–52.

102 Fang Bao highlights several striking examples from the early and mid-fifteenth century as important precedents for later developments in the form. *QSJ* 43–44 and 46.

103 See, for example, the essay by Luo Lun (1431–78) on the topic "Long ago, a former king appointed its ruler to preside over sacrifices to the Eastern Meng," *QSJ* 32–33. An extreme and relatively early version of involuted parallelism appears in Dong Yue's (1431–1502, 1469 *jinshi*) essay "When the Son of Heaven visited the princes, it was called a tour of inspection," which is translated in the appendix to this book and will be discussed in chapter 3. *QSJ* 54–55.

104 Zhu Jian, preface to *ZYCH*, 3.

105 Gu, *Rizhi lu jiaozhu* 16/919.

106 See Zhang Taikai, *Zhangshi lunwen yuezhi*, 9b–10a, and Yu Changcheng's preface to Gui Youguang's essays in Yu, *Keyi tang yibai ershi mingjia zhiyi*.

107 See, for example, Hu Youxin's two very different essays reprinted in Gong, *Mingdai bagu wen shitan*, 430–34.

108 Fang, original introductory remarks to *QSJ*; Yuan Hongdao, "*Zhu dajia shiwen* xu"; Lü Liuliang, *Lü Wancun xiansheng lunwen*, 34a; Cui, *Xuehai jinliang* 2.11b–12a; *ZYCH* 2/40, 3/46; Jiang Guolin, preface to *ZYCH*, 5; Chow, *Publishing, Culture, and Power*, 221.

109 For every case of an innovation that succeeds dramatically, such as involutionary parallelism, there is an example of a stylistic novelty that fell flat: for example, the essay that makes use of the word *ye* twenty-six times in an text under 400 characters in length included in *ZYCH* 5/65–66.

110 *ZYCH* 9/158–59.

111 For critiques of the writing of earlier generations as no longer relevant, and a corresponding emphasis on essays from the most recent examinations, see Gao, "Lunwen zatiao," 19b–20a; *Huayang jijin*.

112 On the proliferation of different terms, see Gong, *Mingdai bagu wen shitan*, 1–49; conversely, even when terms do remain constant, as Zhou Yiqing reminds us, the textual features they reference may have changed substantially. *Xuehai tang ji* 8.32b–33a.

113 Yuan Huang, *Youyi shu wengui* 8/120; *Huayang jijin* 5.1a; introductory remarks to *ZYCH*,, 7.

114 Ko, "Bondage in Time."

115 *Mingshi* 70/1693.

Chapter 1

1 Yuan Mei writes, "Since antiquity essays have expressed one's own beliefs and convictions. Never did writers assume the role of actors and speak on behalf of others [*dairen zuoyu*]. Only *bagu* and the theater value the imitation of another's voice. . . . This is why this form of writing is so lowly." Translated in Roddy, *Literati Identity*, 261. See also Qian Zhongshu, *Tanyi lu*, 32–33, and Jiao Xun's use of theater to criticize poor essay writing by analogy in *Yiyu yuelu* 17.7a. Guan Shiming's comment

appears in *ZYCH* 1/19. Similarly, Lu Longji emphasizes the immediacy of the original setting in an attempt to remind essay writers of what they were meant to recreate. "Lu Jiashu xiansheng lunwen," 4a.

2   *ZYCH* 1/18. Qian Yong (1759–1844) likewise insists that using tone of voice to assess the success or failure of representative speech is very different from making a judgment based on fixed requirements (*dingge*). *Lüyuan conghua* 12.25b. See also Yuan Renlin, *Xuzi shuo*, 36a, and Zhang Shichun's critique of essays that shade into alley lectures when they lose the aesthetic touch. "*Banfang zhai gao* xu," 3038–39.

3   Reprinted in Wu Weifan, *Ming Qing zhiyi jinshuo*, 190–91, from *Xiaoti wuji jingyi*.

4   Yuan Renlin, *Xuzi shuo*, 1b, see also 35b. Caygill, *Art of Judgement*, 152–60; Eagleton, *The Ideology of the Aesthetic*, 13–17, 75–87; Kant, *The Critique of Judgment*, 65.

5   Durand, "L'homme bon et la montagne," 231; Qian Zhongshu, *Tanyi lu*, 33, 361. Qian refers specifically to a passage in Marcel Proust's *À l'ombre des jeunes filles en fleurs*.

6   Kant, *The Critique of Judgment*, 59–60 (emphasis in original).

7   *Mingshi* 70/1693; Liu Dakui, "*Fang Xiyuan shiwen* xu," 97. See also Liu Dakui, "Shiwen lun"; Fang, "Jin sishu wen xuan biao," 286–87; Durand, *Lettrés et pouvoirs*, 79–82; and Gao Dang's margin comments to "Lunwen size" in *LWJC* 9.

8   Although the nineteenth-century scholar Zhou Yiqing distinguishes between these two aspects, writing that speaking on behalf of the Sages and Worthies (*dai shengxian li yan*) like Wang Anshi and Su Zhe and sticking to the tone of the ancients (*dai guren yuqi*) like Yang Wanli are two separate techniques, I have not seen this distinction drawn anywhere else. *Xuehai tang ji* 8.29b.

9   Phrases that mark *daiyan* particularly explicitly include the following examples from *QSJ*: "Confucius replied to Zhong Gong, saying" (23); "I imagine that his intention in enlightening Zigong was as follows" (28); "It was as if Zisi's intention in showing people was" (39); "I once went back and forth in the three hundred poems and got 'don't swerve'" (111).

10 Tang Biao emphasizes this point in *Dushu zuowen pu* 7.7b; see also Cui, *Xuehai jinliang* 3.10b. Some examples drawn from specific essays: in Wu Kuan's "When the Master was in Qi, he heard the Shao," the represented speech begins only in the *guojie* (transition) and yields to assertive speech right after the subsequent parallel section (*QSJ* 16–18); in Gui Youguang's "In the *Book of Poetry* are three hundred pieces," representative speech begins only in the *chuti*, after the end of the first parallel section (*QSJ* 111–12); Xue Yingqi's essay in Wang Kaifu, *Bagu wen gaishuo*, 180–81, has assertive speech in the *poti* and *chengti*, represented speech in the *qijiang* and first parallel section, returns to assertive speech for a *guojie*, then has represented speech again in the *chuti* and the second parallel section, and finally returns to assertive speech for good in the conclusion; Tang Shunzhi's "Jilu asked about serving the spirits of the dead" moves in and out of represented speech, including the use of "first-person" *wu* in the concluding sentence (*QSJ* 143).

11 Wang Ao: "The wife of the prince of a state," in *QSJ* 34–35; Fang Bao: "All the day active and vigilant," reprinted in Wang Kaifu, *Bagu wen gaishuo*, 257–60.

12 Topics belonging to the "narrative" (*jishi*) and "multiple passage" (*lianzhang*) genres generally did not call for responses in the voice of Sages or Worthies. *Xinxuan qijiang*, 1b–2b; Gong, *Mingdai bagu wen shitan*, 69. See, for example, Zhou Sijian's essay on the topic "The wife of the prince of a state," in *QSJ* 160.

13 Dong, *Wenjue jiuze*, 5a.

14 Dong, *Wenjue jiuze*, 5a.

15 Su, "Yilun," 4272.

16 Lau, trans., *Mencius*, 60–61, cited in *Wenzheng*, 5.45a.

17 Lau, trans., *Mencius*, 56, cited in *Wenzheng*, 5.45b. *Mencius* 1A.3 is cited as well, to the same effect.

18 Lau, trans., *Mencius*, 90–91, cited in *Wenzheng*, 5.45a.

19 Huang Qiang, *Bagu wen yu Ming Qing wenxue*, 222–24. In this connection, it is also intriguing to note a genre of text known as *Daiyi bian* (Suspicions compiled on others' behalf) written by the late Ming Christian convert Yang Tingyun (1592 *jinshi*): these "suspicions" about Catholic doctrine are not ones that were necessarily openly articulated at the time, but are questions that Yang anticipates critics could have; he deliberately raises them himself, speaking on behalf of the critics in this text, in order better to counter them. See Chan, *Chinese Books and Documents*, 217.

20 *QSJ* 120.

21 Dong, *Wenjue jiuze*, 5b. The topic begins with Tao Ying's question of what would have happened if Shun's father committed murder. Mencius eventually responds, "Shun looked upon casting aside the Empire as no more than discarding a worn shoe. He would have secretly carried the old man on his back and fled to the edge of the Sea and lived there happily, never giving a thought to the Empire" (Lau, trans, *Mencius*, 190). Fang Bao's imperially commissioned collection of examination essays, *Qinding sishu wen*, includes an essay with a passage that differs from the one quoted here by only a single character and attributes it instead to Wang Ao. Fang discusses the attribution question in his commentary to the essay and tentatively decides to list it as Wang's, despite noting its differences from his usual style. *QSJ* 83–84.

22 Dong, *Wenjue jiuze*, 5b. Following other editions, I read 古 here as 由.

23 Qian Zhongshu, *Tanyi lu*, 360–61, see also 33; Huang Qiang, *Bagu wen yu Ming Qing wenxue*, 359–60. On Tang's reputation as a writer of eight-legged essays, see *ZYCH* 5/74–75, 6/87, and 12/241; Deng, *Qingdai bagu wen*, 212; Gong, *Mingdai bagu wen shitan*, 435; Des Forges, "Industry and Its Motivations."

24 Gui, *Xinkan pishi juye qieyao gujin wenze* 5.15a.

25 Jiao, *Yiyu yuelu* 17.7ab.

26 Jia, *Tongcheng pai wenlun xuan*, 14.

27 Fang, "Jin sishu wen xuan biao," 287. For the circumstances surrounding the compilation of this anthology, see Guy, "Fang Pao and the *Ch'in-ting Ssu-shu-wen*." See also Fang, "*Yang Huangzai shiwen xu*," 49.

28 Preface to *LWJC*, 9; Deng, *Qingdai bagu wen*, 202; Man-Cheong, *Class of 1761*, 92; Durand, *Lettrés et pouvoirs*, 79, 82.

29 Arguments that the Hongwu emperor specifically required "speaking for the Sages" in the fourteenth century turn out to rest on the *Mingshi*, compiled at the turn of the eighteenth century; there is no evidence dating from the early Ming for this requirement. Qian Zhongshu, among others, misses this point: see his discussion of the Qing scholarship on this issue contained in juan 8 of *Xuehai tang ji* (*Tanyi lu*, 32). In fact, the early nineteenth-century scholars whose work is collected in *Xuehai tang ji* turn out on the whole to be rather skeptical of the *Mingshi* claim (*Xuehai tang ji* 8.2ab, 3a, 13b, 27a, 29ab, 43b–44a). For a comprehensive study of the historical doc-

uments relevant to the establishment of the Ming examination system, see Guo Peigui, *Mingdai keju shishi*; see also the original documents reprinted in *Zhengde Da Ming huidian*, juan 77.

30 Qiu, "Qing rushi zhi lu," 61b, 62b, 63a.

31 *LWJC* 9.

32 Gui, *Xinkan pishi juye qieyao gujin wenze* 3.13a, 4.40a, and 5.15a, among others; Yuan Huang, *Youyi shu wengui* 4/74 and 7/113.

33 *JYZY* 4.6b–7a; see also 3.16a and 3.19a for brief mentions of similar techniques that are not formulated specifically in terms of representation (*dai*).

34 Cui, *Xuehai jinliang* 3.10b. Similarly, Tang Biao (1640–1713) writes in the late seventeenth century of *dai* as one technique among several, noting in particular its usefulness as a way to avoid slipping into discussion of the part of the original text that immediately follows the defined topic (a fault known as *fanxia*). *Dushu zuowen pu* 7.7b. It is worth pointing out that Lü passes up a particularly appropriate moment to mention representative speech in *Lü Wancun xiansheng lunwen*, 64b.

35 See Gao Dang's margin comments to Mao Kun's discussion of *renti*, in which he jumps in over two centuries later to explain to the reader that literary writing is about *dai shengxian liyan*, even though Mao Kun did not frame the question in these terms (*LWJC* 9). See also the examination preparation manual *Sanyuan biyao*, in which a section dating from the late Ming presents *dai* as a last resort (4.12b–13a), while a section dating from 1735 explains the task of composition as follows: "writing is nothing other than speaking for the ancients (*ti guren shuohua*)" (2.3b).

36 Liang Zhangju proposes two essays by Yang Wanli (1127–1206) as the first cases of *dai guren yuqi* (*ZYCH* 1/15); these essays are reprinted in Tian, *Bagu wen guanzhi*, 57–63. Five of Ruan Yuan's students, set an assignment to discuss the origins and development of the genre, address this question in detail (*Xuehai tang ji* 8.2ab, 13b, 27a, 29ab, 43b–44a). See also Qian Zhongshu, *Tanyi lu*, 32, and Deng, *Qingdai bagu wen*, 22. Huang Qiang gives an overview of the long tradition of representative speech in a variety of genres in *Bagu wen yu Ming Qing wenxue*, 51–54.

37 Qian Zhongshu, *Tanyi lu*, 31, 360–62; Jiao, *Yiyu yuelu* 17.7ab; Liu Shipei, *Lunwen zaji*, 133. See also Roddy, *Literati Identity*, 261; Huang Qiang, *Bagu wen yu Ming Qing wenxue*, 46–47, 324, 352–80.

38 Gong, *Yaqu cangshu*; Ōki, *Genbun de tanoshimu*, 9–54. See also Yinghui Wu, "Constructing a Playful Space." For condemnation of plays written like *shiwen*, see Huang Qiang, *Bagu wen yu Ming Qing wenxue*, 366–67.

39 For You Tong's use of stereotypes about theatrical performance to highlight the problems he saw in the eight-legged essay format, see his 1663 preface to *Guwen lüshu*, 8ab. You's essay is reprinted in Qi, *Shuo bagu*, 46–48.

40 Cai Jingkang, *Mingdai wenlun xuan*, 289–91. Guo Shaoyu and Wang Wensheng have found three other examples of the claim for aria-writing as a part of the Yuan examinations dating from the late Ming and early Qing. They conclude that despite the apparent lack of evidence for this belief, it was widely held during this period. Guo and Wang, *Zhongguo lidai wenlun xuan* 3:167–73, esp. 168–69. See also Rolston, "Sources of Traditional Chinese Fiction Criticism," 23. For a thorough and perceptive discussion of the complex late Ming claims about the relationship between *zaju* and the examination system, see Sieber, *Theaters of Desire*, 97–111; for a more general

discussion of the relationship between theatrical writing and examination writing through the Ming and Qing, see Huang Qiang, *Bagu wen yu Ming Qing wenxue*, 352–80.

41 Li Yu, *Xianqing ouji* 3/54.

42 Huang Qiang, *Bagu wen yu Ming Qing wenxue*, 358. Liang Zhangju says this is too much (*ZYCH* 1/16).

43 Huang Qiang, *Bagu wen yu Ming Qing wenxue*, 352–54. Representative speech in fact became an explicitly marked area of interest for drama critics only in the Wanli era (Huang Qiang, *Bagu wen yu Ming Qing wenxue*, 324).

44 Shen Shouzheng's "*Hu Xiufu shouping shi yi* xu," 3023, notes the difficulty a male student may have in speaking convincingly for a girl in the fields. Here it is also worth noting Wang Yangming's 1525 "Wansong shuyuan ji," in which he makes use of representative speech to imagine what the students who gather at Wansong Academy must be thinking about the reasons for its founding (269).

45 Small topic questions are discussed in more detail in chapter 2. They first appeared on local examinations in the middle of the fifteenth century; by the end of the Ming, they were common at the provincial level as well. After nearly three centuries of complaint, they were officially accepted by the Ministry of Rites as a legitimate question format during the Qianlong era. See Des Forges, "Industry and Its Motivations." On the representation of nonsagely characters, see also Rolston, "Sources of Traditional Chinese Fiction Criticism," 24.

46 "All reading of literary prose is originally intended to broaden one's knowledge, how could it be the case that small topic essays alone should be different? Such as these are the disputes of petty people and even though the descriptions are highly realistic, they are preserved merely for reference. How could one cause younger generations to copy them down, read them over, and think on them at length, training their hearts to lack scruple or restraint?" Ouyang, *Diankan ji* 2.38b–39a. As we have seen previously in this chapter, the *Wenzheng* suggests that this concern is not without basis: it begins by citing as examples the cicada and pigeon ridiculed in the opening chapter of the *Zhuangzi* for the limited scope of their imagination and goes on to mention a conversation from the *Shuoyuan* between an owl and a pigeon. *Wenzheng* 5.45b–46a.

47 Jiao, *Yiyu yuelu* 17.7b.

48 *QSJ* 229, 233.

49 The Shang Lu essay is reprinted in Wu Weifan, *Ming Qing zhiyi jinshuo*, 121; both Confucius and Guan Zhong are referred to in the third person throughout this essay. In the second case, Wu Weifan claims that Wu Hong is writing from the perspective of Zhu Xi, but based on the vocabulary and the description of the examination system in the essay itself, this seems less likely (180–83).

50 On ideological contestation within and outside of the examination system, see Chow, *Publishing, Culture, and Power*, especially chapters 4 and 5. The phenomenon of *ling jia* is discussed in Lü, *Lü Wancun xiansheng lunwen*, 51b, among other sources.

51 Ai, "*Sijia hezuo zhaimiu* xu," 3037.

52 "Most essays use alley language to stand for the words of the Sages and Worthies (*dai shengxian zhi yan*)." Ai, "Xu Wang Zigong *Guansheng cao*," 3030. See also Zhang Shichun, "*Banfang zhai gao* xu," 3038–39, and Ai, *Tian yongzi ji* 12.10a–13a.

53   See *JYZY* 2.19b, 3.16a, 3.19a; *Xuehai tang ji* 8.8b; and Chow, *Publishing, Culture, and Power*, 222, 227–33, 237.

54   On Ai Nanying's significance, see *Xuehai tang ji* 8.38b, and Chow, *Publishing, Culture, and Power*, 214–18, 230–33. We see this concern for maintaining the integrity of the represented voice in Lu Longji's criticism of "assembled topic" (*dati*) questions, small topic questions cobbled together from different sections of a text, which could break up the "voice of the Sages and Worthies" and lead candidates to substitute their own conclusions for those they were meant to be representing (quoted in *ZYCH* 1/21–22). See also Fang Bao's comments in *QSJ* 561, and "*Yang Huangzai shiwen* xu," 49–50. In the Jiaqing era, Huang Renwan presents a memorial asking to create a sequel to *Qinding sishu wen* that refers to *dai shengxian liyan* as a constraint on superficial and weird writing (Deng, *Qingdai bagu wen*, 202).

55   "The august emperor in teaching officials, caused them to study the words of a generation of Sages; in teaching the educated individuals, caused them to represent the arguments of Sages from two thousand years ago (*dai wei erqian nian qian shengren zhi shuo*)." Ni Yuanlu, "*Yang Boxiang taishi gao* xu," 2984. Intriguingly, although this entire passage appears in the *Ming wen hai* version of the preface, it does not appear in the version reprinted in Ni Yuanlu's own *wenji*. Although the deletion may have been made to soften the tone of the preface, it is also possible that it was an error in transcription resulting from a repeated phrase. Both versions are reprinted in *Bagu wen zonglun bazhong*, 420–21.

56   Ray Huang, "Ni Yüan-lu," 418.

57   Meskill, "Academies and Politics in the Ming Dynasty"; Atwell, "From Education to Politics"; Elman, "Imperial Politics and Confucian Societies"; Chow, *Publishing, Culture, and Power*, 223–40; Gong, *Mingdai bagu wen shitan*, 470–72; Ono, *Minki tōsha kō*.

58   *Xuehai tang ji* 8.8b–9a; see also the comments of his contemporaries Yang Maojian and Hou Kang on this question, *Xuehai tang ji* 8.25a, 49ab, as well as Qian Qianyi, *Muzhai youxue ji* 45/447–48.

59   Gong, *Mingdai bagu wen shitan*, 401–2; Huang Qiang, *Bagu wen yu Ming Qing wenxue*, 96–97.

60   Lu Longji, "Lu Jiashu xiansheng lunwen," 4a.

61   Lü Liuliang, *Lü Wancun xiansheng lunwen*, 14a.

62   *QSJ* 198.

63   This essay is reprinted in Gong, *Mingdai bagu wen shitan*, 362–63.

64   *Chuxue yu linglong* 1.17b; see also *Xinxuan qijiang*, 1b–2b.

65   Shang Yanliu, *Qingdai keju kaoshi shulu*, 255. Shang points in particular to the infiltration of material from later historical sources into the discourse that is supposed to belong to the Sages and Worthies alone.

66   Gong, *Mingdai bagu wen shitan*, 27, 334, 406–7.

67   See, for example, the essay by Wang Shu (1416–1508) on the topic "A man who is loved by all the people of his neighborhood," which shifts in and out of representative speech. *QSJ* 26.

68   "The result is a kind of oblique protest that dares not speak its own name but that is often acceded to if only because its claims are seen to emanate from a powerful spirit and not from the woman herself." Scott, *Domination and the Arts of Resistance*,

141. On the more immediate material benefits that could derive from "speaking for the Sages and Worthies," see Shang, *Rulin waishi and Cultural Transformation*, 59–62.

69 Gu, *Rizhi lu jiaozhu* 16/917–18; *ZYCH* 7/125. See also Chow, "Discourse, Examination, and Local Elite," 185–86; Chow, *Publishing, Culture, and Power*, 182–88, 233–40; Shen Junping, *Juye jinliang*, 136–37; Durand, *Lettrés et pouvoirs*, 84–85; Deng, *Qingdai bagu wen*, 208–9; Elman, *A Cultural History*, 118, 207–13, 407–8.

70 Roddy, *Literati Identity*, 57.

71 Elman, *A Cultural History*, 539–40, 551, 556–57, 563, 565; Man-Cheong, *The Class of 1761*, 82–83 and 91–97.

72 Elman, "Changes in the Confucian Civil Service Examinations," 121, 122, 135–43; Deng, *Qingdai baguwen*, 202–3; Chow, "Discourse, Examination, and Local Elite," 185; Chow, *Publishing, Culture, and Power*, 163–66, 177–88; Gong, *Mingdai bagu wen shitan*, 310, 313, 348–49, 400, 403.

73 Pauline Yu, "Canon Formation in Late Imperial China," 99–100; Elman, *A Cultural History*, 544–62.

Chapter 2

1 Guo Peigui, *Mingdai keju shishi*, 165–66.

2 Gong, *Mingdai bagu wen shitan*, 313.

3 Guo Peigui, *Mingdai keju shishi*, 166–67.

4 Guo Peigui, *Mingdai keju shishi*, 168.

5 Gong, *Mingdai bagu wen shitan*, 313–15.

6 *ZYCH* 1/12. See also the discussion of parallelism in chapter 3 of this book.

7 For a nuanced introduction to the issues involved in contrasting Qing dynasty scholarship with that of the Ming, see Yuming He, *Home and the World*, 1–7. Qian Zhongshu argues that in the Ming and in the Qing, even otherwise innovative critics were very conservative in their approach to examination writing, but the examples he cites are not representative of the full range of critical discourse, and he does not address the actual practice of essay writing. *Tanyi lu*, 353–55. On cultural conservatism in the Qing more generally, see Pei-yi Wu, *The Confucian's Progress*, 235; Burnett, *Dimensions of Originality*, 291–324; Chang and Chang, *Crisis and Transformation*.

8 *QSJ* 776. For Han Tan and Liang Zhangju's comments, see *ZYCH* 12/244–45.

9 "Indeed, the civil examination system remained a tense bureaucratic arena, in which the imperial court gamely tried to maintain control of its elites, and the elites brazenly used the government to enhance their social status and economic assets" (Elman, *A Cultural History*, xix; see also xxx, 245); "The civil service examination was in fact an arena where no one single group could establish absolute dominance" (Chow, *Publishing, Culture, and Power*, 150; see also 11–12); "Yet it is very difficult for even the most scrupulous professional historians to answer fully the question of who actually controlled the examinations upon which the mandarinates were based" (Woodside, *Lost Modernities*, 79). For a rather different take on the stakes and contestants involved in the examination system, inspired by the work of Michel Foucault and by theorists of performance and ritual practice, see Man-Cheong, *The Class of 1761*.

10 Cao Pi, *Dianlun* 1.2a.

11 Quoted in *ZYCH* 1/13.

12 *ZYCH* 6/85–86. It is possible that this is a paraphrase rather than a direct quote from Huang. See also Gong, *Mingdai bagu wen shitan*, 389.

13 *ZYCH* 1/21.

14 "I believe, therefore, that education is a process of living and not a preparation for future living." Dewey, *My Pedagogic Creed*, 7.

15 Elman, *A Cultural History*, 45, and more generally 12–46.

16 Huang Qiang, *Bagu wen yu Ming Qing wenxue*, 347. Writing in the Ming, Wang Wenlu explains this as a combination of Tang dynasty and Song dynasty approaches to selecting candidates. Wang Wenlu, *Wenmai* 1/7.

17 *ZYCH* 1/13, 11/210, 12/230; Gao, "Titi leishuo," 1a. Su Xiangfeng assumed that this shift took place only in the early 1500s: "In the Chenghua and Hongzhi reign periods, the literati did not know of printed anthologies of exam essays, in their bookbags were only the Classics and histories, works of classical prose, and the recorded lectures (*yulu*) of earlier scholars, so they just wrote based on their own opinions and did not borrow from others." Quoted in *ZYCH* 2/38. He Jingming, by contrast, places it several decades earlier. Gong, *Mingdai bagu wen shitan*, 236.

18 Yang Wensun, preface to *ZYCH*, 4.

19 See, for example, Zhang Shichun, "*Banfang zhai gao* xu," 3038–39; Lü, *Lü Wancun lunwen*, 25b–26b and 40b–43a.

20 Zhou Zuoren, *Zhongguo xin wenxue de yuanliu*, 32. Ching-i Tu is cautiously supportive of this assessment in "The Chinese Examination Essay," 405.

21 For a detailed discussion of the complexities of this shift in the Yuan and early Ming, see Elman, *A Cultural History*, 32–37.

22 *Zhengde Da Ming huidian*, vol. 77. See also Tian, *Bagu wen guanzhi*, 1215–17; Guo Peigui, *Mingdai keju shishi*, 5–8, 12–18; Gong, *Mingdai bagu wen shitan*, introduction, 7, 141–42.

23 Huang Qiang writes, "To this day I have not found in any Ming or Qing government sources any regulations stipulating the writing of examination essays in a standard eight-legged format." *Bagu wen yu Ming Qing wenxue*, 111. Similarly, Benjamin Elman concludes that "claims that the form derived from earlier styles served to legitimate the eight-legged essay as the proper harvest of past literature and classical learning. And, as in earlier such cases, the literati themselves, not the imperial court, initially produced this new trend in classical writing." *A Cultural History*, 382.

24 See, for example, Qian Daxin's observation that even after the shift to prose-based examinations in the Song, the literati habit of writing in parallel form persisted. *ZYCH* 1/16. On the complicated question of which "examination essays" attributed to Song dynasty authors by later editors were actually written by those authors in that format, see Huang Qiang, *Bagu wen yu Ming Qing wenxue*, 218–30.

25 See his remarks on the occasion of the 1373 suspension of the examination system, which lasted until 1384. Elman, *A Cultural History*, 43–44.

26 *Zhengde Da Ming huidian* 77.5b; Guo Peigui, *Mingdai keju shishi*, 25; Gong, *Mingdai bagu wen shitan*, 23–24.

27 On the bans and criticisms of the bans, see Lu Longji, "Lu Jiashu xiansheng lunwen," 4b–5a; *Xuehai tang ji* 8.44ab; and *ZYCH* 1/16–17. For examples of subsequent

essays that nonetheless include the "concluding summary" feature, see Wu Weifan, *Ming Qing zhiyi jinshuo*, 180–81, 199–200, and 217–18; Wang Kaifu, *Bagu wen gaishuo*, 269–70; and mentions in *ZYCH* 1/16–17. One way for commentators to mask this defiance was to call the summary *shoujie* (if there was no further text after the topic selection in the original) or *luoxia* (if the original text continued beyond the demarcated topic). Although the name changes, the corresponding practice may in fact remain as it was. See Shang Yanliu, *Qingdai keju kaoshi shulu*, 249; Elman, *A Cultural History*, 391.

28 Chow, *Publishing, Culture, and Power*, 164–65; Gong, *Mingdai bagu wen shitan*, 391–92.

29 *ZYCH* 2/29–31; Man-Cheong, *The Class of 1761*, 22, 57–58.

30 Chow, *Publishing, Culture, and Power*, 149–88; Elman, *A Cultural History*, 442; Gong, *Mingdai bagu wen shitan*, 381–87. On examination preparation books, see Shen Junping, *Juye jinliang*, 42–73, 229–37.

31 Original introductory remarks to *QSJ*, 1; *QSJ* 127; Shen Junping, *Juye jinliang*, 230–31.

32 Pu, "Tan bagu wen," 270. Tang Shunzhi writes that Buddhist sutras can take one's essay writing to another level, and Qu Jingchun credits the *Zhuangzi* for inspiring a breakthrough in his writing. See Yuan Huang, *Youyi shu xu wengui* 1/178–79.

33 *JYZY* 4.29b–34a. See also Wu Zhiwang's instructional canon from two generations later, in Yuan Huang, *Youyi shu xu wengui* 9/276.

34 Gu, *Rizhi lu jiaozhu* 18/1020–23.

35 Gu, *Rizhi lu jiaozhu* 18/1019. The offending writer was Yang Qiyuan; see Yu Changcheng's defense of this usage, quoted in *ZYCH* 5/72.

36 Gu, *Rizhi lu jiaozhu* 18/1023.

37 Gu, *Rizhi lu jiaozhu* 18/1021.

38 See *ZYCH* 3/55, 6/87–88, 7/107, 7/113–14, 7/137; Sakai, "Confucianism and Popular Educational Works," 338–39; Gong, *Mingdai bagu wen shitan*, 380–501; Shen Junping, *Juye jinliang*, 229–37, 261–66. Kai-wing Chow writes of the examination preparation materials on the market in the late Ming that "Commentaries and annotations with accurate philological information would be of little utility to the authors, who were interested in providing the students with as many new and outlandish interpretations as possible." *Publishing, Culture, and Power*, 175. See also 179–82 for an account of the range of possible inspirations for these new interpretations.

39 Gu, *Rizhi lu jiaozhu* 18/1017–18; Guo Peigui, *Mingdai keju shishi*, 175–76; Gong, *Mingdai bagu wen shitan*, 315.

40 Huang Qiang, *Bagu wen yu Ming Qing wenxue*, 97.

41 Wu Kuan (1435–1504, 1472 *zhuangyuan*) uses "enlightenment" (*wu* 悟), as do Tang Shunzhi and Wang Qiao (1521–99, 1547 *jinshi*): *QSJ* 58, 113, 123. Qu Jingchun (1544 *jinshi*) makes reference to Daoist meditation and visualization practices and alludes to the *xinxue* of Wang Yangming ("As for the Way"), *QSJ* 166.

42 See, for example, *QSJ* 39, 181, 239–40.

43 Gui, *Nanhua zhenjing pingzhu* has many annotations with careful attention to the structure of the text, differing in this from the philosophically oriented commentaries to the *Zhuangzi*; see also Gui, *Xinkan pishi juye qieyao gujin wenze*, and his essay on the topic "There is that which even the Sage does not know," *QSJ* 171.

44 In addition to Hu Renyu's essay, see the allusions to the *Daode jing* in essays by Wang Qiao and Xu Fuyuan (*QSJ* 123 and 155, respectively), as well as the use of the *Zhuangzi* by such an unimpeachable authority as Li Guangdi, cited in *ZYCH* 9/149–50; see also 3/55, 5/72, 6/87–88, 7/113–14, 7/137.

45 Zhang Shichun, "*Banfang zhai gao* xu," 3038–39.

46 Quoted in *ZYCH* 8/140. See also Yang Shengwu's similar point about the uses of the various philosophers of the Warring States period, who were affiliated with a wide range of schools. Yang Shengwu, *Lunwen size*, 3a.

47 Gu, *Rizhi lu jiaozhu* 16/921.

48 Zhang Taikai, *Zhangshi lunwen yuezhi*, 1b; Gao, "Wenfa jishuo," 25a.

49 Liu Dakui, "Shiwen lun."

50 Ye Xie, "Yu youren lunwen shu," 268–69. See also the mid-Qing commentator cited by Liang Zhangju as remarking that "*wen* can proceed from unique creativity, but *li* must be based in the ideas of our predecessors." *ZYCH* 11/197.

51 Gu, *Rizhi lu jiaozhu* 18/1023. See also Wang Kentang (1589 *jinshi*) for a similar take on the descent from the Classics to the Masters to the Histories to Buddha and Laozi; although Wang clearly valued Buddhism on its own terms, he sees no place for it in examination writing. *JYZY* 3.26b–27a.

52 The standard commentary to "The wife of the prince of a state" asserts that the meanings of the distinctions between different terms used for the wife of the ruler cannot be traced. After giving a systematic explanation of why these distinctions are in fact significant, Wang concludes his essay with the following words, in case his point might have been missed: "Oh! All of these differences in how one person, the wife of the ruler, is referred to are all set through a tracing of actual feeling (*qing*), and arise through logic (*li*). How could scholars overlook this?" *QSJ* 34. Tang writes of Mencius's critique, "If scholars can begin from words [of the original text] and bring the text together with their minds, examining the traces and using rational principles (*li*) to decide on their validity, then every book in the world is of use to me." *QSJ* 235. On Li Zhi's *Shuoshu*, see *Bagu wen zonglun bazhong*, 241, 251–90, and Huang Qiang, *Bagu wen yu Ming Qing wenxue*, 145–50. Notable in this connection is Feng Qi's 1601 memorial, which presents a general purging of heterodox material from school libraries as the logical next step after the collection and burning of all Li Zhi's books, with the aim of returning *shiwen* production to a more orthodox track. Gu, *Rizhi lu jiaozhu* 18/1023.

53 Writing in the late fifteenth century on the topic "At fifteen, I had my mind bent on learning," Cai Qing (1453–1508) explicitly rejected Cheng Yi's claim in the authorized commentary that Confucius's sagehood was always fully realized and that the original text details stages of learning only as a heuristic guide for the mere humans who would follow. *QSJ* 7–8. Decades later, the well-known stylist Gui Youguang took a similar approach, beginning his essay even more forcefully with the following direct attack on Cheng Yi's claim: "The means by which the Sage reached the Way indeed were only gradual. Now the Way is limitless and inexhaustible, even a Sage is dependent on study; in studying there must be some aspect that is gradual. This is logically necessary; how could it be that this text merely makes a display of excessive humility on the part of the Sage in order to allow those in the world to complete themselves? Such a misunderstanding is due to the fact that people in the world

treated the Sage with excessive reverence and thought he had absolute virtue among all in the world, and did not know that it is the unceasing diligence of the Sage that is in fact our own duty." *QSJ* 112. See also Gong, *Mingdai bagu wen shitan*, 356, and Huang Qiang, *Bagu wen yu Ming Qing wenxue*, 197–99.

54 See, for example, Fang Bao's praise for the subtlety with which an essay on the topic "Between father and son, there should be affection" by Qiu Jun (1418–95) moves back and forth between the commentary's insistence that the virtues in question are inherent in human nature and Mencius's framing of the passage as Shun being so busy ensuring that the people are properly *instructed* in these virtues that he has no time to farm for himself, as well as Gui Youguang's balancing act in his essay on the same topic. *QSJ* 63–64, 161. See also Pu, "Tan bagu wen," 272–73.

55 On the grading of this essay, see *ZYCH* 12/233–34.

56 *QSJ* 146.

57 This translation is taken from Watson (trans.), *Complete Works of Chuang Tzu*, 57–58.

58 Qian Mu, *Zhuzi xue tigang*, 119–29.

59 Gao, "Wenfa jishuo," 13a.

60 *ZYCH* 13/257–58. As we see in *ZYCH* 13/258–59 and elsewhere, "correct" interpretations of the classical canon newly advanced would often be prefaced by citing the range of conventional wisdom against which these new interpretations could distinguish themselves. As with aesthetic excellence, it was now not enough just to be right, it was also important to be distinctive.

61 Ai, "*Huang Zhangqiu jinyi* xu," 3035–36. "The people are the most important element in a nation" is included in *Qinding sishu wen* (*QSJ* 633–34); translations of this essay appear in Lo, "Four Examination Essays," 176–78, and Elman, *A Cultural History*, 407.

62 Xu, "*Tongren hebian* xu," 3044–45.

63 Chow, *Publishing, Culture, and Power*, 2; see also 189. Kent Guy notes that even the *Qinding sishu wen* includes essays by writers who never earned the *jinshi* degree. "Fang Pao and the *Ch'in-ting Ssu-shu-wen*," 167. For an early nineteenth-century discussion of the significance of essay collections in setting and changing standards, see *Xuehai tang ji* 8.7b–9a, 14b.

64 Chow, *Publishing, Culture, and Power*, 86–87, 240.

65 Chow, *Publishing, Culture, and Power*, 163, 201.

66 Chow, *Publishing, Culture, and Power*, 166.

67 Martin Huang, *Literati and Self-Re/Presentation*, 2; Guy, *The Emperor's Four Treasuries*, 18. For a sense of the extent to which essay collections continued to appear in the Qing, see Durand, *Lettrés et pouvoirs*, 84–89, and Shang Yanliu, *Qingdai keju kaoshi shulu*, 258–60. Many essay collections published by academies in the Qing are reprinted in *Zhongguo lidai shuyuan zhi*.

68 See, for example, Ai Nanying's remarks quoted in Gu, *Rizhi lu jiaozhu* 18/1018–19, and his criticism of candidates who draw from Daoist and Legalist texts, as well as from Six Dynasties parallel prose, in Ai, *Tian yongzi ji* 9.19a–21b. On the diversity of stylistic affiliations among *shishang*, see Chow, *Publishing, Culture, and Power*, 222.

69 This preface is quoted in *ZYCH* 2/35–39. See also Ai Nanying's comments on the 1634 examination cycle in "*Jiaxu fangxuan* xu shang" (*Tian yongzi ji* 9.16a–18a).

70 Qiu, "Qing rushi zhi lu," 59a–64a.

71 See, for example, Miyazaki, *China's Examination Hell*; Elman, *A Cultural History*, 277; Chow, *Publishing, Culture, and Power*, 1–2, 93, 187, 189, 201, 219–23; Ge, *The Scholar and the State*, 8–9, 67. For Ai Nanying's preface, see *ZYCH* 6/97–99; on Pu Songling, see Elman, *A Cultural History*, 361, and Allan Barr, "Pu Songling and the Qing Examination System."

72 "Examiners transmitted the authority of the orthodox Tao Learning persuasion in the examination compound. Their efforts to control interpretations in classical essays ensured that the dynasty's cultural conservatism was based on the authority of a fixed canon. Such canonical authority, however, could not always dictate the hermeneutic procedures candidates would apply in their essays. Novelty and literary creativity could not be legislated against." Elman, *A Cultural History*, 422; see also 276–77. Kai-wing Chow writes of a confrontation between the imperial state and a developing public sphere made up of members of the educated elite who were not in office: "What is significant is the challenge [the critics'] poetics posed to the authority of officials and examiners who sought to impose an official standard on all examinees." Chow, *Publishing, Culture, and Power*, 222.

73 I am led to insist on this point in part by the work of James Scott on dynamics of subordination and resistance, in particular by his distinction between "public" and "hidden transcripts." Although examiners in Ming and Qing China were certainly significantly higher in social status than the groups Scott studies in *Weapons of the Weak* and *Domination and the Arts of Resistance*, the structural characteristics of the hierarchy in which they were employed ensured that any changes that they might introduce could be recognized as changes only in negative terms, as problematic deviations from a correct standard. "The public transcript, where it is not positively misleading, is unlikely to tell the whole story about power relations. It is frequently in the interests of both parties to tacitly conspire in misrepresentation." Scott, *Domination and the Arts of Resistance*, 2.

74 Yuan Hongdao, "Xu *Sizi gao*," 8. Zeng Yizhuan also notes the potential for tension between examiners and "decrees from above" in "Xu *Guiyou weidu chao*," 3010–11. On the role of education commissioners and publication models, see Li Tingji's late Ming comments in *JYZY* 2.16b. Shen Cheng's "Wenti ce" includes strong criticism of examiners who undercut decrees that are aimed at rectifying literary style and literati mores, quoted in Gong, *Mingdai bagu wen shitan*, 388–89.

75 "It is fairly clear that the [examinations'] questions and curricular materials were conditioned by the views, not just of emperors, but of hundreds of examiners and 'checking' officials who shaped them by a subtle and variegated repertoire of maneuvers over which they apparently had full discretionary command." Woodside, *Lost Modernities*, 79. See also Gong, *Mingdai bagu wen shitan*, 194–95, 226–27, introduction, 8; Man-Cheong, *The Class of 1761*, 15, 94–95; and Hilde De Weerdt's discussion of a similar question in the Song context (*Competition over Content*, 379).

76 On small topic questions, see Magone, "Once Every Three Years," 196–97; Durand, "L'homme bon et la montagne," 233–35; Gong, *Mingdai bagu wen shitan*, 65–66, 72–81, 87–91, 103–32; Huang Qiang, *Bagu wen yu Ming Qing wenxue*, 13–24; the introductions to the 2009 Wanjuan chuban gongsi reprint of Jin Shengtan, *Xiaoti caizi shu*; Des Forges, "Industry and Its Motivations." For examples and discussions in primary sources, see *ZYCH* juan 22–23 and Ouyang, *Diankan ji*, 45a–47a. A significant portion

of extant examination essay collections include *xiaoti* essays or consist entirely of those essays, with examples ranging from Jin Shengtan's seventeenth-century *Xiaoti caizi shu* to *Qingyun lou xiaoti wen* (1872). Huang Qiang discusses *guanti*, a Song dynasty precedent for this practice, in *Bagu wen yu Ming Qing wenxue*, 72–74.

77 Gong, *Mingdai bagu wen shitan*, 89.

78 For some examples of these combined questions, see Shang Yanliu, *Qingdai keju kaoshi shulu*, 252; Deng, *Qingdai bagu wen*, 142–58.

79 Qiu, "Qing rushi zhi lu," 60ab.

80 Des Forges, "Industry and Its Motivations."

81 *Lunyu jizhu*, 38.

82 Zhao, Li, et al., *Qingdai bagu wen yizhu*, 148–54. The essays collected in this modern work have a particularly interesting source: they had been hand-copied in miniature onto silk for a candidate to smuggle into the examination hall. Although it is likely that they were thought to be fairly good examples of the form, the original authors' names are not included.

83 Wang Fuzhi, *Xitang yongri xulun waipian*, 21b–22a.

84 See, for example, the different treatment of the first chapter of the *Zhongyong* in essays by Cai Qing (covering the whole chapter), Chu Quan (covering two full sentences from the chapter), and Luo Ji (covering one sentence from the chapter). *QSJ* 38, 39, and 40–41.

85 Gong, *Mingdai bagu wen shitan*, 126–27. For another well-known example of a small topic essay that goes beyond the content of the original text, see Yu Yue's "Without the compass and square," reprinted with annotations in Deng, *Qingdai bagu wen*, 136–42, and in Wang Kaifu, *Bagu wen gaishuo*, 280–84.

86 Jiao, *Yiyu yuelu* 8.5a.

87 Quoted in *ZYCH* 1/21–22. A similar point is made contrasting *lianzhang ti* with *jieda ti* in the introductory remarks to *Lianlun lianzhang caifeng ji*, 1a. For extreme examples of *jieda ti*, see Zhang Zhongxin, "*Shuo bagu* buwei," 63–65; Deng, *Qingdai bagu wen*, 199–201. For a discussion of how to manage different types of small topic questions, see Lü, *Lü Wancun xiansheng lunwen*, 59a–61b, 62b–63a.

88 Gao, "Lunwen zatiao," 20b.

89 Guo Peigui, *Mingdai keju shishi*, 69; see also *Zhengde Da Ming huidian* 77.6b.

90 Gong, *Mingdai bagu wen shitan*, 89–90. In a small victory for those who disdained their use, small topic questions were never accepted at the very highest metropolitan level of the examinations, despite their popularity at the local and provincial levels.

91 Quoted in Gong, *Mingdai bagu wen shitan*, 126.

92 Deng, *Qingdai bagu wen*, 199.

93 On the role of education commissioners and publication models, see Li Tingji's late Ming comments in *JYZY* 2.16b, and He Jingming, "Shucheng sankuan," 29b–34a. Outstanding examples of tastemakers who enjoyed examination success that came late if at all include Gui Youguang, Ai Nanying, and Chen Jitai. See Chow, *Publishing, Culture, and Power*, 76–77, 210, 214.

94 See, for example, "[An Early Preface to] *The Fashion System*" in Barthes, *The Language of Fashion*, 70–85.

95 Yuan Huang, *Youyi shu wengui* 8/120; *Huayang jijin* 5.1a; introductory remarks to *ZYCH*, 7.

96 See, for example, Shen Cheng's criticism of insubordinate examiners, quoted in Gong, *Mingdai bagu wen shitan*, 388–89. Unsurprisingly, this phenomenon is framed here in terms of inability on the part of the examiners rather than as a deliberate challenge to imperial decrees. See also Chow, *Publishing, Culture, and Power*, 221.

97 de Certeau, *The Practice of Everyday Life*, 48–49; Scott, *Weapons of the Weak* and *Domination and the Arts of Resistance*. As one example of the kind of deductive work necessary to begin to get a sense of the means by which examiners could effect significant changes in examination practice, see Elman's discussion of the question of whether poetry should be tested on the examinations, raised in Shaanxi and elsewhere in 1759: "The Shen-hsi question reflected the policy question on poetry in the examinations that were asked in other provinces clearly enough that we can see a unified attempt by the examiners to influence imperial policy." Elman, *A Cultural History*, 551.

98 Xu, "*Tongren hebian* xu," 3044.

99 On the significance of commercial publishing as a motive for innovative commentaries in the late Ming, see Chow, *Publishing, Culture, and Power*, 152–89, 201.

100 On the complicated relationship between class formation and reproduction, and the catachresis that is "cultural capital," see Des Forges, "Sleights of Capital"; on the relationship between the market for literati writing and the examination system, see Des Forges, "Industry and Its Motivations."

101 Quoted in *ZYCH* 2/37.

102 Ai, *Tian yongzi ji* 9.16a–18a; Li Tingji cited in *JYZY* 2.16b; Qiu, "Qing rushi zhi lu," 61b; Xia Yan is quoted in Guo Peigui, *Mingdai keju shishi*, 165–66.

103 Zhou Zuoren, "Lun bagu wen," 62–63; see also Ch'en, *Chinese Literature*, 509. An even more egregious example of this kind of performance plays a key role in Chen Duxiu's disillusionment with the examination system (Magone, "The Silence of the Lanes," 327–28). See also Gong, *Mingdai bagu wen shitan*, 254; Shang Wei, *Rulin waishi and Cultural Transformation*, 134–36; and Keulemans, *Sound Rising from Paper*, 247–48, for other examples of the figure of the reader performing to himself.

104 Qiu, "Qing rushi zhi lu," 61b, 62b.

105 Feng Dingyuan, as quoted in *ZYCH* 1/21. See Wu Zhiwang's take on this question: "I say that in cultivating one's mind, one cannot dare to insist that it will resemble the Sages and Worthies in all particulars; only this reading of books and writing of essays is that which our duty requires of us." Yuan Huang, *Youyi shu xu wengui* 9/272.

106 Man-Cheong, *The Class of 1761*, 18, 204; Anderson, *Imagined Communities*, 25, 35.

107 Anderson, *Imagined Communities*, 25; emphasis in original.

108 For a brief sketch of continuities between the examination system and installment fiction as means of imagining communities, see Des Forges, "1890, Fall."

109 Quoted in *ZYCH* 1/23.

110 Gu, *Rizhi lu jiaozhu* 16/921–22.

111 Kant, *Critique of Judgment*, 176–78, 186–87.

112 For an account of the stages through which the individual moves in this internalization process, see the essay by Zhang Yongqi discussed in chapter 4 of this book. Fang Bao refers to the *Zhuangzi* in his comment to an essay by Tang Shunzhi to make a similar point about internalization of standards. *QSJ* 101.

113 See Eagleton, *The Ideology of the Aesthetic*, esp. 31–69.

114 Chow, *Publishing, Culture, and Power*, 104ff.

115 As Benjamin Elman puts it, "The regimen for reading described above for civil examination candidates was not intended to make them members of a 'reading public,' although a 'reading elite' certainly was a by-product of their training. They were in training, via memorization and calligraphy practice, to become members of a 'writing elite' whose essays would mark each as a classically trained literatus who could write his way to fame, fortune, and power via essays on the local, provincial, metropolitan, and palace examinations." Elman, *A Cultural History*, 276–77. For a detailed discussion of these points, see Des Forges, "Sleights of Capital" and "Industry and Its Motivations."

116 According to Marx, "In a communist society there are no painters but at most people who engage in painting among other activities" (*The German Ideology*, Part 1, 109). Of particular interest in this regard is John Guillory's wistful commentary on this statement: "The utopia of production Marx imagines reproduces Bourdieu's domain of 'restricted production'—production for other producers—*as a condition of the entire society*" and "The point is not to make judgment disappear but to reform the conditions of its practice.... Socializing the means of production and consumption would be the condition of an aestheticism unbound, not its overcoming. But of course, this is only a thought experiment." Guillory, *Cultural Capital*, 338, 340.

117 See Kant on the relation between genius and taste: ultimately "if there is a conflict between these two properties in a product, and something has to be sacrificed, then it should rather be on the side of genius." Kant, *Critique of Judgment*, 179–89.

118 On ghost-writing, see Chow, *Publishing, Culture, and Power*, 103, 106, 110.

119 See, for example, Chen Longzheng, *Juye suyu*, 21b–23a. Essays on the Four Books were reduced in number and seem to have appeared in the second session rather than the first session between 1663 and 1667; the format in which these essays were written may also have been looser during this period. *Benchao Zhewei sanchang quanti beikao; ZYCH* 9/152; Elman, *A Cultural History*, 530–33.

120 Elman, *A Cultural History*, 277.

Chapter 3

1 *Mingshi* 70/1693.

2 See, for example, Ch'en, *Chinese Literature*, 508; Nivison, "Protest against Conventions," 194; Ropp, *Dissent in Early Modern China*, 92–93; Deng, *Qingdai bagu wen*, 10; the journal editor's introduction to Lo, "Four Examination Essays," 167–68; Elman, *A Cultural History*, 394–95. Tu Ching-i allows for a greater degree of stylistic variability generally speaking, but nonetheless emphasizes parallelism in the main body of the essay as an "essential characteristic." Tu, "The Chinese Examination Essay," 398. Pierre-Henri Durand presents a similarly nuanced account in "L'homme bon et la montagne," esp. 238–41.

3 See, for example, Cheng, "Some Reflections on Chinese Poetic Language." Andrew Plaks suggests that although hardly unique to Chinese literature, "the workings of parallelism seem to go farther in Chinese usage than in most comparable cases." Plaks, "Where the Lines Meet," 47; on vernacular fiction and drama see 57–60. See

also Plaks, "Bones of Parallel Rhetoric," 163–73, and Owen, "Liu Xie and the Discourse Machine," 175–91.

4 Writing at the turn of the nineteenth century, Ruan Yuan revisits the Six Dynasties discussions of *wen* and *bi* (筆) in three essays that remained highly influential down to the Republican period: "Wenyan shuo," "Wenyun shuo," and "Shu 'Liang Zhaoming Taizi *Wenxuan* xu' hou." See also *Xuehai tang ji* juan 7; Liu Shipei, *Zhongguo zhonggu wenxue shi* and *Lunwen zaji*; and Huters, "From Writing to Literature," 83–96.

5 *ZYCH* 1/16. On Song examination essays, see Zhu Shangshu, *Songdai keju yu wenxue*, 321–49; on the place of classical prose in Song examination writing, see De Weerdt, "Canon Formation and Examination Culture," 91–111.

6 Plaks, "The Prose of Our Time," 209.

7 *QSJ* 39. See also Gui Youguang's famous essay on the topic "The Son of Heaven constituted one dignity," which primarily consists of two extended sections over 240 characters in length. Half of each section is perfectly parallel to the other, and the other halves are as close to perfectly parallel as the assigned topic selection allows. *QSJ* 220–21; Gong, *Mingdai bagu wen shitan*, 346–47.

8 *Tang Song ba da jia wenchao*, 445–51; Plaks, "Where the Lines Meet," 50. On this point, see also Ping Buqing, *Xiawai junxie*, 460, and Huang Qiang, *Bagu wen yu Ming Qing wenxue*, 57–59. Hilde De Weerdt notes the continued use of parallel structures among writers of classical prose in *Competition over Content*, 73.

9 Another good example of this technique appears in an essay by Chen Xianzhang (1428–1500, *juren* 1447), "Anciently, the establishment of the frontier-gates," which includes the following lines: "I do not regret that the moderns do not study the ancients; but when it comes to the people of today not being able to obtain guidance from the government of the ancients I am particularly saddened by the misfortune they encounter"—ten characters in the first line matched by eighteen in the second. *QSJ* 86.

10 Tang Xianzu, *Tang Xu er huiyuan zhiyi*, comment to an essay on the topic "If the scholar be not grave." For other examples, see *JYZY* 2.36a and 3.17ab; Cui, *Xuehai jinliang* 2.14a, 3.9a; Zhang Taikai, *Zhangshi lunwen yuezhi*, 8b–9a, 18a; Gao, "Wenfa jishuo," 3b; *ZYCH* 6/88, 7/120–21; introductory remarks to *Xiaoti zhenggu*, 1a; *Huayang jijin* 2.14a; Huang Qiang, *Bagu wen yu Ming Qing wenxue*, 40, 102.

11 *ZYCH* 7/106; Gao, "Lunwen zatiao," 10b–11a. Similarly, Chen Hongxu (1597–1665) lets us know that excessive parallelism is "vulgar." Gong, *Mingdai bagu wen shitan*, 418. See also Gao Dang's discussion of "two wing" topics in "Titi leishuo," 41b–42b.

12 Quoted in Cui, *Xuehai jinliang* 2.14b.

13 *ZYCH* 3/56, 2/47. See also Lü Liuliang's praise for lines that "seem to be parallel but are not parallel; seem to be loose but are not loose" (*Lü Wancun xiansheng lunwen*, 38a); Liu Dakui's comment that "Literary writing values unevenness; of all things created by heaven, there is none that is not matched and none that is perfectly balanced" (*Lunwen ouji*, 10); and Chen Longzheng, *Juye suyu*, 21b.

14 Huang Qiang, *Bagu wen yu Ming Qing wenxue*, 102–3.

15 Gu, *Rizhi lu jiaozhu* 16/919–20; Zhu Jian, preface to *ZYCH*, 3. Intriguingly, Gao Dang's 1786 version of Zhang Taikai's remarks on parallelism interpolates a new criticism of students for following You Tong, who Guo claims is known for his parallel prose, not for his examination essays, and strongly asserts that mastery of parallelism alone did not qualify a writer for imitation by examination candidates. Since

this particular point does not appear in Zhang's original version, composed in 1752, it is likely that the intervening years had seen an increased emphasis on parallel writing by examination candidates. For Gao Dang's version of Zhang's comments, see Zhang Taikai, "Zhang Youtang lunwen," 17b.

16 The sessions cited are provincial level examinations in 1804, 1812, and 1831. *ZYCH* 2/41; see also 11/209.

17 "The people are the most important element in a nation" appears in *QSJ* 633–34. Translations of this essay appear in Lo, "Four Examination Essays," 176–78, and Elman, *A Cultural History*, 407. "To the mind belongs the office of thinking" appears in *QSJ* 616–17.

18 *QSJ* 9, 32–33.

19 The former appears in Wang Kaifu, *Bagu wen gaishuo*, 257–58; the latter in Wu Wei-fan, *Ming Qing zhiyi jinshuo*, 208–9.

20 Gao, "Wenfa jishuo," 14b.

21 Preface to *Xiaoti zhenggu*, 2a.

22 *JYZY* 3.17b.

23 de Certeau, *The Practice of Everyday Life*, 97.

24 Plaks, "Where the Lines Meet," 47ff.

25 *QSJ* 129–30.

26 The relationship between N_1 and N_2 does differ slightly between the two lines. In the first line, either Bo Yi or Shu Qi would become a feudal lord, but in the second line it is the realm itself that resembles a worn-out sandal.

27 "Discarding the realm like a worn-out sandal" refers us to *Mencius* 7A.35, which also deals with the complications of family relations and political power; ironically *qie* also appears in this same passage (where Shun would steal away with his father on his back), but with rather a different meaning.

28 Mair and Mei, "The Sanskrit Origins of Recent Style Prosody." Similar to examination essays referred to as "modern prose," regulated verse was known as "recent style poetry" (*jinti shi*) and, as Mair and Mei remind us, was central to the Tang examination system.

29 According to one eighteenth-century manual, even and oblique tones should harmonize (*xie*). Gao, "Wenfa jishuo," 4b. Although this could mean simply matching single characters against each other by tone, other longer and more complicated patterns were common. See Deng, *Qingdai bagu wen*, 121, and Qi, *Shuo bagu*, 22–23, 40–45.

30 See, for example, Yuan Renlin's discussion of the addition of empty words in the recital of poetry: "Formerly Master Ch'eng . . . pleased himself by adding one or two empty words when he recited a poem, and the whole poem came alive, suddenly articulated and charged with internal transformations. Master Chu . . . proceeded in the same manner when he explained a poem." Translated in Cheng, "Some Reflections on Chinese Poetic Language," 39. Original in Yuan Renlin, *Xuzi shuo*, 38ab.

31 Quoted in *ZYCH* 6/86.

32 *QSJ* 142. For an example of "carried characters," see the following match: "through transcendence it is illuminated, preserved in *that* person, those who feel it do so through heaven, those who attend to it do so through heaven . . . through transformation it is tailored, preserved through change, those who follow it do so through

heaven, those who do *not* exceed it do so through heaven" in "At fifteen, I had my mind bent on learning," *QSJ* 112.

33 *QSJ* 108.

34 *QSJ* 143.

35 For a description of this technique, see Gao, "Wenfa jishuo," 3b–4a.

36 Dong, *Wenjue jiuze*, 13a. Wu Zhiwang also emphasizes the importance of "criss-crossing" (*cuozong*) to complicate the flow of the argument. See Wu Zhiwang, "Wu Shuqing lunwen," 1a.

37 Qi, *Shuo bagu*, 22. See also Huang Qiang, *Bagu wen yu Ming Qing wenxue*, 36, where a similarly structured passage from another essay is merely noted in passing to have "rather large discrepancies."

38 *QSJ* 27–28.

39 For a simpler example of this technique, which would not have posed a challenge to most readers, see Wang Yangming, "The determined scholar and the benevolent person," *QSJ* 31. Wang Ao and the other authors discussed here push this approach to an extreme.

40 For other examples of involutionary parallelism in essays by Wang Ao, see *QSJ*, 21, 25, 27–28, 34 (the comment about "unevenness" comes in response to this last one). For essays by other authors, see *QSJ* 23, 32–33, 170, 201, 674–76, among others. See also Deng, *Qingdai bagu wen*, 162.

41 *QSJ* 54–55.

42 "The operation of walking, wandering, or 'window shopping,' that is, the activity of passers-by, is transformed into points that draw a totalizing and reversible line on the map. They allow us to grasp only a relic set in the nowhen of a surface of projection. Itself visible, it has the effect of making invisible the operation that made it possible." De Certeau, *The Practice of Everyday Life*, 97.

43 See, for example, the discussion in Wu Zhiwang, "Wu Shuqing lunwen," 1a.

44 Quoted in *ZYCH* 3/47.

45 *Tang Song ba da jia wenchao*, 2788–89. This brief piece was a touchstone for later advocates for the reform of decadent writing, such as Ai Nanying. See Ai, *Tian yongzi ji* 2.4a. For an overview of the different meanings that the term *guwen* assumed over the centuries, see Feng Shugeng, *Guwen tonglun*, 1–83.

46 *Tang Song ba da jia wenchao*, 2111–12. Han Yu refers to *guwen* in his essay "Shi shuo," but it is unclear here whether he means a genre that is still actively productive, or is merely referring to texts that date from an earlier and better era.

47 Ruan, "Shu Liang Zhaoming taizi 'Wenxuan xu' hou," 106. See also Bao, *Yizhou shuang ji* 2.38b–41b. On the relationship between examination writing and classical prose in the Song, see Feng Shugeng, *Guwen tonglun*, 25, 42–52.

48 Gao, "Lunwen zatiao," 11a. See also the claim elsewhere in the same text that classical prose is concerned primarily with material force and modern prose with technique; classical prose influences only one's spirit and not the formal aspects of one's writing. Gao, "Lunwen zatiao," 1a.

49 Introductory remarks to *Mingshi wenzong*, 1b. See also Ruan, "Yu youren lun guwen shu," 107.

50 See, for example, Qian Zhonglian, "Tongcheng pai guwen yu shiwen de guanxi wenti." Qian represents the two types of writing as essentially different (79), allowing only

that modern prose could have a negative effect on classical prose, while "the influence of classical prose on modern prose was a means for raising the latter's level" (78).

51 Chongzhen preface to *Mingshi wenzong*, 5b. Indeed, Huang Qiang notes that Song anthologies of classical prose could include examination essays from that same dynasty. Huang Qiang, *Bagu wen yu Ming Qing wenxue*, 452.

52 Fang, "Yu Han Mulu xueshi shu," 333; Liu Dakui, "Shiwen lun," 2a; Yao Nai's preface to his own *Xibao xuan shiwen*; Yao, "Xibao xuan yu," 2b; Lü Xinchang, *Gui Zhenchuan ji qi sanwen*, 113–14; Huang Qiang, *Bagu wen yu Ming Qing wenxue*, 453.

53 Huang Zongxi, "*Li Gaotang wenchao xu*"; Dai Mingshi, "*Xiaoxue lunxuan xu*," 90–92.

54 1609 edition of *Wenzhang guifan*; this preface is standard in later reprint editions of the *Wenzhang guifan*, such as the 1883 edition, reproduced in 1991 by Zhongzhou guji chuban she.

55 Ai, *Tian yongzi ji* 2.3b–4b; Bao, preface to *Yizhou shuangji*, 4a. Ruan Yuan makes a similar point in "Shu Liang Zhaoming taizi '*Wenxuan* xu' hou."

56 On Ouyang Xiu as examiner, see Bol, "*This Culture of Ours*," 191–94, and De Weerdt, "Canon Formation and Examination Culture," 93–111.

57 Gong, *Mingdai bagu wen shitan*; Huang Qiang, *Bagu wen yu Ming Qing wenxue*; Chow, "Discourse, Examination, and Local Elite," 183–96.

58 Huang Qiang, *Bagu wen yu Ming Qing wenxue*, 428–29, 452. See also De Weerdt, "Canon Formation and Examination Culture," 99–100.

59 Gong, *Mingdai bagu wen shitan*, 301; Shen Junping, *Juye jinliang*, 42–73, 229–37.

60 Original introductory remarks to *QSJ*, 1; *QSJ* 127; Shen Junping, *Juye jinliang*, 230–31.

61 Jiao, *Yiyu yuelu* 17.7a; Liu, *Lunwen zaji*, 133.

62 Gao, "Lunwen zatiao," 11a. See also Ruan, "Shu Liang Zhaoming taizi '*Wenxuan* xu' hou," which locates the shift to longer sentences in exam essays to the Hongzhi and Zhengde reign periods; these longer sentences resemble those found in classical prose of the Tang and Song. Fang Bao (along with Han Tan) is cited as an example of a writer who can combine *guwen* and *shiwen* in one written hand. *ZYCH* 9/158.

63 Zhang Zhongxing, "*Shuo bagu huwei*," 63. See also Deng, *Qingdai bagu wen*, 220, as well as De Weerdt's discussion of the use of parallelism in a Song-dynasty exposition (*lun*) by Huang Huai. De Weerdt, *Competition over Content*, 73–74.

64 *QSJ* 8.

65 *QSJ* 9. The parallel match runs as follows: "Thinking is sought in the mind, measuring carefully in order to explore its subtlety, tracing out in order to search out one's interest; who could abandon thinking? Now [the object of] thinking is logic. Logic must be conveyed through things; things are the material for learning, and the way of learning is none other than practice. If one does not practice then the mind will not be pleased; thus thinking depends on learning to yield real effects. Otherwise, although one may reflect in detail, it will not be true vision based on evidence; investigation will merely be precise to no purpose, and not realized in distinctive actions. The appropriateness of the logic of things will end in perplexity and apprehension; how could one hope that things will be contentedly put in good order?" *QSJ* 8. A similar, although slightly freer structure appears in Gu Xiancheng's "It requires a perfectly benevolent prince to be able, with a great country, to serve a small one," to be discussed in more detail in chapter 4. Gong Duqing remarks of this essay that it is single-line writing in parallel form. *Mingdai bagu wen shitan*, 480.

66 In 1110 CE, examiners were asked to "accept essays whose logic succeeds and dismiss those that are forced into a parallel structure." *ZYCH* 1/15.

67 Owen, "Liu Xie and the Discourse Machine."

68 *ZYCH* 7/111.

69 Dividing one meaning into two layers (*yiyi fenchu liangceng*); overturning one meaning to yield a second layer (*yiyi fanchu liangceng*); supplementing one layer with a second (*yiceng chenchu liangceng*). Quoted in *ZYCH* 2/41. This same explanation, attributed to a different authority, also appears in Gao, "Wenfa jishuo," 3b. See also *Huayang jijin* 1.49a, which discusses transforming one meaning into two (*yiyi hualiang*), and Gong, *Mingdai bagu wen shitan*, 33.

70 Bao, *Yizhou shuangji* 2.39b.

71 Zhou Zuoren, *Zhongguo xin wenxue de laiyuan*, 31. See also Dai Shadi, "Xinhai zhi ji wenlun," 584–85. Ironically, as Rui Magone points out, the canonical May Fourth story "Kong Yi Ji," written by Zhou Zuoren's older brother, shows distinct structural correspondences with the eight-legged essay. Magone, "Silence of the Lanes," 351–52.

72 This dynamic resembles the organization of order and disorder into a higher-level order that Steven Sangren finds to be characteristic of popular religious practice in *History and Magical Power*, 171.

73 For example, Gao, "Wenfa jishuo," 1b, 5a; "Shen Hongtai lunwen," 1b. "Odd and even mutually engender" appears in Gao, "Wenfa jishuo," 16b and Ruan, "Shu Liang Zhaoming taizi 'Wenxuan xu' hou." Not to mention, at a more abstract level, "the spirit of the self" balanced by "the spirit of the Sages and Worthies." Liu Dakui, "Shiwen lun," 1b–2a, and Bao, *Yizhou shuangji* 1.1b ("Although the physical form is parallel there is oddness at its heart in order to shake the material force awake; although the force is loose, there is parallelism at its heart in order to plant its bones firmly"). See also Lü Liuliang, *Lü Wancun xiansheng lunwen*, 21a. For other examples of pairs of contrasting stylistic qualities in the modern prose essay, see Durand, "L'homme bon et la montagne," 245–46.

74 "In particular, if one takes the 'map' in its current geographical form, we can see that in the course of the period marked by the birth of modern scientific discourse . . . the map has slowly disengaged itself from the itineraries that were the condition of its possibility." De Certeau, *The Practice of Everyday Life*, 120.

75 See, for example, chapter 3 of Wu Jingzi, *Rulin waishi*.

76 Elman, *A Cultural History*, 403–7. "When compared to the rule-like, perfect parallelism in Wang Ao's beautifully crafted essays, Ai Nan-ying's politically charged essay reveals that, as the eight-legged essay increased in length from 500 to over 600 characters in the late Ming, its strict balance and symmetrical structure were compromised in practice if not in literary spirit" (407). Huang Qiang writes of Tang Shunzhi's "To give entire credit to the *Book of History*" (which will be discussed in more detail later in this chapter) that it shows that "form is in service to content, and when someone talented writes even an eight-legged essay, it will not constitute an exception." Huang Qiang, *Bagu wen yu Ming Qing wenxue*, 197. Similarly, Wu Weifan explains that Fang Bao's "The Master was wishing Qidiao Kai to enter on employment" (also discussed in detail later in this chapter) gives a sense of "unevenness and disorder," concluding that although this is a conscious stylistic choice on the part of

the author, showing that the examination essay form is not rigid and ossified, "use of neat parallel organization would show even greater attention to artistic detail."

77	Original introductory remarks to *QSJ*, 1. For examples of Fang's influence later in the Qing, see the discussions of the origins and development of the essay genre collected in *Xuehai tang ji* juan 8.

78	"As for literary form, there were few in the Wanli period who showed interest in the strict requirements and norms that had governed the standard eight-legged format previously; many used two *gu*, four *gu*, or even divided up the structure of the essay into first and second halves according to the meaning of the topic, and quite a few simply transformed parallel prose into single-line prose, employing the loose construction of classical prose." Gong, *Mingdai bagu wen shitan*, 381.

79	For example, see Hu Ding's essay on the topic "Those who are fleeing from the errors of Mo naturally turn to Yang," which is as clearly *san* as "Feng Fu of Jin." The comments to this essay in *Qinding sishu wen* note that it "makes parallel sets into single-line prose, using an old form to write in the contemporary format." *QSJ* 237–38.

80	*QSJ* 9, 12.

81	Han's essay appears in *QSJ* 909–10; Fang's essay is reprinted in Wu Weifan, *Ming Qing zhiyi jinshuo*, 208–13.

82	*QSJ* 303–4. Gong Duqing comments of this essay that it is "purely a piece of classical prose." Gong, *Mingdai bagu wen shitan*, 423–25.

83	Feng Yuanyang's essay is reprinted in Gong, *Mingdai bagu wen shitan*, 421–23; Zhu Shixiu's essay is excerpted in *ZYCH* 16/318. For a discussion of this excerpt as an example of "using classical prose to write modern prose," see Huang Qiang, *Bagu wen yu Ming Qing wenxue*, 441.

84	*QSJ* 155–56.

85	Wu Weifan, *Ming Qing zhiyi jinshuo*, 208–9. Wu remarks that the three parallel sets in this essay give one a sense of "unevenness and disorder," as they are not "well-turned parallels" (209). Han Tan employs similar offset echoes and inserted clauses in slightly different fashion, also with the effect of disorienting the reader, in "The Master said to Yan Yuan," where the problematic echo "Oh, Hui!" comes after the first parallel set, at the beginning of the *chuti*. See *QSJ* 732 and Wang Kaifu, *Bagu wen gaishuo*, 228.

86	*QSJ* 235. Huang Qiang remarks that this essay can barely be said to meet even the basic requirements of the genre—"there are no *gu* into which to divide it." Huang Qiang, *Bagu wen yu Ming Qing wenxue*, 196. For another, somewhat earlier instance of displaced parallelism (in this case, between the start of the *chuti* and the start of the *dajie*) see Gu Qing's turn-of-the-fifteenth-century essay "The Master said of the Shao that it was perfectly beautiful," *QSJ* 13.

87	*QSJ* 713–14. Wang Kaifu divides this essay into two large *gu* without marking off the parallel set mentioned here; in his reading, that parallel set is contained in the first *gu*, and there is no corresponding element to balance it in the second *gu*. Wang Kaifu, *Bagu wen gaishuo*, 253–56.

88	For example, see Wu Weifan's and Wang Kaifu's different parsings of Tang Xianzu's essay on the topic "I have not seen one who loves virtue" (Wu Weifan, *Ming Qing zhiyi jinshuo*, 158–59; Wang Kaifu, *Bagu wen gaishuo*, 202–3), and Mao Kun's "When the villagers were drinking together" (Wu Weifan, *Ming Qing zhiyi jinshuo*, 155–56;

Wang Kaifu, *Bagu wen gaishuo*, 184–85). Similarly, Liu Zizhuang's "Let the superior man never fail reverentially to order his own conduct" is punctuated differently in Wang Kaifu, *Bagu wen gaishuo*, 216–18, and *QSJ* 778. See also Qi, *Shuo bagu*, 41, where Qi Gong notes that readers may differ on whether the essay he analyzes has a separate *yuanti*, or whether the part in question belongs instead to the *qijiang*. Unusually lengthy *guojie* and *chuti* can add to the confusion under these circumstances —are they not *gu* themselves? See Hu Renyu's "Dian, what are your wishes?," in which the *guojie* is comparable to the *bi* in length. *QSJ* 776.

89 For example, see *QSJ* 131–32, 136, 169, 193, 212.

90 *ZYCH* 7/111.

91 *Huayang jijin* 2.14a, 2.17a. See also Zhang Taikai, *Zhangshi lunwen yuezhi*, 8b ("The particular accomplishments of *wen* are in the division of *gu*"), and Gao, "Wenfa jishuo," 3ab.

92 Plaks, "The Prose of Our Time," 209.

93 Quoted in *Xuehai tang ji* 8.35b.

94 Cheng, "Some Reflections on Chinese Poetic Language," 44. As Yuan Renlin points out, the use of what is ordinarily a *shizi* as a *xuzi* instead—a particularly effective rhetorical device—is a shift that can be perceived only in the context of a sentence or paragraph; we can add to this point that in the case of strict parallelism, the most important part of that context is likely to be the character that appears to be positioned as parallel to the one in question. Yuan Renlin, *Xuzi shuo*, 39ab, 40a.

95 For an example of one strong reader—Qiu Jun—who turns out to be exactly right about what comes next when grading Wang Ao's metropolitan session exam paper in 1475, see *ZYCH* 12/233. The essay in question appears in *QSJ* 70–71.

96 *ZYCH* 6/97. See also an example drawn from *Qilu deng*, cited in Rolston, "Sources of Traditional Chinese Fiction Criticism," 24.

97 Huang Qiang, *Bagu wen yu Ming Qing wenxue*, 8–9. See, for example, Bao, *Yizhou shuangji* 2.38b–41b; Zhang Yushu's Kangxi-era preface to *Tieli wenqi*, reprinted in *Xuxiu Siku quanshu* 1714:265; Qian Zhongshu, *Tanyi lu*, 32. Indeed, it seems that references to *babi* may predate the earliest uses of *bagu*: Shen Defu's *Wanli yehuo bian* refers only to *babi* and *sigu* (23/595, 25/649, 25/650, 27/687).

98 *QSJ* 90.

99 Cited in Gao, "Wenfa jishuo," 6a. For Gao Dang's explanation, see "Wenfa jishuo," 10a, 11b.

100 Gao, "Wenfa jishuo," 11a, 11b; *ZYCH* 10/185, 10/188, 10/194, 10/195, 11/202, 11/213, among others. See also Zeng, "Xu *Guiyou weidu chao*," 3010–11, the preface to *Xiaoti zhenggu*, and the citation from a Qing author in Deng, *Qingdai bagu wen*, 10.

101 For example, see Wu Weifan, *Ming Qing zhiyi jinshuo*, in which the term *bi* is used interchangeably to refer to the following five distinct types of passages: (1) a parallel set of two paragraphs in a broader essay structure (127, 135, 124–25, 143–44, 147–48); (2) a single paragraph-length prose passage that happens to have a parallel set (151); (3) a single paragraph-length element in a more broadly parallel essay, in the place of the parallel set that a more ordinary essay would have there (170–71, 204–5); (4) a pair of *nonparallel* lines in a more broadly parallel essay, in the place of the parallel set that a more ordinary essay would have there (208–9); and (5) two basically parallel paragraph-length elements that make up most of an essay taken

together (121). Gong Duqing maintains a certain degree of interchangeability between *bi* defined as single or double. See Gong, *Mingdai bagu wen shitan*, 31–44, and Gong, *Bagu wen baiti*, 31–32, 37ff.

102 "*Bagu* are also called *babi*. Actually, '*babi*' is illogical as a *bi* is a pair of things arranged together, so *babi* would in fact be sixteen *gu*." Zhao, Li, et al., *Qingdai bagu wen yizhu*, 23. Huang Qiang (*Bagu wen yu Ming Qing wenxue*, 8–9) and Qi (*Shuo bagu*, 5) also note this paradox.

103 On the *gu* as the intermediary level between sentence and essay, see Gao, "Titi leishuo," 2a.

104 See, for example, Ping, *Xiawai junxie*, 699, which ties together the usage of *gu* to indicate stocks or shares in late nineteenth-century Shanghai with earlier references that gloss the word in terms of a division into parts, and Yu Yingshi's discussion of *gu* in the context of investment in enterprises in Ming and Qing in *Shi yu Zhongguo wenhua*, 568ff.

105 Gui, *Xinkan pishi juye qieyao gujin wenze* 2.1a.

106 Gao, "Wenfa jishuo," 14b.

107 Gao, "Wenfa jishuo," 15a. Note the similarity to Gu Yanwu's comment on this same question. Gu, *Rizhi lu jiaozhu* 16/901.

108 Cui, *Xuehai jinliang* 2.10b–11a.

109 Comment to the essay "Although I could not be a disciple of Confucius himself." *QSJ* 76; Tang Biao, *Dushu zuowen pu* 9.2b–3a.

110 Bao, *Yizhou shuangji* 1.1b–2a. See also the discussion of Jin Sheng's essays in *Xuehai tang ji* 8.23b.

111 One further instance of parallelism at the conceptual level can be seen in the understanding of the *poti* and *chengti* as forming a balanced system, in which a stylistic or structural choice made in one should be met by the complementary choice in the other. See *ZYCH* 23/436.

112 Amariglio and Callari, "Marxian Value Theory," 186–216, esp. 206.

113 Von Glahn, *Fountain of Fortune*; Lin, *China Upside Down*.

114 Des Forges, "Sleights of Capital" and "Industry and Its Motivations."

115 Gates, *China's Motor*.

116 The problematic aspects of the concept of "cultural capital" are discussed in more detail in Des Forges, "Sleights of Capital."

117 Zhu Shou, *Zhizhi tang wenji* 2.1a.

118 See Qian Zhongshu, *Tanyi lu*, 355–59, for this quote and many similar statements from a variety of other genres.

119 See *JYZY* 4.20a.

120 Brokaw, *The Ledgers of Merit and Demerit*, 68, 230–32; Ge, *The Scholar and the State*, 70–74; Elman, *A Cultural History*, 299–311. Elman notes of the story of Xu Zhongxing, whose good deed led to his examination success: "This clear moral inversion of the corrupt uses of gold and silver to buy examination success by paying off examiners could also take the form of 'spirit-money' used in temples and shrines to honor the dead and to redeem one's moral debts." Elman, *A Cultural History*, 305. See also Barr, "Pu Songling and the Qing Examination System," 100–102; Yuan Huang, *Youyi shu wengui* 1/18–22; *ZYCH* 12/238.

121 Qi, *Shuo bagu*, 22–23 and 51. For a general study of anthologies of parallel phrases through the ages, see Liang Zhangju, *Jingjiao qiaodui lu*.

122 Cui, *Xuehai jinliang* 4.11b–12a; Gao, "Wenfa jishuo," 1a; Huang Qiang, *Bagu wen yu Ming Qing wenxue*, 256–58.

123 Cui, *Xuehai jinliang* 2.19a, 3.9a; Yuan Huang, *Youyi shu xu wengui* 6/244; *JYZY* 4.10a; Lü, *Lü Wancun xiansheng lunwen*, 47a; Gao, "Lunwen zatiao," 14b–15b; Gao, "Wenfa jishuo," 27a; *Huayang jijin* 2.17a, 3.16a; *ZYCH* 2/40.

124 Gao, "Lunwen zatiao," 18a; Jin Xuelian, *Shu'an wenlun bielu*, 23ab; Bao, *Yizhou shuangji* 1.2ab. For more general uses of sequences of *zi* drawn from elementary primers and famous poems to order objects and locations, see Des Forges, "Burning with Reverence," 148.

125 Magone, "Once Every Three Years," 180–81.

126 Meskill, *Academies in Ming China*, 119–22, 140.

127 Des Forges, "Burning with Reverence," 149.

128 On the necessity for careful verification in the duplication process, see *Zhengde Da Ming huidian* 77.8b; Magone, "Once Every Three Years," 208–14; and Huang Qiang, *Bagu wen yu Ming Qing wenxue*, 88.

129 Lü Liuliang, *Lü Wancun xiansheng lunwen*, 50a. See also the remarks on different types of *gu* in "Shen Hongtai lunwen," 3a.

Chapter 4

1 The culture of the late Ming has inspired too much scholarship to list exhaustively; the following is a representative sample: Widmer, "The Epistolary World"; Chang and Chang, *Crisis and Transformation*, 162–77, 345–49; Wai-yee Li, *Enchantment and Disenchantment*, 47–88; Ko, *Teachers of the Inner Chambers*; Bai, *Fu Shan's World*; Shang and Wang, *Dynastic Crisis and Cultural Innovation*; Volpp, *Worldly Stage*; Handler-Spitz, *Symptoms of an Unruly Age*. On the "individual" in the late Ming: de Bary, "Individualism and Humanitarianism"; Pei-yi Wu, *The Confucian's Progress*, xii; Brokaw, *Ledgers of Merit and Demerit*; Wai-yee Li, "The Collector, the Connoisseur"; Martin Huang, *Literati and Self-Re/Presentation*, 5; Tina Lu, *Persons, Roles, Minds*; Burnett, *Dimensions of Originality*. For comparative perspective, see Watt, *The Rise of the Novel*; Armstrong, *Desire and Domestic Fiction*; Greenblatt, *Renaissance Self-Fashioning*; Plaks, *The Four Masterworks of the Ming Novel*, esp. chap. 1; Hegel, *The Novel in Seventeenth-Century China*; Ma, *The Age of Silver*.

2 Wu Kuan, *Paoweng jiacang ji* 41.6b–7a.

3 Ai, "*Jin Zhengxi gao xu*," 3032; Durand, *Lettrés et pouvoirs*, 82; Roddy, *Literati Identity*, 261; Jiao, "Shiwen shuo," 154; Bao, *Yizhou shuangji* 2.39ab. Among Western scholars, Georges Margouliès was one of the earliest to argue for the quality "bien personnel et bien intime" of *guwen* from the Tang dynasty forward. See Margouliès, *Le kou-wen chinois*, xxxiii–xxxiv.

4 Huang Qiang, *Bagu wen yu Ming Qing wenxue*, 129. Similarly, Andrew Plaks notes several specific examples of "the highlighting of personal perspective and literary self-consciousness" in late Ming examination essays. Plaks, *The Four Masterworks of the Ming Novel*, 34.

5 Wu Zhiwang, *Juye zhiyan* (1588 edition) 2.5ab.

6 *QSJ* 125–26.

7 On Tang Shunzhi's advocacy of *bense* (true color) as a literary value, see his letter to Mao Kun, *Tang Jingchuan xiansheng wenji* (1553 edition) 4.51b–54b, a selection of

which was also included in the influential late Ming examination preparation handbook edited by Yuan Huang, *Youyi shu xu wengui* 9/175–76. David Pollard translates several paragraphs of this letter in *A Chinese Look at Literature*, 62–64. For a useful warning against overreading Tang's concept of *bense*, see Clifford, "The Rules of Prose."

8 On the possibility that Li Zhi is taking a "deliberately provocative stand" with his advocacy of the examination essay in "Tongxin shuo," see Plaks, "The Prose of Our Time," 206. For Li Zhi's own remarks on *Shuoshu*, see "Zixu," 1; for more on *Shuoshu* and Li Zhi's attitude toward the eight-legged essay generally, see Huang Qiang, *Bagu wen yu Ming Qing wenxue*, 141–50.

9 Ai, "*Qianli shijuan zixu*," 3032; see also *ZYCH* 6/99.

10 Bao, *Yizhou shuangji* 2.40ab.

11 See Qian Mu, *Zhuzi xue tigang*, 119–29, as well as David Hall and Roger Ames's discussion of the contrast in early Confucian texts between *ji* (associated with *li* 利) and the "exalted self (*wo*)" associated with *yi*. Hall and Ames, *Thinking through Confucius*, 93.

12 Huang Qiang, *Bagu wen yu Ming Qing wenxue*, 358.

13 Liu Dakui, "Shiwen lun," 1b–2a. See also Yu Changcheng's comments on Wang Anshi's prose, quoted in *ZYCH* 3/47.

14 Yuan Hongdao, "Da Li Yuanshan," 330; this translation adapted from Burnett, *Dimensions of Originality*, 95.

15 Quoted in Huang Qiang, *Bagu wen yu Ming Qing wenxue*, 139.

16 Dong, *Juye beilei*, 1a–4b. See also Yuan Huang, *Youyi shu wengui* 1/12. On the modern prose stylist Tao Wangling's role as link between Dong Qichang and Yuan Hongdao, see Son, "Publishing as a Coterie Enterprise," 99.

17 *JYZY* 1.2a, 1.23a. This edition of *Juye zhiyan* includes some brief words from the oldest of the three Yuan brothers, Yuan Zongdao, about "brilliant enlightenment" in literature.

18 On the pivotal nature of the 1588–89 examination season, see Gong, *Mingdai bagu wen shitan*, 108–10.

19 Quoted in *ZYCH* 2/39. An alternative ending to the last sentence in this paragraph—"they will count only as slaves, as they are not able to create their own positions (*zizuo zhuzhang*)"—appears in the version quoted in Yuan Huang, *Youyi shu xu wengui* 1/180.

20 This passage is quoted or referenced in *JYZY* 4.13b; Dong, *Juye beilei*, 4b–5b; Cui, *Xuehai jinliang* 2.10a; Tang Biao, *Dushu zuowen pu* 1.6b; Gao, "Lunwen zatiao," 2a; and *ZYCH* 2/39. The entire text of the "Kunhu Qu xiansheng lunwen" is included in Yuan Huang, *Youyi shu xu wengui* 1/179–82. For Qu's influence on later writers more generally, see also *QSJ* 159.

21 *QSJ* 211–12. Neither the original passage from the *Mencius* nor the standard commentary had addressed the question of what agency or subjectivity is involved in movement of the hands and feet.

22 For example, see Luo Wanzao and Jin Sheng's essays on the pine and the cypress (*QSJ* 443–44; Wu Weifan, *Ming Qing zhiyi jinshuo*, 147–48).

23 Yuan Huang, *Youyi shu xu wengui* 1/180.

24 Yuan Huang, *Youyi shu xu wengui* 1/181.

25 *QSJ* 166.

26 *QSJ* 214. See also Qu's essay "It is said in the *Book of Poetry*, 'What needs no display is virtue.'" Reprinted in Tian, *Bagu wen guanzhi*, 431–32.

27 Original introductory remarks to *QSJ*, 1. Fang's formulation has been particularly inspirational for later scholars who argue that there is a place for originality in *shiwen*. For example, see *ZYCH* 1/19, and chapter 4 of Huang Qiang, *Bagu wen yu Ming Qing wenxue*.

28 *QSJ* 543, 446. See also Fang's praise of one essay as *zichu jingyi* "naturally putting forth his own fine meaning." *QSJ* 179.

29 *QSJ* 742–44. See also Chen Longzheng's comment on this question: "The most marvelous writing is that which suddenly begins, and suddenly is complete; it is not under my control . . . not knowing how it comes to be so and it nonetheless comes to be so, this is the means by which one places [in the examination]." Chen Longzheng, *Juye suyu*, 26a.

30 *QSJ* 743.

31 *Mengzi*, 2. This translation is drawn from Legge, *The Works of Mencius*, 128.

32 *QSJ* 909–10.

33 For examples of essays from the late fifteenth and early sixteenth centuries that show great interest in *xin*—beyond that suggested by the standard commentaries to the original passages from which the topics were drawn—and often connect *xin* to naturalness, see *QSJ* 72, 73, 74, 75–76, 165. See also Hu Ding's introduction of the new construction "proceeding from the bottom of one's heart to reach outside" (*youzhong yi da yu wai*) as a parallel to the canonical resonances in "cultivating one's words to attain sincerity" (*xiuci yi da qi cheng*). *QSJ* 239–40. Gui Youguang's essay on the topic "While there are no stirrings of pleasure, anger, sorrow, or joy" (*QSJ* 167) includes the following line: "Now many of those who discuss the Way seek it in an unchecked breadth of range, and do not know the merit of returning to the self and effecting restraint, finding [the Way] in my own mind and that being sufficient." Also of interest is Wang Ao's essay on the topic "Learning without thought is labor lost," in which an otherwise straightforward rephrasing of the Zhu Xi commentary on this line is altered by the insertion of "from oneself" (*yu ji*) to constitute the *poti*. See Wu Weifan, *Ming Qing zhiyi jinshuo*, 135.

34 Quoted in Yuan Huang, *Youyi shu xu wengui* 1/175.

35 Tang Shunzhi, *Tang Jingchuan xiansheng wenji* (1555 edition) 4.14a. Similarly, Tang highlights the necessity for distinctiveness in writing: "there must be a part that shines brightly and cannot be worn down; one opens one's mouth and speaks a few phrases that could not have been said in a thousand ages." Tang Shunzhi, *Tang Jingchuan wenji* (1573 edition) 7.25ab. See also Tang's statement about the uniqueness of each person's *bense* in a letter to Mao Kun mentioned previously in this chapter, which Yuan Huang takes as an inspiration for his examination writing. For this and other instances of Tang's influence, see Yuan Huang, *Youyi shu xu wengui* 1/175, 176; *JYZY* 4.29ab; Cui, *Xuehai jinliang* 2.9b.

36 *QSJ* 153.

37 *QSJ* 146. Yuan Huang seems to have been moved by this tendency in Tang's writings to interpolate a key phrase (marked below in italics) into a letter Tang wrote urging his brother to commit himself to his studies at home as fully as he would if he were

at a mountain retreat: "If you concentrate on getting it in your mind when you read *and on letting it flow forth from your mind when you write*, how is [studying at home] any different from in the mountains?" Yuan Huang, *Youyi shu xu wengui* 1/177. An earlier version of this letter, in the 1553 and 1555 editions of Tang Shunzhi, *Tang Jingchuan xiansheng wenji* 4.40b–41a, as well as in the 1573 edition of Tang Shunzhi, *Tang Jingchuan wenji* does not include the italicized phrase.

38 *QSJ* 201.

39 On narrative point of view in fiction, see Chen Pingyuan, *Zhongguo xiaoshuo xushi moshi*, 67; Plaks, "Terminology and Central Concepts," 108. In drama, see Li Yu, *Xianqing ouji* 1/17. On autobiographical representation see Martin Huang, *Literati and Self-Re/Presentation*; for examples of roman-à-clef readings of this type of fiction, Li Hanqiu, *Rulin waishi ziliao*, 197–246. More subjective modes of narration are often thought to come to Chinese vernacular fiction only in the twentieth century: Chen Pingyuan, *Zhongguo xiaoshuo xushi moshi*, 65–105; Egan, "Characterization in *Sea of Woe*," 170–73; Hanan, *The Sea of Regret*, 9–10.

40 Wang Mengruan and Shen Ping'an, *Honglou meng suoyin*, 1–2.

41 See, for example, Wu Weifan, *Ming Qing zhiyi jinshuo*, 155–58, and Wang Kaifu, *Bagu wen gaishuo*, 184–88, which discuss the same essay by Mao Kun on the topic "When the villagers drank wine": Wu argues that the speech represented is that of Confucius; Wang feels differently, concluding that the essay does not contain representative speech. Similarly, the *chengti* of Tang Shunzhi's "Ziwen thrice took office" includes a first-person usage (*wu*) that we would expect from its position in the essay to refer to Tang himself but actually makes more sense as a reference directly to Confucius. *QSJ* 127. In this connection, it is worth noting Judith Zeitlin's distinction between the clear fictionality of vernacular narrative and the ambiguous status of tales written in the literary language. Zeitlin, *Historian of the Strange*, 5.

42 For example, see Xu Fuyuan's "Is our Master for the ruler of Wei?," *QSJ* 129–30. One story by Pu Songling shows how this can work: it is claimed that Confucius cannot be the speaker in question in one passage of the *Analects* because the phrase refers to one of his disciples by *zi* rather than by *ming*; the passage begins "The Master said, 'Filial indeed is Min Ziqian!'" (cited in Huang Qiang, *Bagu wen yu Ming Qing wenxue*, 383–84). The standard Zhu Xi commentary does not catch this point, but a comparison with parallel passages in early sources other than the *Analects* suggests that this argument cannot be dismissed out of hand. See *ZYCH* 14/281–82 for several different opinions on this question.

43 Mao Kun, "Mao Lumen lunwen size," 1a.

44 *QSJ* 137; see also Wu Weifan, *Ming Qing zhiyi jinshuo*, 155, and Wang Kaifu, *Bagu wen gaishuo*, 185.

45 *QSJ* 61. See also Zhou Yanru's essay on the topic "O ye, my little children," reprinted in Gong, *Mingdai bagu wen shitan*, 669–70, and Liu Dakui's comments in "*Xu Lishan shiwen* xu," 93–94.

46 Zhang Taikai, *Zhangshi lunwen yuezhi*, 12a.

47 *QSJ* 112.

48 Jiao, *Yiyu yuelu* 1.10ab. On Cheng Yi's critique of "enmirement," see Van Zoeren, *Poetry and Personality*, 204–5.

49 *QSJ* 543. Similarly, Tang Shunzhi uses *wu* in one essay to model a position from which one neither dares to claim kinship with the Sage nor dares to not claim kinship

with the Sage. *QSJ* 169. In this connection it is worth noting that Fang Bao praises Wang Ao and Gui Youguang for their appropriation of phrases from the Classics in such a way as to make it seem that they themselves had written them. *QSJ* 95.

50 *ZYCH* 6/100–101; see also Huang Qiang, *Bagu wen yu Ming Qing wenxue*, 136–37. Here James Scott's discussion of spirit possession as a means of social critique—opinions are attributed to a powerful spirit rather than to the individual who gives voice to that spirit—seems apposite. Scott, *Domination and the Arts of Resistance*, 140–42.

51 See Gui Youguang's essay on the topic "The ancients who wished to illustrate illustrious virtue throughout the kingdom," *QSJ* 98–99, and Wang Yangming's essay on the topic "The determined scholar and the benevolent person," *QSJ* 30–31. Also worth noting is the trickiness with which *ziyong* (oneself make use of) and *ziwo* (oneself) are set up as parallel in an early Qing essay on "A transmitter and not a maker," excerpted in *ZYCH* 9/174.

52 Lacan writes of the "series of gestures" in which a child "playfully experiences the relations of the assumed movements of the image to the reflected environment, and of this virtual complex to the reality it reduplicates—the child's own body, and the persons or even things in his proximity" ("The Mirror-Phase," 72). "The fact is that the total form of the body by which the subject anticipates in a mirage the maturation of his power is only given to him as *Gestalt*, that is to say in an exteriority in which this form is certainly more constituent than constituted, but in which it appears to him above all in a contrasting size that fixes it and a symmetry that inverts it which are in conflict with the turbulence of the motions which the subject feels animating him." Lacan, "The Mirror-Phase," 73.

53 "The crucial thing is when reading the writings of the ancients to use this body to speak for the ancients, now swallowing now spitting out, all of this coming from them and not from me. Once this has been done thoroughly, my spirit is in fact the spirit of the ancients, and the rhythms of the ancients are all in my throat and mouth; that which suits my throat and mouth is none other than that which resembles the spirit and rhythm of the ancients. After a long while, the tones of metal and stone are manifested in sonorous fashion." Liu Dakui, *Lunwen ouji* (1959 reprint), 12.

54 Guan is quoted in *ZYCH* 1/19.

55 Rolston, "Sources of Traditional Chinese Fiction Criticism," 24.

56 "Strictly speaking, the authorial self can never be directly revealed; rather, it is presentable only as metaphor. . . . In other words, self-representation always has to be mediated through the representation of others because the moment one thinks or writes about one's self, that self has already become an 'other' (a character), a phenomenon that arises from the paradoxical nature of self-writing." Martin Huang, *Literati and Self-Re/Presentation*, 49. See also Huang's discussion of "self-allegorizing" and "self-comparison," *Literati and Self-Re/Presentation*, 11, 45–48.

57 Yuan Renlin, preface to *Xuzi shuo*, 1ab. See also Winkler, *Gelehrte Worte über leere Wörter*, 67.

58 Zhang Taikai, *Zhangshi lunwen yuezhi*, 10a; Liu Dakui, *Lunwen ouji*, 18–19. See also Gao Dang's margin comments to Mao Kun, "Mao Lumen lunwen size," 1a, and to Gao Dang, "Titi leishuo," 2b.

59 Yuan Renlin, preface to *Xuzi shuo*, 1ab.

60 Mao Kun, "Mao Lumen lunwen size," 1a.

61 See Zheng and Mai, *Gu Hanyu yufa xue ziliao*, 147; Ji, *Gu Hanyu judu*, 204, 207–8. François Cheng includes pronouns in his categorization of "empty words" in "Some Reflections," 38. For examples of first-person pronouns matched against other *xuzi* in parallel sets, see *QSJ* 16–17, 19, 98–99, 742–44; *ZYCH* 9/174.

62 *QSJ* 30–32.

63 Des Forges, "Paratexts, Collected Works."

64 The topic of that essay is "When kindred spirits come from afar"; Plaks reads *wuren* as "every individual" in the *qijiang*, *wu* as "their own" in the *qigu*, and *wu* as "individual" in the *xugu*. Plaks, "The Prose of Our Time," 211–12. See also Ai Nanying's usage in "*Wuchen fangshu shanding* xu": "Now candidates tag along after the language of the Classics in order to satisfy the topic, and then force 'their own' intention (*wuyi*) to satisfy the language of the Classics" (3025).

65 A similar example appears in another essay by Wang Yangming, on the topic "Zi Kuai had no right to give Yan to another man." *QSJ* 60.

66 *QSJ* 25.

67 Tu, "The Chinese Examination Essay," 401. Ch'en Shou-yi translates this passage similarly in *Chinese Literature*, 507.

68 Elman, *A Cultural History*, 390.

69 *QSJ* 317.

70 *QSJ* 940–41. In You Ying's essay on the topic "In the government of my kingdom," Mencius uses *wu* to ask whether he may imagine a strategy for King Hui of Liang (*wu qing wei wang ce yan*), which strikes the reader as strange. As it turns out, there is no case in the *Mencius* itself where Mencius asks "May I . . ." (*wu qing*); requests of this sort that aim to faithfully represent Mencius's habitual speech should be made with *qing* only, or with *chen qing* ("May your servant . . .") (*QSJ* 196). See also Liu Jieyuan's 1711 essay on the topic "To be able to practice five things everywhere under heaven constitutes perfect virtue," in which the first-person *wu* appears repeatedly and insistently, in distinct contrast with the original text and the standard commentary. *ZYCH* 12/246.

71 In an essay on the topic "Ziwen thrice took office," drawn from book five of the *Analects*, Tang Shunzhi directly quotes from book fourteen of the *Analects* in the *chengti*, which is ordinarily supposed to be in the voice of the author, not that of the Sage, and uses *wu* nonetheless, provoking us to wonder whether he is speaking as himself or whether the Sage is speaking; later in the essay he switches in mid-sentence from speaking for the Sage to speaking for Ziwen. *QSJ* 127.

72 Kneale, *Romantic Aversions*.

73 Gui Youguang's essay on the topic "While there are no stirrings of pleasure, anger, sorrow, or joy" includes several instances of these sudden, but not necessarily problematic, appearances of the first person (*QSJ* 167).

74 See Pascal, *The Dual Voice*, esp. 8–21. Dorrit Cohn writes of "the seamless junction between narrated monologues and their narrative context. Note how, in the Joyce passage, the text weaves in and out of Stephen's mind without perceptible transitions, fusing outer with inner reality, gestures with thoughts, facts with reflections." Cohn, *Transparent Minds*, 103.

75 Doležel, *Narrative Modes in Czech Literature*, 21–28, 32–33; Pascal, *The Dual Voice*, 10; Hagenaar, *Stream of Consciousness*, 23. For a detailed discussion of tense in particular and free indirect discourse in English, French, and German, see Fludernik, *The Fictions of Language*, 178–226.

76 Doležel, *Narrative Modes in Czech Literature*, 15–55; Banfield, *Unspeakable Sentences*, 65–108.

77 Cohn, *Transparent Minds*, 113. See also Pascal, *The Dual Voice*, on "the depiction of states of mind, temperaments, moods rather than external actions" (34). On free indirect discourse in twentieth-century Chinese literature, see Hagenaar, *Stream of Consciousness*, 34–41.

78 Similarly, Cohn points out that successful use of free indirect discourse in fiction requires the author "to plant sufficient clues for its recognition." Cohn, *Transparent Minds*, 106.

79 *QSJ* 31.

80 Tang Shunzhi: "Zimo holds a medium between these" ("Mengzi criticizes his fault in order to set the standard of my/our Way"); Gui Youguang: "In regard to inferior creatures, the superior man"; Hu Ding: "Those who are fleeing from the errors of Mo naturally turn to Yang." *QSJ* 233, 234, and 237; He Zhuo: "When the villagers were going through their ceremonies to drive away pestilential influences," quoted in *ZYCH* 10/181. For other examples from the early and mid-Qing, see *ZYCH* 9/153, 10/181, 10/189, 10/190, and 11/209. Slightly more complex but still quite readable is Luo Lun's mid-fifteenth-century "This condoling, on being three months unemployed by a ruler," which includes the following sentence toward the end: "It is not only that there is no way to see their ruler (*qijun*), but in the end there is no way to practice my Way (*wudao*)" (*QSJ* 67). Such shifts also appear in essays that make more insistent use of the first-person pronoun throughout, and in these essays are not as noticeable. See, for example, Gui Youguang's essay on "The Way of Great Learning," as well as an essay on the topic "Zizhang asked what constituted intelligence" by his slightly younger contemporary Wang Qiao (*QSJ* 95, 147).

81 Dong, *Wenjue jiuze*, 1a–4a. See also Shen Hongtai's claim that in literary writing, "You and I must take shape against each other," which appears first in "Shen Hongtai lunwen," 2a, and is later cited in Zhang Taikai, *Zhangshi lunwen yuezhi*, 12b–13a.

82 Ai, "*Jin Zhengxi gao* xu," 3032.

83 Quoted in Watt, *The Rise of the Novel*, 176. Writing specifically of free indirect discourse, Dominick LaCapra argues that "this 'style' involves a dialogue between narrator and character that assumes changing positions on the threshold between 'self' and 'other.'" *Madame Bovary on Trial*, 135.

84 Fu, "*Qingxi huiye* xu," 3047.

85 Dong, *Wenjue jiuze*.

86 For Wang Ao, see the essay on the topic "If the people have plenty, their prince will not be left to want alone" discussed earlier in this chapter; for Tang Shunzhi, see *QSJ* 127–28, 212–13, 233.

87 This translation is based in part on translations by David Hawkes in *The Story of the Stone*, 2:132, and Haun Saussy in "Unspoken Sentences," 432–33. See also Wang and Shen, *Honglou meng suoyin*, 383.

88 Saussy, "Unspoken Sentences," 432–33.

89   In Anthony Yu's translation of this passage from *Honglou meng* into English, we see some of the same struggles to smooth out difficult turns that were evident in the essay translations cited earlier in this chapter. Anthony Yu, "Self and Family in the *Hung-lou Meng*," 215. It is no surprise that the early twentieth-century commentators Wang Mengruan and Shen Ping'an would write that the author of *Dream of the Red Chamber* must have been "skilled at writing eight-legged essays." Wang Mengruan and Shen Ping'an, "*Honglou meng suoyin* tiyao," 7.

90   *Qianlong chaoben bai nian hui Honglou meng gao*, 372.

91   Taken from *Xixiang zhiyi*.

92   Compare the rhetoric in these essays with the discourse of "conquering the self" found in the standard Song commentaries to the "Yan Yuan asked about perfect virtue" chapter of the *Analects*.

93   "When I was eleven years old I entered the village school to study for the exams, and after I spent some time at it, and learned something of it, I began to suspect that exam-compound writings, with their forced parallelism and rigid sound scheme, constrain people's brushes, which are unable to rush about and freely express that which they wanted to say; leaving one's private mind unhappy." Wu Kuan, *Paoweng jiacang ji* 41.6b.

94   *QSJ* 616.

95   *QSJ* 616: "Now the eyes and ears act through the movement of material force, and the mind's reflection responds to them with material force; [these types of actions] are equally material force. It is only that the mind's function is reflection and [one] is vigilant with it by means of reflection, using *li* to steer material force, then traveling along the road of emotional response without fault." The distinctiveness of Ai's approach in the late Ming context becomes even clearer when his essay is contrasted with another essay on this same topic, by his contemporary Zhang Shichun (*QSJ* 617–18).

96   Wang Ao quoted in Yuan Huang, *Youyi shu xu wengui* 1/175; see also *Youyi shu xu wengui*, 1/173 for a similar remark by Wang Ao, and Yuan Huang's approving comment on the formulation "in awe of oneself rather than in awe of the Sages," *Youyi shu wengui* 4/66. Gu Yanwu is quoted in *Xuehai tung ji* 8.44a and in *ZYCH* 23/433; original in Gu, *Rizhi lu jiaozhu* 16/920. Zhang Xuecheng is quoted in Huang Qiang, *Bagu wen yu Ming Qing wenxue*, 140. See also the discussion of *zide* (getting it oneself), including how this figure mediates between the assigned essay topic and the contemporary society in which the candidate is writing, in Chen Longzheng, *Juye suyu*, 8a–9a, as well as comments by Liu Dakui, "In modern prose one's own spirit must reach an accommodation with the spirit of the Sages and Worthies" ("Shiwen lun," 1b–2a) and Jiang Zuolin, "I therefore say that although examination essays speak for the sages and worthies, in fact each [writer] speaks of what his own mind has obtained" (preface to *ZYCH*, 5). For a more concrete and technical discussion of the contrast between representative speech and *jiyi* (one's own intention), see *Chuxue yu linglong* 1.17ab. In some cases, literati would publish essays with their "own notes" *ziji* (自記) attached; a further occasion for the "self-expression" that the essay form seems to call forth. For example, see *ZYCH* 10/178–79, 190, 192–94, 11/206.

97   Lu Longji, "Lu Jiashu xiansheng lunwen," 3a.

98   Zhu Shangshu, *Songdai keju yu wenxue*, 328.

99 Quoted in Gu, *Rizhi lu jiaozhu* 16/913.
100 Huang Qiang, *Bagu wen yu Ming Qing wenxue*, 93–94; see also *ZYCH* 1/15.
101 Chen Jitai (1567–1641): "by means of the spirit of the single individual self (*yiji*) and penetrating the meaning of the Sages and Worthies." Quoted in *ZYCH* 7/120. See also Cui, *Xuehai jinliang* 2.9b.
102 Gong, *Mingdai bagu wen shitan*, 126; *ZYCH* 22/426-27.
103 Cited in Gao, "Lunwen zatiao," 1b. See also Gao Dang's comment on this, that it is necessary to study both those one agrees with and those one does not, which refers throughout to a self (*ji*) that is presumed to have distinctive qualities.

Chapter 5

1 See, for example, *Xinxuan qijiang*, 3a–4b.
2 *ZYCH* 5/80; Yang Wensun preface to *ZYCH*; Fang, "Jin sishu wen xuan biao," 286–87. For a more general argument that the uniqueness of each writer's work is evident to the competent reader, see Nivison, *The Life and Thought of Chang Hsüeh-ch'eng*, 178. An examiner convinced that he has guessed the identity of a candidate from his essay but who turns out to have been mistaken would be a source of some amusement to his colleagues. See *ZYCH* 7/117.
3 Magone, "Once Every Three Years," 208–14. On the examination situation generally as a type of dramatic production, see Magone, "Who Wants to Be a Bureaucrat?" Essays written for the palace examination, which were not *shiwen*, were not recopied, reintroducing the candidate's calligraphic style as a factor at that point. Iona Man-Cheong notes that candidates often sent poetry to potential palace examiners before the session in order to make their handwriting recognizable; *The Class of 1761*, 64–65.
4 On the significance of networks (and the role of paratexts in articulating them), as well as the value of having a recognized name attached to a text, see Chow, *Publishing, Culture, and Power*, 110–19; Meyer-Fong, "Packaging the Men of Our Times"; Durand, "Le péritexte comme lieu de sociabilité"; Son, "Publishing as a Coterie Enterprise."
5 For a more detailed discussion of this function of prefaces, especially those designated as "gift prefaces" (*zengxu*), see Des Forges, "Paratexts, Collected Works."
6 Huang Zongxi's *Ming wen hai* includes eighty-one of these prefaces in volumes 307–13 (it should be noted that quite a few of these prefaces were deleted from the version of the *Ming wen hai* included in the *Siku quanshu*). Ming and Qing authors also regularly include such prefaces in their collected works.
7 On the significance of the examination trope in vernacular fiction, see Ge, *The Scholar and the State*, esp. 67–97.
8 For an overview of strategies for and defenses against cheating, see Elman, *A Cultural History*, 196–97. See also *ZYCH* 23/434-35.
9 On the Qianlong emperor's attempts to root out collusion, see *ZYCH* 2/29-31; Man-Cheong, *The Class of 1761*, 22, 57–58.
10 For a discussion of these stories, see Elman, *A Cultural History*, 299–326. On discourses of fate and examination success in the Song dynasty, see Zhu Shangshu, *Songdai keju yu wenxue*, 492–519.

11 Even in the palace examination, it was not impossible to "reanonymize" one's writing by choosing a calligraphic hand that one was not known for; see Man-Cheong, *The Class of 1761*, 138–41. For a critical assessment of the discourse of a corrupt and scandal-ridden system, see Ho, *The Ladder of Success*, 93–94; and Magone, "The Silence of the Lanes," 330–34, and "The Corruption that Wasn't There." The mechanics by which literary recognition in general could sometimes translate into examination success are necessarily complicated. From the work of Kurahashi Keiko, it seems likely that candidates' literary fame would in most cases be mediated through greater access to current trends in examination writing to yield examination success, rather than working in their favor more directly through name recognition. Kurahashi, *Chūgoku dentō shakai no erītotachi*.

12 Fish, "No Bias, No Merit."

13 Foucault, "What Is an Author?," esp. 114: "When I speak of Marx or Freud as founders of discursivity, I mean that they made possible not only a certain number of analogies, but also (and equally important) a certain number of differences. They have created a possibility for something other than their discourse, yet something *belonging* to what they founded" (emphasis added). As Fish writes of "Geoffrey Hartman's Wordsworth"—the use of the possessive here is telling—"When Geoffrey Hartman speaks on Wordsworth, is his just another voice, or is it the voice of someone who is in great measure responsible for the Wordsworth we now have, insofar as by that name we understand an array of concerns, formal properties, sources, influences, and so on?" Fish, "No Bias, No Merit," 168.

14 See, for example, Gui, *Zhenchuan xiansheng ji, bieji* 6.1ab.

15 "Ours is a hierarchical profession in which some are more responsible for its products than others; and since one of those products is the standard of merit by which our labors will, for a time, be judged, there will always be those whose words are meritorious (that is, important, worth listening to, authoritative, illuminating) simply by virtue of the position they occupy in the institution." Fish, "No Bias, No Merit," 166–67.

16 On this question, see Des Forges, "Sleights of Capital."

17 Des Forges, "Sleights of Capital," 112–13. See in particular Bourdieu, *Distinction*, 13–18, 35, 512–18.

18 Chow, "Discourse, Examination, and Local Elite," 198. As we have seen in the previous chapters, there was often significant leeway even in *shiwen* to indicate one's intellectual leanings.

19 As Yuan Hongdao argues, even examiners who were philosophically committed to rejecting outstanding and original (*qi*) writing would find themselves with no choice but to select such essays because choosing the plain and balanced (*ping*) writing instead would not sufficiently narrow down the field. Yuan Hongdao, "Xu *Sizi gao*," 8.

20 The most significant of these was the creation of the small topic essay questions, in response to which candidates were required to restrict their answers to address only a sentence fragment rather than the larger argument from which the fragment was selected, or write a "bridge" essay linking two such fragments from unrelated passages in a coherent fashion. See chapter 2 for more detail.

21 Standard language warning against smuggling books into the exam compound appears in the preface to *Qingyun lou xiaoti wen*, 1a, and *Lianglun lianzhang caifeng ji*,

2a. See also Plaks, "Research on the Gest Library 'Cribbing Garment,'" 10–11. The intriguing question of how the proper bounds of the individual for the purposes of the examinations are determined partly through physical searches is too complicated to address here.

22 There has been a great deal of research on families and social reproduction through the examination system: see, among others, Ho, *The Ladder of Success*; Waltner, "Building on the Ladder of Success"; Elman, *A Cultural History*; Man-Cheong, *The Class of 1761*, esp. chapter 4; and Kurahashi, *Chūgoku dentō shakai no erītotachi*. Specifically, on wealthy families' attempts to "relocate" the site of essay productivity by contracting in advance for sets of essays written to order, see Gu, *Rizhi lu jiaozhu* 16/913; on literary societies and *shegao*, see Chow, *Publishing, Culture, and Power*, 211, 223–29. Compare the emphasis on the individual in the exam compound with Watt's understanding of the "new economic order" in eighteenth-century Britain that he considered central to the appearance of the novel in Britain: "the effective entity on which social arrangements were now based was no longer the family, nor the church, nor the guild, nor the township, nor any other collective unit, but the individual." Watt, *The Rise of the Novel*, 61.

23 Jiao, "Yu Wang Qinlai lunwen shu," 687.

24 Zito, *Of Body and Brush*, 101: "The location of subjectivity within a single, biological individual is a modern, Western phenomenon. The traditional Chinese ritualist sensibility did not limit and locate consciousness in such a way." Although Zito's assertion is insufficiently nuanced, it does remind us that different discursive contexts within Ming and Qing China will assume correspondingly distinct levels of emphasis on the bounded individual; contrary to what one might assume, it turns out that the examination system is predicated on the concept of the bounded individual to an extent that other discursive contexts generally fail to match. For a discussion of how this individual is to be identified, see Magone, "Brown Eyes—Black Hair—Beard/No Beard."

25 Ye, "Yu youren lunwen shu," 268; Tian, *Bagu wen guanzhi*, 382.

26 Dong, *Wenjue jiuze*, 7a; Dong, *Dong Sibai juye peilei*, 8b. The latter passage is also quoted in Gao, "Lunwen zatiao," 11b.

27 By the middle of the Qing, greater attention is paid to differentiation in scholarly terms as well. Even in these circumstances, where one might have thought that the aim was simply to supply a correct understanding of the original, the appreciation of this correctness depends on and is presented in a narrative of its unique distinction from other, incorrect understandings. See, for example, *ZYCH* 13/258–59.

28 Ye Xie writes that "If these words come from oneself then they stand (*li* 立); if they do not then they cannot stand; when there is nothing to lean against that is called standing; alone doing what is right is what is called standing." Ye Xie, "Yu youren lun wenshu," 270.

29 See, for example, Fang, "Jin sishu wen xuan biao," 287, and "*Yang Huangzai shiwen xu*," 50; *ZYCH* 1/17, 9/148, 9/152, 13/258; Ai, *Tian yongzi ji* 12.11b; Liu Shixiang's attached note ("Ke Fang xiansheng quangao fuji") to Fang, *Fang Linghao quangao*; Zhu Jian, preface to *ZYCH*, 3; Yang Wensun, preface to *ZYCH*, 4.

30 Yuan Huang, *Youyi shu wengui* 5/78; see also Yuan Huang, *Youyi shu xu wengui* 8/264.

31 Gao, "Lunwen zatiao," 3a; Li Yu, *Xianqing ouji* 3/66; *Huayang jijin* 2.7a and preface.

32 On the importance of freshness and *xing* (awakening) as qualities of exam essays, see *ZYCH* 2/39–40; Gao, "Wenpin zashuo," 6ab includes an entire paragraph on novelty and how crucially important it is at all levels of the essay; Yuan Huang notes not only the importance of novelty but also originality (*qi*), in the proper balance with stability and plainness, of course (Gao, "Lunwen zatiao," 16a). Writing in the seventeenth century, Li Yu equated these two values directly: "the new is just another name for what is original," *Xianqing ouji* 1/15. On *qi* in particular, see the references in a wide variety of works collected in *JYZY* 2.9b, 10a, 12b, 14b–15a, 18a, 20ab, 22b, 3.16b, 20ab, 26b–27a, 4.6b, 7b, 11b. See also Yuan Huang, *Youyi shu wengui* 4/75, 5/78. On *qi* in late Ming culture and beyond, see Zeitlin, *Historian of the Strange*, 5–6, and Bai, *Fu Shan's World*, 11–20.

33 Burnett, *Dimensions of Originality*, 16, 45, 58–60; for a detailed analysis of the place of *qi*, see 135–200.

34 Yu Changcheng is particularly emphatic on this point: see his assessment of Wang Anshi's essays cited in chapter 3 (*ZYCH* 3/47) and his comments to Gui Youguang's essays in *Keyi tang yibai ershi mingjia zhiyi*.

35 Ni, "Ma Xunqian *Jinshi shuyi* xu," 17a. See also Wang Heng in *JYZY* 2.9b and *ZYCH* 6/94. Similarly, one late Ming art critic remarks: "Some may compete by wielding the unusual (*qi*) to show off to their contemporaries, but what they do is nothing more [permanent] than raising ripples and waves in water." Burnett, *Dimensions of Originality*, 145.

36 Quoted in Yuan Huang, *Youyi shu xu wengui* 7/249. This quote also appears in *JYZY* 2.15a–16a.

37 Wu Weifan, *Ming Qing zhiyi jinshuo*, 147–48. See also Luo Wanzao's late Ming essay on this topic, in which pine and cypress are an ideal because of their self-completeness (*cheng yu ji*) and their lack of concern for being known, in *QSJ* 443–44.

38 *QSJ* 89. See also his comment on the potential for "gradual" change in literary preferences over time, *QSJ* 165.

39 *Xuehai tang ji* 8.6a.

40 Quoted in Gong, *Mingdai bagu wen shitan*, 695.

41 Gong, *Mingdai bagu wen shitan*, 383–87; see also Bai, *Fu Shan's World*, 18–19. This approach has interesting resonances with Watt's argument for the development of a "concept of individualism" in connection with the rise of the novel in Britain. Watt, *The Rise of the Novel*, 60–61.

42 Des Forges, "Industry and Its Motivations."

43 Shang Yanliu, *Qingdai keju kaoshi shulu*, 249–50, 255. "On further reflection, we realize that the intense competition and high degree of sophistication in essay criticism over the years would certainly be good incentive to innovation." Rolston, "Sources of Traditional Chinese Fiction Criticism," 20. See also Plaks, *The Four Masterworks*, 33–34.

44 *Huayang jijin* 2.34a. Examiners "looking at flowers from horseback" appear already in Shen Wei's late Ming comments on *wen*, in *JYZY* 3.17a.

45 Chen Longzheng, *Juye suyu*, 26b–27a.

46 *Yinzhi wen zhiyi*, 25a–26a.

47 Pollard, *A Chinese Look at Literature*, 62–64.

48 *JYZY* 4.29ab. Li Guangdi is quoted in *ZYCH* 1/18.

49 *JYZY* 4.24b–25a.

50 Quoted in *ZYCH* 5/80. The innovative playwright Xu Wei is cited as an example to substantiate this claim. See also 7/124, 11/223 and 225, and Roddy, *Literati Identity*, 52. The rare exceptions to this rule stand out: see *ZYCH* 5/72 and 9/172–73. One of the most detailed examples of this type of reasoning appears in Qu Jingchun's remarks on literary writing, recorded by Yuan Huang, in which he gives a careful assessment of Tang Shunzhi's and Xue Yingqi's writings, with a particular focus on their examination essays, and explains how the distinctive qualities found in their work relate to their individual natures. Yuan Huang, *Youyi shu xu wengui* 1/180. This degree of individuating detail already goes several steps beyond Jiang Yingke's more stereotyped general explanation of the links between literary types and personality types. See Chaves, "The Expression of Self," on Jiang's relatively schematic approach.

51 In connection with this point, see also Bai, *Fu Shan's World*, 11–13.

52 See, for example, Fang, "Jin sishu wen xuan biao." Conversely, for Huang Zongxi, the failure of the Ming to have individuals (*ren*) to match up to the texts (*wen*) produced during the dynasty is a strong reason to be critical of the examination system. Huang Zongxi, "*Ming wen an* xu," 94–95.

53 Nivison, *The Life and Thought of Chang Hsüeh-ch'eng*, 178.

54 Lou, "*Zhang Boyu gao* xu," 3018.

55 Fang, "Jin sishu wen xuan biao," 286. In more critical accounts of the modern prose genre, we find the transformative effects of writing to be rather more problematic. See, for example, Gu, *Rizhi lu jiaozhu* 16/913.

56 Fu, "*Qingxi huiye* xu," 3047. See also *Zhangshi lunwen yuezhi*, 2b–3a, reprinted in "Zhang Youtang lunwen," 2b–3a.

57 Mei, "Zashuo," 284.

58 Bao, *Yizhou shuangji* 2.40b.

59 On this point, see Pu, "Tan bagu wen," 279.

60 Dong, *Wenjue jiuze*; Cui, *Xuehai jinliang* 2.9b.

61 Wu Zhiwang, *Juye zhiyan* (1588 edition) 2.14a; this passage is quoted in Yuan Huang, *Youyi shu xu wengui* 9/273.

62 See, for example, Fu, "*Qingxi huiye* xu"; Dong, *Wenjue jiuze*; Lü, *Lü Wancun xiansheng lunwen*; Fang Bao's commentary in *QSJ* 234; Yang Wensun, preface to *ZYCH*, 4; introductory remarks to *ZYCH*, 8; *ZYCH* 1/19, 1/21–23, 14/287.

63 *ZYCH* 1/21–22 (quoting Lu Longji), 2/38 (quoting Su Xiangfeng). Of Ai Nanying, Liang remarks, "His understanding of the canonical texts is not always correct, but his writing is simple and dignified; he must be recommended as an author (*zuozhe*)." *ZYCH* 6/97.

64 P'ei-yi Wu, *The Confucian's Progress*, 8.

65 P'ei-yi Wu, *The Confucian's Progress*, 84.

66 *JYZY* 4.6b–7a; Yuan Huang, *Youyi shu xu wengui* 6/243.

67 P'ei-yi Wu, *The Confucian's Progress*, 163–64; Martin Huang, *Literati and Self-Re/Presentation*, 7–8.

68 Li Zhi, "Zhuowu lunlüe," 1a–6a; P'ei-yi Wu, *The Confucian's Progress*, 19–24.

69 Translated in Peterson, *Bitter Gourd*, and Owen, *Remembrances*, 131–41, respectively.

70 See Huang Qiang, *Bagu wen yu Ming Qing wenxue*, 137–38.

71 Original introductory remarks to *QSJ*, 1. For a reference to a modern prose essay Fang wrote to express his melancholy at being on the road, see Wang Sihao, *Fang Bao*, 35.

72 See, for example, Greenblatt, *Renaissance Self-Fashioning*, 9.

73 "Shen Hongtai lunwen," 2a. Zhang Taikai, *Zhangshi lunwen yuezhi*, 12b–13a; this discussion is reprinted in Zhang Taikai, "Zhang Youtang lunwen," 13a–14a.

74 Yuan Huang, *Youyi shu xu wengui* 1/179–81.

75 In this connection, see Nivison's discussion of the habitual forms that protests against the examination system tended to take in "Protest against Conventions."

76 P'ei-yi Wu, *The Confucian's Progress*, xii, 163–64; Martin Huang, *Literati and Self-Re/Presentation*, 6–8. Jaroslav Průšek takes a slightly different approach to these questions, in which he argues that individual literary subjectivities in the premodern period have a particular class basis. Like Wu and Huang, however, he does argue that "Strongly subjective, intimate and individualistic traits characterized the novel in [the Qing]." Průšek, "Subjectivism and Individualism," 11.

77 Des Forges, "Paratexts, Collected Works."

Epilogue

1 See, for example, the lengthy dispute between Philip C. C. Huang and Kenneth Pomeranz in the *Journal of Asian Studies*, volumes 62.1 and 62.3, a dispute that drew in a number of other scholars in the field. For the participants in this conversation, "involution" and "development" are taken to be settled terms; the debate for them is centered on the question of which societies display these traits in what combination at what point in time. On the tributary mode of production, see Gates, *China's Motor*.

2 Hegel, *Philosophy of History*, 116. See also 124: "In China, we have the reality of absolute equality, and all the differences that exist are possible only in connection with that administration, and in virtue of the worth which a person may acquire, enabling him to fill a high post in the Government."

3 Frank, *ReORIENT*; Arrighi, *Adam Smith in Beijing*; Ma, *The Age of Silver*, 21–25.

4 "On this conceptual basis, I shall argue that the novel in the East and the West co-evolved toward a socioeconomically informed and nationally allegorical mode of 'realism' due to transregional conditions of cultural displacement during the Age of Silver." Ma, *The Age of Silver*, 28; Moretti, *The Novel*.

5 Ma, *The Age of Silver*, 22. On the anxieties this attraction caused in Britain, see Porter, *Ideographia*, 193–98.

6 The mere fact of gathering individuals to provide and take local, provincial, and metropolitan examinations was, in Rui Magone's words, a "major logistical and financial act"; Magone, "Once Every Three Years," 34, 83, 116. See also Elman, *A Cultural History*, xxviii, xxxiv.

7 See also Ho, *The Ladder of Success*; Elman, *A Cultural History*.

8 Anderson, *Imagined Communities*, 12–29, 25. Anderson writes more specifically of newspaper reading that "each communicant is well aware that the ceremony he performs is being replicated simultaneously by thousands (or millions) of others of whose existence he is confident, yet of whose identity he has not the slightest no-

tion" (35). Man-Cheong, *The Class of 1761*, 18, 204. See also Des Forges, "1890, Fall."

9 Woodside, *Lost Modernities*.

10 Qian Zhongshu, "China in the English Literature." David Porter writes of the "convergence in the civil service examinations of political and linguistic legitimizing functions" that could serve for British authors as a "crucial source of exemplars in the service of pressing domestic needs." Porter, *Ideographia*, 47.

11 Batchelor, "Concealing the Bounds," 82–83, 87; Webb, *An Historical Essay*, 92–93, 133–35; Temple, "Of Heroic Virtue," 343–44, 330.

12 Temple, "Of Heroic Virtue," 336. "In the seventeenth and eighteenth centuries, an extensive Dutch and Jesuit literature with an eye toward commerce and conversion described China as populous, urbanized, commercial society with strong institutions devoted to the cultural replication of merit, namely, the examination system and the civil cult of Confucius." Batchelor, "Concealing the Bounds," 80. Defoe's famous critique of China is a direct reaction to this literature; see Porter, *Ideographia*, esp. 237–40.

13 Webb, *An Historical Essay*, 133–34.

14 Turgot refers to the "profession of letters" to which future administrators devote themselves, and Quesnay presents an image of the Chinese state in which pedagogical practice is woven into the fabric of government at every level. See Maverick, *China: A Model for Europe*, 49, 193–203.

15 Lin, *China Upside Down*; Chin, *Savage Exchange*.

16 Ma, *The Age of Silver*, 24.

17 *QSJ* 104.

18 *Zhouyi benyi*, 64.

19 *Xinyi Sanzijing*, 41; see also 38–39 for examples of diligent individuals.

20 As John Dardess writes of Taihe County in the Ming: "It was not wealth, not high office, but education that perpetuated a patriline." Dardess, *A Ming Society*, 117.

21 van der Sprenkel, "The Chinese Civil Service," 11, 20. See also Webb, *An Historical Essay*, 92–93, 95, and 133.

22 Temple, "Of Heroic Virtue," 341; see also 333 on diligence in service of self-improvement.

23 Teng, "Chinese Influence"; van der Sprenkel, "The Chinese Civil Service"; Woodside, *Lost Modernities*.

24 Reprinted in Yuan Huang, *Youyi shu xu wengui* 6/234–35.

25 The 1699 edition of Tang Biao's *Dushu zuowen pu*, in Harvard-Yenching Library.

26 Reprinted in Yuan Huang, *Youyi shu xu wengui* 9/273.

27 Quoted in Huang Qiang, *Bagu wen yu Ming Qing wenxue*, 358.

28 On this question, see Volpp, *Worldly Stage*, 49–54.

29 Huang Qiang, *Bagu wen yu Ming Qing wenxue*, 342–43. "The concept of 'wenzi' does not deny the differences between eight-legged essays and other literary forms and styles, but it particularly emphasizes what the eight-legged essay does have in common with them." Lü Liuliang defends *shiwen* as *wenzi* in the preface to *Wancun tiangai lou ouping*.

30 Des Forges, "Burning with Reverence"; Dai Shadi, "Xinhai wenlun de chengqian qihou."

31 McDermott, *Social History of the Chinese Book*, 182–85; Des Forges, "Burning with Reverence."

32 Translation from Lewis, *Writing and Authority*, 272.

33 Ledderose, *Ten Thousand Things*.

34 Wang and Shen, *Honglou meng suoyin*.

35 Williams, *Marxism and Literature*.

36 See, for example, Watt, *The Rise of the Novel*, 35–59.

37 See Chow, *Publishing, Culture, and Power*; Rolston, "Sources of Traditional Chinese Fiction Criticism," 24; Durand, *Lettrés et pouvoirs*, 84–89; for a discussion of some examination essay collections, see *ZYCH* 1/24–27; Wu Jingzi, *Rulin waishi*, gives an unparalleled sense of how the publishing trade could work for individual characters in long vernacular fiction.

38 Chen Pingyuan, *Zhongguo xiaoshuo xushi moshi*, 17.

39 Watt, *The Rise of the Novel*, 53.

40 Des Forges, "Industry and its Motivations."

41 Des Forges, "Sleights of Capital." On seventeenth-century literati's careful adaptation of print publication in ways that would maintain class status distinctions rather than challenging them, see Son, "Publishing as a Coterie Enterprise."

42 Des Forges, "Sleights of Capital," 116.

43 Geertz, *Agricultural Involution*, 79. See also Mark Elvin's discussion of the "high-level equilibrium trap" in *The Pattern of the Chinese Past*, 285–319.

44 Goldenweiser, "Loose Ends of Theory," 102–3; see also Geertz, *Agricultural Involution*, 81.

45 Hayami, "A Great Transformation," and *Kinsei Nihon no keizai shakai*. Ping-ti Ho likewise notes "the permeation of society" by an ideology of mobility and advancement through effort; *Ladder of Success*, 86–89. See also de Vries, *The Industrious Revolution*.

Appendix

1 Reprinted in Wu Weifan, *Ming Qing zhiyi jinshuo*, 190–91, from *Xiaoti wuji jingyi*.

2 *QSJ* 776.

3 Wu Weifan, *Ming Qing zhiyi jinshuo*, 151; this essay also appears in *Tang Shunzhi, Tang Jingchuan gao*.

4 *QSJ* 54–55.

BIBLIOGRAPHY

Ai Nanying 艾南英. *"Huang Zhangqiu jinyi* xu 黃章丘近義序." In *MWH* 312/3035–36.

Ai Nanying 艾南英. *"Jin Zhengxi gao* xu 金正希稿序." In *MWH* 312/3032–33.

Ai Nanying 艾南英. *"Qianli shijuan* zixu 前歷試卷自序." In *MWH* 312/3030–32.

Ai Nanying 艾南英. *"Sijia hezuo zhaimiu* xu 四家合作摘謬序." In *MWH* 312/3036–38.

Ai Nanying 艾南英. *Tian yongzi ji* 天傭子集. 1688. Reprinted in *Siku jinhui shu congkan bubian* 四庫禁毀書叢刊補編, vol. 72. Beijing: Beijing chuban she, 2005.

Ai Nanying 艾南英. *"Wang Kanghou hebing gao* xu 王康侯合并稿序." In *MWH* 311/3025–27.

Ai Nanying 艾南英. *"Wuchen fangshu shanding* xu 戊辰房書刪定序." In *MWH* 311/3024–25.

Ai Nanying 艾南英. "Xu Wang Zigong *Guansheng cao* 序王子鞏觀生草." In *MWH* 312/3029–30.

Alt, Wayne. "The Eight-Legged Essay: Its Reputation, Structure, and Limitations." *Tamkang Review* 17.2 (1986): 155–74.

Amariglio, Jack, and Antonio Callari. "Marxian Value Theory and the Problem of the Subject: The Role of Commodity Fetishism." In *Fetishism as Cultural Discourse*, edited by Emily Apter and William Pietz, 186–216. Ithaca, NY: Cornell University Press, 1993.

Anderson, Benedict. *Imagined Communities: Reflections on the Origin and Spread of Nationalism*. Rev. ed. London: Verso, 1991.

Armstrong, Nancy. *Desire and Domestic Fiction: A Political History of the Novel*. New York: Oxford University Press, 1987.

Arrighi, Giovanni. *Adam Smith in Beijing: Lineages of the 21st Century*. London: Verso, 2007.

Atwell, William S. "From Education to Politics: The Fu She." In *The Unfolding of Neo-Confucianism*, edited by Wm. Theodore de Bary, 333–67. New York: Columbia University Press, 1975.

Bagu wen zonglun bazhong 八股文總論八種. Edited by Zhang Siqi 張思齊. Wuhan: Wuhan daxue chuban she, 2009.

Bai, Qianshen. *Fu Shan's World: The Transformation of Calligraphy in the Seventeenth Century*. Cambridge, MA: Harvard University Asia Center, 2003.

Banfield, Ann. *Unspeakable Sentences: Narration and Representation in the Language of Fiction*. London: Routledge and Kegan Paul, 1982.

Bao Shichen 包世臣. *Yizhou shuangji* 藝舟雙楫. 1846. Reprinted in *Xuxiu siku quanshu* 續修四庫全書, vol. 1082. Shanghai: Shanghai guji chuban she, 1995.

Barr, Allan. "Pu Songling and the Qing Examination System." *Late Imperial China* 7.1 (1986): 87–111.

Barthes, Roland. *The Language of Fashion*. Translated by Andy Stafford. Oxford: Berg, 2006.

Batchelor, Robert. "Concealing the Bounds: Imagining the British Nation through China." In *The Global Eighteenth Century*, edited by Felicity A. Nussbaum, 79–92. Baltimore, MD: Johns Hopkins University Press, 2005.

Benchao Zhewei sanchang quanti beikao 本朝浙闈三場全題備考. Qing dynasty. Institute for Advanced Studies on Asia Library, Tokyo University.

Bol, Peter K. "Examinations and Orthodoxies: 1070 and 1313 Compared." In *Culture & State in Chinese History: Conventions, Accommodations, Critiques*, edited by Theodore Huters, R. Bin Wong, and Pauline Yu, 29–57. Stanford, CA: Stanford University Press, 1997.

Bol, Peter K. *"This Culture of Ours": Intellectual Transitions in T'ang and Sung China*. Stanford, CA: Stanford University Press, 1992.

Bourdieu, Pierre. *Distinction: A Social Critique of the Judgement of Taste*. Translated by Richard Nice. Cambridge, MA: Harvard University Press, 1984.

Bourdieu, Pierre. "The Market of Symbolic Goods." *Poetics* 14 (1985): 13–44.

Brokaw, Cynthia J. *The Ledgers of Merit and Demerit: Social Change and Moral Order in Late Imperial China*. Princeton, NJ: Princeton University Press, 1991.

Burnett, Katharine P. *Dimensions of Originality: Essays on Seventeenth-Century Chinese Art Theory and Criticism*. Hong Kong: Chinese University Press, 2013.

Cai Jingkang 蔡景康, ed. *Mingdai wenlun xuan* 明代文論選. Beijing: Renmin wenxue chuban she, 1993.

Cao Pi 曹丕. *Dianlun* 典論. Longxi jingshe, 1917 reprint.

Caygill, Howard. *Art of Judgement*. Oxford: Blackwell, 1989.

Chan, Albert. *Chinese Books and Documents in the Jesuit Archives in Rome: A Descriptive Catalog*. Armonk, NY: M. E. Sharpe, 2002.

Chang, Chun-shu, and Shelley Hsueh-lun Chang. *Crisis and Transformation in Seventeenth-Century China: Society, Culture, and Modernity in Li Yü's World*. Ann Arbor: University of Michigan Press, 1992.

Chaves, Jonathan. "The Expression of Self in the Kung-an School: Non-Romantic Individualism." In *Expressions of Self in Chinese Literature*, edited by Robert E. Hegel and Richard C. Hessney, 123–50. New York: Columbia University Press, 1985.

Chen Jiajun 陳佳君. *Xushi zhangfa xilun* 虛實章法析論. Taipei: Wenjin chuban she, 2002.

Chen Longzheng 陳龍正. *Juye suyu* 舉業素語. 1631. Institute for Advanced Studies on Asia Library, Tokyo University.

Chen Pingyuan 陳平原. *Zhongguo xiaoshuo xushi moshi de zhuanbian* 中國小說敘事模式的轉變. Shanghai: Shanghai renmin chuban she, 1988.

Ch'en, Shou-yi. *Chinese Literature: A Historical Introduction*. New York: Ronald Press, 1961.

Cheng, François. "Some Reflections on Chinese Poetic Language and Its Relation to Chinese Cosmology." In *The Vitality of the Lyric Voice: Shih Poetry from the Late Han to the T'ang*, edited by Shuen-fu Lin and Stephen Owen, 32–48. Princeton, NJ: Princeton University Press, 1986.

Chin, Tamara. *Savage Exchange: Han Imperialism, Chinese Literary Style, and the Economic Imagination*. Cambridge, MA: Harvard University Asia Center, 2014.

Chou, Chih-p'ing. *Yüan Hung-tao and the Kung-an School*. Cambridge: Cambridge University Press, 1988.

Chow, Kai-wing. "Discourse, Examination, and Local Elite: The Invention of the T'ung-ch'eng School in Ch'ing China." In *Education and Society in Late Imperial China, 1600–1900*, edited by Benjamin A. Elman and Alexander Woodside, 183–219. Berkeley: University of California Press, 1994.

Chow, Kai-wing. *Publishing, Culture, and Power in Early Modern China*. Stanford, CA: Stanford University Press, 2004.

Chuxue yu linglong 初學玉玲瓏. Zhiyi tang, 1835 reprint. Bibliothèque nationale de France.

Clifford, Timothy R. "The Rules of Prose in Sixteenth-Century China: Tang Shunzhi (1507–1560) as an Anthologist." *East Asian Publishing and Society* 8.2 (2018): 145–82.

Cohn, Dorrit. *Transparent Minds: Narrative Modes for Presenting Consciousness in Fiction*. Princeton, NJ: Princeton University Press, 1978.

Cui Xuegu 崔學古. *Xuehai jinliang* 學海津梁. 1695. Shanghai Library.

Dai Mingshi 戴名世. "*Song Songnan zhiyi* xu 宋嵩南制義序." In *Dai Mingshi ji* 戴名世集, 113–14. Beijing: Zhonghua shuju, 1986.

Dai Mingshi 戴名世. "*Xiaoxue lunxuan* xu 小學論選序." In *Dai Mingshi ji* 戴名世集, 90–92. Beijing: Zhonghua shuju, 1986.

Dai Mingshi 戴名世. "*You Ming lichao xiaoti wen xuan* xu 有明歷朝小題文選序." In *Tongcheng pai wenlun xuan* 桐城派文論選, edited by Jia Wenzhao 賈文昭, 14–19. Beijing: Zhonghua shuju, 2008.

Dai Shadi 戴沙迪 [Alexander Des Forges]. "Xinhai zhi ji wenlun de chengqian qihou 辛亥之際文論的承前啟後." In *Shuqing chuantong yu weixin shidai* 抒情傳統與維新時代, edited by Wu Shengqing 吳盛青 and Ko Chia Chian 高嘉謙, 584–98. Shanghai: Shanghai wenyi chuban she, 2012.

Dardess, John W. *A Ming Society: T'ai-ho County, Kiangsi, Fourteenth to Seventeenth Centuries*. Berkeley: University of California Press, 1996.

de Bary, Wm. Theodore. "Individualism and Humanitarianism in Late Ming Thought." In *Self and Society in Ming Thought*, edited by Wm. Theodore de Bary, 145–247. New York: Columbia University Press, 1970.

de Certeau, Michel. *The Practice of Everyday Life*. Translated by Steven Rendall. Berkeley: University of California Press, 1984.

Deng Yunxiang 鄧雲鄉. *Qingdai bagu wen* 清代八股文. Beijing: Renmin daxue chuban she, 1994.

Des Forges, Alexander. "1890, Fall: *Lives of Shanghai Flowers*, Dialect Fiction, and the Genesis of Vernacular Modernity." In *A New Literary History of Modern China*, edited by David Der-wei Wang, 133–39. Cambridge, MA: Harvard University Press, 2017.

Des Forges, Alexander. "Burning with Reverence: The Economics and Aesthetics of Words in Qing (1644–1911) China." *PMLA* 121.1 (2006): 139–55.

Des Forges, Alexander. "Industry and Its Motivations: Reading Tang Xianzu's Examination Essay on the Problem of Excess Cloth." *Harvard Journal of Asiatic Studies* 80.1 (2020).

Des Forges, Alexander. "Opium / Leisure / Shanghai: Urban Economies of Consumption." In *Opium Regimes: China, Britain, and Japan, 1839–1952*, edited by Timothy Brook and Bob Tadashi Wakabayashi, 167–85. Berkeley: University of California Press, 2000.

Des Forges, Alexander. "Paratexts, Collected Works (*wenji*), and the Literary Critical Enterprise." Paper presented at the conference "Paratexts in Late Imperial Chinese Book Culture." Heidelberg, October 1, 2010.

Des Forges, Alexander. "Sleights of Capital: Fantasies of Commensurability, Transparency, and a 'Cultural Bourgeoisie.'" *differences* 24.3 (2014): 101–26.

de Vries, Jan. *The Industrious Revolution: Consumer Behavior and the Household Economy, 1650 to the Present*. Cambridge: Cambridge University Press, 2008.

De Weerdt, Hilde. "Canon Formation and Examination Culture: The Construction of *Guwen* and *Daoxue* Canons." *Journal of Sung-Yüan Studies* 29 (1999): 91–134.

De Weerdt, Hilde. *Competition over Content: Negotiating Standards for the Civil Service Examinations in Imperial China (1127–1279)*. Cambridge, MA: Harvard University Asia Center, 2007.

Dewey, John. *My Pedagogic Creed*. New York: Kellogg, 1897.

Doležel, Lubomir. *Narrative Modes in Czech Literature*. Toronto: University of Toronto Press, 1973.

Dong Qichang 董其昌. *Dong Sibai lunwen zongzhi* 董思白論文宗旨 and *Juye beilei* 舉業蓓蕾. 1681 preface. Shanghai Library.

Dong Qichang 董其昌. *Huachan shi suibi* 畫禪室隨筆. In *Siku quanshu* 四庫全書, vol. 867. Taipei: Shangwu yinshu guan, 1983 reprint.

Dong Qichang 董其昌. "Huating jiuzi jue 華亭九字訣." In *LWJC* 41–56.

Dong Qichang 董其昌. *Wenjue jiuze* 文訣九則. In *JYZY* 3.1a–14a.

Durand, Pierre-Henri. "L'homme bon et la montagne. Petite contribution en trois temps à l'étude de la prose moderne." *Études chinoises* 18.1–2 (1999): 223–88.

Durand, Pierre-Henri. *Lettrés et pouvoirs: un procès littéraire dans la Chine impériale*. Paris: Éditions de l'École des hautes études en sciences sociales, 1992.

Durand, Pierre-Henri. "Le péritexte comme lieu de sociabilité. Préfaceurs et correcteurs au siècle de Kangxi." Paper presented at the conference "Paratexts in Late Imperial Chinese Book Culture." Heidelberg, September 30, 2010.

Eagleton, Terry. *The Ideology of the Aesthetic*. Oxford: Blackwell, 1990.

Egan, Michael. "Characterization in *Sea of Woe*." In *The Chinese Novel at the Turn of the Century*, edited by Milena Doleželová-Velingerová, 165–76. Toronto: University of Toronto Press, 1980.

Elman, Benjamin A. "Changes in the Confucian Civil Service Examinations from the Ming to the Ch'ing Dynasty." In *Education and Society in Late Imperial China, 1600–1900*, edited by Benjamin A. Elman and Alexander Woodside, 111–49. Berkeley: University of California Press, 1994.

Elman, Benjamin A. *A Cultural History of Civil Examinations in Late Imperial China*. Berkeley: University of California Press, 2000.

Elman, Benjamin A. "Imperial Politics and Confucian Societies in Late Imperial China: The Hanlin and Donglin Academies." *Modern China* 15.4 (1989): 379–418.

Elvin, Mark. *The Pattern of the Chinese Past: A Social and Economic Interpretation*. Stanford, CA: Stanford University Press, 1973.

Fang Bao 方苞. *Fang Linghao quangao* 方靈皋全稿. National Library, Beijing.

Fang Bao 方苞. "Jin sishu wen xuan biao 進四書文選表." In *Fang Wangxi quanji* 方望溪全集, 286–87. Beijing: Zhongguo shudian, 1991 reprint.

Fang Bao 方苞. "*Yang Huangzai shiwen* xu 楊黃在時文序." In *Fang Wangxi quanji* 方望溪全集, 49–50. Beijing: Zhongguo shudian, 1991 reprint.

Fang Bao 方苞. "*Yang Qianmu wengao* xu 楊千木文稿序." In *Fang Wangxi quanji* 方望溪全集, 300–301. Beijing: Zhongguo shudian, 1991 reprint.

Fang Bao 方苞. "Yu Han Mulu xueshi shu 與韓慕廬學士書." In *Fang Wangxi quanji* 方望溪全集, 332–34. Beijing: Zhongguo shudian, 1991 reprint.

Feng Shugeng 馮書耕. *Guwen tonglun* 古文通論. Taipei: Zhonghua congshu, 1966.

Fish, Stanley E. "No Bias, No Merit: The Case against Blind Submission." In *Doing What Comes Naturally: Change, Rhetoric, and the Practice of Theory in Literary and Legal Studies*, 163–79. Durham, NC: Duke University Press, 1989.

Fludernik, Monika. *The Fictions of Language and the Languages of Fiction: The Linguistic Representation of Speech and Consciousness*. London: Routledge, 1993.

Foucault, Michel. "What Is an Author?" In *The Foucault Reader*, edited by Paul Rabinow, 101–20. New York: Pantheon Books, 1984.

Frank, Andre Gunder. *ReORIENT: Global Economy in the Asian Age*. Berkeley: University of California Press, 1998.

Fu Zhanheng 傅占衡. "*Qingxi huiye* xu 清溪會業序." In *MWH* 313/3047–48.

Gao Dang 高璥, ed. *Lunwen jichao* 論文集鈔. 1788 edition with 1786 preface. East China Normal University Library. Beijing: Beijing tushuguan chuban she, 2006 reprint. (*LWJC*)

Gao Dang 高璥. "Lunwen zatiao 論文雜條." In *LWJC* 113–52.

Gao Dang 高璥. "Titi leishuo 題體類說." In *LWJC* 153–271.

Gao Dang 高璥, ed. "Wenfa jishuo 文法集說." In *LWJC* 273–336.

Gates, Hill. *China's Motor: A Thousand Years of Petty Capitalism*. Ithaca, NY: Cornell University Press, 1996.

Ge, Liangyan. *The Scholar and the State: Fiction as Political Discourse in Late Imperial China*. Seattle: University of Washington Press, 2015.

Geertz, Clifford. *Agricultural Involution: The Processes of Ecological Change in Indonesia*. Berkeley: University of California Press, 1966.

Goldenweiser, Alexander. "Loose Ends of Theory on the Individual, Pattern, and Involution in Primitive Society." In *Essays in Anthropology: Presented to A. L. Kroeber in Celebration of his Sixtieth Birthday*, 99–104. Berkeley: University of California Press, 1936.

Gong Duqing 龔篤清. *Bagu wen baiti: jieshi bagu wen yinbi de lishi mianmu* 八股文百題: 揭示八股文隱蔽的歷史面目. Changsha: Yuelu shushe, 2010.

Gong Duqing 龔篤清. *Mingdai bagu wen shitan* 明代八股文史探. Changsha: Hunan renmin chuban she, 2006.

Gong Duqing 龔篤清, ed. and annot. *Yaqu cangshu: "Xixiang ji" quyu ti bagu wen* 雅趣藏書: 西廂記曲語題八股文. Changsha: Hunan renmin chuban she, 2008.

Greenblatt, Stephen. *Renaissance Self-Fashioning: From More to Shakespeare*. Chicago: University of Chicago Press, 1984.

Gu Yanwu 顧炎武. *Rizhi lu jiaozhu* 日知錄校注. Edited and annotated by Chen Yuan 陳垣. Hefei: Anhui daxue chuban she, 2007.

Gui Youguang 歸有光, annot. *Nanhua zhenjing pingzhu* 南華真經評註. National Library, Beijing.

Gui Youguang 歸有光. *Xinkan pishi juye qieyao gujin wenze* 新刊批釋舉業切要古今文則. 1572. Beijing University Library.

Gui Youguang 歸有光. *Zhenchuan xiansheng du guwen fa* 震川先生讀古文法. 1734. National Library, Beijing.

Gui Youguang 歸有光. *Zhenchuan xiansheng ji* 震川先生集. 1675 edition; edited by Qian Qianyi 錢謙益. Harvard-Yenching Library.

Guillory, John. *Cultural Capital: The Problem of Literary Canon Formation.* Chicago: University of Chicago Press, 1993.

Guo Peigui 郭培貴. *Mingdai keju shishi biannian kaozheng* 明代科舉史事編年考證. Beijing: Kexue chuban she, 2008.

Guo Shaoyu 郭紹虞 and Wang Wensheng 王文生, eds. *Zhongguo lidai wenlun xuan* 中國歷代文論選. Shanghai: Shanghai guji chuban she, 1980.

"Guwen xiaopu 古文小譜." In *Jingxuan zengru wenquan zhuru aolun cexue tongzong* 精選增入文筌諸儒奧論策學統宗. 1332 preface. Microfilm in National Central Library, Taipei.

Guy, R. Kent. *The Emperor's Four Treasuries: Scholars and the State in the Late Ch'ien-lung Era.* Cambridge, MA: Harvard University Asia Center, 1987.

Guy, R. Kent. "Fang Pao and the *Ch'in-ting Ssu-shu-wen.*" In *Education and Society in Late Imperial China, 1600–1900,* edited by Benjamin A. Elman and Alexander Woodside, 150–82. Berkeley: University of California Press, 1994.

Hagenaar, Elly. *Stream of Consciousness and Free Indirect Discourse in Modern Chinese Literature.* Leiden: Centre of Non-Western Studies, 1992.

Hall, David L., and Roger T. Ames. *Thinking through Confucius.* Albany: State University of New York Press, 1987.

Hanan, Patrick, trans. *The Sea of Regret: Two Turn-of-the-Century Chinese Romantic Novels.* Honolulu: University of Hawai'i Press, 1995.

Handler-Spitz, Rivi. *Symptoms of an Unruly Age: Li Zhi and Cultures of Early Modernity.* Seattle: University of Washington Press, 2017.

Handler-Spitz, Rivi, Pauline C. Lee, and Haun Saussy, eds. and trans. *A Book to Burn and a Book to Keep (Hidden): Selected Writings of Li Zhi.* New York: Columbia University Press, 2016.

Hawkes, David, trans. *The Story of the Stone.* Volume 2. London: Penguin Books, 1977.

Hayami, Akira. "A Great Transformation: Social and Economic Change in Sixteenth- and Seventeenth-Century Japan." *Bonner Zeitschrift für Japanologie* 8 (1986): 3–13.

Hayami Akira 速水融. *Kinsei Nihon no keizai shakai* 近世日本の経済社会. Tokyo: Reitaku daigaku shuppankai, 2003.

He Jingming 何景明. "Shucheng sankuan 書程三款." In *JYZY* 4.29b–34a.

He, Yuming. *Home and the World: Editing the "Glorious Ming" in Woodblock-Printed Books of the Sixteenth and Seventeenth Centuries.* Cambridge, MA: Harvard University Asia Center, 2013.

Hegel, Georg Wilhelm Friedrich. *The Philosophy of History.* Translated by J. Sibree. New York: Dover, 1956.

Hegel, Robert E. *The Novel in Seventeenth-Century China.* New York: Columbia University Press, 1981.

Ho, Ping-ti. *The Ladder of Success in Imperial China: Aspects of Social Mobility, 1368–1911.* New York: Columbia University Press, 1962.

"*Huachan shi suibi* mulu 畫禪室隨筆目錄." In *Siku quanshu* 四庫全書, vol. 867. Taipei: Shangwu yinshu guan, 1983 reprint.

Huang, Martin W. *Literati and Self-Re/Presentation: Autobiographical Sensibility in the Eighteenth-Century Chinese Novel*. Stanford, CA: Stanford University Press, 1995.

Huang Qiang 黃強. *Bagu wen yu Ming Qing wenxue lungao* 八股文與明清文學論稿. Shanghai: Shanghai guji chuban she, 2005.

Huang Qiang 黃強, ed. *Youxi bagu wen jicheng* 遊戲八股文集成. Wuhan: Wuhan daxue chuban she, 2009.

Huang Qiang 黃強 and Wang Ying 王穎, eds. *Youxi bagu wen yanjiu* 遊戲八股文研究. Wuhan: Wuhan daxue chuban she, 2015.

Huang, Ray. "Ni Yüan-lu: 'Realism' in a Neo-Confucian Scholar-Statesman." In *Self and Society in Ming Thought*, edited by Wm. Theodore de Bary, 415–82. New York: Columbia University Press, 1970.

Huang Zongxi 黃宗羲. "*Li Gaotang wenchao* xu 李杲堂文鈔序." 1678. Reprinted in *Qingdai wenlun xuan* 清代文論選, 80–81. Beijing: Renmin wenxue chuban she, 1999.

Huang Zongxi 黃宗羲. "*Ming wen an* xu 明文案序." 1675. Reprinted in *Qingdai wenlun xuan* 清代文論選, 94–95. Beijing: Renmin wenxue chuban she, 1999.

Huayang jijin 花樣集錦. 1844. National Central Library, Taipei.

Huters, Theodore. "From Writing to Literature: The Development of Late Qing Theories of Prose." *Harvard Journal of Asiatic Studies* 47.1 (1987): 51–96.

Ji Yongxing 季永興. *Gu Hanyu judu* 古漢語句讀. Beijing: Shangwu yinshu guan, 2001.

Jiao Xun 焦循. "Shiwen shuo 時文說." In *Diaogu ji* 雕菰集, 154–55. Shanghai: Shangwu yinshu guan, 1937 reprint.

Jiao Xun 焦循. *Yiyu yuelu* 易餘籥錄. 1819 preface; 1886 printing. Reprint.

Jiao Xun 焦循. "Yu Wang Qinlai lunwen shu 與王欽萊論文書." In *Qingdai wenlun xuan* 清代文論選, 687–88. Beijing: Renmin wenxue chuban she, 1999.

Jin Kemu 金克木. "Bagu xinlun 八股新論." In Qi Gong, *Shuo bagu* 說八股, 74–165. Beijing: Zhonghua shuju, 2000.

Jin Shengtan 金聖歎. *Xiaoti caizi shu* 小題才子書. 1889 edition. Shenyang: Wanjuan chuban gongsi, 2009 reprint.

Jin Xuelian 金學蓮. *Shu'an lunwen bielu* 述庵論文別錄. 1795. Shanghai Library.

Kant, Immanuel. *The Critique of Judgement*. Translated by Werner S. Pluhar. Indianapolis: Hackett, 1987.

Keulemans, Paize. *Sound Rising from Paper: Nineteenth-Century Martial Arts Fiction and the Chinese Acoustic Imagination*. Cambridge, MA: Harvard University Asia Center, 2014.

Kneale, J. Douglas. *Romantic Aversions: Aftermaths of Classicism in Wordsworth and Coleridge*. Montreal: McGill University Press, 1999.

Ko, Dorothy. "Bondage in Time: Footbinding and Fashion Theory." In *Modern Chinese Literary and Cultural Studies in the Age of Theory: Reimagining a Field*, edited by Rey Chow, 199–226. Durham, NC: Duke University Press, 2000.

Ko, Dorothy. *Cinderella's Sisters: A Revisionist History of Footbinding*. Berkeley: University of California Press, 2005.

Ko, Dorothy. *Teachers of the Inner Chambers: Women and Culture in Seventeenth-Century China*. Stanford, CA: Stanford University Press, 1994.

Kurahashi Keiko 倉橋圭子. *Chūgoku dentō shakai no erītotachi: bunkateki saiseisan to kaisō shakai no dainamizumu* 中国伝統社会のエリート達：文化的再生産と階層社会のダイナミズム. Tokyo: Fūkyōsha, 2011.

Lacan, Jacques. "The Mirror-Phase as Formative of the Function of the I." *New Left Review* 51 (1968): 71–77.

LaCapra, Dominick. *Madame Bovary on Trial*. Ithaca, NY: Cornell University Press, 1982.

Lau, D. C., trans. *Mencius*. London: Penguin Books, 1970.

Ledderose, Lothar. *Ten Thousand Things: Module and Mass Production in Chinese Art*. Princeton, NJ: Princeton University Press, 1998.

Legge, James, trans. *The Works of Mencius*. Volume 2 of *The Chinese Classics: With a Translation, Critical and Exegetical Notes, Prolegomena, and Copious Indexes*, edited by James Legge. Taipei: Southern Materials Center, 1985 reprint.

Lewis, Mark Edward. *Writing and Authority in Early China*. Albany: State University of New York Press, 1999.

Li Hanqiu 李漢秋, ed. *Rulin waishi ziliao* 儒林外史資料. Shanghai: Shanghai guji chuban she, 1984.

Li, Wai-yee. "The Collector, The Connoisseur, and Late-Ming Sensibility." *T'oung Pao* 81.4 (1995): 269–302.

Li, Wai-yee. *Enchantment and Disenchantment: Love and Illusion in Chinese Literature*. Princeton: Princeton University Press, 1993.

Li Yu 李漁. *Xianqing ouji* 閒情偶記. Taipei: Dingwen shuju, 1974 reprint.

Li Zhi 李贄. "Daogu lu 道古錄." In *Li Wenling ji* 李溫陵集, juan 18 and 19. Reprinted in *Xuxiu siku quanshu* 續修四庫全書, vol. 1352. Shanghai: Shanghai guji chuban she, 1995.

Li Zhi 李贄. "Shiwen houxu 時文後序." In *Li Wenling ji* 李溫陵集 11.2b–3a. Reprinted in *Xuxiu siku quanshu* 續修四庫全書, vol. 1352. Shanghai: Shanghai guji chuban she, 1995.

Li Zhi 李贄. "Tongxin shuo 童心說." In *Li Wenling ji* 李溫陵集 9.1a–3b. Reprinted in *Xuxiu siku quanshu* 續修四庫全書, vol. 1352. Shanghai: Shanghai guji chuban she, 1995.

Li Zhi 李贄. "Zhuowu lunlüe 卓吾論略." In *Li Wenling ji* 李溫陵集, 8.1a–6a. Reprinted in *Xuxiu siku quanshu* 續修四庫全書, vol. 1352. Shanghai: Shanghai guji chuban she, 1995.

Li Zhi 李贄. "Zixu 自序." In Li Zhi 李贄, *Fenshu Xu fenshu* 焚書 續焚書. Beijing: Zhonghua shuju, 1975.

Lianglun lianzhang caifeng ji 兩論聯章採風集. 1873. National Central Library, Taipei.

Liang Zhangju 梁章鉅. *Jingjiao qiaodui lu* 精校巧對錄. 1849 preface. Fudan University Library.

Liang Zhangju 梁章鉅, ed. *Zhiyi conghua Shilü conghua* 制藝叢話 試律叢話. Shanghai: Shanghai shudian, 2001 reprint. (*ZYCH*)

Lin, Man-houng. *China Upside Down: Currency, Society, and Ideologies, 1808–1856*. Cambridge, MA: Harvard University Asia Center, 2006.

Lin, Shuen-fu, trans. "The Chapter Comments from the Wo-hsien ts'ao-t'ang Edition of *The Scholars*." In *How to Read the Chinese Novel*, edited by David L. Rolston, 252–94. Princeton, NJ: Princeton University Press, 1990.

Liu Dakui 劉大櫆. "*Fang Xiyuan shiwen* xu 方晞原時文序." In *Liu Dakui ji* 劉大櫆集, 97–98. Shanghai: Shanghai guji chuban she, 2008 reprint.

Liu Dakui 劉大櫆. *Lunwen ouji* 論文偶記. 1832 edition. Shanghai Library.

Liu Dakui 劉大櫆. *Lunwen ouji* 論文偶記. Beijing: Renmin wenxue chuban she, 1959 reprint.

Liu Dakui 劉大櫆. "*Shiwen lun* 時文論." In *Liu Haifeng quanji* 劉海峰全集, 1a–2b. 1875 edition. National Library, Beijing.

Liu Dakui 劉大櫆. "*Xu Lishan shiwen* xu 徐笠山時文序." In *Liu Dakui ji* 劉大櫆集, 93–95. Shanghai: Shanghai guji chuban she, 2008 reprint.

Liu Shipei 劉師培. *Zhongguo zhonggu wenxue shi; Lunwen zaji* 中國中古文學史論文雜記. Beijing: Renmin wenxue chuban she, 1959 reprint.

Lo, Andrew. "Four Examination Essays of the Ming Dynasty." *Renditions* 33/34 (1990): 168–81.

Lou Jian 婁堅. "*Zhang Boyu gao* xu 張伯隅稿序." In *MWH* 311/3018–19.

Lu Longji 陸隴其. "*Lu Jiashu xiansheng lunwen* 陸稼書先生論文." In *LWJC* 61–70.

Lu, Tina. *Persons, Roles, and Minds: Identity in* Peony Pavilion *and* Peach Blossom Fan. Stanford, CA: Stanford University Press, 2001.

Lunyu jizhu 論語集注. In *Sishu zhangju jizhu* 四書章句集注. Beijing: Zhongguo shudian, 1985 reprint.

Lü Liuliang 呂留良. *Lü Wancun xiansheng lunwen huichao* 呂晚邨先生論文彙鈔. 1714. Reprinted in *Siku jinhui shu congkan* 四庫禁毀書叢刊, Zibu vol. 36. Beijing: Beijing chuban she, 2000.

Lü Liuliang 呂留良. *Wancun tiangai lou ouping* 晚邨天蓋樓偶評. Reprinted in *Siku jinhui shu congkan* 四庫禁毀書叢刊, Jingbu vols. 5–6. Beijing: Beijing chuban she, 1997.

Lü Xinchang 呂新昌. *Gui Zhenchuan ji qi sanwen* 歸震川及其散文. Taipei: Wenjin chuban she, 1998.

Ma, Ning. *The Age of Silver: The Rise of the Novel East and West*. New York: Oxford University Press, 2017.

Magone, Rui. "Brown Eyes—Black Hair—Beard/No Beard: Official Criteria and Data of Human Identification in Pre-Photographic China." Paper presented at the Max Planck Institute for the History of Science, Berlin, February 23, 2010.

Magone, Rui. "The Corruption that Wasn't There: Fraud Prevention and Its Limits in Qing Civil Examinations." In *Über Himmel und Erde: Festschrift für Erling von Mende*, edited by Raimund Kolb and Martina Siebert, 155–71. Wiesbaden: Harrassowitz, 2006.

Magone, Rui. "Examination Culture and the Non-Commercial Book: The Case of Liang Zhangju's (1775–1849) *Zhiyi conghua* (Collected words on the eight-legged essay)." In *Imprimer sans profit? Le livre non commercial dans la Chine impériale*, edited by Michela Bussotti and Jean-Pierre Drège, 637–74. Geneva: Librairie Droz, 2015.

Magone, Rui. "Once Every Three Years: People and Papers at the Metropolitan Examination of 1685." Ph.D. diss., Freien Universität Berlin, 2001.

Magone, Rui. "The Silence of the Lanes: Traditional Examination Culture and the Emergence of Modern Chinese Literature." In *Paths toward Modernity: Conference to Mark the Centenary of Jaroslav Průšek*, edited by Olga Lomová, 320–57. Prague: Charles University, 2008.

Magone, Rui. "Who Wants to Be a Bureaucrat? The Performative Dimension of Civil Service Examinations in Late Imperial China." *Études asiatiques* 58.3 (2004): 581–95.

Mair, Victor, and Tsu-lin Mei. "The Sanskrit Origins of Recent Style Prosody." *Harvard Journal of Asiatic Studies* 51.2 (1991): 375–470.

Man-Cheong, Iona. *The Class of 1761: Examinations, State, and Elites in Late Imperial China*. Stanford, CA: Stanford University Press, 2004.

Mao Kun 茅坤. "Mao Lumen lunwen size 茅鹿門論文四則." In *LWJC* 9–13.

Mao Zedong. *Oppose the Party "Eight-Legged Essay."* Beijing: Foreign Languages Press, 1955.

Margouliès, Georges. *Le kou-wen chinois*. Paris: Librairie Orientaliste Geuthner, 1926.

Marx, Karl. *The German Ideology*. Part 1. Edited by C. J. Arthur. New York: International, 1947.

Maverick, Lewis A. *China: A Model for Europe*. San Antonio, TX: Paul Anderson, 1946.

McDermott, Joseph P. *A Social History of the Chinese Book: Books and Literati Culture in Late Imperial China*. Hong Kong: Hong Kong University Press, 2006.

Mei Zengliang 梅曾亮. "*Taiyi zhou shanfang wenji* xu 太乙舟山房文集序." In *Jindai wenlun xuan* 近代文論選, 21–22. Beijing: Renmin wenxue chuban she, 1999.

Mei Zengliang 梅曾亮. "Zashuo 雜說." In *Tongcheng pai wenlun xuan* 桐城派文論選, edited by Jia Wenzhao 賈文昭, 284–86. Beijing: Zhonghua shuju, 2008.

Mengzi zhangju jizhu 孟子章句集注. In *Sishu zhangju jizhu* 四書章句集注. Beijing: Zhongguo shudian, 1985 reprint.

Meskill, John T. "Academies and Politics in the Ming Dynasty." In *Chinese Government in Ming Times: Seven Studies*, edited by Charles Hucker, 149–74. New York: Columbia University Press, 1969.

Meskill, John T. *Academies in Ming China: A Historical Essay*. Tucson: University of Arizona Press, 1982.

Meyer-Fong, Tobie. "Packaging the Men of Our Times: Literary Anthologies, Friendship Networks, and Political Accommodation in the Early Qing." *Harvard Journal of Asiatic Studies* 64.1 (2004): 5–56.

Mingshi 明史. Beijing: Zhonghua shuju, 1974 reprint.

Mingshi wenzong 名世文宗. 1628. Seikadō Library, Tokyo.

Ming wen hai 明文海. Airusheng digital version of Qing dynasty Hanfen lou manuscript edition. (*MWH*)

Miyazaki, Ichisada. *China's Examination Hell: The Civil Service Examinations of Imperial China*. Translated by Conrad Schirokauer. New Haven, CT: Yale University Press, 1981.

Moretti, Franco, ed. *The Novel*. Princeton, NJ: Princeton University Press, 2007.

Ni Yuanlu 倪元璐. "*Ma Xunqian Jinshi shuyi* xu 馬巽倩進士書義序." In *Ni Wenzhen gong wenji* 倪文貞公文集 17.7ab. 1772. Harvard-Yenching Library.

Ni Yuanlu 倪元璐. "*Yang Boxiang taishi gao* xu 楊伯祥太史稿." In *MWH* 307/2983–84.

Nivison, David S. *The Life and Thought of Chang Hsüeh-ch'eng (1738–1801)*. Stanford, CA: Stanford University Press, 1966.

Nivison, David S. "Protest against Conventions and Conventions of Protest." In *The Confucian Persuasion*, edited by Arthur Wright, 177–200. Stanford, CA: Stanford University Press, 1960.

Ōki Yasushi 大木康. *Genbun de tanoshimu Min-Shin bunjin no shōhin sekai* 原文で楽しむ明清文人の小品世界. Fukuoka: Chūgoku shoten, 2006.

Ono Kazuko 小野和子. *Minki tōsha kō: Tōrin tō to Fukusha* 明季党社考:東林党と復社. Kyoto: Dōhō sha, 1996.

Ouyang Quan 歐陽泉. *Diankan ji* 點勘記. Institute for Advanced Studies on Asia Library, Tokyo University.

Owen, Stephen. "Liu Xie and the Discourse Machine." In *A Chinese Literary Mind: Culture, Creativity, and Rhetoric in* Wenxin diaolong, edited by Cai Zong-qi, 175–91. Stanford, CA: Stanford University Press, 2001.

Owen, Stephen. *Remembrances: The Experience of the Past in Classical Chinese Literature*. Cambridge, MA: Harvard University Press, 1986.

Pascal, Roy. *The Dual Voice: Free Indirect Speech and its Functioning in the Nineteenth-Century European Novel*. Manchester: Manchester University Press, 1977.

Peterson, Willard J. *Bitter Gourd: Fang I-Chih and the Impetus for Intellectual Change*. New Haven, CT: Yale University Press, 1979.

Ping Buqing 平步青. *Xiawai junxie* 霞外攟屑. Shanghai: Shanghai guji chuban she, 1982.

Plaks, Andrew H. "Bones of Parallel Rhetoric in the *Wenxin diaolong*." In *A Chinese Literary Mind: Culture, Creativity, and Rhetoric in* Wenxin diaolong, edited by Zong-qi Cai, 163–73. Stanford, CA: Stanford University Press, 2001.

Plaks, Andrew H. *The Four Masterworks of the Ming Novel: Ssu ta ch'i-shu*. Princeton, NJ: Princeton University Press, 1987.

Plaks, Andrew H. "The Prose of Our Time." In *The Power of Culture: Studies in Chinese Cultural History*, edited by Willard J. Peterson, Andrew H. Plaks, and Ying-shih Yü, 206–17. Hong Kong: Chinese University Press, 1994.

Plaks, Andrew H. "Research on the Gest Library 'Cribbing Garment': A Very Belated Update." *East Asian Library Journal* 11.2 (2004): 1–39.

Plaks, Andrew H. "Terminology and Central Concepts." In *How to Read the Chinese Novel*, edited by David L. Rolston, 75–123. Princeton, NJ: Princeton University Press, 1990.

Plaks, Andrew H. "Where the Lines Meet: Parallelism in Chinese and Western Literatures." *CLEAR* 10.1–2 (1988–89): 43–60.

Pollard, David E. *A Chinese Look at Literature: Chou Tso-jen in Relation to the Tradition*. Berkeley: University of California Press, 1973.

Porter, David. *Ideographia: The Chinese Cipher in Early Modern Europe*. Stanford, CA: Stanford University Press, 2001.

Průšek, Jaroslav. "Subjectivism and Individualism in Modern Chinese Literature." In *The Lyrical and the Epic: Studies of Modern Chinese Literature*, edited by Leo Ou-fan Lee, 1–28. Bloomington: Indiana University Press, 1980.

Pu Yanguang 蒲彥光. "Tan bagu wen ruhe quanshi jingdian 談八股文如何詮釋經典." *Disan jie Zhongguo wenzhe dangdai zhi quanshi xueshu yantao hui huiqian lunwen ji* 第三屆中國文哲當代之詮釋學術研討會會前論文集, 261–82. 2007.

Qi Gong 啟功. *Shuo bagu* 說八股. Beijing: Zhonghua shuju, 2000.

Qian Mu 錢穆. *Zhuzi xue tigang* 朱子學提綱. 1971. Beijing: Sanlian shudian, 2014 reprint.

Qian Qianyi 錢謙益. *Muzhai youxue ji* 牧齋有學集. 1663. Shanghai: Shangwu yinshu guan, 1922? reprint.

Qian Yong 錢泳. *Lüyuan conghua* 履園叢話. 1823. University of California Berkeley Library.

Qian Zhonglian 錢仲聯. "Tongcheng pai guwen yu shiwen de guanxi wenti 桐城派古文與時文的關係問題." Reprinted in *Mengtiao'an Qingdai wenxue lunji* 夢苕庵清代文學論集, 78–82. Jinan: Qilu shushe, 1983.

Qian Zhongshu (Ch'ien Chung-shu). "China in the English Literature of the Seventeenth Century." 1940. Reprinted in *The Vision of China in the English Literature of the Seventeenth and Eighteenth Centuries*, edited by Adrian Hsia, 29–68. Hong Kong: Chinese University Press, 1998.

Qian Zhongshu 錢鐘書. *Tanyi lu (buding ben)* 談藝錄 (補訂本). Beijing: Zhonghua shuju, 1984.

Qianlong chaoben bai nian hui Honglou meng gao: Yang ben 乾隆抄本百廿回紅樓夢稿: 楊本. Beijing: Renmin wenxue chuban she, 2010.

Qinding sishu wen jiaozhu 欽定四書文校注. Wuhan: Wuhan daxue chuban she, 2009. (*QSJ*).

Qingyun lou xiaoti wen 青雲樓小題文. 1872. National Central Library, Taipei.

Qiu Jun 丘濬. "Qing rushi zhi lu 清入仕之路." In *Huang Ming mingchen jingji lu* 皇明名臣經濟錄. 1551 edition, 26.59a–64a. Harvard-Yenching Library.

Qu Jingchun 瞿景淳. "Kunhu Qu xiansheng lunwen 昆湖瞿先生論文." In *Youyi shu xu wengui* 遊藝塾續文軌, edited by Yuan Huang 袁黃, 1/179–82. Wuhan: Wuhan daxue chuban she, 2009 reprint.

Roddy, Stephen J. *Literati Identity and Its Fictional Representations in Late Imperial China*. Stanford, CA: Stanford University Press, 1998.

Rolston, David L. "Sources of Traditional Chinese Fiction Criticism." In *How to Read the Chinese Novel*, edited by David L. Rolston, 3–34. Princeton, NJ: Princeton University Press, 1990.

Rolston, David L. *Traditional Chinese Fiction and Fiction Commentary: Reading between the Lines*. Stanford, CA: Stanford University Press, 1997.

Ropp, Paul S. *Dissent in Early Modern China: Ju-lin wai-shih and Ch'ing Social Criticism*. Ann Arbor: University of Michigan Press, 1981.

Ruan Yuan 阮元. "Shu Liang Zhaoming taizi '*Wenxuan* xu' hou 書梁昭明太子文選序後." In *Jindai wenlun xuan* 近代文論選, 105–6. Beijing: Renmin wenxue chuban she, 1999.

Ruan Yuan 阮元. "*Sishu wen hua* xu 四書文話序." In *Xuehai tang ji* 8.52ab.

Ruan Yuan 阮元. "Wenyan shuo 文言說." In *Jindai wenlun xuan* 近代文論選, 100–101. Beijing: Renmin wenxue chuban she, 1999.

Ruan Yuan 阮元. "Wenyun shuo 文韻說." In *Jindai wenlun xuan* 近代文論選, 102–4. Beijing: Renmin wenxue chuban she, 1999.

Ruan Yuan 阮元. "Yu youren lun guwen shu 與友人論古文書." In *Jindai wenlun xuan* 近代文論選, 107–8. Beijing: Renmin wenxue chuban she, 1999.

Rusk, Bruce. *Critics and Commentators: The Book of Poems as Classic and Literature.* Cambridge, MA: Harvard University Asia Center, 2012.

Sakai Tadao. "Confucianism and Popular Educational Works." In *Self and Society in Ming Thought*, edited by Wm. Theodore de Bary, 331–66. New York: Columbia University Press, 1970.

Sangren, P. Steven. *History and Magical Power in a Chinese Community.* Stanford, CA: Stanford University Press, 1987.

Sanyuan biyao 三元必要. Qing edition. Shanghai Library.

Saussy, Haun. "Unspoken Sentences: A Thought-Sequence in Chapter 32 of *Honglou meng*." In *Studies in Chinese Language and Culture in Honour of Christoph Harbsmeier*, edited by Christoph Anderl and Halvor Eifring, 427–33. Oslo: Hermes, 2006.

Scott, James C. *Domination and the Arts of Resistance: Hidden Transcripts.* New Haven, CT: Yale University Press, 1990.

Scott, James C. *Weapons of the Weak: Everyday Forms of Peasant Resistance.* New Haven, CT: Yale University Press, 1985.

Shang, Wei. Rulin waishi *and Cultural Transformation in Late Imperial China.* Cambridge, MA: Harvard University Asia Center, 2003.

Shang, Wei, and David Der-wei Wang, eds. *Dynastic Crisis and Cultural Innovation: From the Late Ming to the Late Qing and Beyond.* Cambridge, MA: Harvard University Asia Center, 2005.

Shang Yanliu 商衍鎏. *Qingdai keju kaoshi shulu ji youguan zhuzuo* 清代科舉考試述錄及有關著作. Tianjin: Baihua wenyi chuban she, 2004.

Shen Defu 沈德符. *Wanli yehuo bian* 萬曆野獲編. Beijing: Zhonghua shuju, 1959 reprint.

"Shen Hongtai lunwen 沈虹臺論文." In *LWJC* 15–19.

Shen Junping 沈俊平. *Juye jinliang: Ming zhongye yihou fangke zhiju yongshu de shengchan ji liutong* 舉業津梁：明中葉以後坊刻制舉用書的生產及流通. Taipei: Xuesheng shuju, 2009.

Shen Shouzheng 沈守正. "*Hu Xiufu shouping shi yi* xu 胡休復手評詩義序." In *MWH* 311/3023–24.

Sieber, Patricia. *Theaters of Desire: Authors, Readers, and the Reproduction of Early Chinese Song-Drama.* New York: Palgrave Macmillan, 2003.

Son, Suyoung. "Publishing as a Coterie Enterprise: Zhang Chao and the Making of Printed Texts in Early Qing China." *Late Imperial China* 31.1 (2010): 98–136.

Spence, Jonathan D. *Treason by the Book.* New York: Viking, 2001.

Su Xun 蘇洵. "Yilun 易論." In *Tang Song ba da jia wenchao jiaozhu jiping* 唐宋八大家文鈔校注集評, 4272. Xi'an: San Qin chuban she, 1998.

Tang Biao 唐彪. *Dushu zuowen pu* 讀書作文譜. Guangqi tang, 1699. Harvard-Yenching Library.

Tang Shunzhi 唐順之. *Tang Jingchuan gao* 唐荊川稿. No date. Fudan University Library.

Tang Shunzhi 唐順之. *Tang Jingchuan wenji* 唐荊川文集. 1573 edition. Shanghai: Shangwu yinshu guan 1922 reprint.

Tang Shunzhi 唐順之. *Tang Jingchuan xiansheng wenji* 唐荊川先生文集. 1553 edition. Harvard-Yenching Library.

Tang Shunzhi 唐順之. *Tang Jingchuan xiansheng wenji* 唐荊川先生文集. 1555 edition. Beijing: Guojia tushu guan chuban she, 2012 reprint.

Tang Song ba da jia wenchao jiaozhu jiping 唐宋八大家文鈔校注集評. Xi'an: San Qin chuban she, 1998.

Tang Xianzu 湯顯祖, ed. *Tang Xu er huiyuan zhiyi* 湯許二會元制義. 1610 preface. National Central Library, Taipei.

Tang Yin 唐寅. *Liuru jushi quanji* 六如居士全集. 1801 edition. Institute for Advanced Studies on Asia Library, Tokyo University.

Temple, William. "Of Heroic Virtue." In *The Works of Sir William Temple, Bart: To Which is Prefixed the Life and Character of the Author, Considerably Enlarged*, vol. 3, 325–45. Rivington, 1814.

Teng, Ssu-yü. "Chinese Influence on the Western Examination System." *Harvard Journal of Asiatic Studies* 7.4 (1943): 267–312.

Tian Qilin 田啟霖, ed. *Bagu wen guanzhi* 八股文觀止. Haikou: Hainan chuban she, 1996.

Tu, Ching-i. "The Chinese Examination Essay: Some Literary Considerations." *Monumenta Serica* 31 (1974–75): 393–406.

van der Sprenkel, Otto. "The Chinese Civil Service." *East Asian History* 11 (1996): 17–32.

Van Zoeren, Steven. *Poetry and Personality: Reading, Exegesis, and Hermeneutics in Traditional China*. Stanford, CA: Stanford University Press, 1991.

Volpp, Sophie. *Worldly Stage: Theatricality in Seventeenth-Century China*. Cambridge, MA: Harvard University Asia Center, 2011.

Von Glahn, Richard. *Fountain of Fortune: Money and Monetary Policy in China, 1000–1700*. Berkeley: University of California Press, 1996.

Waltner, Ann. "Building on the Ladder of Success: The Ladder of Success in Imperial China and Recent Work on Social Mobility." *Ming Studies* 17 (1983): 30–36.

Wang Fuzhi 王夫之. *Xitang yongri xulun waipian* 夕堂永日緒論外篇. In *Chuanshan yishu* 船山遺書. Jinling, 1864.

Wang Kaifu 王凱符. *Bagu wen gaishuo* 八股文概說. Beijing: Zhonghua shuju, 2002.

Wang Mengruan 王夢阮 and Shen Ping'an 沈瓶庵. "*Honglou meng suoyin* tiyao 紅樓夢索隱提要." In *Honglou meng suoyin* 紅樓夢索隱, edited by Wang Mengruan and Shen Ping'an, 5–27. Beijing: Beijing daxue chuban she, 2011 reprint.

Wang Mengruan 王夢阮 and Shen Ping'an 沈瓶庵, eds. *Honglou meng suoyin* 紅樓夢索隱. 1916. Beijing: Beijing daxue chuban she, 2011 reprint.

Wang Sihao 王思豪. *Fang Bao* 方苞. Nanjing: Jiangsu renmin chuban she, 2016.

Wang Wenlu 王文祿. *Wenmai* 文脈. Reprint in *Congshu jicheng* 叢書集成. Shanghai: Shangwu yinshu guan.

Wang Yangming 王陽明. "Wansong shuyuan ji 萬松書院記." In *Wang Yangming quanji xin bian ben* 王陽明全集新編本, 269. Hangzhou: Zhejiang guji chuban she, 2010.

Wang Yunxi 王運熙 and Gu Yisheng 顧易生, eds. *Zhongguo wenxue piping shi xinbian* 中國文學批評史新編. Shanghai: Fudan daxue chuban she, 2001.

Watson, Burton, trans. *The Complete Works of Chuang Tzu.* New York: Columbia University Press, 1968.

Watt, Ian. *The Rise of the Novel: Studies in Defoe, Richardson, and Fielding.* Berkeley: University of California Press, 1965.

Webb, John. *An Historical Essay Endeavoring the Probability that the Language of the Empire of China is the Primitive Language.* London: Printed for Nath. Brook, 1669.

Wenjin yingji hexuan 文津迎機合選. 1838. 1883 reprint. National Library, Beijing.

Wenzhang guifan 文章軌範. 1609 edition. Seikadō Library, Tokyo.

Wenzhang guifan 文章軌範. 1883 edition. Zhongzhou guji chuban she, 1991 reprint.

Wenzheng 文徵. Institute for Advanced Studies on Asia Library, Tokyo University.

Widmer, Ellen. "The Epistolary World of Female Talent in Seventeenth Century China." *Late Imperial China* 10.2 (1989): 1–43.

Williams, Raymond. *Marxism and Literature.* Oxford: Oxford University Press, 1977.

Winkler, Roland. *Gelehrte Worte über leere Wörter: Das* Xuzi shuo *von Yuan Renlin und die Partikeln in der traditionellen chinesischen Philologie, Stilistik und Sprachwissenschaft.* Heidelberg: Groos, 1999.

Woodside, Alexander. *Lost Modernities: China, Vietnam, Korea, and The Hazards of World History.* Cambridge, MA: Harvard University Press, 2006.

Wu Jingzi 吳敬梓. *Rulin waishi* 儒林外史. Beijing: Renmin wenxue chuban she, 1977 reprint.

Wu Kuan 吳寬. *Paoweng jiacang ji* 匏翁家藏集. 1508. Harvard-Yenching Library.

Wu, Pei-yi. *The Confucian's Progress: Autobiographical Writings in Traditional China.* Princeton, NJ: Princeton University Press, 1990.

Wu Weifan 吳偉凡. *Ming Qing zhiyi jinshuo: "bagu wen" de xiandai chanshi* 明清制藝今說：「八股文」的現代闡釋. Beijing: Xueyuan chuban she, 2009.

Wu, Yinghui. "Constructing a Playful Space: Eight-Legged Essays on *Xixiang ji* and *Pipa ji*." *T'oung Pao* 102.4–5 (2016): 503–45.

Wu Zhiwang 武之望, ed. *Juye zhiyan* 舉業巵言. 1588 edition (2 juan); 1835 reprint. Harvard-Yenching Library.

Wu Zhiwang 武之望, ed. *Juye zhiyan* 舉業巵言. 1599 edition (5 juan). Shanghai Library. (*JYZY*)

Wu Zhiwang 武之望. "Wu Shuqing lunwen 武叔卿論文." In *LWJC* 35–40.

Xiaoti jianfeng 小題尖峰. 1841. Fudan University Library.

Xiaoti zhenggu 小題正鵠. 1843. Fudan University Library.

Xijian Mingren wenhua ershi zhong 稀見明人文話二十種. Shanghai: Shanghai guji chuban she, 2016.

Xinxuan qijiang 新選起講. National Central Library, Taipei.

Xinyi Sanzi jing 新譯三字經. Taipei: Sanmin, 2003.

Xixiang zhiyi 西廂制義. Institute for Advanced Studies on Asia Library, Tokyo University.

Xu Shipu 徐世溥. "*Tongren hebian* xu 同人合編序." In *MWH* 313/3044–45.

Xuehai tang ji 學海堂集. Nanjing: Jiangsu jiaoyu chuban she, 1995 reprint.

Yang Shengwu 楊繩武. *Lunwen size* 論文四則. In *Zhaodai congshu* 昭代叢書. *Congshu jicheng xubian* 叢書集成續編 vol. 157: 205–7. Shanghai: Shanghai shudian, 1994.

Yao Nai 姚鼐. *Xibao xuan shiwen* 惜抱軒時文. In *Liu Haifeng quanji* 劉海峰全集. 1875 edition. National Library, Beijing.

Yao Nai 姚鼐. "Xibao xuan yu 惜抱軒語." In Liu Dakui 劉大櫆, *Lunwen ouji* 論文偶記. 1832 edition. Shanghai Library.

Ye Chuyan 葉楚炎. *Mingdai keju yu Ming zhongqi zhi Qing chu tongsu xiaoshuo yanjiu* 明代科舉與明中期至清初通俗小說研究. Nanchang: Baihua zhou wenyi chuban she, 2009.

Ye Xie 葉燮. "Yu youren lunwen shu 與友人論文書." In *Qingdai wenlun xuan* 清代文論選, 257–70. Beijing: Renmin wenxue chuban she, 1999.

Yinzhi wen zhiyi 陰騭文制義. Institute for Advanced Studies on Asia Library, Tokyo University.

Yokota Terutoshi 横田輝俊. "Hakkobun ni tsuite 八股文について." *Bungaku* (Hiroshima University Studies) 24.3 (1965): 144–60.

You Tong 尤侗. *Guwen lüshu* 古文律書. 1663. Institute for Advanced Studies on Asia Library, Tokyo University.

You Tong 尤侗. "*Jichou zhenfeng* xu 己丑真風序." In *Qingdai wenlun xuan* 清代文論選, 143–44. Beijing: Renmin wenxue chuban she, 1999.

Yu, Anthony C. "Self and Family in the *Hung-lou Meng*: A New Look at Lin Tai-yü as Tragic Heroine." *CLEAR* 2.2 (1980): 199–223.

Yu Changcheng 俞長城. *Keyi tang yibai ershi mingjia zhiyi* 可儀堂一百二十名家制義. 1699. National Library, Beijing.

Yu, Pauline. "Canon Formation in Late Imperial China." In *Culture & State in Chinese History: Conventions, Accommodations, Critiques*, edited by Theodore Huters, R. Bin Wong, and Pauline Yu, 83–104. Stanford, CA: Stanford University Press, 1997.

Yu Yingshi 余英時. *Shi yu Zhongguo wenhua* 士與中國文化. Shanghai: Shanghai renmin chuban she, 1987.

Yu Yue 俞樾. *Yu Yue sishu wen* 俞樾四書文. Manuscript. Nanjing University Library.

Yuan Hongdao 袁宏道. "Da Li Yuanshan 答李元善." In *Mingdai wenlun xuan* 明代文論選, 330. Beijing: Renmin wenxue chuban she, 1993.

Yuan Hongdao 袁宏道. "Xu *Sizi gao* 敘四子稿." In *Yuan Zhonglang quanji* 袁中郎全集, 8–9. Taipei: Shijie shuju, 2009.

Yuan Hongdao 袁宏道. "*Zhu dajia shiwen* xu 諸大家時文序." In *Yuan Hongdao ji jian jiao* 袁宏道集箋校, 184–87. Shanghai: Shanghai guji chuban she, 1981.

Yuan Huang 袁黄. *Youyi shu wengui* 遊藝塾文軌. Wuhan: Wuhan daxue chuban she, 2009 reprint.

Yuan Huang 袁黄. *Youyi shu xu wengui* 遊藝塾續文軌. Wuhan: Wuhan daxue chuban she, 2009 reprint.

Yuan Renlin 袁仁林. *Xuzi shuo* 虛字說. 1710 preface. 1746 edition reprinted in *Xuxiu Siku quanshu*, vol. 195, 503–25. Shanghai: Shanghai guji chuban she, 1995.

Zeitlin, Judith T. *Historian of the Strange: Pu Songling and the Classical Chinese Tale*. Stanford, CA: Stanford University Press, 1993.

Zeng Yizhuan 曾異撰. "Xu *Guiyou weidu chao* 序癸酉闈牘抄." In *MWH* 309/3010–11.

Zeng Yizhuan 曾異撰. "Xu *Wenjiang zhiyi* xu 徐文匠制義序." In *MWH* 309/3004–5.

Zeng Yizhuan 曾異撰. "Zixu *Sishu lunshi* 自序四書論世." In *MWH* 309/3005–6.

Zhang Chao 張潮. "*Bagu shi* zixu 八股詩自序." In *Xinzhai liaofu ji* 心齋聊復集. Reprinted in *Siku jinhui shu congkan bubian* 四庫禁毀書叢刊補編, vol. 85. Beijing: Beijing chuban she, 2005.

Zhang Shichun 章世純. "*Banfang zhai gao* xu 半舫齋稿序." In *MWH* 312/3038–40.

Zhang Taikai 張泰開. *Zhangshi lunwen yuezhi* 張氏論文約旨. 1838. 1891 reprint edition. Shanghai Library.

Zhang Taikai 張泰開. "Zhang Youtang lunwen yuezhi 張有堂論文約旨." Compiled in 1742. In *LWJC* 71–111.

Zhang Yushu 張玉書. Preface to *Tieli wenqi* 鐵立文起. Reprinted in *Xuxiu Siku quanshu* 續修四庫全書, vol. 1714. Shanghai guji chuban she, 1995.

Zhang Zhongxing 張中行. "*Shuo bagu* buwei 說八股補微." In Qi Gong 啟功, *Shuo bagu* 說八股, 59–73. Beijing: Zhonghua shuju, 2000.

Zhao Jiyao 趙基耀, Li Xu 李旭, et al., eds. *Qingdai bagu wen yizhu* 清代八股文譯注. Shanghai: Shanghai guji chuban she, 2011.

Zheng Dian 鄭典 and Mai Meiqiao 麥梅翹, eds. *Gu Hanyu yufa xue ziliao huibian* 古漢語語法學資料彙編. Hong Kong: Zhonghua shuju, 1972 reprint.

Zhengde Da Ming huidian 正德大明會典. Tokyo: Kyuko shoin, 1989 reprint.

Zhongguo lidai shuyuan zhi 中國歷代書院志. Nanjing: Jiangsu jiaoyu chuban she, 1995.

Zhou Xunchu 周勛初. *Zhongguo wenxue piping xiaoshi* 中國文學批評小史. Hubei: Changjiang wenyi chuban she, 1982.

Zhou Zuoren 周作人. "Lun bagu wen 論八股文." In *Zhongguo xin wenxue de yuanliu* 中國新文學的源流, 60–65. Reprinted in *Zhou Zuoren zibian wenji: Ertong wenxue xiaolun, Zhongguo xin wenxue de yuanliu* 周作人自編文集: 兒童文學小論, 中國新文學的源流. Shijiazhuang: Hebei jiaoyu chuban she, 2002.

Zhou Zuoren 周作人. *Zhongguo xin wenxue de yuanliu* 中國新文學的源流. Reprinted in *Zhou Zuoren zibian wenji: Ertong wenxue xiaolun, Zhongguo xin wenxue de yuanliu* 周作人自編文集: 兒童文學小論, 中國新文學的源流. Shijiazhuang: Hebei jiaoyu chuban she, 2002.

Zhouyi benyi 周易本義. In *Sishu zhangju jizhu* 四書章句集注. Beijing: Zhongguo shudian, 1985 reprint.

Zhu Shangshu 祝尚書. *Songdai keju yu wenxue* 宋代科舉與文學. Beijing: Zhonghua shuju, 2008.

Zhu Shou 朱綬. *Zhizhi tang wenji* 知止堂文集. 1850. Seikadō Library, Tokyo.

Zito, Angela. *Of Body and Brush: Grand Sacrifice as Text/Performance.* Chicago: University of Chicago Press, 1997.

CHARACTER LIST

This list is sorted alphabetically by syllable.

babi	八比
bagu wen	八股文
Baochai	寶釵
Baoyu	寶玉
bense	本色
bi	比
biejing	別境
bie li yi men	別立一門
biezhan xinsi	別展新思
bin/zhu	賓主
Bo Yi	伯夷
bu	不
bu de zizhi ye	不得自知也
buren	不忍
"Bu yi guiju"	不以規矩
cai	才
Cai Qing	蔡清
caizi jiaren	才子佳人
celun	策論
cenci	參差
changren zhi jian	常人之見
changwei	嘗謂
changwu zhi wen	場屋之文
Chen Jitai	陳際泰
chen qing	臣請
Chen Xianzhang	陳獻章
chenzi	襯字
cheng	承
Cheng Duanli	程端禮
Chenghua	成化

chengti	承題
Cheng Yi	程頤
Chongzhen	崇禎
Chu Quan	儲巏
chuti	出題
Chuanjia bao	傳家寶
chuanqi	傳奇
Chunqiu lun	春秋論
ci	詞
Ci	賜
Congxian wenjue neipian	從先文訣內篇
cong ziji xiongzhong liuchu	從自己胸中流出
Cui Xian	崔銑
cun	存
cuozong	錯綜
dajiang	大講
dajie	大結
dati	搭題
dai	代
dai guren yuqi weizhi	代古人語氣為之
dai juzi zuo	代舉子作
dairen zuoyu	代人作語
dai shengren xianren zhi yan	代聖人賢人之言
dai shengxian liyan	代聖賢立言
dai shengxian zhi kouyu	代聖賢之口語
dai shengxian zhi yan	代聖賢之言
dai shengxian zhi zhi	代聖賢之旨
dai taren shuohua	代他人說話
dai wei erqian nian qian shengren zhi shuo	代為二千年前聖人之說
daiyan	代言
Daiyi bian	代疑編
danhang	單行
dang bagu wen	黨八股文
dangshi kouqi	當時口氣
Daode jing	道德經
Daogu lu	道古錄

Daoxue	道學
de	的
Deng Xi	鄧析
Dian	點
ding	定
dingge	定格
dong/jing	動靜
Donglin	東林
Dong Yue	董越
douqi	鬥奇
Du Fu	杜甫
duanzuo	斷作
dui	對
fa	法
fan	反
Fang Yizhi	方以智
Fang Zhou	方舟
Feng Ban	馮班
Feng Fu	馮婦
Feng Qi	馮琦
Feng Yuanyang	馮元颺
fu	賦
fufen	傅粉
Fushe	復社
Fu Xiaqi	傅夏器
gan	感
ge	格
Ge	葛
Gong'an	公案
gongfu zaozuo	功夫造作
gongming bagu wen	功名八股文
Gongsun Chou	公孫丑
Gongsun Long	公孫龍
Gu Dashao	顧大韶
Gu Qing	顧清
Gu Xiancheng	顧憲成
Gu Xianzheng	顧咸正

gu	股
guwen	古文
Guan Shiming	管世銘
Guan Zhong	管仲
"Gui qu lai ci"	歸去來辭
guojia	國家
guojie	過接
Han Feizi	韓非子
Han Tan	韓菼
Han Yu	韓愈
haoran zhi qi	浩然之氣
he	合
hezhang zhi bing	合掌之病
He Zhuo	何卓
Hongwu	洪武
hougu	後股
Hou Kang	侯康
Hu Ding	胡定
Hu Renyu	胡任與
Hu Shi	胡適
huanzi fa	換字法
Huang Hongxian	黃洪憲
hui	慧
huiyuan	會元
huo	活
huoju	活局
ji	機
jijian	己見
"Ji jiuben Hanwen hou"	記舊本韓文後
Jilu	季路
jishi	記事
jishi ti	記事題
jiyi	己意
jiyi zaozuo	己意造作
jiyu	寄寓
Ji Yun	紀昀
Jiagui ji	甲癸集

Jiajing	嘉靖
Jiang Guolin	江國霖
Jiangnan	江南
Jiangnan diyi fengliu caizi	江南第一風流才子
jiangxue	講學
Jiaoshi yilin	焦氏易林
jieda ti	截搭題
Jin	晉
Jin Ping Mei	金瓶梅
jinri zhi wen	今日之文
Jin Sheng	金聲
jinshi	進士
jinti shi	近體詩
jingjie	境界
Jingling	竟陵
jingshen	精神
jingyi	經義
juye	舉業
juzi ye	舉子業
juan	卷
jun	鈞
junzi	君子
Kangxi	康熙
kaozheng	考證
keji fuli	克己復禮
kinben kakumei	勤勉革命
kong	空
"Kong Yi Ji"	孔乙己
kouqi	口氣
kuang	狂
Kunyi	昆夷
Laozi	老子
li	理
Li Bai	李白
lide	立德
Li Dongyang	李東陽
ligong	立功

Li Guangdi	李光地
Li He	李賀
Li Tingji	李廷機
lixiang	里巷
liyan	立言
lianzhang	連章
lianzhang ti	連章題
Liang Qichao	梁啟超
Liezi	列子
Liezi	列子
Lin Daqin	林大欽
Lin Daiyu	林黛玉
ling jia	凌駕
liushui	流水
Liu Zizhuang	劉子壯
Longqing	隆慶
Lu Xiangshan	陸象山
lüshi	律詩
lun	論
Lunwen jiujue	論文九訣
Luo Lun	羅倫
Luo Wanzao	羅萬藻
luoxia	落下
maiwen wei sheng	賣文為生
Mei Lanfang	梅蘭芳
Min Ziqian	閔子騫
ming	名
ming jiao	名教
Mudan ting	牡丹亭
Nan Wu jiuhua lu	南吳舊話錄
ni	你
ou	偶
Ouyang Xiu	歐陽修
pifu ziyou zhi zhi	匹夫自有之志
pianti wen	駢體文
Pianzi leibian	駢字類編
pingdian	評點

"Pingwen"	評文
ping/ze	平仄
pocheng	破承
poti	破題
Pu Songling	蒲松齡
qi	奇
Qi	齊
qicai	奇才
qi-cheng-zhuan-he	起承轉合
Qidiao Kai	漆雕開
qigu	起股
qijiang	起講
qijun	其君
qipi	奇僻
qiren	奇人
qishen	其身
qiwen	奇文
qixin	其心
Qianlong	乾隆
Qian Youwei	錢有威
Qian Zhenguang	錢振光
qie	且
qiefu	且夫
qin	勤
Qin	秦
qing	情
qing zishen	情自深
Qiu Yi	丘義
Qu Yuan	屈原
ren	仁
renti	認題
ru	儒
ruhe	如何
ruti	入題
ruoyue	若曰
san	散
sanxing	散行

Shanhai jing	山海經
Shao	韶
Shao Guijie	邵圭潔
shegao	社稿
shen	神
Shen Buhai	申不害
Shen Cheng	沈承
Shen Hongtai	沈虹臺
Shen Tong	沈同
Shen Wei	沈位
Shenglü qimeng	聲律啟蒙
shi	時
Shi Chengjin	石成金
shihua	詩話
Shiji	史記
shimao	時髦
shiren zhi ye	士人之業
shishang	士商
"Shishuo"	師說
shiwen	時文
shiyi	時藝
shou	售
shoujie	收結
Shu Qi	叔齊
shu er bu zuo	述而不作
shu suohuai zhi fenji	抒所懷之憤激
shu zi xingling	抒自性靈
Shuihu zhuan	水滸傳
Shun	舜
Shuoshu	說書
Shuoyuan	說苑
"Sibai Dong xiansheng lunwen"	思白董先生論文
sidui budui	似對不對
sigu babi	四股八比
Sima Qian	司馬遷
sishu wen	四書文
sixin	私心

Song	宋
su	俗
Su Shi	蘇軾
Su Xiangfeng	蘇翔鳳
Su Zhe	蘇轍
Sun Kuang	孫鑛
suo	所
suoyi ran	所以然
ta gu wei xia bian ye	他固未暇辨也
ta gu wei zu xin ye	他固未足信也
Tan Yuanchun	譚元春
Tang	唐
Tao Shizheng	陶世徵
Tao Wangling	陶望齡
Tao Ying	桃應
Tao Yuanming	陶淵明
tige	體格
ti guren shuohua	替古人說話
tian	天
Tongcheng	桐城
Wan Guoqin	萬國欽
Wanli	萬曆
Wang Anshi	王安石
Wang Ao	王鏊
Wang Heng	王衡
Wang Kentang	王肯堂
Wang Qiao	王樵
Wei	衛
wei jin zhi juzi ye	為今之舉子業
Wei Xi	魏禧
weiyan	危言
weiyi	微意
wen	文
Wenchang	文昌
wenda ti	問答題
wenhua	文話
wenhua xianxiang	文化現象

wenji	文集
wenshi	文勢
"Wenti ce"	文體策
Wenxin diaolong	文心雕龍
wenxue shi	文學史
wenxue zuopin	文學作品
wen yao er wo xiangxing	文要爾我相形
wenzhang	文章
wen zhi zhengtong	文之正統
wenzi	文字
wo	我
woxuan	斡旋
wu	吾
wucai	吾財
wudao	吾道
wuguan	吾觀
Wu Hong	吳鴻
Wu Kuan	吳寬
Wu Qiao	吳喬
wu qing wei wang ce yan	吾請為王策焉
wuren	吾仁
wuren zhi shi	吾人之事
wushen	吾身
wusheng	吾生
wuxin	吾心
wuyi	吾意
wu yiwei	吾以為
wuyou	吾有
wuzhi	吾知
Xixiang ji	西廂記
xiyin hui	惜陰會
xizi hui	惜字會
Xia Yan	夏言
xian	鮮
xiangxiang shengren zhi yi dai wei liyan	想像聖人之意代為立言
xiaoti	小題

Xiaoti wuji jingyi	小題五集精詣
xin	心
xinxue	心學
xin yang	新樣
xinzhai	心齋
xiongzhong	胸中
xiuci yi da qi cheng	修辭以達其誠
xu	虛
Xu Fuyuan	許孚遠
xugu	虛股
Xu Guangqi	徐光啟
xu/shi	虛實
xuzi	虛字
xuzi yan	虛字眼
xuan	玄
Xue Xuan	薛瑄
Xue Yingqi	薛應旂
Yan	燕
Yan Shizhang	顏士璋
Yan Yuan	顏淵
yang bagu wen	洋八股文
Yang Huo	陽貨
Yang Maojian	楊懋建
Yang Qiyuan	楊起元
Yang Wanli	楊萬里
Yang Wensun	楊文蓀
Yang Xiong	楊雄
yangzhi	養志
ye	也
yi	義
yiceng chenchu liangceng	一層襯出兩層
yi cun zhiji zhi gan	以存知己之感
yi guwen wei shiwen	以古文為時文
yijia zhi dao	一家之道
yijia zhi wen	一家之文
yili	義理
yilun	議論

yiwei	意謂
"Yiwen zhi"	藝文志
yi wo wei shiwen	以我為時文
yiyi fanchu liangceng	一意翻出兩層
yiyi fenchu liangceng	一意分出兩層
yiyi hualiang	一意化兩
Yin	殷
yingchou	應酬
yingchou zhi wen	應酬之文
yongbi	用筆
Yongle	永樂
Yongzheng	雍正
you wei ji zhi xin	有為己之心
youxi zhi bi	遊戲之筆
you zhong yi da yu wai	由衷以達於外
you zhu zhi xin	有主之心
yu	予
yu ji	於己
yulun	輿論
yuqi	語氣
Yuzhang Society	豫章社
Yuan	元
Yuan Cuijun	元崔君
"Yuandao"	原道
Yuanqu xuan	元曲選
yuanti	原題
Yuan Zhongdao	袁中道
Yuan Zongdao	袁宗道
zaju	雜劇
zai ji zhe	在己者
zai wo zhe	在我者
Zang Cang	臧倉
Zang Maoxun	臧懋循
ze	則
Zeng Xi	曾晳
Zengzi	曾子
Zhang Dai	張岱

Zhang Juzheng	張居正
Zhang Yongqi	張永祺
Zhang Yuan	張元
Zhao Nanxing	趙南星
Zhaoshi bei	照世杯
zhe	這
zhen	真
Zheng Haoruo	鄭灝若
Zheng Xie	鄭燮
Zheng Zhenduo	鄭振鐸
zhi	之
Zhiju wen jiufa	制舉文九法
zhijuye zhi dao	制舉業之道
zhishi renren	志士仁人
zhonggu	中股
Zhou Yanru	周延儒
Zhou Yiqing	周以清
zhu bu yi chuan zhi shen	著不易傳之神
Zhu Jian	朱琦
Zhu Shixiu	朱士琇
Zhu Xi	朱熹
Zhu Xie	諸燮
zhuan	轉
zhuangyuan	狀元
Zhuangzi	莊子
zhuoran	卓然
zhuoyue	卓越
zi	字
zicheng yijia zhi yan	自成一家之言
zichu jingyi	自出精意
zide	自得
zide zhi jian	自得之見
zidong	自動
Zigong	子貢
ziji	自己
ziji jingshen	自己精神
ziji yan	自己言

ziji zhen jingshen	自己真精神
zijia benlai lingxing	自家本來靈性
zijia shen	自家神
zijia xingling	自家性靈
ziju	字句
zili	自力
Zimo	子莫
zineng	自能
ziqiang	自強
Ziqin	子禽
zi shi jiyi	自適己意
zishuo	自說
zishuo jiyi	自說己意
Zisi	子思
ziwo	自我
zixian	自限
zixie	自寫
Ziyan bianyong	字眼便用
ziyi	自易
ziyong	自用
ziyuan	自遠
Zizhang	子張
zizuo zhuzhang	自作主張
zuo	作
zuozhe	作者

INDEX

Adam Smith in Beijing (Arrighi), 171
aesthetic, the: and anonymity, 151, 154–55; and autobiography, 167; and class, 58, 81, 82; of consumption vs. production, 81–82, 139, 154, 182–83, 184; of Daoism and Buddhism, 64–65; and economic development, 151, 186; and formalism of *shiwen*, 22, 25, 83, 103, 106; and ideology, 9, 30, 57–62, 64–65, 67, 68, 75, 83, 157; and literati class, 58, 60, 80; vs. morality, 56, 57; originality in, 3, 24–25, 67–68, 157; and politics, 24, 29, 36, 46, 48, 57, 70; and representative speech, 54, 79–80; and small topic questions, 74–75; and social exchange, 182; and tone of voice (*yuqi*), 2, 35, 134; in the West, 2, 3, 35, 36, 81, 82, 83, 151, 154–55; and *xu*, 2, 14, 15, 25, 36
aesthetic autonomy, 3, 30, 61–62, 65, 68–84
Age of Silver (Ning Ma), 171
Ai Nanying, 27, 238n64, 245n63; and Buddhism, 63; and examination anonymity, 154; on examiners, 68–69, 70, 71, 78; and "friend who knows your true self" (*zhiji*), 122, 145; and *guwen* vs. *shiwen*, 99, 208n81; and individual subjectivity, 120, 147, 240n95; and interpretive labor, 111; parallelism of, 89, 229n76; and representative speech, 48, 50, 82; and shifting discourse, 143, 146
Akira Hayami, 186
Amariglio, Jack, 115
Analects, 51, 132, 238n71; and authentic self, 126–27, 129; and representative speech, 41, 236n42; and small topic questions, 72–73
Anatomy of Melancholy (Burton), 176
Anderson, Benedict, 79–80, 172

anonymity, 150–69; and authentic voice, 161–64; and autobiography, 164–69; in blind peer review, 153–54; in examination system, 151–57; vs. originality, 150, 157–61
anthologies (collections of examination essays), 204n37; copying from, 72, 217n17; and essay criticism, 17–19; as instruction manuals, 18, 69, 70, 100, 156; prefaces to, 152; punctuation in, 104; small topic essays in, 222n76
Arrighi, Giovanni, 171
Austen, Jane, 140, 141
autobiography, 164–69; and fiction, 130, 165, 168; and *shiwen*, 1, 8, 125, 165, 166, 167–68

Bao Shichen, 117, 201n4, 206n63; on authentic voice, 163; on *guwen* vs. *shiwen*, 99, 102; on individual subjectivity, 120–21, 122; on nonstandard structure, 114
Barthes, Roland, 10, 76
Bo Yi, 91
Book of Poetry (*Shijing*), 127, 128, 208n82
Bourdieu, Pierre, 21, 36, 81–82, 154–55, 168, 183, 224n116
Braudel, Fernand, 174
Britain, 81, 166; and Chinese bureaucracy, 173, 247n10; nobility in, 173, 176; the novel in, 143, 171, 243n22, 244n41
Buddhism, 20, 218n32; Chan, 30, 63–64; in examination essays, 7, 56, 62–68, 80; as heterodoxy, 24, 43, 50, 67–68, 70, 219n51
bureaucracy, Chinese: and examination system, 53, 58, 59, 69, 75–76, 77, 173; and involution, 186; as literate administration, 170, 172–76; and

parallel prose (*pianti wen*), Six Dynasties, 86, 103, 108, 112
Party eight-legged essay (*dang bagu wen*), 4
Peony Pavilion (*Mudan ting*; Tang Xianzu), 17
Pianzi leibian (A collection of matching words in categories), 117
Plaks, Andrew, 9, 14, 19, 110, 135, 224n3, 233n4, 238n64
poetry: *ci*, 108; in examinations, 54, 59; and interpretive labor, 110; linked-verse, 94; parallelism in, 85–86; prefaces to, 151; recent style (*jinti shi*), 8, 226n28; regulated verse (*lüshi*), 8, 59, 86, 92, 108, 226n28; *shihua* criticism of, 18; Tang, 8, 16. See also *Book of Poetry*
policy essays (*celun*), 6, 9, 83, 203n23
politics: and the aesthetic, 24, 29, 36, 46, 48, 57, 70; factional, 126, 155; and representative speech, 49, 53, 54, 68; and *shiwen*, 1, 7–8, 10, 23, 83, 229n76; in small-topic essays, 73
poti (topic-breaker; introductory element), 37, 60–61, 63, 100, 131, 150, 159, 232n111
prefaces, 151–52, 168, 184, 241n6
Pu Songling, 71, 236n42
publishing industry, 62, 69, 181; and commodity exchange, 115–16; and examination preparation, 77, 182; production and consumption in, 3, 154

Qi Gong, 94
Qian Qianyi, 201n8
Qian Yong, 211n2
Qian Youwei, 106
Qian Zhenguang, 132–33
Qian Zhongshu, 14, 17, 35, 208n75, 216n7
Qianlong emperor, 57, 61–62, 152
Qianzi wen (Classic of a thousand characters), 117
qijiang (initiation of discourse), 37, 51, 56, 100, 130, 138
Qijie (Seven solutions; Fang Yizhi), 165
Qing dynasty: Daoism and Buddhism in, 64; and *guwen* vs. *shiwen*, 98, 99,

103; individual subjectivity in, 31, 32, 120, 123, 125, 133; the literary in, 15–23; parallelism in, 86, 88, 89; political factions in, 46, 49; representative speech in, 44–45; *shiwen* in, 4–5, 6, 9, 10, 15, 61; transition to, 3, 105, 126, 173
Qiu Jun, 44, 71, 72, 74, 78, 79, 220n54
Qiu Yi, 14
Qu Jingchun, 8, 139, 218n32, 245n50; and authentic self, 124–25, 128; on autobiography, 166–67
Qu Yuan, 62
Quanxue wen (Encouragement of learning), 177
Quesnay, François, 174, 247n14

Random Writings from Zen Painting Studio (*Huachan shi suibi*; Dong Qichang), 20, 21
readers: and authentic voice, 162–63; and authors, 178; and drama, 45; examiners as, 78, 111, 137, 155, 178; and *guwen* vs. *shiwen*, 180; interpretive labor of, 3, 109–14, 155, 170, 185, 187; and narrative voice, 137; oral, 78–79, 91–92; and parallelism, 31, 96–97, 109–14; as producers vs. consumers, 21, 31, 32, 77–84, 139, 151, 154, 171, 181–83, 184, 224nn115–16
Renaissance Self-Fashioning (Greenblatt), 166
Renewal Society (*Fushe*), 49, 53
ReORIENT: Global Economy in the Asian Age (Frank), 171
Republican period, 103
Richardson, Samuel, 143
Roddy, Stephen, 19
Rolston, David, 19, 133, 160, 209n96
Ruan Yuan, 16, 98, 206n59, 225n4
Rusk, Bruce, 208n82
ruti (entrance into the topic), 107

Saintsbury, George, 143, 144
Sanzi jing (Three character classic), 176, 177
Saussy, Haun, 145
Scholars, The, 133, 177

Harvard-Yenching Institute Monograph Series

(most recent titles)